THE BIG BASICS BOOK OF
MICROSOFT® OFFICE

by Sherry Kinkoph
Joe Kraynak
Ed Guilford

A Division of Macmillan Computer Publishing
201 West 103rd Street, Indianapolis, Indiana 46290 USA

International Standard Book Number: 1-56761-6232

Library of Congress Catalog Card Number: 96232-6

98 97 96 95   8 7 6 5 4 3 2 1

Interpretation of the printing code: the rightmost double-digit number is the year of the book's first printing; the rightmost single-digit number is the number of the book's printing. For example, a printing code of 95-1 shows that this copy of the book was printed during the first printing of the book in 1995.

Publisher
Roland Elgey

Vice-President and Publisher
Marie Butler-Knight

Publishing Manager
Barry Pruett

Director of Editorial Services
Elizabeth Keaffaber

Managing Editor
Michael Cunningham

Senior Development Editor
Seta Frantz

Senior Production Editor
Michelle Shaw

Copy Editor
San Dee Phillips

Designer
Barbara Kordesh

Cover Designer
Jay Corpus

Technical Specialist
Cari Skaggs

Indexers
Virginia Munroe
Debra Myers

Production Team
Angela D. Bannan
Claudia Bell
Brian Buschkill
Chad Dressler
Rich Evers
Bryan Flores
Hartman Publishing
Bob LaRoche
Bobbi Satterfield
Michael Thomas
Scott Tullis
Jody York

➤ *Special thanks to Marty Wyatt for ensuring the technical accuracy of this book.*

Contents

Part 2   Do-It-Yourself

Combining Excel Data and Charts with Your Word Document — 381

Find a Job with Microsoft Office — 403

Organize Your Home and Personal Finances — 433

On the Job with Microsoft Office — 471

Part 3   101 Quick Fixes

Part 4   Quick References

Introduction

Have you seen those commercials that try to show how technology can make your life easier? A woman claps and a lamp turns off or on. A man points to his garage door and then presses a button on his garage door opener to open the door. Simple. That's the goal of PC and software makers everywhere: make the computer as easy to use as possible... for example, as easy as it is to drive a car. To drive a car, you don't have to know how a car works. You start it up, put it in drive, and head out on the highway.

Unfortunately, computers and the computer software have a long, long, long way to go to become simple to use. Sure, programs and computers have gotten somewhat easier to use since their arrival on the market in the 1980s, but it's still not simple to use a software program. You need some help.

When you purchase the programs for your computer, you may receive a fat old manual written by someone who obviously knows the program really well. The manual includes all the features in an order that is logical to someone who knows the program, but what about the beginner?

Most manuals don't explain the *why* of a feature. Why would I use this feature? What's the benefit? Give me an example! Also, most manuals include a lot of text with perhaps one figure (or picture). That figure may have many callouts that explain each and every option you can select. You are left to muddle through all the confusing text and hope you don't make a misstep.

While this book can't make programs any more intuitive, it can help you learn the program in the easiest way possible. Here are the top five reasons why this book is so easy to use:

1. This book explains the *why* of a feature and gives you examples of when that feature might come in handy. If you read something that sounds like it might make your work easier, you can read through the steps. If not, you can skip the section.

2. This book includes easy-to-follow *illustrated* steps called Guided Tours. The design of the book is similar to popular how-to books for home repair, cooking, and gardening. This book presents each step clearly; plus, you see what your screen should look like for each step. You don't have to wonder whether you got off track. You can follow along with the figures step-by-step.

3. The How-To section consists of manageable topics so you can find what you need to know. For example, you don't have to read an entire chapter's worth of material just to find out how to insert page numbers in a document. You can quickly go to the topic on page numbers and follow the steps.

4. This book covers more than just the basic, simple features that can get you only so far in a program. It also covers the more advanced features and concepts that will help you build your skills and get the most from your Microsoft Office 95 programs.

5. This book anticipates common problems that may pop up and includes a handy problem-solving section called 101 Quick Fixes. If you encounter a problem, you can look it up and find an answer. You can also look up reference information.

What Is Microsoft Office 95?

Microsoft Office 95 is a group of powerful programs designed to easily share information and utilize the new Windows 95 operating system. Two versions of this package are sold: Standard and Professional. The Standard version includes Microsoft Word, Excel, PowerPoint, and Schedule+. The Professional version includes those same four programs with the addition of Access, a powerful database program. This book focuses mainly on Word, Excel, PowerPoint, and Schedule+.

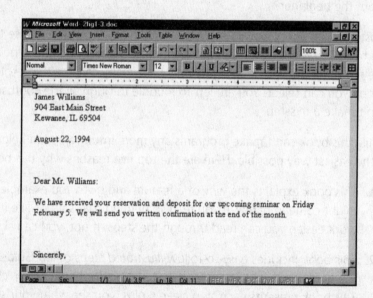

Word is a word-processing program that enables you to create all kinds of documents: letters, memos, reports, newsletters, and more.

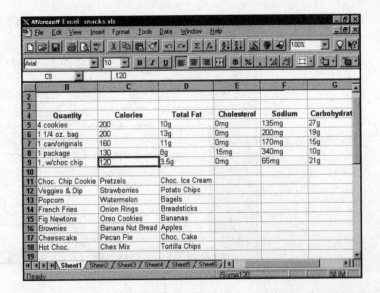

Excel is a spreadsheet program that enables you to track data. You can perform calculations on this data and even create charts from it. You can use this program to present numerical and other kinds information; you can also use it to build databases.

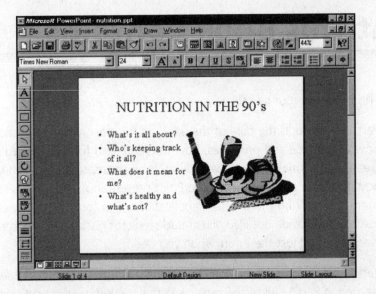

PowerPoint is a presentation graphics program that enables you to set up information in a graphic format for use in slide shows and other business presentations.

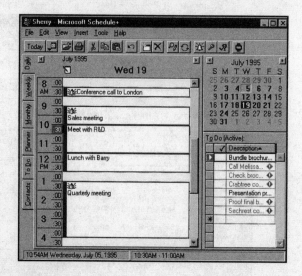

Schedule+ is an electronic calendar program that helps you organize appointments and meetings, much like a daily organizer or planner. You can also use Schedule+ to compile To Do lists and keep a database of addresses and phone numbers.

What This Book Contains

This book has four parts:

Part 1, How To, is the core of the book. In this part, you find sections on Office 95 basics, how to manage and print files, how to create and format a Word document, how to create and format an Excel worksheet, how to create an Excel chart and Excel database, how to create and format a PowerPoint presentation, how to use Schedule+, and how to share data among the different applications. The sections clearly explain when a feature is useful and provide detailed, illustrated steps for each task. You can turn to the topic you want and find just the information you need.

Part 2, Do-It-Yourself, provides real-world examples of how you can use the skills you learned in Part 1. All of the projects in this section involve using one or more of the Office 95 programs to create a finished product. By trying out the projects, you will learn how to harness the power of Microsoft Office 95 to quickly create polished documents.

Part 3, 101 Quick Fixes, provides answers to 101 common questions and problems that you may encounter. You can use this troubleshooting section to pinpoint and solve problems as they occur. Use the QuickFinder table at the beginning of this section to go directly to the answer you need.

Part 4, Handy References, includes all the reference information you need in one easy-to-find spot. Here, you will find lists of keyboard shortcuts as well as a description of the toolbar buttons in each of the programs. Also included is a list of Excel functions along with explanations of what each one does.

You can do so many exciting, wonderful things with Microsoft Office 95. And with this book, you can take advantage of all that Microsoft Office 95 offers now.

A Word About Conventions

This book was specially designed to make it easy to use. In each task you'll find an explanation about the task and examples of how and why you use it. Immediately following is a *Guided Tour*, which shows you step-by-step how to perform the task. The following figure shows you how the Guided Tour works.

There are a few special conventions that make the book easier to use:

Typed text appears bold. For example, if you read, type **win** and press **Enter**, type the command "win" and press the Enter key on your keyboard.

You will use Key+Key combinations when you have to press two or more keys to enter a command. When you encounter one of these combinations, hold down the first key while pressing the second key.

Menu names and commands are also bold. When told to open a menu and select a command, move the mouse pointer over it, and press and release the left mouse button.

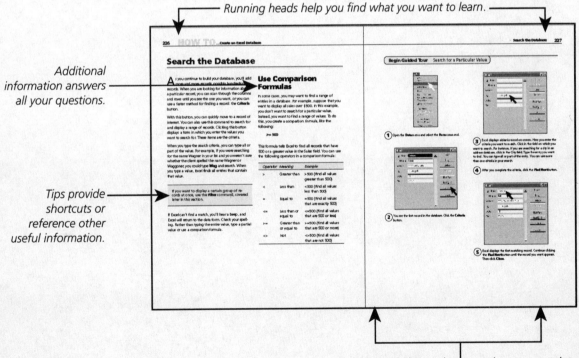

Running heads help you find what you want to learn.

Additional information answers all your questions.

Tips provide shortcuts or reference other useful information.

The Guided Tour shows you how to complete a computer task step-by-step.

Acknowledgments

When you read a book, it is easy to assume that the author is the person responsible for creating what you hold in your hands. But that's not true; the book is really the result of the efforts of many individuals.

First and foremost, the credit for the concept for this book goes to the Publisher, Marie Butler-Knight. Marie is constantly thinking of innovative ways to best meet the needs of you, the buyer. Thanks also go to Barry Pruett, Faithe Wempen, and Martha O'Sullivan for all their brainstorming and administrating.

Finally, extra special thanks go to all the editors for their work on this project. Unless you've written a book, you have no idea how much work the editors do to ensure that all the pieces and parts come together and that the manuscript is readable and free from mistakes. The editors often give up their weekends and holidays to make sure a book gets done on time and gets done right. Many thanks go to editors Seta Frantz, Heather Stith, San Dee Phillips, Liz Keaffaber, and all the production department for putting this book together.

PART 1

How To...

The first part of this book is a How To guide covering all the basic operations needed to use the Microsoft Office 95 programs. Plus, you'll learn how to use the new elements of Windows 95, how to install the Office 95 programs, and how to manage the files you create. Each section is jam-packed full of information about using each of the Office 95 programs individually. You'll learn all the details needed to put Word, Excel, PowerPoint, and Schedule+ to work for you. You'll find important information about each program and how it functions, which will come in handy later when you learn how to integrate them all.

If you're ready to master Microsoft Office 95, then dive into these topics:

What You will Find in This Part

HOW TO...

Use Basic Windows 95 Elements

Before you begin learning all about using Microsoft Office for Windows 95, you need to learn a few things about Microsoft's new Windows 95. Microsoft has made quite a few changes to the Windows interface since Windows 3.1. Windows 95 looks a lot different, works a lot differently, and it has many new features to learn about. One way to learn the detailed ins and outs of this new operating system is to buy a book about the subject—but if you're just looking for instructions about the essentials of Windows 95, then this first section of the *Big Basic Book of Microsoft Office* is just for you.

In this section of the book, you learn how to start and stop Windows 95, familiarize yourself with some of the new features, such as the taskbar and the Programs menu, and find out how to manipulate windows on your screen. These basic skills are fundamental for using the Office 95 programs. (If you're already an experienced Windows 95 user, you can skip ahead to the next section of the book and start using Microsoft Office 95.)

What You Will Find in This Section

Use Windows 95

Microsoft Windows 95 can greatly enhance the way you run your computer system. Because it's so different from the old Windows (version 3.1), software companies are creating new software programs or versions to run on Windows 95—and "everybody" includes the Microsoft Office creators. Microsoft Office for Windows 95 (or Office 95, for short) is a whole new set of Office applications created to run on the new Windows 95 interface.

To help you understand the new Windows 95 system, you first have to know a little about its history. Windows originated as a graphical user interface program, called GUI ("GOO-ey"), that ran on top of DOS—an operating system that tells your computer to act like a computer. DOS was around long before Windows and is command-driven, which means you have to type in cryptic words and abbreviations at a strange-looking prompt symbol to get the computer to do anything.

Thankfully, the Microsoft people designed the Windows GUI to run on top of DOS to make the computer easier to use and much nicer to look at. Instead of text commands, you control the computer using visual graphics—hence the name *graphical user interface*. All you have to do is click on icons (little pictures), select commands from pull-down menus (lists), and open dialog boxes (miniwindows) to make the computer perform various tasks.

Eventually, the Microsoft people decided they could improve Windows, making it even better and easier to use—eliminating its dependence on DOS. That improvement comes in the form of Windows 95. With Windows 95, you never have to deal with command-driven DOS again. Windows 95 is faster, more powerful, and gives you better performance when doing several computer things at the same time.

Begin Guided Tour   New Windows 95 Features

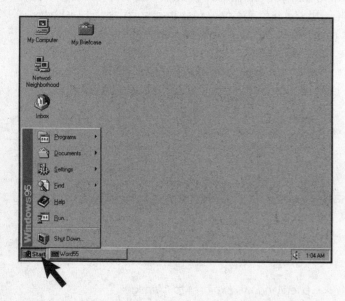

1 You can open any program or document by clicking on the **Start** button, which is on a convenient taskbar at the bottom of your Windows 95 screen.

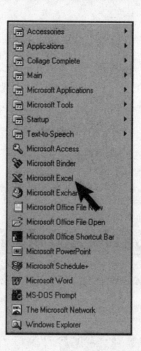

2 Instead of arranging programs and files into program group boxes and directories, you now arrange them in folders in a **Programs** menu. To open any program or folder on the menu, click on its name.

Guided Tour   New Windows 95 Features

3 Microsoft replaced Windows 3.1 File Manager with the **Windows Explorer**. You can use it to manage files, just like the old File Manager, but you access it from the **Start** menu.

5 The Control Panel is still around; you can find it by opening the **Start** menu and choosing **Settings**.

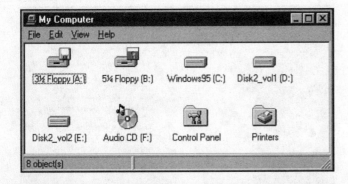

4 You can easily view the contents of your computer's drives by opening the **My Computer** icon. You can also access your Windows 95 Control Panel and Printers folder using this icon.

6 Print Manager's still around, too, using a new name. Access it through the **Start** menu by choosing **Settings** and **Printers**. You'll be happy to know that printing is a major area of improvement in Windows 95. It's easier to add new printers and change settings with the Add Printer Wizard feature.

(continues)

Guided Tour New Windows 95 Features

(continued)

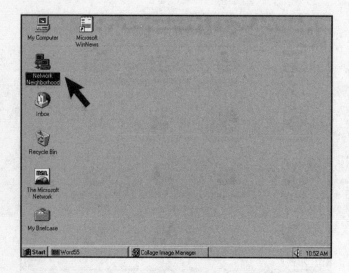

7 Networking is easier now with the Windows 95 **Network Neighborhood** icon. This is handy when you're hooked up to other computers in an office situation.

9 Windows 95 makes full use of Plug and Play hardware technology. With it, you can easily install new hardware devices, without all the headaches of hardware/software clashes. Microsoft also made it easier to install software, too.

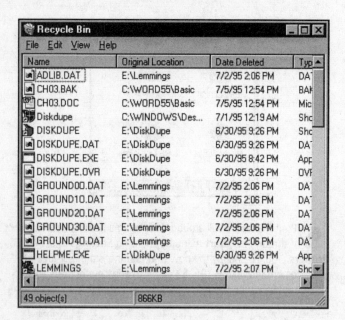

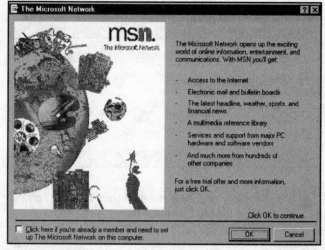

8 You can dump files you no longer want by tossing them, electronically, into the **Recycle Bin**, a temporary storage place for items you're cleaning off your system. The great thing about the Recycle Bin is you can get any files back that you accidentally deleted (if you haven't turned off your computer yet).

10 You can jump into cyberspace without much fuss using Microsoft's online service, aptly named **The Microsoft Network**. You'll also find built-in Internet support on Windows 95.

Start and Stop Windows 95

The new Windows 95 starts immediately whenever you turn on your computer system. Mind you, *immediately* isn't necessarily a fast thing on a computer. Most computers, when started, hum and whir for a few seconds, and strange text appears on the screen. After that, the Windows 95 opening screen appears; then you're presented with a logon box.

The *logon box* is new to Windows 95. You can setup your logon box so that you have to use a password in order to use your computer. This feature is for people who want to safeguard their computers from others and keep computer data protected. If you have important files that you don't want tampered with, then it's a good idea to set up a password. If you're using a networked computer, you'll also have to use a password to access the network.

After you log onto the computer with the logon box, Windows 95 opens up. From your Windows 95 desktop, you can run other applications, use other Windows 95 features, and proceed with your own computer business. You'll always start from this opening screen, which you can think of as your Windows 95 lobby.

When you're ready to turn off your computer, there's a new way to exit. You'll find a Shut Down option when you click on the Start button on the taskbar. It opens a dialog box containing various exiting routes to apply. If you haven't saved your Windows work, Windows will ask you to do so before exiting. A little dialog box pops up with several choices about saving.

Change Your Windows 95 Password

One of the new features used in Windows 95 is a logon box. You can use the box to set up a password to log on with. You can use the password to keep

other people from using your computer. Once you assign yourself a password, however, you'll have to remember it every time you open Windows 95.

Passwords are quite common in computer programs today; you can even use one in your Microsoft Office Schedule+ program. People use passwords to help keep important data safe. It's a good idea to change your password often, every few weeks or so, to keep your computer data secure. If you're using your computer at home, you may not have to be so diligent in computer security, unless you're trying to keep family members from deleting important files.

Use these steps to change your Windows 95 password:

1. To change your Windows 95 password, click the **Start** button; select **Settings** and **Control Panel**.

2. Double-click the **Passwords** icon in the Control Panel box.

3. This opens a dialog box that lets you change the password. Click the **Passwords** tab to bring its information to the front of the box; then click the **Change Windows Password** button.

4. In the Change Windows Password dialog box, type in your old password (if applicable), type in a new password, and then retype the new password again in the Confirm dialog box.

5. Click **OK** to exit the box. The next time you log onto Windows 95, you can use your new password.

Be sure to consult your Windows 95 manual for help with setting up your own logon box with a password. If you set up a password the first time you used Windows 95, you'll have to type it in exactly as you designated it each time you log onto your computer.

Begin Guided Tour   Start Windows 95

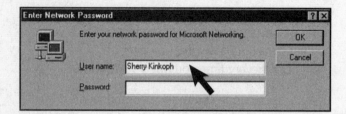

1 Turn on your computer. Windows 95 loads itself without any prompting. When the logon box appears, type in your password (if applicable). If you didn't set up a password, you can proceed directly to Step 2.

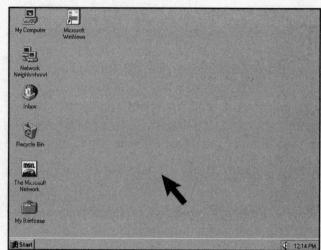

2 Click **OK** or press **Enter** and the Windows 95 desktop opens onto your screen.

Begin Guided Tour   Exit Windows 95

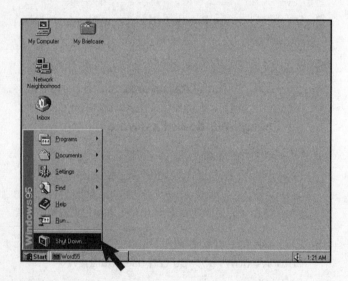

1 Open the **Start** menu and choose **Shut Down**.

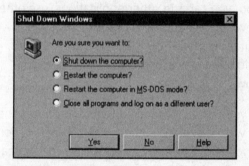

2 In the Shut Down Windows dialog box, choose an appropriate exit option (typically the first one), and then click **Yes**. Your computer prepares for shutdown and prompts you when it's safe to turn off the computer.

If you haven't saved your work, you'll be prompted to do so before turning off the computer.

Move Around in Windows 95

One of the primary tools for navigating Windows 95 and Windows-based programs is the *mouse*. You can use your mouse to point at items on-screen and move them around. You can also use your mouse buttons to select items and perform tasks.

Ever use a mouse before? Don't worry. It gets easier and easier each time you work with it. The mouse is a piece of hardware (as is your printer and keyboard). As you move the mouse around on your desktop, a little arrow appears on-screen and moves as well. That's your *mouse pointer*. It seems a little disorienting at first, but keep at it; using your mouse will become a natural part of your computer life.

There are four mouse actions to learn about:

Click   To quickly tap lightly on the mouse button, usually the left button unless otherwise specified.

Double-click   To lightly tap on the left mouse button twice in quick succession.

Right-click   To quickly tap lightly on the right mouse button.

Drag   To move the mouse while simultaneously holding down the left mouse button.

Although the vast majority of people use a mouse to work with Windows 95, you can use the keyboard to navigate the many windows, too. You have to memorize keystrokes to perform certain tasks.

Here's what you need to know for keyboarding around:

- **Selection letters**   Underlined letters found on menu commands.

- **Shortcut keys**   Keystroke combinations you use to perform tasks.

- **Arrow keys**   Use to move up, down, left, and right on your screen.

- **The helpful Ctrl and Alt keys**   Use to open menus and carry out commands.

The Ctrl key and the Alt key are commonly used in conjunction with other keys to activate commands. All of the menu bars and most of the menu commands have underlined letters in them, called *selection letters*. If you press the Alt key and one of these selection letters, it's the same as opening the menu or selecting the command with the mouse. For example, you can press **Alt+F** to open the File menu. Look for selection letters throughout the Microsoft Office 95 programs.

Also on the menu lists, you'll find keypress combinations, called *shortcut keys*, for activating commands. If available, these are located right next to the menu commands, and they will come in handy as you become more familiar with the programs. Because they're shortcuts, you can save time and effort in selecting commands.

You'll find yourself using the arrow keys quite a bit, too. They move you around the screen and up and down menu lists. (For more information about keyboard commands, check your Windows 95 or Microsoft Office 95 manuals.) Although the rest of this book focuses on mouse actions, you can still utilize the keyboard whenever applicable.

Begin Guided Tour   Move Around with the Mouse

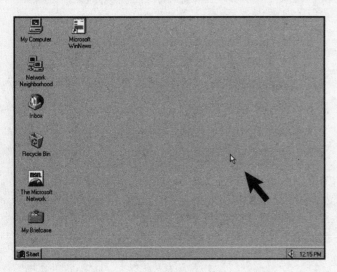
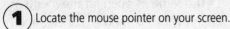
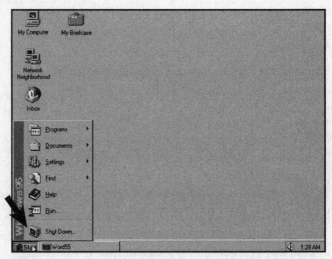

1   Locate the mouse pointer on your screen.

2   To move the mouse pointer, simply move your mouse. To select an item on-screen, move the pointer over the item and click on the left mouse button. For example, if you move the pointer over the **Start** button on the taskbar (the bar at the bottom of the Windows 95 desktop) and click, the Start menu opens. To open an icon on the desktop (a small picture representing a feature, command, or program), move your pointer over the icon and double-click.

Begin Guided Tour   Move Around with the Keyboard

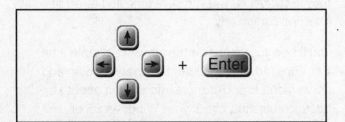
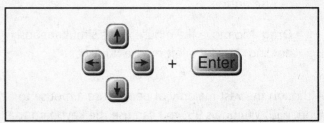

1   To move around on the Windows 95 desktop using the keyboard, use the arrow buttons to move from icon to icon. When you've selected an icon, it appears highlighted. You can then press the **Enter** key to open the feature.

3   Use the arrow keys to move up and down the Start menu and highlight options. To select an option, highlight it and press **Enter**.

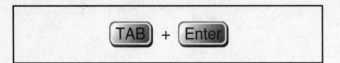

2   Press the **Tab** key to move back and forth from the desktop to the taskbar. Once you highlight the **Start** button, which appears to have a dotted outline of a box around the button's edge, you can press **Enter** to open the Start menu.

View the Windows 95 Desktop

Windows 95 focuses on a desktop look, which means that the most common elements appear on your screen much like your own office elements, such as you arrange your stapler, phone, pens, and paper on your desk. Here are some common elements you'll find on your Windows 95 desktop:

My Computer This icon opens to reveal all of the drives you have on your computer. You can use this feature to open each drive's contents and find out what folders and files you have. For example, to find out what's on your floppy disk, you can put the disk in your floppy drive, open the My Computer window, and select the floppy disk drive. It will list what's on the disk in the drive. It also lets you access the Control Panel and Printers folders.

Network Neighborhood Use this icon when you're connected to a network of other computers. It displays the various elements found on your network and lets you use them.

Recycle Bin This is where you toss things you no longer want on your system, such as old files. When you're ready to remove items, open this icon up and confirm the deletions.

The Microsoft Network This icon helps you get online with Microsoft's commercial online service. You'll need a modem to use this feature and a credit card to pay for the service.

Taskbar Use the taskbar to open and use one or more programs at the same time. For every program you open, a button for it appears on the taskbar. You can easily click on the buttons to switch to other programs.

Start button To start any program, use this button. It displays a Start menu for launching programs, accessing the Control Panel, finding files, finding online help, and shutting down the computer.

In Windows 3.1, you access a Task List for switching between programs you are working with. You press **Ctrl+Esc** to see the list because it isn't readily visible. Windows 95 lets you do this with the taskbar, which is always on your screen (unless you choose to hide it).

Use Windows Accessories

There's more to Windows 95 than the items found on the desktop. Windows 95 comes with several applications, although you can certainly add others such as Microsoft Office for Windows 95. The Accessories folder contains some fun Windows 95 features, such as a painting program and a calculator. You don't absolutely need to know about these accessories, but they may come in handy. I'll describe these for you, and then you can explore them at your leisure.

WordPad A simple word processing program that lets you work with text. It's not as sophisticated as Word for Windows 95, but it can handle basic word processing tasks. (WordPad is the replacement for the old Windows 3.1 Write program.)

Paint A drawing and painting program for creating computer graphics. Paint has various tools for illustrating, making shapes, and using colors and patterns.

Calculator An on-screen calculator for handling simple operations such as addition, subtraction, division, and multiplication.

Calendar Helps you keep track of your schedule (kind of like a streamlined version of Schedule+, which comes with your Office 95 pack). You'll only have this accessory if you upgraded from Windows 3.1.

Cardfile   A very simple database program that resembles a card catalog or Rolodex. Use it to keep track of information such as addresses, phone numbers, and so on. (You'll only have this accessory if you upgraded from Windows 3.1.)

HyperTerminal   Helps you use your modem to dial online services. HyperTerminal is a new Windows Terminal (a feature from Windows 3.1).

Be sure to check your Windows 95 manual for more information about using each of these accessories.

Begin Guided Tour   Tour the Windows 95 Desktop

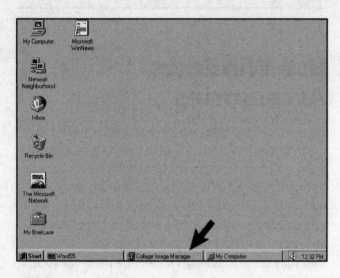

1 Windows 95 taskbar lets you switch back and forth between open programs. The program names appear as buttons on the taskbar.

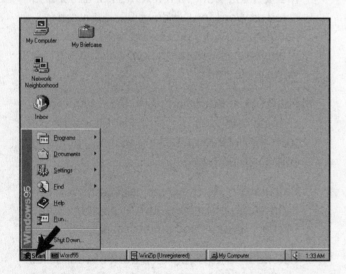

2 Also located on the taskbar is the **Start** button. When you click on the **Start** button, a menu appears with various options you can select.

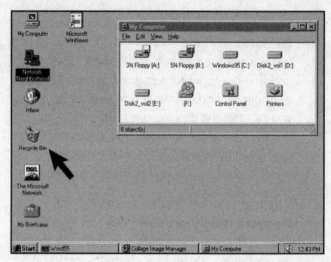

3 The rest of the Windows 95 desktop holds icons representing various features such as the Recycle Bin or My Computer. To open any feature on the desktop, double-click on the icon.

Use My Computer to View Your Drives

The My Computer icon presents you with another way to look at your drives and the files they contain. To open the My Computer feature, double-click on its icon. It opens into a window revealing all of your drives. The My Computer window lets you see your drives' contents and find out how much space they each have. It also provides quick access to the Control Panel (for controlling Windows 95 settings), and the Printers folders (for handling printers).

To see how much space your hard drive is using, click on the drive icon to select it; then look at the bottom of the My Computer window to see how much free space you have left. You'll also see what your drive's capacity is, listed in megabytes.

To open a drive and see its contents, just double-click on the drive's icon. To close the window at any time, click on the **Close** button—the button with an **X** on it in the upper right corner of the opened window.

Begin Guided Tour   Open My Computer

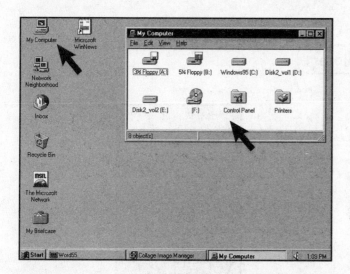

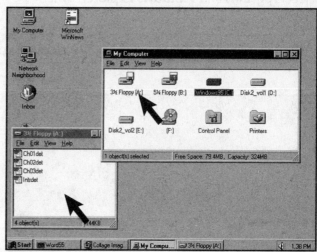

1 Double-click the **My Computer** icon to open a window revealing the contents of your computer. You see an icon for each drive on your computer, plus the Control Panel and Printers folders.

2 To see what's in a drive, double-click the drive icon. This opens a window revealing the contents of the drive.

You can open as many drive windows as you want. You can even move and copy files and folders from window to window. To close the My Computer window or drive windows you've opened, click the **Close** button in the upper right corner. The button with the **X** on it is the Close button.

Use Windows Explorer to Manage Files

Windows 95 does not have a File Manager like Windows 3.1; it has been replaced with the Windows Explorer. You can do the same things with the Explorer that you did with File Manager, including moving and copying files to new locations, deleting files, printing files, and even launching programs. You can view your computer's file structure and folder hierarchy with Explorer. Windows Explorer looks very much like the old File Manager, with a few stylish touches added.

To find the Windows Explorer, you must first click on the **Start** button to display the Start menu, then select **Programs** and **Windows Explorer**. When

selected, it opens the Explorer window. Inside this window, you'll find menus, toolbar buttons, and a listing of your computer's file and folder hierarchy. To change the folders in view, click on the drop-down list and choose a drive or folder you want to display. You can use the toolbar buttons to quickly view files; expand or collapse the folder hierarchy; delete files; cut, copy, or paste, and more.

To open a folder and view its contents, double-click on the folder icon or name. Use the scroll bars to move back and forth along the list of folders or files displayed.

Begin Guided Tour   Open Windows Explorer

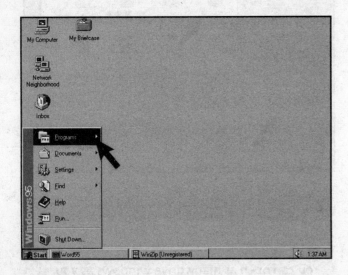

1 Open the **Start** menu and choose **Programs**. The Programs menu appears.

2 Locate the Windows Explorer at the end of the Programs menu list, and click on it to select it.

Guided Tour   Open Windows Explorer

To close the Windows Explorer window, click the **Close (X)** button in the upper right corner of the window.

3 The Exploring - Windows 95 window appears, which looks very much like the Windows 3.1 File Manager. From here, you can use the menu bar to manage your files and folders.

Work with Windows

Microsoft appropriately named Windows 95 because of all the windows (also called boxes) that open up to reveal programs, tools, and other computer information. The windows you encounter may be program windows, or Windows 95 features, such as My Computer. Each window has some common elements you'll need to know about. You can use these elements to manipulate the window's size, move around inside the window, and open and close the window.

For example, each window has a *border* that you can use to resize the window. Move your mouse pointer over a border; when the pointer becomes a directional arrow, you can click-and-drag a new border shape. You can drag any of the four sides of your window to change its size in that direction. You can drag any of the corners with the mouse to make the window bigger or smaller in two directions at the same time. You'll need to know how to resize windows when you start working with two or more open windows on your screen.

In the upper right corner of your windows, you'll find three buttons. Those are your *Minimize*, *Maximize*, and *Close* buttons. You can click on any of these buttons to control your window. The Minimize button, when selected, reduces your window into a button on the taskbar (which you can open again by clicking on it). The Maximize button enlarges your window to take up the entire screen space. Once a window has been maximized, a *Restore* button appears. Click the Restore button to reduce the window to its original size. The Close (**X**) button does just as its name implies; it closes the window completely.

In the upper left corner of most windows is a *Control-menu* icon. It sits to the left of the window title. If you click your mouse pointer on the **Control-menu** icon, it reveals a menu for controlling the window. You'll find commands listed for changing the window's size or closing the window. You can also double-click on the **Control-menu** icon to close the window completely.

Another window element to know about are *bars*. The typical window can have several bars, each pertaining to a certain aspect of the window. You can use the bars to open menus, view different portions of the window, and even check a task's status. For example, a window's title bar tells what program or feature it is, and the menu bar lists all of the menu groups you can choose from. A window's status bar might display information about the task you're performing. A window's scroll bar lets you move backward and forward in a list of items.

Work with Multiple Windows

The useful feature about Windows is that you can open as many windows as you want. You can also move from window to window by clicking on each one. (You can use the taskbar to do this, too.) Multiple-opened windows make it easier than ever to move items from one window and place them in another. However, there's a downside to multiple windows. The more you open, the more cluttered your desktop becomes. Each time you open a window, it will sit on top of the previous window. This makes things a little messy sometimes. If you're opening all kinds of folder windows, for example, a stack of opened windows piles up fast.

The active window's title bar is always a solid color so you always know which one you're currently using.

There are some options for tidying up these multiple windows. If you're working with multiple program windows, you can tidy them up using the program's Windows menu commands (the Windows menu is on the program's main menu bar). If you're working with windows from My Computer or Network Neighborhood, you can tidy up multiple windows with the Options dialog box:

1. Open your window's **View** menu and select **Options**. This opens the Options dialog box with tabs for controlling windows.

2. Click the **Folders** tab to bring it to the front of the dialog box. There are two options for viewing your windows. The first option opens a new window for every folder you view. The second option replaces the previous window with the new window's contents. In other words, when you select this option, only one window appears on-screen no matter how many you open—only the window's contents change.

3. Choose an option, and click **OK** to exit the box. You can open the Options dialog box at any time and change the selection for viewing your folder windows.

Another way to keep things tidy is with a Shortcut menu (a menu that appears when you right-click) on the taskbar. If you're working with multiple windows opened on your screen, you can arrange them neatly by *tiling* or *cascading* them on your desktop. To do so:

1. Move your mouse pointer down to the taskbar and right-click. This opens a Shortcut menu for arranging windows.

2. Select a command from the menu, such as **Cascade** (stacks the windows nicely) or one of the **Tile** (displays the windows side-by-side) commands, and the windows will appear neatly on-screen for you.

3. If you want to minimize all the windows opened on your desktop, select the **Minimize All Windows** command from the Shortcut menu. This will reduce all the opened windows to buttons on your taskbar.

> If you're looking for more detailed information about using Windows 95, pick up a copy of *The Big Basics Book of Windows 95*.

Begin Guided Tour   Use the Window Elements

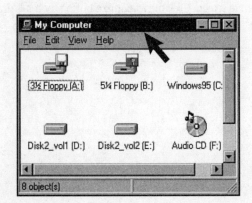

1 At the top portion of the window is a *title bar* that displays the program or file name. If you're not sure which program or window you're in, look at the title bar for a clue. You can move a window by pointing at the title bar, holding down the left mouse button, and dragging the mouse.

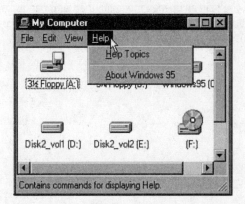

2 Located below the title bar, the *menu bar* displays a row of menu names. To open a menu, click on the menu name, and a list of commands will appear. To select a command, click on it.

(continues)

Guided Tour Use the Window Elements

(continued)

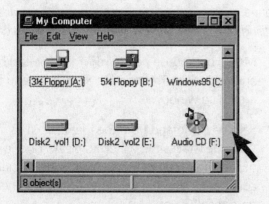

3 You can find *scroll bars* along the right side or bottom of the window (or both), which you can use to view other parts of the window that aren't currently visible on-screen.

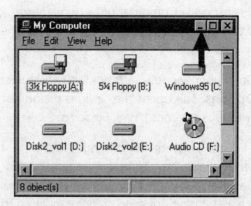

5 Clicking the **Minimize** button reduces the window to a button on your taskbar. (Click the button on the taskbar to open the window again.)

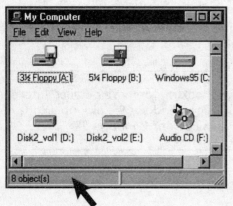

4 At the bottom of your screen (which you might encounter if you're in an opened program), the *status bar* displays information about the file you're working on. In some programs, the status bar may even contain buttons you can activate.

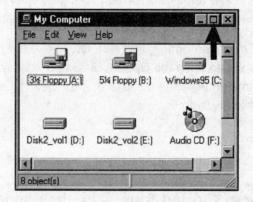

6 Maximizing enlarges the window so that it takes up the entire screen. Click the **Maximize** button for a full-size window.

Guided Tour   Use the Window Elements

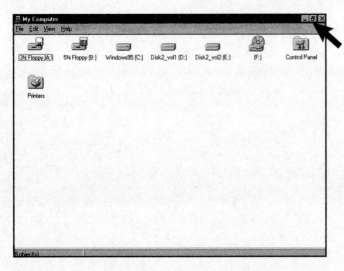

9 If you click your mouse pointer on the **Control-menu** icon, it reveals a menu for controlling the window. You'll find commands listed for changing the window's size or closing the window. You can also double-click the **Control-menu** icon to close the window completely.

7 When you maximize a window, a **Restore** button appears. You can click it to restore the window to its original size.

In Windows 3.1, you used a Minimize, Maximize, and Restore button to control the window's size. Those buttons are still around, they just look different.

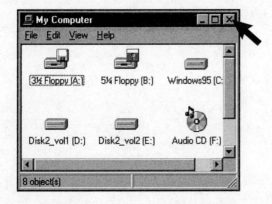

8 The **Close** button stands out because it has a big **X** in its box. Click it to close the window.

HOW TO

Perform Basic Office Skills

f you're already familiar with the new Windows 95 operating environment, then you're ready to dive in and start using Microsoft Office. If you're a new Windows user, you might want to back up and read the previous section for fundamental information about using the Windows 95 features.

If you're a seasoned veteran of the old Microsoft Office programs, you'll feel right at home using Office 95. All of your favorite features from the other programs are still around, plus there are plenty of new ones to try. The installation procedures are a little different, but simple and easy to handle. If you're a brand new user of the Office suite of applications, don't worry, this book will show you in detail how to use each program to its fullest, regardless of your comfort level.

In this section, you learn how to set up Microsoft Office 95, open and close applications, and understand the on-screen elements that will help you use the programs. With these skills, you can start using any of the Office 95 applications. The following tasks are covered

What You Will Find in This Section

Install Microsoft Office 95

Before you can take advantage of all the great things you can do with Microsoft Office 95, you first have to install the programs. If you have already installed Windows 95 on your system, you're ready to go. If you are installing Microsoft Office for Windows 95 using floppy disks, you'll have a bunch of disks to juggle. Each disk, however, is labeled so you'll know which one to insert. If you purchased a CD-ROM version of Office 95, you'll just have the one CD. If you're installing Office 95 from a network, however, you'll need to ask your network administrator for assistance. Network installation works a little differently, depending on the type of network you have.

To make it as easy as possible to install Microsoft Office 95, the package includes a setup program that will lead you through the installation process, asking you to make and confirm selections. You can choose to install the entire Office 95 package or just a single program. This same setup program can help you uninstall Office 95 programs later.

The setup program offers you three installation options: Typical, Custom, or Compact. If you are installing the system on a desktop computer (not a laptop), the best choice is Typical. The Custom installation is for users who like to customize the setup of their Office 95 programs. The Compact installation is useful if you don't have much hard disk space to install onto. You can always go back later and make changes or customize how the programs are set up.

During installation, the setup program will prompt you to select the drive and folder where you want to place the program files. You can select the default suggestions or change the folder, if necessary. You can also select which programs you want to install. After you make your choices, the setup program will prompt you to insert the appropriate disks. Simply follow the on-screen instructions as necessary. When the installation is complete, restart your computer.

> To install a single program, find the first disk, usually called the setup disk, for the program. Then follow the Guided Tour for installing Microsoft Office 95.

Begin Guided Tour   Install Microsoft Office 95

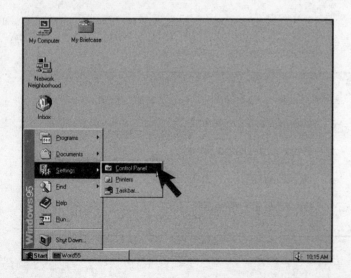

1 Start Windows 95, if it isn't up and running already. Click the **Start** button; select **Settings** and **Control Panel**.

Guided Tour   Install Microsoft Office 95

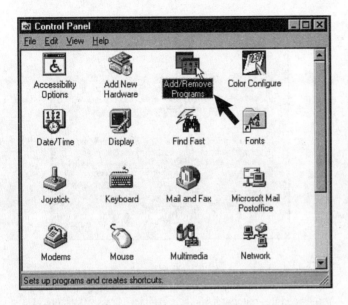

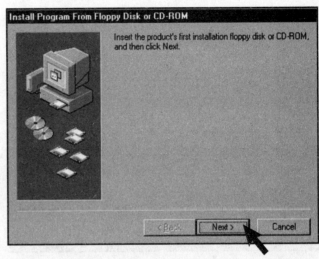

2 The Control Panel window opens on your screen. Double-click the **Add/Remove Programs** icon.

4 A series of boxes will appear (called a wizard) to lead you through selecting a drive and program to install. Insert the Office Setup disk into the appropriate drive. Click the **Next** button to continue.

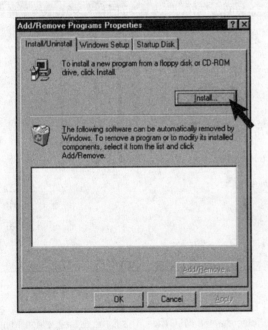

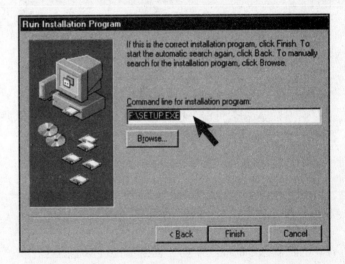

3 The Add/Remove Programs Properties dialog box appears. Click the **Install/Uninstall** tab to bring its information to the front of the dialog box, if it's not already at the front. Click the **Install** button to start the procedure.

5 Your computer searches your drives to locate the disk or CD-ROM. When it finds the setup program, its location appears in the box. (If your computer is having trouble finding the setup program, you can use the **Browse** button to look for it.) Click the **Finish** button to open the setup program.

(continues)

Guided Tour Install Microsoft Office 95

(continued)

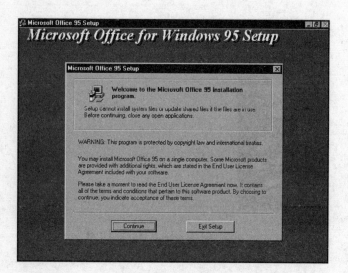

6 You see the initial Microsoft Office Setup screen. Read the information and click the **Continue** button.

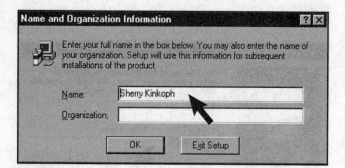

7 In the Name and Organization Information box, type in your name and company; then click **OK**. A confirmation box appears where you can check the information. If you need to edit your entry, click the **Change** button. If everything's correct, click **OK**.

If you're installing from a CD-ROM, the next box that appears prompts you to enter the CD's 10-digit key code found on the CD liner notes or sleeve. Type the number in and click **OK** to continue to step 8.

8 In the next box, you'll confirm your product ID number. Be sure to write this number down and keep it in a safe place. You'll need this number if you ever contact Microsoft's technical support people. Click **OK** to continue installing.

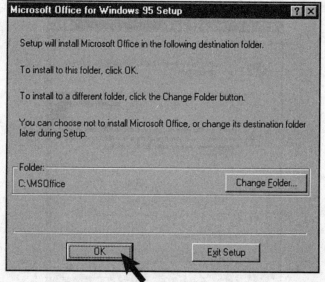

9 The setup program prompts you to install Office 95 in a folder named **MSOffice**. This is the default folder. To install the program files to this folder, click **OK**. If you prefer to install Office to another folder or drive, click the **Change Folder** button and designate another destination for the program files.

Guided Tour   Install Microsoft Office 95

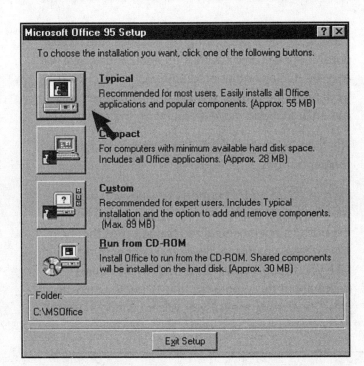

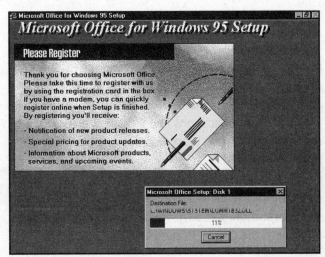

12 Finally, the installation process begins in earnest, copying program files onto your computer. Just follow the on-screen prompts, inserting each disk as needed. A little installation-gauge box appears on-screen, indicating how much of the program is installed.

10 The next setup box lets you pick an installation option: Typical, Compact, Custom, or Run from CD-ROM. Click the option button to select the installation type you want. For most users, the **Typical** installation is the best option to choose; it installs the most common features the average computer user wants to have access to.

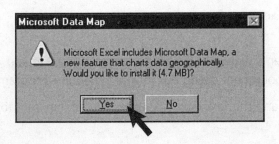

11 Depending on the installation option you selected in the previous step, more on-screen prompts may appear. Read the instructions and make the appropriate choices for you and your computer. One of the prompts you'll encounter will ask if you want to install the DataMap feature. This feature charts data geographically on your system—it's actually a collection of maps from all over the world. Click on Yes to install this feature.

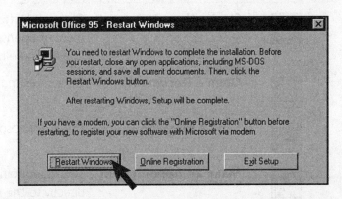

13 When you have installed everything, Setup displays a Restart Windows box. You'll have to restart Windows 95 in order to complete the installation. Click on the **Restart Windows** button.

If you prefer, you can stop and register your copy of Microsoft Office 95 electronically with your modem. All you have to do is click on the **Online Registration** button and follow the prompts. When finished, you can restart Windows and complete the installation.

Use the Office Shortcut Bar

One of the first things you'll notice after installing the Office 95 programs is the *Office Shortcut bar*. This toolbar appears on-screen, in the upper right corner, as soon as you start Windows 95. The Office Shortcut bar is a unique feature that connects all of the Office 95 applications and literally acts as a manager, delegating work and bossing the other programs around. You can open documents with it, set up appointments, quickly access online help, and even launch the various applications with it. Basically, the Shortcut bar can save you time and effort as you work with the Office 95 programs.

When you start Windows, the Office Shortcut bar feature starts up by default You'll see the toolbar regardless of what program you're using (unless you choose to hide it or close it). For instance, the toolbar doesn't appear only in Office 95 applications; you will also see it in any other programs you have running. By default, the toolbar is quite small, however, you can enlarge it and move it around on the screen.

The following table explains each of the default toolbar buttons.

Each of your Shortcut buttons provides you with a shortcut to starting a program or document. Some of the buttons open generalized dialog boxes that help you choose a particular file or task. Other buttons take you to familiar windows such as Schedule+ (more about this program in the "How to Use Schedule+" section) or the Answer Wizard window (learn

Icon	Name	Description
	Start a New Document	Click this button when you're ready to start a new Office 95 document. It opens the New dialog box for choosing among Word, Excel, and PowerPoint documents.
	Open a Document	Opens existing Office documents you've already created and saved.
	Send a Message	Opens Microsoft Exchange for sending e-mail messages.
	Make an Appointment	Sets up appointments with your Schedule+ program; it takes you directly to the Appointment dialog box in your Schedule+ program.
	Add a Task	Opens Schedule+ and the Task dialog box; lets you add an item to your To Do list.
	Add a Contact	Opens Schedule+ and lets you add a contact name to your list with the Contact dialog box.
	Getting Results Book	Accesses the CD-ROM documentation for maximizing your Office 95 usage.
	Office Compatible	Use this button to view demonstrations of programs that work with Office 95.
	Answer Wizard	Opens the online Help system and displays the Answer Wizard dialog box where you can get help fast.

to use this feature under the heading "Get Help" in this section).

When you click on an Office Shortcut bar button, the appropriate program starts. You can customize the buttons to represent each Office application you've installed or other common tasks you'll use frequently. With some modifications, this toolbar will let you open any of the Office 95 programs by simply clicking on the respective icon. You can also add other buttons to this toolbar, even buttons for other non-Microsoft programs that you use frequently.

I highly recommend that you customize your Shortcut bar to include each of the Office 95 applications. When you do, you can easily open any of the Office programs at any time with a simple click on the appropriate button on the toolbar.

Customize the Office Toolbar

If you click on the **Microsoft Office** icon in the Shortcut bar (the puzzle icon at the very left of the bar), the Microsoft Office menu drops down. If your Shortcut bar is floating (not touching any of the four sides of the monitor screen), you can right-click on the title bar, or right-click on any empty space on the bar to see the menu. You can use the Microsoft Office menu to perform a variety of tasks, including opening the Customize dialog box or turning off the Shortcut bar (covered in a Guided Tour later in this task).

Here's what's on your menu:

Restore, **Move**, and **Minimize**   Commands for controlling your Shortcut bar. For example, when you choose the Minimize command, your Shortcut bar becomes an icon button on the Windows 95 taskbar.

Auto Hide   Instructs your computer to automatically conceal the Shortcut bar when you open a program.

Customize   Opens a dialog box for retooling (customizing) your Shortcut bar.

Add/Remove Office Programs   Opens the setup program (which you used to install the Office applications). You can use the setup program to add and delete Office 95 programs.

Microsoft Office Help Topics   Hooks you up with the online Help system.

About Microsoft Office   Displays some copyright information about the Office 95 product version and serial numbers.

Exit   Removes the Shortcut bar from your screen.

Add Non-Microsoft Program Buttons to the Shortcut Bar

Microsoft Office programs aren't the only applications you can add to the Shortcut bar. You can also add non-Microsoft programs that you use frequently. You can even add Windows 95 features, such as the Windows Explorer to the bar. To do any of these things, you first have to open the Customize dialog box.

To find the Customize dialog box, you first have to open the Office menu. In the left corner of your Office Shortcut bar is a tiny icon. Click on the icon to display a menu of Office commands. One of those commands is the Customize command, which you can use to customize how your Office Shortcut bar is set up. Follow these steps to customize your own Shortcut bar:

1. Click the **Microsoft Office** icon to access the Office menu.

2. Select the **Customize** command.

3. In the Customize dialog box, click the **Buttons** tab to bring the button options to the front of the box.

4. Click on the **Add File** button. The Add File dialog box appears.

5. In the Add File dialog box, select the program file you want to add to the Shortcut bar. Use the Look in drop-down list to locate the program, or use the File name text box to look it up directly.

6. Once you select the program file, click on the **Add** button to close the dialog box and return to the Buttons tab.

7. Make sure the check box for the newly added program has a check mark in it, and then click **OK** to close the Customize dialog box.

> You can use the **Add Folder** button in the Add File dialog box to add a folder to your Shortcut bar. For example, if you want speedy access to your My Documents folder, add it to the bar following the steps above (except click on the **Add Folder** button instead of the Add File button). Then whenever you click its icon, the folder window opens on your screen.

Moving Your Shortcut Buttons Around

By default, your Office Shortcut bar buttons appear in a set order. However, you can customize the buttons to be in any order that you want. Once again, you'll have to utilize the Customize dialog box to carry out your customizing tasks. You'll find the Customize command located on the Office menu. You can access the menu by clicking on the **Microsoft Office** icon in the corner of the Shortcut bar.

In the **Buttons** tab in the Customize dialog box, you can designate what order the Shortcut bar buttons appear, from left to right. Why would you want to rearrange the buttons? Perhaps you're used to clicking on the first icon on a toolbar, or maybe you want similar icons and tasks grouped together. You can designate which button appears where on the bar. It's easy to move the buttons to other locations on the bar, so you can place the buttons you use the most in the places you'll click most often.

Use these steps to change the order of your Shortcut bar buttons:

1. Click the **Microsoft Office** icon to access the Microsoft Office menu.

2. Select the **Customize** command.

3. In the Customize dialog box, click on the **Buttons** tab to bring the button options to the front of the box.

4. Select the name of the button you want to move.

5. Click the up or down **Move** arrow to move the program to another place on the list. (Don't click on the scroll bar arrows; that won't do the trick.)

6. When you're all done, click **OK**. The Shortcut bar reflects your icon changes.

> If you want to delete buttons from the bar and from the list of buttons in the Customize dialog box, access the Buttons tab of the Customize dialog box, select the program, and click on the **Delete** button.

Begin Guided Tour   Start and Close the Office Shortcut Bar

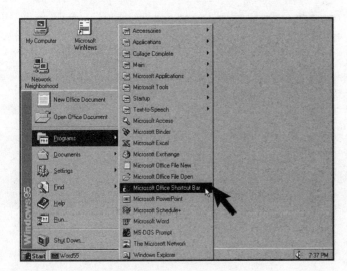

1 Click on the Start button on your Windows 95 taskbar, then select Programs and Microsoft Office Shortcut Bar.

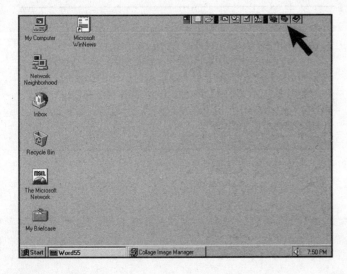

2 The Microsoft Office Shortcut bar opens and places the toolbar in the upper right corner of your Windows 95 desktop.

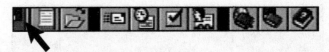

3 To close the Shortcut bar and remove it from your screen, click on the Microsoft Office icon (the little puzzle icon at the very left of the bar).

4 The Microsoft Office menu drops down. Click on the Exit command to close down the Shortcut bar.

Begin Guided Tour   Move the Office Shortcut Bar

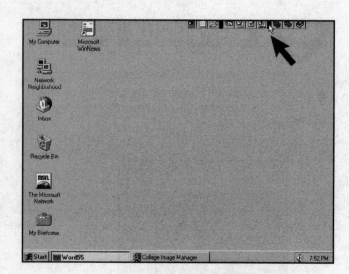

1 By default, the Shortcut bar starts out anchored in the upper right corner of your screen. You can turn the Shortcut bar into a floating toolbar on your screen. Move your mouse pointer over a blank part of your Shortcut bar, such as in between buttons.

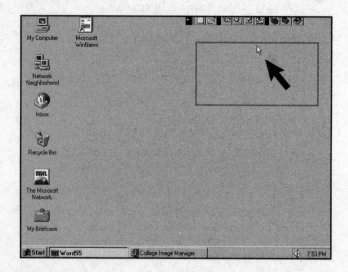

2 Drag your Shortcut bar (hold down the left mouse button and move the mouse) to a new location on the screen.

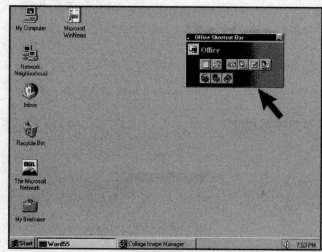

3 Let go of the mouse button when the Shortcut bar is in place.

To re-anchor the Shortcut bar back into its default position in the upper right corner of the screen, double-click on the title bar. You can also drag the bar back up to the corner. As soon as you near the edge of the screen, let go of the bar and, like a magnet, it finds its way back to the edge.

Begin Guided Tour　Change Your Shortcut Bar's Button Size

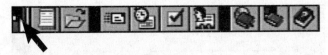

1 Click the **Microsoft Office** icon (it looks like a tiny puzzle shape at the far left of your bar) on the Shortcut bar.

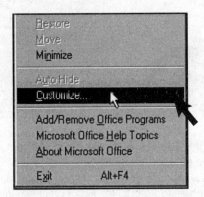

2 From the menu that appears, choose **Customize**.

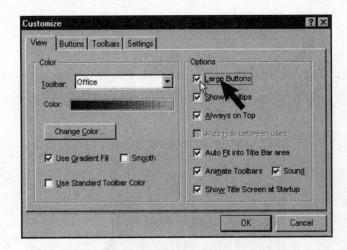

4 Click the **Large Buttons** check box under the Options heading in the tab. When you finish with the View options, click **OK** to put them into effect.

Any time you want your buttons small again, just follow the steps above and deselect the Large Buttons option.

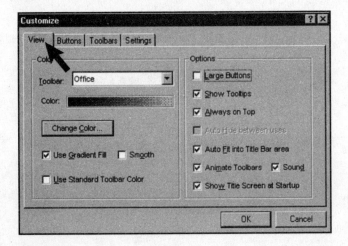

3 When the Customize dialog box opens, click the **View** tab to bring the View options to the front of the box.

Begin Guided Tour Customize the Shortcut Bar

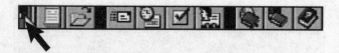

1 Click the **Microsoft Office** icon to access the Microsoft Office menu.

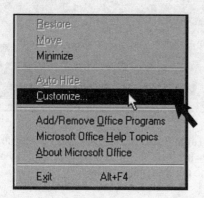

2 Select the **Customize** command from the menu.

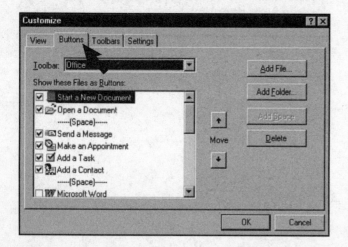

3 In the Customize dialog box, click on the **Buttons** tab to bring the button options to the front of the dialog box.

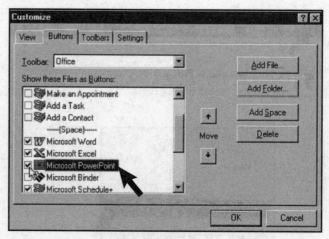

4 From the list of possible buttons, you can select or unselect to add and subtract icons from the Shortcut bar. To customize your toolbar to show all of the Office 95 applications as buttons, you first have to select all the buttons representing your Office 95 programs in this dialog box. When you select a button to appear on the bar, it has a check mark in its box. Then turn off the buttons you don't want to use.

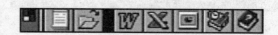

5 When you finish redoing your buttons, click **OK**, and the Shortcut bar reflects your changes.

You can use the Add Space button in the dialog box to add spacers between your Shortcut bar buttons. Click on the button list (in the Customize box) where you want space, and then click the **Add Space** button.

Begin Guided Tour Adding Tools to Your Shortcut Bar

1 First, turn your Office Shortcut bar into a floating bar (see earlier Guided Tour steps). You don't have to float the bar to do this task; however, it certainly makes it easier to see what's going on.

The Office Shortcut bar isn't the only toolbar you can use with Windows 95. Other programs use toolbars, too; even Windows 95 has a desktop toolbar you can display to quickly access Windows 95 accessory programs.

3 Once you add a toolbar, your Office Shortcut bar icons move over to make room for the new addition.

To see the Office Shortcut bar buttons again, click on the Office side of the floating toolbar. You can easily get rid of the additional toolbars by opening the menu again and deselecting the bars you no longer want to see.

2 On the floating Shortcut bar, right-click on an empty space on the bar and select which toolbar you want to add from the menu of available toolbars.

Start and Exit an Office 95 Application

Starting up an application is one of the easiest things you can do with your computer. To start an application, click on the Start button, open the Programs menu and click on the application's icon. If the Office Shortcut bar appears on your screen, you can also start programs using the toolbar buttons. Aside from the startup methods just described, you can also launch your Office applications from the Windows Explorer or My Computer windows by double-clicking on the application's executable file. With Windows 95, you can have several programs running at the same time. You can switch back and forth between them as needed using the taskbar.

When you finish working with a program, be sure to save all your work (the next chapter covers saving), and then exit the program. Why is it important to exit when you can have a lot of programs running? It's a good idea to exit the program to conserve memory and ensure your system runs as efficiently as possible. You can think of exiting a program as clearing off your desk. When you clear off the desk, you have more working room. If you exit a program without saving your work, you will be prompted to save it.

There are many different ways to exit an Office application:

- Double-click the program window's **Control-menu** icon (that tiny icon in the upper left corner of the window on the title bar with a tiny icon in it).

- Click on the **Close** button (that tiny box with an **X** in it in the upper right corner of the window).

- Pull down the program's **File** menu and select **Exit**.

- Press **Alt+F4** on your keyboard.

Begin Guided Tour Start a Program

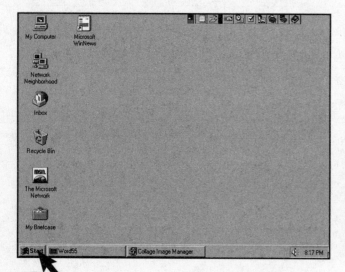

1 Click on the **Start** button on the Windows 95 taskbar.

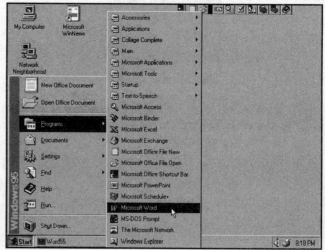

2 Select **Programs** from the Start menu; then in the Programs menu click on the Office 95 program you want to open. The application opens onto your screen.

Begin Guided Tour   Exit a Program

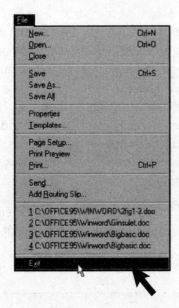

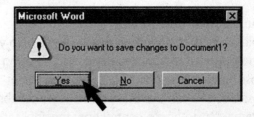

2 If you have saved the document, you exit the program and return to the Windows 95 desktop. If you didn't save, you are prompted to save. Click the **Yes** button to save the document, the **No** button to exit without saving, or the **Cancel** button to cancel the exit.

1 From any open program window, open the **File** menu and choose the **Exit** command. (You can also click on the program's **Close** button.)

When you finish working with the computer and want to turn it off, make sure you exit Windows 95 properly. You shouldn't turn off your computer with Windows 95 still running because Windows 95 takes care of some housekeeping (getting rid of temporary files and other things) when you exit. Use the exit steps you learned in the previous chapter. Click on the **Start** button, select **Shut Down**; then click **Yes** to turn off your computer.

Use Basic Office 95 Program Elements

The program creators have put several basic elements in the application window to help you get the most out of your programs, so that using Microsoft Office 95 applications is as convenient as possible. You can use these elements to tell the program what to do, to control how the application appears on your screen, and to speed up your work. In every Office 95 application, you'll find tools to resize the window, select commands, use formatting features, and much more. You'll find these basics in each Office program, so once you've learned to use them in one program, you know how to use them for all the programs.

Keep in mind that when you are working in a document in an application, you actually have two windows open: the application window and the document window. Each window has its own set of controls: the standard windows controls. The windows include the Minimize, Maximize, and Close buttons used for controlling the windows. The document window may include scroll bars for scrolling the window.

Let's take a look at each of the common elements you'll see on your own Office program screens.

Begin Guided Tour   Basic Office 95 Elements

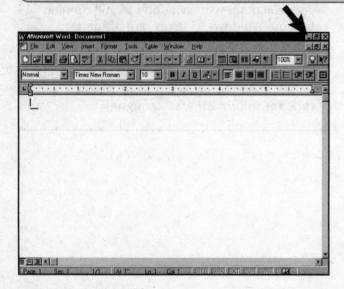

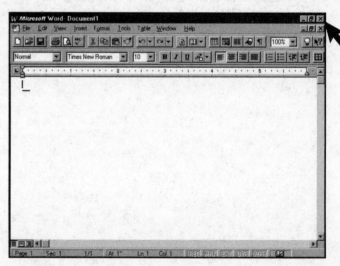

1 Click the **Minimize** button to turn the window into an icon that appears on the taskbar. With some programs, such as Microsoft Word, you're working with a program window and a document window on-screen at the same time, so you will see two sets of window control buttons.

Click the **Maximize** button to expand the window to fill the entire screen. When you maximize a window, you see the Restore button, which you can then use to restore the window to its original size.

2 Click the **Close** button to exit the program at any time. As mentioned, in some programs, you're working with a program window and a document window, so you'll see two sets of window control buttons. If you click on the document window's **Close** (**X**) button, you'll close the document you were working on, but the program stays open. If you click on the program window's **Close** (**X**) button, you'll close the entire program.

Guided Tour   Basic Office 95 Elements

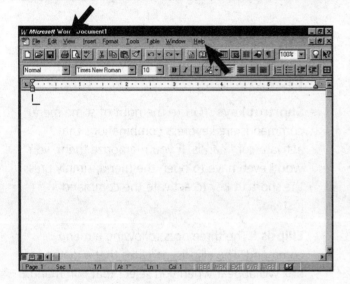

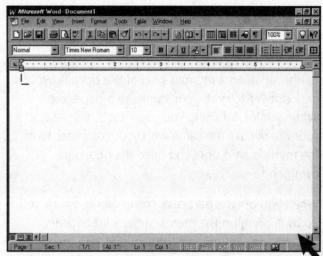

3 The *title bar* shows you the name of the program or file you're currently working on. The *menu bar* lists the menu names that contain commands for controlling tasks and features in your program.

5 Use the *scroll bars* to view other portions of your file. You can scroll up and down, or right and left to view your document. Use the scroll arrows to move in specific directions. To scroll quickly, drag the scroll box in the appropriate direction.

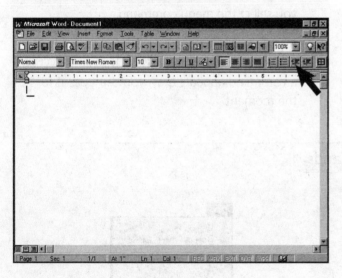

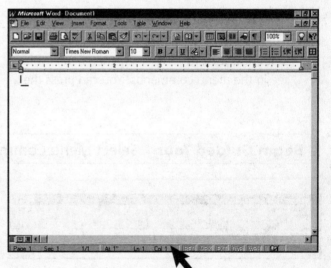

4 The *toolbars* include buttons for frequently used commands. These buttons can speed up your computer work. You can click on the appropriate button to select a command.

6 The *status bar* contains information about the current document, such as what page you are on. For example, in Word, you can see what page you're working on, and the current location in the document. In PowerPoint, the status bar even contains buttons for activating commands.

Use Menu Commands

Menus are where most of your Office 95 commands hang out. Because menus contain all of the necessary tools for making the computer do things, opening a menu is kind of like opening your desk drawer to grab your stapler or a paper clip. When you're not using your desk tools, they stay in your drawer. It's the same with your computer tools: the menu is shut until you need the necessary command.

When you open a particular menu group, which you do by clicking on the menu name, a list appears revealing related menu commands. (These menus are said to *drop down* because the menu list literally drops down from the menu bar.) To select a command from the menu list, click on it with your mouse. After you choose a command, the menu disappears until you pull it down again.

Here's what you'll encounter on your Office 95 menus:

Selection letters The underlined letters you see in the menu commands. You can press the selection letter to choose a command with the keyboard (instead of clicking on the screen with the mouse).

Shortcut keys Off to the right of some menu commands are keypress combinations that activate commands. If you memorize them, you won't even have to open the menu; simply press the shortcut key to activate the command instead.

Ellipsis The three dots following a menu command. The ellipsis indicates that a dialog box will appear when you select that command. (See "Work with Dialog Boxes" on page 45.)

Arrow to the right of a menu command Indicates there are more menus to view (a submenu). The additional menu appears after you select the menu command.

Inactive commands Any faded-looking or grayish-colored commands on the menu. When a command appears gray, you can't use it for the moment.

Begin Guided Tour   Select Menu Commands

1 Click on the name of the menu you want to open.

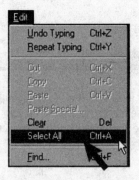

2 The menu drops down, and you see a list of commands. Click on the command you want to execute. (Some menu commands open dialog boxes asking for additional information before executing the task.)

Work with Dialog Boxes

O n many occasions when you select a command, the computer needs additional information from you before it can carry out the task. When it does, a dialog box pops up on your screen. A dialog box is like a miniwindow within your program window for making additional decisions. It presents you with a bunch of options from which to choose, places in which to type text, and buttons for activating the options.

To make selections in a dialog box, click on the various options with your mouse. In some cases, selecting something might open yet another dialog box. When you finish with the dialog box, click the **OK** button (or whichever activating button resides in the box), or press the **Enter** key to put your changes into action. If you change your mind about the dialog box selections, click the **Cancel** button (or press **Esc**).

A dialog box contains quite a variety of components, as shown in the guided tour.

Begin Guided Tour   Use Dialog Boxes

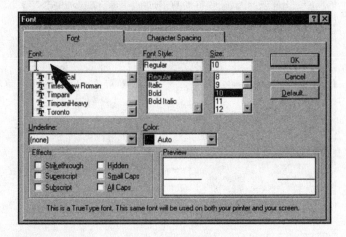

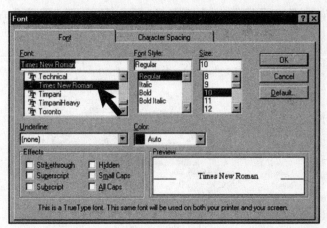

1 **Text box**   An area in which you type text such as a file name. When you click inside the text box, the mouse pointer becomes a cursor for typing.

2 **List boxes**   Exactly what their name implies: lists in a box. To select an item in a list, click on it to highlight it. If the list is a long one, scroll bars may appear. Use them to move backward and forward in the displayed list.

(continues)

Guided Tour   Use Dialog Boxes

(continued)

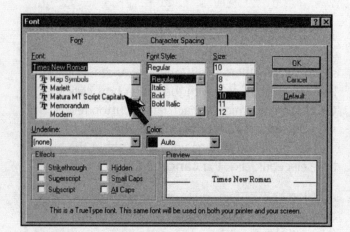

3 **Scroll bars**   Use to move back and forth through a list. Click on the arrows to move up or down.

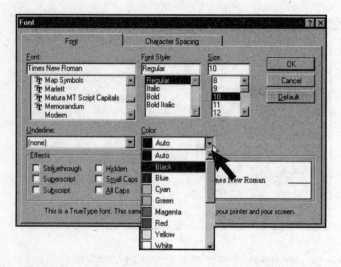

4 **Drop-down lists**   Have a downward-pointing arrow next to the first list item. When you click on the arrow, a continuation of the list appears for you to view and choose from.

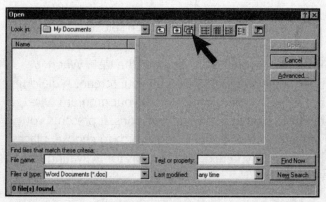

5 **Toolbars**   May appear in some of the dialog boxes you use. Toolbars have icon buttons that act as shortcuts for performing tasks. Click the icon to activate the task.

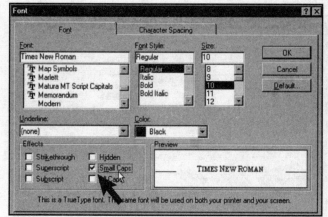

6 **Check boxes**   Tiny square boxes that turn a feature on or off. A check mark in a check box means the option is on; no check mark means it's off. You can turn on as many of these check boxes as you want. There's no limit.

Guided Tour   Use Dialog Boxes

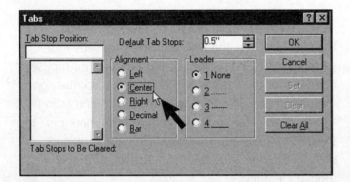

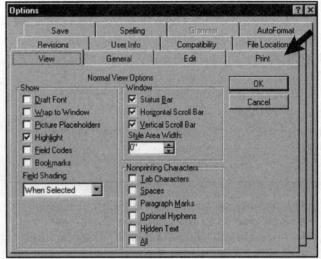

7 **Option buttons**   Little round buttons that turn a feature on or off. A black dot in the option button means the feature is turned on. Option buttons usually represent a group of choices from which you can choose only one at a time.

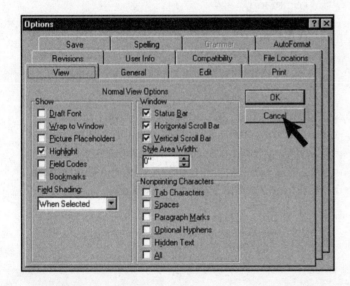

9 **Tabs**   Appear in some dialog boxes. You'll know them when you see them because they look like they have little folders tabs at the top of them. Each tab has a name on it describing its options. In order to select options from one of the hidden folders, you must click on its tab name to move it to the front of the dialog box.

To quickly close a dialog box, click the **Close** button (if available) in the upper right corner of the dialog box or press **Esc**.

8 **Command buttons**   Look like real buttons that you can click on with the mouse to make things happen. Just about every dialog box has a command button that says **OK**. Click the **OK** button to have the computer carry out all of the dialog box selections you've made. Some command buttons even open additional dialog boxes.

Use Toolbars

Icons are little pictures or symbols. *Buttons* are small squares that you click on with your mouse. Combine icons and buttons, and you have a *toolbar*. Toolbars are a part of every Microsoft Office for Windows 95 program. So what's so hot about toolbars? Toolbars are collections of icon buttons that represent specific computer tasks, and they're the fastest way to select frequently used commands.

> **The pictures on the toolbar buttons give you a visual clue as to what task the button performs. However, discerning what these pictures mean isn't always easy. If you're ever in doubt about what task the button performs, move your mouse pointer over it, and the button's name appears. This is a *ToolTip*. (This won't work if the ToolTip feature is turned off. By default, it's on when you first use the Office 95 programs. If it is off, open the View menu, select Toolbars and select the Show ToolTips check box.)**

You'll find several toolbars available for every Office 95 application. For example, Word has nine toolbars to choose from. When any of the Office 95 programs first start up, the default toolbar will appear. With some of the Office 95 programs, such as Word and Excel, there are two or more default toolbars.

As you work with the program, you can change toolbars to access the icon buttons that meet your current needs. To change toolbars, move your mouse pointer over the toolbar and right-click (click the *right* mouse button). This displays a shortcut menu listing all of the available toolbars, with a check mark next to the one that currently appears. To change toolbars, click on the one you want from the list, and your toolbar changes.

You can also change toolbars through the View menu, if available.

1. Open the **View** menu and select the **Toolbar** command.

2. A dialog box appears from which you can select which toolbars to show. You can select none at all, or you can display every toolbar available.

Microsoft has tried to come up with every possible toolbar combination you could want, but they've also made it easy for you to tailor the toolbars to fit your needs. You can edit the toolbars with the **Customize** button found in the Toolbars dialog box.

Begin Guided Tour   Select a Button from a Toolbar

1 Move your mouse pointer over the toolbar button you want to activate.

2 Click on the button, and it's activated.

Get Help in Office 95

When you can't remember how to do something in an application, you can use online help to refresh your memory. All Microsoft Office 95 applications include a Help menu and various ways to access the help features. You look up a topic in online help just like you do in a book: you can look up a topic in a table of contents or in the index. Unlike a book, though, you can also use the Help system to search for a particular topic. Which method you use depends on which you prefer—which you find easiest.

There's even a Help button on your Office toolbars which you can use to access help concerning other on-screen items. For example, if you're confused about what a toolbar button does, click on the Help button, this turns the mouse pointer into an arrow with a question mark. Move the pointer over the button in question and click to reveal online help about the function of the button.

A new Help feature Microsoft added to the Office 95 suite is the *Answer Wizard*. The Answer Wizard can help you find specific information that you want to know more about. You simply type in your question in the Answer Wizard box, and the Answer Wizard presents you with a list of related topics, or even a tutorial that explains how to complete a task.

> To get help on a particular on-screen element or command, click on the **Help** button (the button with the question mark icon) on the program's toolbar. Then click on the item or command for which you want help. For instance, you can click on the **Help** button and then click on the **Save** command to get help on saving. Another way to get help is press **F1** on the keyboard.

Let's look through each of the help methods you can use to assist you with your work.

Begin Guided Tour   Use Help

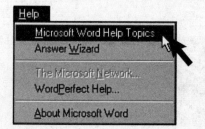

1 First open the **Help** menu and select the **Help Topics** command from any Office 95 program.

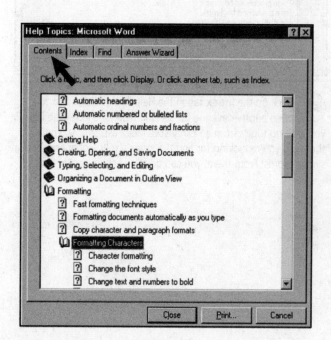

2 Click the **Contents** tab to view a list of topics.

(continues)

3 To choose a topic, double-click on its name or icon. In many instances, this reveals a sublist of more topics. Keep double-clicking to find the exact topic you want to view information about. You'll note several different Help icons among the lists.

A closed book icon next to a topic means there's a more-detailed list to view.

An opened book icon next to a topic means the topic is selected.

A question mark icon next to a topic means there's detailed text to view about the topic.

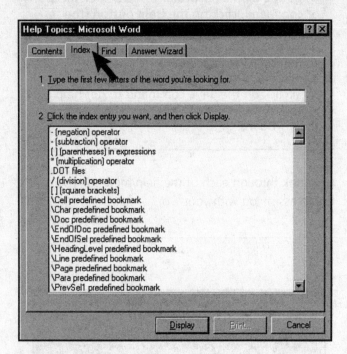

4 Click on the **Index** tab in the Help Topics dialog box to open another avenue for seeking help. The Index tab lets you look up topics from an exhaustive index list. Simply type in the word you're looking for and the index scrolls alphabetically to similar words. From there, you can double-click to display topics.

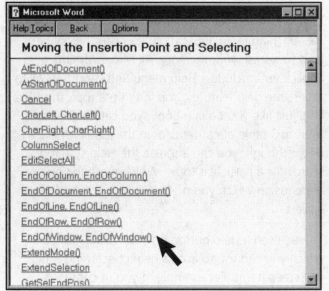

5 Some topics you'll run across in the help text appear underlined and in a different color. You can jump to that topic by clicking on it. Some topics appear underlined with a dotted line; click these hot spots to display a definition of the term.

6 You can also look up things with the **Find** tab, which is also part of Microsoft's wizard collection. The Find feature can help you look up a specific topic based on words you type in. It leads you to your information through a series of dialog boxes.

Guided Tour   Use Help

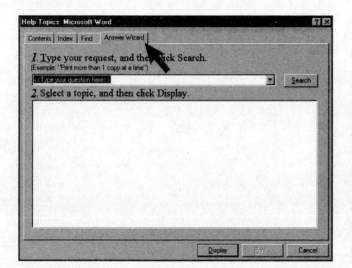

7 By far, the hippest help on the system comes from the **Answer Wizard**. To open the Answer Wizard, you can click on its tab in the Help dialog box or choose it directly from the Help menu. Inside the Answer Wizard tab, all you do is type in your request, click on the **Search** button, and the list box displays the results.

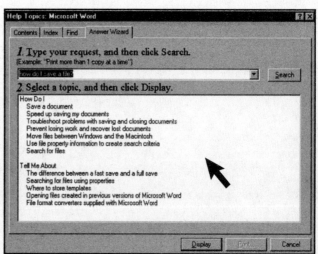

9 Answer Wizard may answer you with a list box of related topics, or it may lead you through a tutorial on how to perform the requested task. If a list box appears after typing in your question, look through the topics. When you see something close to your request listed in the box, double-click on it to see detailed information about the subject matter.

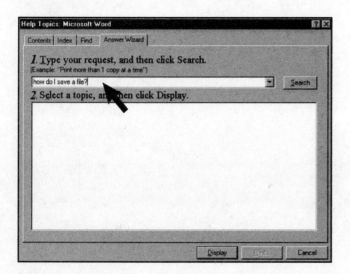

8 For example, let's say you're having trouble saving a file. You can type in a question like "**how do I save a file?**" and Answer Wizard will answer you. You can type in any kind of question, and Answer Wizard tries to answer it.

HOW TO...

Manage Files

One of the best things about using a suite of applications such as Microsoft Office 95 is that you can perform many common tasks the same way—for example, saving a file. Once you learn how to save a file in one application, you will know how to save a file in any of the applications. This section of the book covers common file management tasks.

Microsoft has radically changed the appearance of the dialog boxes associated with saving and opening files. If you've used Microsoft Office programs in the past, the new Save As and Save As Open dialog boxes used in Office 95 may confuse you a little. In Windows 95, you no longer store files in directories, but in *folders*. The hierarchy of a drive's contents appears the same way as before, but the way in which you display a drive works a little differently. But don't worry, this section will show you how to use each dialog box and its new features.

What You will Find in This Section

Save a File

When you create a file (a letter, memo, budget, database), also called a *document*, your computer stores that information only temporarily in its memory. To make a permanent copy, you need to save the file to your hard disk or onto a floppy disk. It's important that you remember to save often. Why? Because if you don't and something happens to the power (such as an outage or an interruption in power just long enough to make the lights blink), all your hard work will be lost.

There are several different ways you can save files with the Office 95 programs:

- You can save a new file to a folder on your hard disk drive or save the file onto a floppy disk.

- You can save previously saved files, and even give them new names.

- You can save files of different types to use with non-Microsoft Office programs.

The first time you save a file, you need to enter a file name. For the file name, you can type up to 255 characters. In Windows 3.1, you could only use 8 characters in a file name, which was very limiting. Windows 95's new capacity for longer file names will go a long way in helping you clearly identify your documents.

Also, if you've worked with Windows 3.1, you might remember using three-letter file extensions in previous versions of Office. A file extension provides a unique way of identifying which program you created the file in and what type of file it was. File extensions are still around in Windows 95, however, they do not appear by default. Instead, you can identify files by icons next to the file name. For example, when you create a file in Word, a Word icon appears in front of the file name as it appears in a list of saved files. Knowing the Office-related icons will help you recognize files and file types in the lists you may come across, especially when you're looking at files in the Windows Explorer or My Computer windows.

You can still choose to view extensions, when needed. For example, if you want to view file extensions again while in the Windows Explorer, open the **View** menu, select **Options**. Click on the **View** tab. Make sure you deselect the **Hide MS-DOS file extensions** check box. This will display the file names with their extensions.

By default, the following extensions are assigned by Office 95 applications:

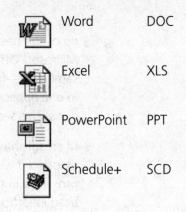

	Word	DOC
	Excel	XLS
	PowerPoint	PPT
	Schedule+	SCD

When you save a file, the application will automatically save the document to the current folder or drive. If you want to put the document in a different location, you can use the **Save in** drop-down list in the Save As dialog box to change drives or folders.

It's a good idea to get in the habit of saving every 5 or 10 minutes so that your computer updates the disk version with the changes you make. After you've saved the first time, you simply select the **Save** command in the **File** menu to save again. You won't be prompted for the name.

All of the applications include a **Save** button in the toolbar. You can also use the keyboard shortcut **Ctrl+S** to save a file.

New Features in the Save As Dialog Box

The Save As dialog box has changed quite a bit from the previous versions of Office. There are new elements to learn about and new ways to save your data. In Windows 3.1, you saved files in directories, but in Windows 95, you save files in *folders*—which are just like the old Windows 3.1 directories. Folders can hold files and other folders (*subfolders*). Each of the Office programs appear as folders on your computer.

The toolbar buttons inside the Save As box let you view folders and files in various detail, and even let you create new folders. Click a button to apply its function. Each button has a specific function, as shown in this table.

Button	Button Name	Function
	Up One Level	Moves your drive's hierarchy list back one level.
	Look in Favorites	Opens the Favorites folder: a folder you can use to store your most popular document files in.
	Create New Folder	Creates a new folder.
	List	Lists the folders and files by name.
	Details	Lists the files by details such as when the files were created, how much disk space they consume, their file type, and so on.
	Properties	Lists each file's individual details such as how many pages, name of the original author, what template the file's based on, and so on.
	Commands and Settings	Opens a submenu with commands for viewing properties, sorting files, and mapping your network drive.

Begin Guided Tour   Elements of the Save As Dialog Box

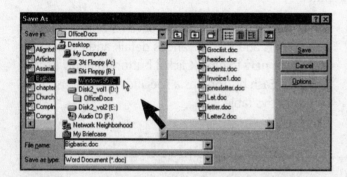

When you want to choose a drive or folder to save your file to, you can open the **Save in** drop-down box. From the list that appears, you select a specific drive or folder to save the file in. To select an item from the list, click on its name.

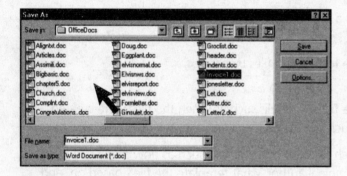

As you select items from the **Save in** drop-down box, the list box in the middle displays files and folders currently in the selected drive or folder. To open a folder and view its contents in the list box, double-click on the folder name.

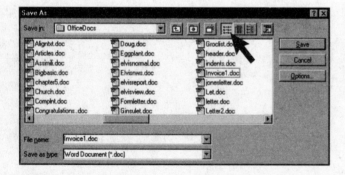

The toolbar buttons in the Save As dialog box allow you to see different levels of your drive's folder hierarchy, view folder contents in different ways, and create new folders.

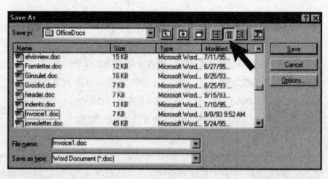

Use these three buttons to change how files and folders appear in the list box.

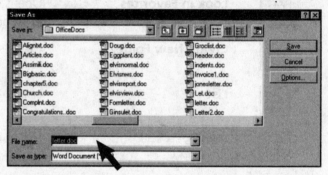

You can type in names for your files in the **File name** text box.

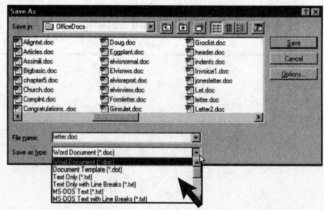

To save a file in a different format or type, use the **Save as type** drop-down list to choose a file type.

Guided Tour   Elements of the Save As Dialog Box

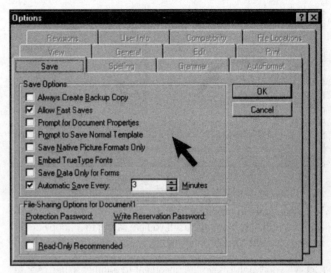

The command buttons let you actually save the file, close the dialog box, or open yet another dialog box containing file-saving options. Click on the **Save** button to save the file under the file name you typed into the **File name** text box. If you change your mind about saving the file, or just want to close the dialog box, click the **Cancel** button.

To view a dialog box of file-saving options, click the **Options** button.

Begin Guided Tour   Save a File

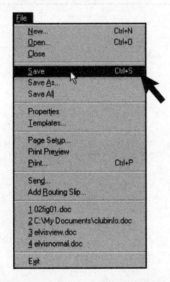

1 Open the **File** menu and select the **Save** command. (You can also click the **Save** button on your application's toolbar.)

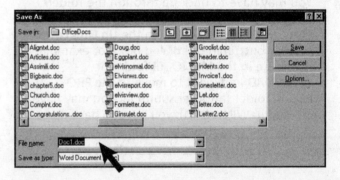

2 You see the Save As dialog box. Type a name for your document in the **File name** text box. You can type up to 255 characters.

(continues)

Guided Tour   Save a File   *(continued)*

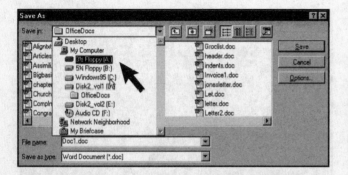

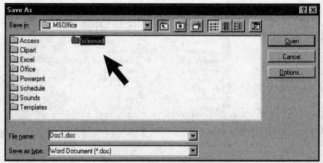

3 If you want to save the document to another drive, click on the **Save in** drop-down arrow, and click on the drive you want from the list that appears. If you are saving to a floppy drive, be sure to insert the disk into the floppy drive.

4 If you want to save the document to another folder, choose one from the list box. To do so, click on the folder name and click the **Open** button, or double-click on the folder name to open it. You can also choose a folder from the **Save in** drop-down list. Click the **Save in** drop-down arrow; select a folder from the list by clicking on its name.

You may have to back up through the folder/ directory tree to get to the folder you want. You can do so by clicking on the **Up One Level** toolbar button in the dialog box. For example, if you are in the MEMO subfolder of WINWORD and want to move to the PROPOSAL folder (another subfolder you may have created in WINWORD), you have to back up to WINWORD and then change to PROPOSAL.

5 Once you give the file a name and decide which folder to save it in, click the **Save** command button. The application saves the document. You see the new file name in the title bar of the application.

To save a previously saved file you're working on, simply click the **Save** button on your application's toolbar. If you want to rename the file, open the **File** menu, select **Save As**, and then type in a new file name for the document.

Save a File Using Other Names and Options

If you don't like the name you originally used to save a file, or if you want to make a copy of the file, you can use the **File Save As** command. The Save As command lets you rename existing files. For example, suppose that you wrote a letter that you want to use again, with some changes. You can open the original letter, save it with a new name, and modify the new version. Meanwhile, the original version remains intact. You'll find detailed steps for using the Save As command in the Guided Tour in this task.

Another option you can use when saving a file is to save it as a different file type (also called format). In the world of computer files, there are many different types. Just to illustrate this point, think of all the word processing programs available today. Microsoft Word for Windows is just one of many. Each different word processing program creates a specific file type, even though the content focus (creating text pages) is the same. When it comes to word processing file types, you'll find choices such as Word for Windows, Word for DOS, WordPerfect, Word Pro, and Word for Macintosh, just to name a few. Unfortunately, not every program recognizes files from other programs.

If you share documents with users who have different programs, you may want to save a document as another file type. For example, if a co-worker uses WordPerfect for Windows, you can save your Word document as a WordPerfect file that your co-worker can use. Your co-worker won't be able to use the file you've created unless it's converted to a usable format. Thankfully, most programs today let you convert a file's format. You can easily save your Word documents as other file types using the Save dialog box. You can also save Excel worksheets in different file formats, and PowerPoint presentations as different file types.

Use the Options Dialog Box

In the Save As dialog box, there's an Options button you can press. If you click on this button, you'll open the Options dialog box. In the Save tab, you can select from the many save options and even set up a password to protect your file.

Pay careful attention to the **Automatic Save Every** option. You can set up your Office 95 application so it automatically saves the file you're working on every few minutes. In case of a power failure or surge that occurs while you're in the middle of creating an important file, your computer will save the file contents automatically, without any instructions from you. This is a good safeguard to use for all of your Office 95 programs.

When in the Save tab of the Options dialog box, make sure to select the **Automatic Save Every** option, and set a minute increment from the **Minutes** box. I suggest **3** minutes as a good choice.

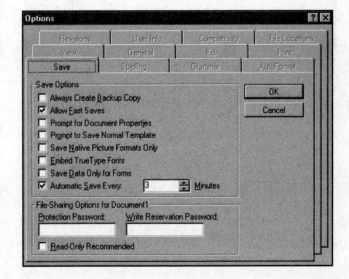

Begin Guided Tour   Save a File Under a New Name

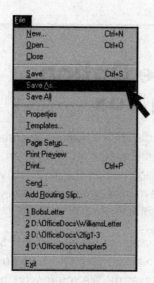

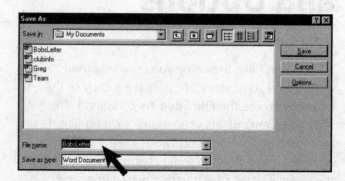

2 In the Save As dialog box, type in a new name in the File name text box. The existing name already appears in the box, but you can type right over it.

3 Click on the **Save** button, and the existing file is saved under the new name.

1 Open the **File** menu and select **Save As**.

Begin Guided Tour   Save a File Under a New Format

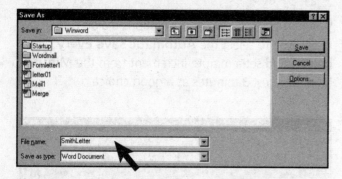

1 Open the Save As dialog box. To do so, select **File Save** (if you're saving for the first time) or **File Save As** (if you're saving an existing file). The Save As dialog box appears. If necessary, give the file a name using the File name text box.

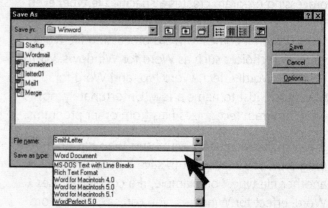

2 To save the file as another file type, display the **Save as type** drop-down list. Click on its drop-down arrow to see the list. From the list that appears, select the appropriate file type.

3 Click the **Save** button and the file is saved in a different file format.

Open a File

The purpose of saving a file is so that you can open it and work on it again. You open a file you previously saved because you may want to edit, reuse, or print the document. Opening a file is fairly straightforward: select the **File Open** command and double-click the file name from the Open dialog box.

The key is getting the Open dialog box to display the document name you want to open. You'll find the Open dialog box looks very similar to the Save As dialog box. Files and folders appear in the list box, and you can change the display at any time. If the file you want is in the current drive or folder, you'll see it listed. If it's not, you can switch to the appropriate drive or folder using the **Look in** drop-down list or by clicking open any of the folders listed in the list box.

> You can also use the **Open** button in the toolbar to display the Open dialog box. If you like keyboard shortcuts, use the **Ctrl+O** key combination for opening a file. Another shortcut is to open the **File** menu; notice the last files you worked on appear at the bottom of the menu. To open one of these files, click on the name.

You can also open documents in another file format. For example, in Word, you can open WordPerfect, Word Pro, and several other document types. To display other file types in the Open dialog box, use the **Files of type** drop-down list and select the file format you want.

Once you find the file you want to open and select it, you can click on the **Open** button to display the file on your application screen.

Use the Open Dialog Box

Like the Save As dialog box you learned about previously, Microsoft Open dialog box differs from the previous versions of Office you may have worked with. The dialog box displays files and folders in a new format. A new edition to the box are toolbar buttons. These buttons let you view folders and files in various detail, and even let you create new folders. Click on a button to apply its function. Each button controls a specific function, as shown in this table.

Work with More than One File Open

Just like you can have several papers on your desk, you can have several files open on your "electronic" desktop—the computer screen. You may need to review information in one document to create a second document. You may need to copy information from one document to another. With Office 95, you can have as many documents open as your computer memory allows.

To work on more than one document, open the first document you want to work with. Then follow the same steps to open the next document. The application displays the last document you opened on top. You can use the following features to move among the different open documents:

- To switch to a different document, open the **Window** menu. You see the names of the open documents displayed. Click on the one you want.

Button	Button Name	Function
	Up One Level	Moves your current drive's hierarchy list back one level.
	Look in Favorites	Opens the Favorites folder: a folder you can use to store your most popular document files in.
	Add to Favorites	Moves the selected file into the Favorites folder.
	List	Lists the folders and files by name.
	Details	Lists the files by details such as when the files were created, how much disk space they consume, their file type, and so on.
	Properties	Lists each file's individual details such as how many pages, name of the original author, what template the file's based on, and so on.
	Preview	Lets you preview the selected file, if applicable.
	Commands and Settings	Opens a submenu with additional file commands.

- To arrange the documents so that you can see at least part of each of them on-screen at the same time, open the **Window** menu. For Word, select the **Arrange All** command. For Excel, select the **Arrange** command, select how you want the windows arranged in the Arrange Windows dialog box, and then click **OK**. In PowerPoint, select **Arrange All**.

- To return a document to a full-screen display, move to the document window you want to expand and click on the **Maximize** button.

- If you have several files open at once, you can minimize the ones you aren't using. If you click on the **Minimize** button, the file window reduces to a button on the Windows 95 taskbar. To open the window again, click on its button on the taskbar.

You can also resize windows using the techniques you learned about in the first section of this book. Turn to page 22 and follow the instructions under "Work with Windows" to learn about resizing.

Begin Guided Tour   Elements of the Open Dialog Box

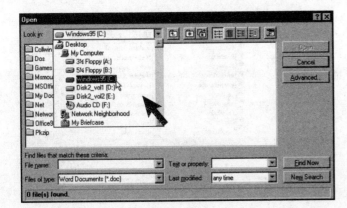

If the file you want to open doesn't appear when you first open the Open dialog box, click on the **Look in** drop-down box. From the list, you can select a specific drive or folder containing the file you want to open. To select an item from the drop-down list, click on its name.

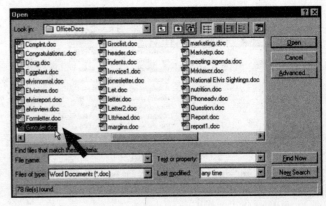

When you locate the file you're looking for, click on its name to select it. You can then proceed to preview the file by clicking on the **Preview** toolbar button in the Open dialog box (more about the toolbars next), or you can open the file directly into your application by clicking on the **Open** button.

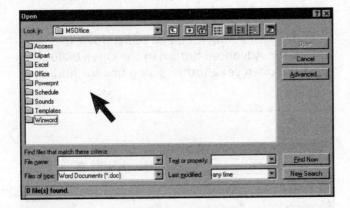

As you select items from the **Look in** drop-down box, the list box in the middle displays files and folders currently in the selected drive or folder. To open a folder and view its contents in the list box, double-click on the folder name.

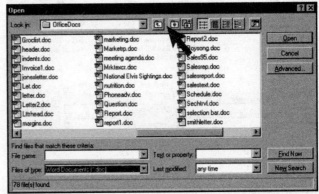

The toolbar buttons in the Open dialog box allow you to see different levels of your drive's folder hierarchy, view folder contents in different ways, and even preview a file before selecting it.

(continues)

Guided Tour   Elements of the Open Dialog Box   *(continued)*

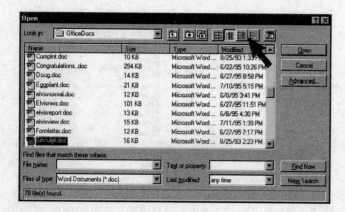

Use these three buttons to change how files and folders appear in the list box.

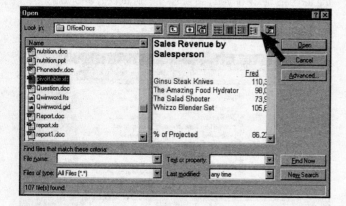

Click on the **Preview** button in order to see what the selected file looks like before opening it into your application. You may not be able to preview the file, depending on what kind of file it is.

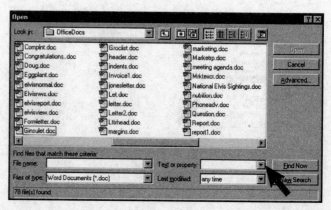

If you have trouble locating the file you want to open, you can use the Find commands in the dialog box to help you. Use the text boxes and command buttons at the bottom of the Open dialog box to search for specific files or file elements. Type in the information about the file you're looking for and click the **Find Now** button.

> To perform a more detailed search for a file, click the **Advanced** button in the Open dialog box to open yet another dialog box for finding files.

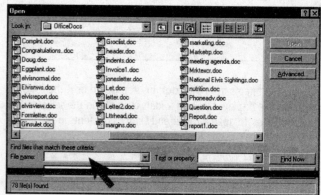

If you know the name of the file you're looking for, you can type it in the **File name** text box; then click the **Open** button.

Guided Tour   Elements of the Open Dialog Box

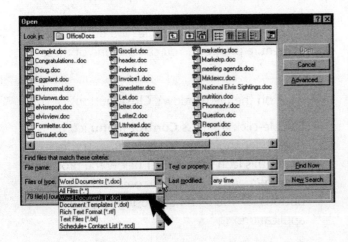

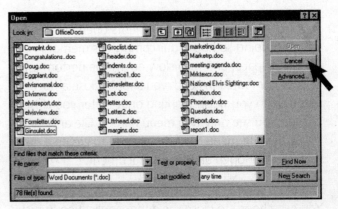

To list files of different types, use the **Files of type** drop-down list.

The command buttons let you open the file, close the dialog box, or use advanced file-finding options. Click the **Open** button to open the selected file. Click the **Cancel** button to exit the box.

Begin Guided Tour   Open a File

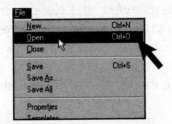

1 Open the **File** menu and select the **Open** command.

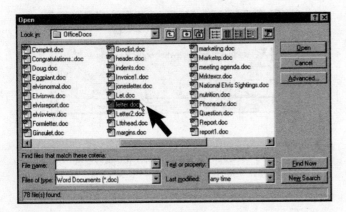

2 You see the Open dialog box. If you see the file you want to open listed, double-click on the name. If you don't see the document you want listed, follow the next step.

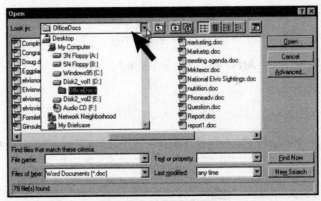

3 If the document is in another folder or drive, click on the **Look in** drop-down list to locate the file. When the document appears in the list, double-click on it. The document will appear on-screen.

Close a File

You can have a lot of documents open at once, but doing so hogs your computer's memory (working space) and may slow down the performance of your computer. Instead, you should close a document when you finish working on it. After you close all files, you see only two menu names: File and Help. Using the **File** menu, you can choose to create a new document or open an existing document.

There are several different ways you can close a file. You can choose to close the entire application, which also closes the file, or you can choose to close only the opened application. If you're closing the entire program, you can use any of these methods:

- Click on the application's **Close** (**X**) button in the upper right corner.·

- Open the **File** menu and select **Exit**.

- Double-click the program's **Control-menu** icon located in the upper left corner.

- Press **Alt+F4** on the keyboard.

If you're only closing the open file, you don't have to close the entire program. You can use one of these methods:

- Click on the file window's **Close** button.

- Double-click the file's **Control-menu** icon. Again, depending on what program you're using, this icon may appear below the program's Control-menu icon. (Don't confuse the two buttons, or you'll end up closing the entire application.)

- Open the **File** menu, and select **Close**.

If you haven't saved your work before closing the file or application, the program will prompt you to do so before exiting. A dialog box pops up on your screen with three choices: Yes, No, and Cancel. If you don't want to save your work, click **No** to close the file. If you want to save your work, click the **Yes** button, the Save As dialog box appears, and you can give the file a name. If you change your mind about exiting, click the **Cancel** button and you'll return to the application window.

Begin Guided Tour Close a File Using the File Menu

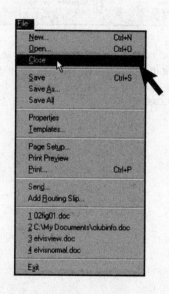

1 Open the **File** menu and select **Close**.

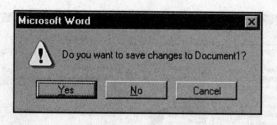

2 If you haven't saved your work, a box appears prompting you to do so. Click on **No** to exit without saving. Click on **Yes** to save your file first.

Create a New File

When you start Word and Excel, both display a new document for you to start working in. In Word, you can start typing away. In Excel, you can start entering the figures and data for the worksheet. If you want to create another new document, you can do so using the **New** button in the toolbar—a button found on most of the Office programs.

Another way to start a new file is to use the New dialog box. To access this box, open the **File** menu and select **New**. In the dialog box that appears, you'll see tabs that list sample documents and templates you can use to help you build your file. A *template* is simply a premade design and structure for a file.

Some of the samples you see are, in fact, wizards, special templates that walk you step by step through the process of building a file design and structure. For more information on templates and wizards, see the "Use Templates and Wizards" task on page 135.

PowerPoint works differently. When you start PowerPoint, you see the startup dialog box. Here, you can select to create a new presentation from scratch, use a wizard or template, or open an existing presentation. For information on setting up a new presentation, see the "Creating a New Presentation" task in the "How to Create a PowerPoint Presentation" section.

Begin Guided Tour   Close a File Using the File Menu

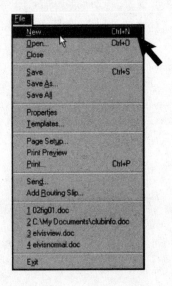

1 Open the **File** menu and select the **New** command.

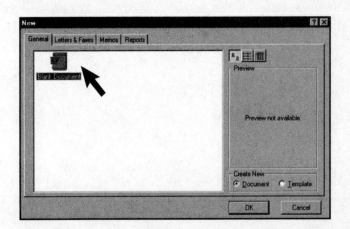

2 The New dialog box appears on-screen. Look through the various tabs to see sample documents you can use to base your file on. (You can even choose from wizards that will lead you through the steps for building a document.) Use the Preview area to see what the document sample looks like (if applicable).

3 Select the template you want to use (if you haven't already) and click the **OK** button. You see a new document on-screen.

HOW TO...

Print Files

The purpose of creating most documents is to create a printed copy to review yourself, to give to someone else, or to distribute to a group of people. You can print a letter you created with Word, a budget you created with Excel, or a presentation you created with PowerPoint. You can even print out portions of your daily schedule from Schedule+. When it comes right down to it, a computer isn't much use without the ability to print out the things you create.

Printers are often a source of difficulty and aggravation among many computer users. Some people use two or more different printers to print on, others have to share a printer with co-workers. People aren't the only ones confused by printers, it sometimes seems that computers themselves are a little confused by printers too. Getting your computer to send a file to your printer, and getting the printer to understand the file and print it out can sometimes become a major ordeal. Thankfully, computer hardware and software manufacturers have come a long way in making sure that computers and printers get along, electronically speaking. Printing files is easier than ever with Windows 95, as you'll see in the tasks to come.

This section of the book covers how to preview and print your files.

What You Will Find in This Section

Preview a Document

When you are working in a file, you see only the part you are working on. You can't tell how the page numbers look, for instance, or how the document will appear on the page. Are the margins okay? Do you need to add a header or footer? Is the page layout pleasing to the eye? You can try and see how these features look by scrolling back and forth, but that doesn't really help. You need a way to view the entire page on your screen without wasting paper by printing a hard copy. With the Preview feature, you can do just that.

Before you print your document, you should preview it to see how it will look when printed. This will save you time and paper because you can get an overall sense of the document, make any necessary changes, and then print. In preview mode, you see a full-page view of the document. Depending on the application, you see different on-screen tools for working with the preview.

> You can click the **Print Preview** button to quickly preview a document.

When you preview a document in Word, you see a toolbar, and the buttons have icons or words on them. Use the buttons to perform the following tasks.

Use This Button	To
🖨	Print the document.
🔍	Magnify portions of the document. Click the button; then click on the area of the document you want to get a closer look.
▣	View a single page (the default view).

Use This Button	To
⊞	View multiple pages. Click the button and then drag across the number of pages in the drop-down palette.
34% ▼	Change the zoom percentage of the view. Display the drop-down list and click on the zoom you want.
🖼	Display horizontal and vertical rulers. You can use the rulers to change the margins.
📑	Shrink the document to fit in one window.
▣	Hide the menu bar and toolbar.
Close	Close the preview window. Click this button to return to the Word document window.
▶?	Get help on the different preview options.

In Excel, the toolbar buttons have names, so you can easily understand them. The following table explains what each button does.

Use This Button	To
Next	View the next page. If your worksheet uses more than one page, you can click on this button to view other pages.
Previous	View the previous page. Click this button to go back and view the previous page (if your worksheet uses multiple pages).

Use This Button	To
Zoom	Zoom the preview to make it larger. You can do the same thing by clicking the mouse on the worksheet. (The pointer should look like a magnifying glass when you point to the worksheet.)
Print...	Print the worksheet.
Setup...	Display the Page Setup dialog box and make changes to the layout of the page. See "Setting Up the Page" on page [7TBD].
Margins	Display on-screen margin indicators. You can then drag the margin indicators to change the margins.
Close	Closes the preview window.
Help	Display help on preview.

Note: For information on previewing a PowerPoint presentation, see "View the Slide Show" on page 275.

Zoom In and Out

In addition to previewing, you can also zoom a document in or out, much like you can zoom in and out with a camera. You may want to zoom in to see a close-up, magnified view of the document. You may want to zoom out to see more of the document. You can do either of these things without having to use the Preview feature. The Office programs also have a Zoom feature that lets you view your document up close or view the entire page. When you select the **Zoom** command, you select the percentage you want. To return to the regular view, select the **Zoom** command and select **100%**.

Begin Guided Tour Zoom In and Out

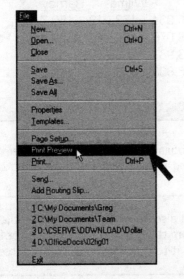

1 Open the **File** menu and select the **Print Preview** command.

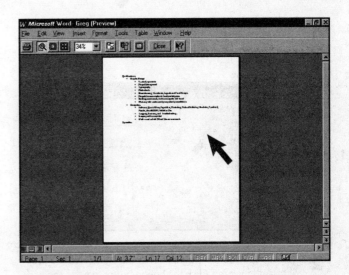

2 You see a full-page preview. You can click on any of the toolbar buttons on the Preview toolbar to adjust your preview of the document. See the tables on the previous pages for a description of the buttons.

(continues)

Guided Tour   Zoom In and Out   *(continued)*

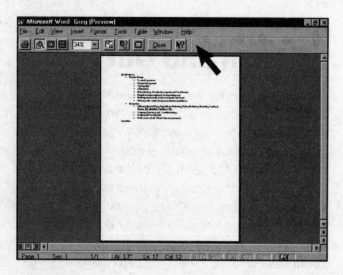

3 To exit Print Preview, click the **Close** button.

Begin Guided Tour   Zoom a Document

1 Open the **View** menu and select the **Zoom** command.

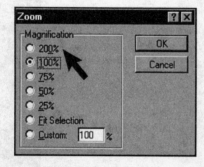

2 You see the Zoom dialog box. (The dialog box looks a little different in Word.) Click the option button next to the amount to zoom. To select a different percentage, type it in the text box (usually called Custom) or use the spin arrows to set the zoom percentage. Click the **OK** button.

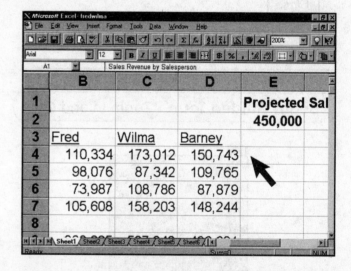

3 The document appears using the zoom percentage you selected. Here the worksheet is zoomed to 200%.

> You can also zoom a document by clicking on the Zoom drop-down list on your toolbar. You can use it to quickly select zoom percentages.

Print a Document

All your hard work pays off when you can print your final document. You may want to print a copy to review and mark up editing changes, or you may print a copy to distribute to others.

> Use the **Print** button in the toolbar to print, or if you want to use a keyboard shortcut, press **Ctrl+P**.

Note that before you can print, you must set up the printer using the Windows 95 Control Panel. Windows 95 needs to know certain information about the type of printer and fonts that you have. Once you set up the printer, it is available to all Windows 95 programs. Read about changing the printer setup on page 75.

To print an entire file, you can simply click on the Print button on the toolbar. To control what parts of the file are printed, and to control how the file is printed, you'll need to open the Print dialog box. You can access the box by pulling down the File menu and selecting Print. Inside the Print dialog box, you'll find all kinds of options for printing, including paper size and orientation.

In a long document, you may need to print only certain pages. Rather than waste paper, you can print just the pages you need. If you need to make several copies of a document, you should use a copier machine to avoid too much wear and tear on your printer. If you just need a couple of copies, though, you can have the application print multiple copies.

Begin Guided Tour   Print a File

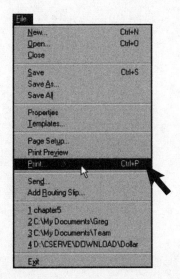

1 Open the **File** menu and choose the **Print** command.

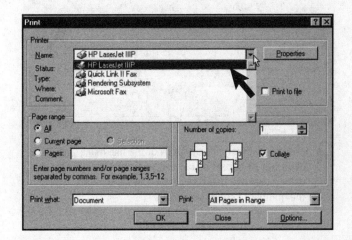

2 You see the Print dialog box. To change which printer the file is sent to, click on the Name drop-down list under the Printer options, then select the printer from the list. If you rely on just one printer, and it's listed in the Name text box, you don't need to choose another printer to use.

(continues)

Guided Tour Print a File *(continued)*

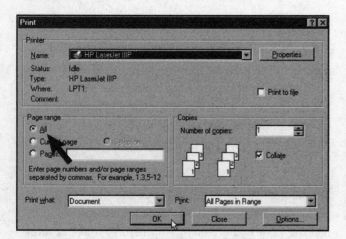

3 To print the entire file, make sure the **All** option is selected under the Page Range options.

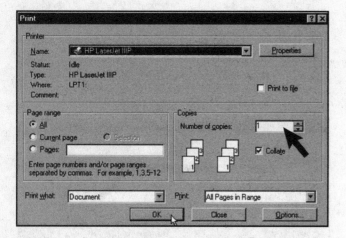

4 If you're printing just one copy of the file, make sure the **Number of copies** box under the Copies options says 1. If you want more than one copy, in the Copies spin box, type or select the number of copies you want.

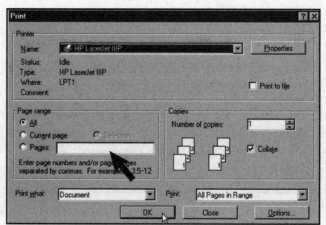

5 If you're using Word, select **Current Page** under the Page Range options to print the current page. To print other pages, select **Pages**, and enter the pages you want to print in the text box. If you're printing more than one page, you can use commas to separate the page numbers, such as 1,2,3. If you're printing a range of pages, you can use hyphen, such as 1-5. To print just the selected text in your file, choose the **Selection** option.

6 Click the **OK** button to print out your file.

Change Your Printer Setup

Microsoft Office 95 applications always print to the default printer. In some situations, you may have more than one printer available, and you can select which printer is the default. For example, if you work in an office and are hooked up to a network, you may be able to select which network printer you want to use. If you work at home, you may have a printer and a computer fax machine. Your computer treats the fax machine like a printer; to fax something, you select the fax as a printer source.

You can control which printer you use in the Print dialog box. To access the Print dialog box, open the **File** menu and select **Print**. In this box, you'll find controls for determining which printer to use, as well as other printing options, such as controlling which pages will print from your document. The Print dialog box looks slightly different depending on which program you use.

You can also change certain default options for your printer, such as the page size and orientation. What you want to remember is that changing the printer setup this way changes the options for all documents and applications. While in the Print dialog box, you can choose the **Properties** button to change default printing options, such as page orientation. If you want to change the page orientation for just one document (for example, use landscape for a document), use the **Page Setup** command instead, covered in the "Format a Word Document" section, which starts on page 107.

Remember that once you change the default, all Microsoft Office 95 applications will use this default printer—even if you didn't change the printer in that application.

Set Printer Default Options

To set the printer default options for a selected printer, follow these steps:

1. Open the **File** menu and choose the **Print** command.

2. You see the Print dialog box. To change default options for the selected printer (follow the previous Guided Tour to change printers), click the **Properties** button.

3. This opens the printer's Properties dialog box. Click on the Paper tab to bring it to the front of the box. Here you can change the default options for paper size and orientation. Make any changes and click the **OK** button.

> You can restore the default printer options at any time by returning to the Properties dialog box and clicking on the **Restore Defaults** button.

4. You return to the Print dialog box. Click **OK** to print the document. Click **Cancel** to close the dialog box without printing.

Begin Guided Tour   Change Printer Setup

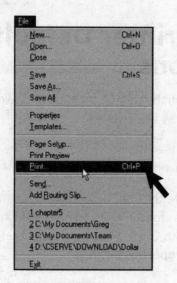

1 Open the **File** menu and choose the **Print** command.

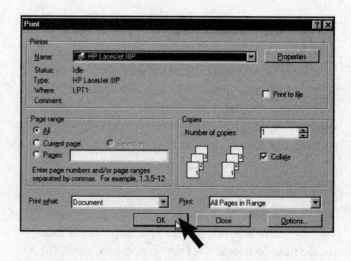

3 To print the document on the selected printer, click the **OK** button. To close the dialog box without printing, click the **Cancel** button.

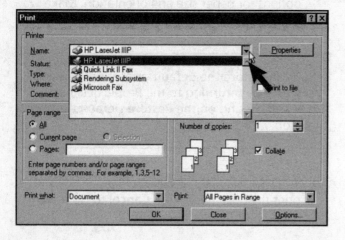

2 You see the Print dialog box. Under the Printer options, click on the **Name** drop-down list and select a printer to use from the list of available printers.

> To see additional options, click on the Options button. This opens yet another dialog box with options for printing things like hidden text.

HOW TO...
Create a Word Document

The most popular type of computer program is a word processing program, and Microsoft Word is the most popular Windows word processing program. You can use this program to create any type of document you want—from simple memos to multipage reports, from flyers to newsletters. To open Word, click on the **Start** menu; select **Programs** and **Microsoft Word**.

The basics of creating a document are simple; you just type the text you want in your document. Word includes many features that not only make typing the text easier but that also help you with the finer points of document creation, such as proofreading and revising your document. In this section, you learn about these features.

What You Will Find in This Section

Type in Text

In the simplest terms, a word processing program such as Word is similar to a typewriter; you type on the keyboard just like you type on a typewriter. However, a word processing program offers many advantages over manual typing.

For one thing, the words appear on-screen as you type. A flashing vertical line, called the *insertion point*, indicates the place where new text will appear. As you type, the insertion point moves to the right. If you make a mistake, you can easily correct it by using the Backspace or Delete key. You can press **Backspace** to delete characters to the left of the insertion point, or press **Delete** to delete characters to the right of the insertion point.

With a typewriter, you have to be careful not to type past the end of the line. When the carriage reaches the end of the line, you must press the carriage return key to go to the next line. With Word, you don't— and shouldn't—press the carriage return key (called the Enter key on the keyboard) at the end of each line. Just keep typing. Word will wrap the words that won't fit to the next line. Because of this feature, called *word wrap*, you can easily add or delete text. Word will move the existing text over to make room for new text or fill in the gap left when you delete text. You should press **Enter** *only* when you want to end one paragraph and start another and when you want to insert a blank line.

Aside from the insertion point, there's also a horizontal line on your Word screen, called the *end of document* line. The end of document line marks the end of your document, the point where you typed your last line of text. Both the insertion point and the end of document line start out at the same place on your screen, until you start typing in text. The end of document line will always be under the last line of text in your document, but the insertion point can be anywhere.

Just like Word adjusts line breaks, the program also automatically inserts page breaks, as necessary. If you add or delete text to one of the pages, Word automatically adjusts the page breaks.

Also, because the words aren't committed to paper, you can easily make changes—move text around, copy text, and make formatting changes. This section covers making editing changes to existing text; see the next section for help on all the available formatting features.

By default, Word 7 is set up to start you out in Normal view mode. Word lets you view your documents in several different modes such as Page Layout and Outline view. Normal view lets you see a simplified version of your document. Page Layout view shows you how your document will actually appear on paper. Outline view lets you see how your document looks in an outline format. To switch to the different views, click on one of the three view buttons on the bottom of the window.

Begin Guided Tour Enter Text

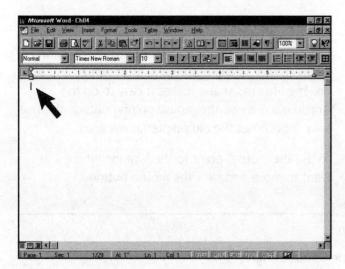

1 When you start Word, you see a new blank document on-screen with the insertion point at the top. To begin, just start typing.

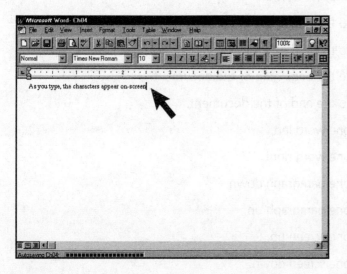

2 As you type, the characters appear on-screen and the insertion point moves to the right. If you make a mistake, press **Backspace** to delete characters to the left of the insertion point.

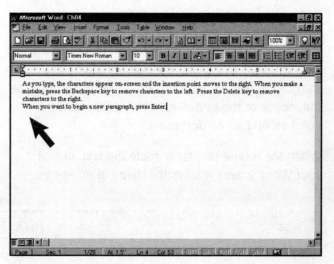

3 When you want to begin a new paragraph or insert a blank line, press **Enter**. Word inserts a hidden paragraph marker and moves the insertion point to the beginning of the next line. Continue typing your document.

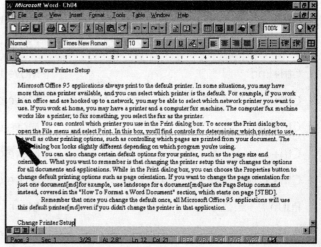

4 When a page fills up, Word inserts a break and creates a new page. On-screen you see a dotted line.

Move Around the Document

You can think of the insertion point as the "You Are Here" arrow. When you want to add text or delete text, you start by moving the insertion point to the start of the text where you want to work. You can use the mouse or the keyboard to move the insertion point around in the document.

When the mouse pointer is inside the text area of your Word screen, it takes the shape of an I-beam, also known as the *cursor*. It looks like a capital I. You can click the I-beam, or *cursor*, into place for editing between characters, before and after words, and so on. The I-beam's shape makes it easy to do this. Anytime you move the mouse pointer outside the text area, it becomes the old pointer arrow again.

To use the mouse, point to the location where you want to move and click the mouse button.

Press	To Do This
→	Move one character right.
←	Move one character left.
↑	Move one line up.
↓	Move one line down.
Home	Move to the beginning of the line.
End	Move to the end of line.
Ctrl+Home	Move to the beginning of the document.
Ctrl+End	Move to the end of the document.
Ctrl+←	Move one word left.
Ctrl+→	Move one word right.
Ctrl+↓	Move one paragraph down.
Ctrl+↑	Move one paragraph up.
PgUp	Move one screen up.
PgDn	Move one screen down.
Ctrl+PgDn	Move to the bottom of screen.
Ctrl+PgUp	Move to the top of screen.
Shift+F5. You can press Shift+F5 up to four times. The first three times you move to the previous three locations. The fourth time, you move back to the original location of the insertion point.	Move to the last location of the insertion point.
Ctrl+G	Display the Go To dialog box.

The insertion point jumps to that spot. If you can't see the place you want, you can use the scroll arrows to scroll to a different section or page. Click the up arrow to scroll up and the down arrow to scroll down; or drag the scroll box the relative distance you want to move. Use the horizontal scroll arrows to scroll left or right in the document. Remember that the insertion point remains at the same spot until you click to position it. If the insertion point is on page 1 and you scroll to page 3, the insertion point is still on page 1 until you click somewhere on page 3.

Sometimes, it is faster to move using the keyboard, especially if you are a fast typist and don't like to take your hands away from the keyboard. You can use any of the key or key combinations listed in the table to move around in the document. Note that if the key combination is joined with a plus sign, you must

press and hold the first key and then press the second key.

If you have not typed anything on-screen (or pressed the Spacebar or Enter), you cannot move the insertion point. Word doesn't permit the insertion point to move where nothing exists. Only after you enter text or spaces on-screen can you move the insertion point. The small horizontal line indicates the end of the document; you cannot move past this point.

In a long document, you can quickly move to a particular page using the **Go To** command. This method is much faster than scrolling through the document. You can jump to any page in the document by typing the page number.

Begin Guided Tour Use the Mouse

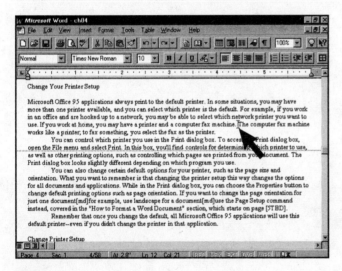

1 Point to where you want the insertion point.

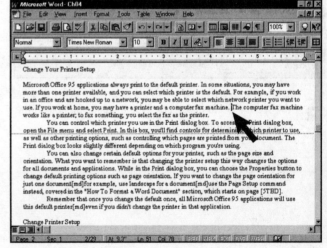

2 Click the left mouse button. The insertion point jumps to this spot.

Begin Guided Tour   Use the Go To Command

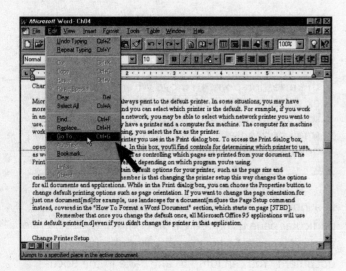

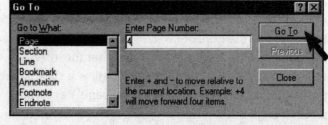

3 When you type a page number, the **Next** button changes to the **Go To** button. Click the **Go To** button. You move to that page. Word also places the insertion point at the top of the page.

1 Open the **Edit** menu and select the **Go To** command.

2 You see the Go To dialog box. Type the page number in the **Enter Page Number** text box.

Select Text

As you edit your documents, you will eventually find that you need to move, delete, or copy text. To edit in this way, you have to learn how to *select* text. You have to grab it somehow to manipulate it, and there's only one way to do it—electronically.

You can use the mouse or the keyboard to select text. Selecting with the mouse is similar to dragging a highlighter pen over the text. Selected text appears *highlighted* on the screen in reverse: white type on a black background instead of black text on a white background. To use the keyboard, hold down the **Shift** key and use the arrow keys to highlight the text you want. When all the text you want is highlighted, release the Shift key.

If you select text by mistake, you can deselect it. To do so, click anywhere outside the selected text or press any arrow key.

Because selecting text is such a common task, Word offers some selection shortcuts. You can do any of the following:

- To select a word, double-click anywhere within the word.

- To select a sentence, hold down the **Ctrl** key and click anywhere within the sentence.

- To select a line, click once in the selection bar, the thin border to the left of the text. (You can tell when the pointer is in the selection bar because it looks like a northeast-pointing arrow.)

- To select a paragraph, click three times within the paragraph or double-click in the selection bar.

- To select the entire document, open the **Edit** menu and choose the **Select All** command, press the **Ctrl+A** key combination, or triple-click in the selection bar.

Begin Guided Tour   Select Text with the Mouse

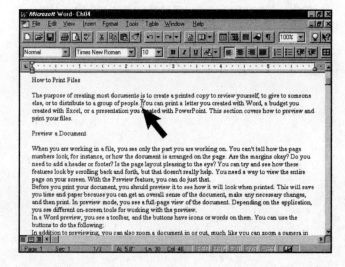

1 Point to the beginning of the text you want to select. Hold down the left mouse button and drag across the text you want to select.

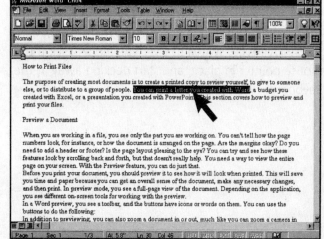

2 As you drag, the text appears white on black. After you highlight all the text you want, release the mouse button.

Add and Delete Text

Have you ever typed a document and then remembered something you wanted to add? With Word, you can easily add or delete text from your document. Word provides two modes for entering text: *Insert mode* and *Overtype mode*. When you type using Insert mode, any existing text on your screen moves to the right to make room for the new text you're typing. (It's like a bulldozer, pushing your old text out of the way to make room for the new.) When you first start Word, you're in Insert mode (it's the default setting). Insert mode is ideal for inserting new words into the middle of existing sentences. In Insert mode, you can simply click the mouse into place and start typing.

When you type using Overtype mode—also called *Typeover* mode in some circles—the new text replaces the existing text you're typing. (Overtype mode is like a tank that runs over all the characters that are in its way.) Overtype mode is effective for deleting existing text by simply typing over it.

As I mentioned, by default, Word is set up to let you type in Insert mode. However, you can turn the Insert and Overtype modes on or off. To switch between Insert and Overtype modes, press the **Ins** (or **Insert**) key on your keyboard. When the Overtype mode is in effect, you'll see the bold letters **OVR** on the status bar (at the bottom of your screen). When you're ready to use Overtype, switch to Overtype mode, click the mouse pointer in place, and start pecking away at the keyboard.

However, you should be careful when using Overtype: although it works well when you want to replace text, you have to remember to turn it off when you're done so you don't accidentally replace more text than you intended. Most often, you will turn on Overtype by mistake and wonder what's happening when characters disappear when you start typing. If this happens, check the status bar for **OVR**. You probably pressed **Ins** by mistake. Simply press **Ins** again to turn off Overtype.

Two Ways to Delete

Another way of deleting text is with the **Backspace** or **Delete** keys. Backspace deletes characters to the left; delete removes characters to the right of the insertion point. If you have a lot of text to remove, it's faster to select the text and then delete it all at once by simply pressing the **Delete** key.

Make a mistake? If you delete text by accident, you can undo the deletion by using the **Undo** command in the **Edit** menu or by using the **Undo** button in the toolbar. It's best to use the Undo command immediately after making the mistake.

Begin Guided Tour Add Text

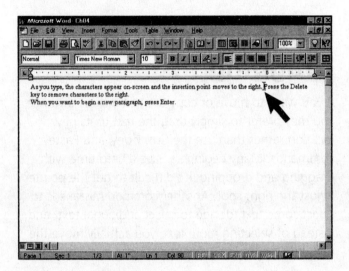

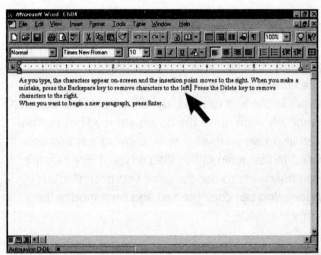

1 Move the insertion point to the spot where you want the new text. Type the new text.

2 The existing text moves over to make room.

Begin Guided Tour Delete Text

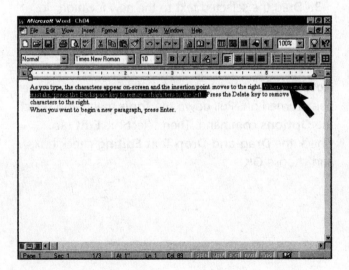

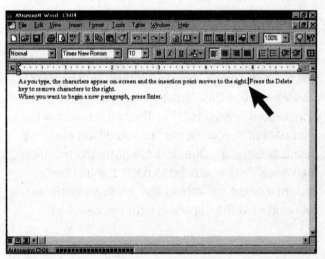

1 Select the text you want to delete and press the **Delete** key. See the preceding section for help on selecting text.

2 Word deletes the text, and existing text moves over to fill in the gap.

Move and Copy Text

The ability to copy and move text from one place to another in your document can really come in handy as you edit your Word documents. One of the editing changes you may make is to change the order of the text to make the document flow more smoothly or to make the document read better. You can also save yourself time by copying text that you need to use again rather than retype it. For example, you may want to use the same text or similar text again. You can copy the text and then modify the copy.

When you are moving or copying text, think of scissors and paste. That's the analogy used for these procedures. With a move, you cut the text from the original location and paste it in the new location, using the Cut and Paste commands. With a copy, you copy and then paste using the Copy and Paste commands. You can find these commands in the Edit menu or you can use the buttons in the toolbar.

When you cut or copy text, Word places it in the *Clipboard*, a temporary holding spot. (The Clipboard is a Windows 95 feature, which means you can copy text from one application to another. Sharing data is covered in "Use Data Together from Different Office Applications" on page 345.) The text remains in the Clipboard until you cut or copy something else. That means two things. One, you can paste the text more than once. Two, you need to paste the text before you copy or cut something else; otherwise, the text is overwritten in the Clipboard with the new text.

> Press the **Ctrl+X** key combination to select the Edit Cut command. Press **Ctrl +C** to select the Edit Copy command. Press the **Ctrl+V** key combination to select the Edit Paste command.

Move and Copy by Dragging

If you want to move or copy the text a short distance, you may prefer to simply drag the text to its new location rather than use the Cut, Copy, and Paste commands. Many beginners have a hard time with dragging and dropping; it's difficult to get the pointer in just the right spot. Another common mistake is to select some text, decide to select additional text, and instead of selecting more text, you actually move the text. If this happens, undo the change and start over.

To move and copy by dragging, follow these steps:

1. Select the text to move or copy. Release the mouse button.

2. Point to the selected text.

3. Drag the selected text to the new location. To drag a copy, hold down the **Ctrl** key as you drag.

Note: If dragging doesn't work, the feature may have been turned off. Pull down the **Tools** menu and select the **Options** command. Then select the **Edit** tab. Check the **Drag-and-Drop Text Editing** check box and choose **OK**.

Begin Guided Tour　Move Text

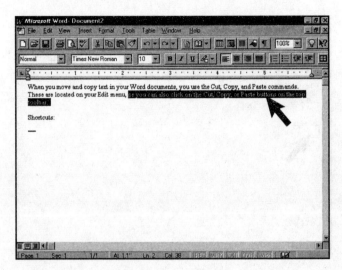

1 Select the text you want to move.

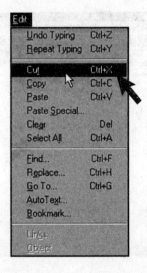

2 Open the **Edit** menu and select the **Cut** command. Word removes the text from the document and places it on the Clipboard.

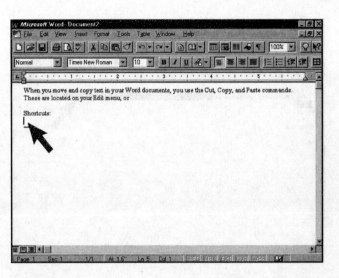

3 Move the insertion point to where you want to paste the cut text.

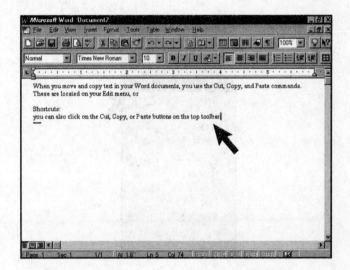

4 Open the **Edit** menu again, and this time select the **Paste** command. Word pastes the cut text at the new location.

Begin Guided Tour Copy Text

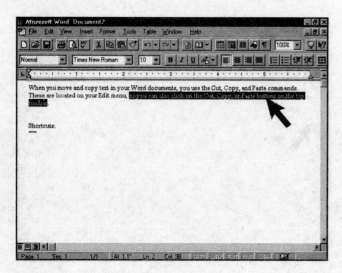

1 Select the text you want to copy.

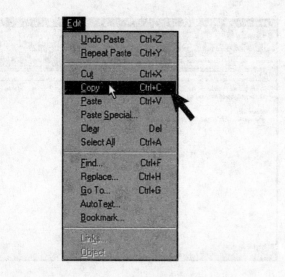

2 Open the **Edit** menu and select the **Copy** command.

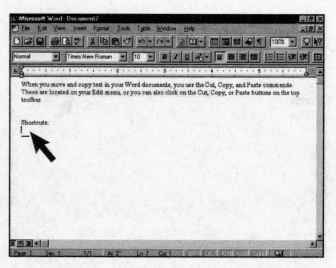

3 Nothing changes on-screen, but Word has placed a copy of the text in the Clipboard. Move the insertion point to where you want to paste the text.

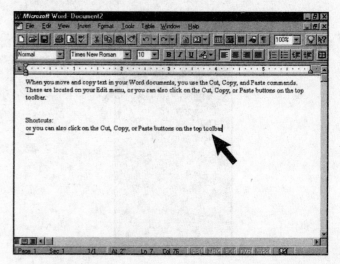

4 Open the **Edit** menu again, and this time select the **Paste** command. Word pastes the copy at the new location.

Don't forget that you can also use the Cut, Copy, and Paste buttons on your Standard toolbar.

Find and Replace Text

Sometimes, you can read a document over and over looking for a particular word or phrase. Where is it? Are you going blind? If you are looking for a particular word or phrase or section of a document, you can move there more quickly using the **Find** command. Find is particularly useful for moving around in a long document. Imagine scanning a 20-page document looking for the one occurrence of the word **dog**.

A companion to the Find command is the Replace command. You can use this command to find one word or phrase and replace it with another. Suppose that you used the not-so-politically correct term "spokesman" in a document. You decide that "spokesperson" is a better word choice. You can look for each occurrence and replace the word manually, or you can have Word find all occurrences and make the changes for you. The latter is definitely going to save you some time and effort.

Find and Replace sound great until you search for a common letter combination such as **not** and have to stop at 15 words until you find the word you want, or until you make a replacement and end up with replacements you didn't intend. To make Find and Replace work best, consider the following suggestions:

- If you are trying to find a section in a document, think of a unique word. If you search for a common word, you'll have to stop on several occurrences until you find the one you want. For example, suppose that you have a document describing different cooking classes offered and you want to move to the section on Italian Cooking. If you search for **cooking** or **class**, you may have to stop on several sections before you find the one you want. If you search for the word **Italian**, on the other hand, you have a better chance of moving directly to the section you want.

- Use the **Find Whole Words Only** check box when you want to stop on whole words. For example, if you type **man**, Word will stop on **man**, **manager**, **chairman**, and any other words that contain **man**. If you check Find Whole Words only, Word will stop only on **man**.

- Another way to limit the search is to use the **Match Case** check box. If you check this, Word will find only words that match exactly. If you type **FIG**, Word will stop only on **FIG**—not **fig** or **Fig**.

- Even though you can make all the replacements at once, go through a few and confirm the change one by one to make sure the replace works as you intended. Suppose that you want to change all occurrences of hat to cap in your document. Sounds easy enough. But did you think that those three letters—**hat**—may appear in other words? If you replace without checking, you may end up with cCAPter instead of cHATter.

- To repeat a search, press **Shift+F4**.

- When Word has searched the entire document, you see a message saying so. If you did not find the match, try changing the search options.

- If Word does not find the text, you see an alert message. Click **OK** and try the search again. Be sure to type the search string correctly.

- You can use the **Special** button in the dialog box to search for and/or replace special characters. For example, you can search for all the tabs in your document. To do this, click on the **Special** button. From the pop-up list that appears, click on the item you want to find.

- You can also search for and/or replace formatting. To do so, click on the **Format** button. From the drop-down menu that appears, click on the type of formatting you want to find: Font, Paragraph, Language, or Style. Word displays the appropriate dialog box. Make selections in the dialog box and click **OK**. (The next section covers formatting features.)

Begin Guided Tour Find Text

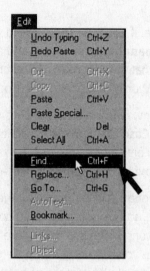

1 Open the **Edit** menu and select the **Find** command.

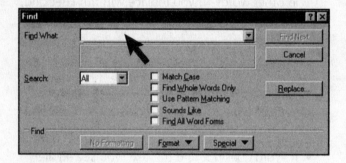

2 You see the Find dialog box. In the **Find What** text box, type the text you want to find. You can type as much or as little text as you want. If you have searched previously in this document, the last text you searched for may appear in the **Find What** text box. If so, simply delete the current entry and type the new one.

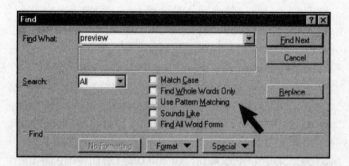

3 Below the **Find What** text box are the search options. Set any options you want to use by clicking the appropriate check boxes to select them. If you want Word to match the case as you've typed it, select the **Match Case** check box. If you want Word to flag only whole words as opposed to partial words, select the **Find Whole Words Only** check box.

4 Click on the **Find Next** button to start the search.

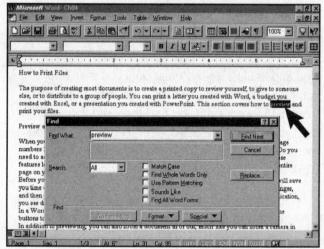

5 Word moves to the first match and highlights the found word or phrase. If this is the text you want, click the **Cancel** button to close the dialog box. If this isn't the text, click the **Find Next** button to find the next match. Continue to do so until you find the match you want.

Begin Guided Tour Replace Text

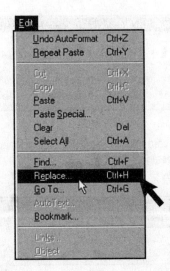

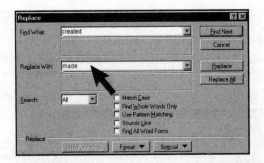

1 Open the **Edit** menu and select the **Replace** command.

3 You see the search text entered. Click in the **Replace With** text box and type the text you want to use as the replacement. If you want to delete the found text, you can leave the **Replace With** text box blank.

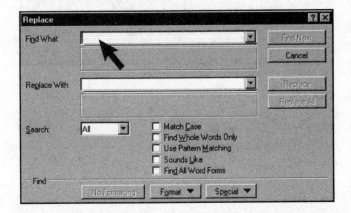

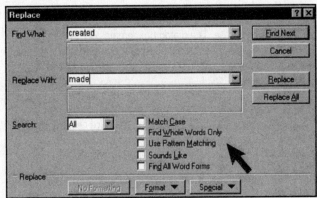

2 You see the Replace dialog box. In the **Find What** text box, type the text you want to find. (You may have to delete the current entry if one appears. Select the text and press **Delete**.)

4 Set any of the replace options by clicking the appropriate check box. For example, if you want Word to match the case as you've typed it, check the **Match Case** check box. If you want Word to flag only whole words as opposed to partial words, check the **Find Whole Words Only** check box.

5 Click the **Find Next** button to start the search.

(continues)

Guided Tour   Replace Text

(continued)

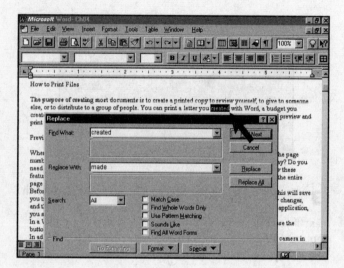

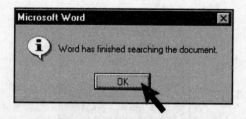

8 When Word finishes searching the document, you see an alert message. Click **OK**.

6 Word moves to the first match and highlights the found word or phrase. The dialog box remains open. If you want to make the replacement, click the **Replace** button. (To leave this text as is and move to the next match, click the **Find Next** button.)

7 Word makes the replacement and moves to the next occurrence. Continue clicking on **Replace** or **Find Next** until you go through each occurrence. You can also click the **Replace All** button to make all the replacements at once.

9 Click the **Cancel** button to close the Replace dialog box.

Have Word Type Often-Used Phrases for You

Suppose that you work for the State University Division of Continuing Studies, and you have to type this phrase A LOT. Want to save some time? Instead of typing the text each time, you can create a shortcut version, called *AutoText*. You can then type the shortcut name and press a shortcut key to insert the AutoText.

AutoText is one of the handiest time-saving features you can use. You can use it for boilerplate phrases or paragraphs that you use again and again. For instance, you may have a paragraph that you use to describe your company. You can create an AutoText entry to ensure the statement appears precisely the same way each time you use it. Or maybe you tire of typing in your company name and address onto every letter. You can save this information as an AutoText entry, too.

The first step to use AutoText is to create the entry. (You only have to do this once.) You can assign a short name (as short as one character) to the entry or a longer name. When assigning a name, keep in mind that you have to type the shortcut name into your document in order to insert the AutoText, so you won't save much time if the name you use is long. I tend to use a one letter name; for example, I might use just **s** for State University Division of Continuing Studies. After you create the entry, you can insert the Autotext whenever you need it.

> If you forget the name, you can select it from a list. To do so, open the **Edit** menu and choose the **AutoText** command. From the dialog box that appears, click the entry you want to insert and click on the **Insert** button.

Begin Guided Tour   Create an AutoText Entry

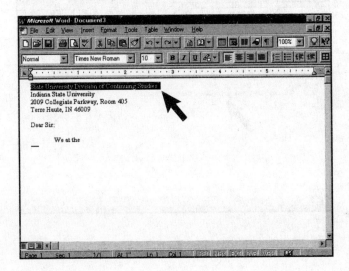

1 Select the text you want to use as the AutoText entry.

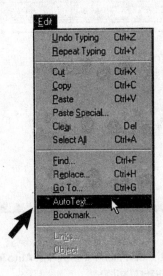

2 Open the **Edit** menu and select the **AutoText** command.

(continues)

Guided Tour   Create an AutoText Entry

(continued)

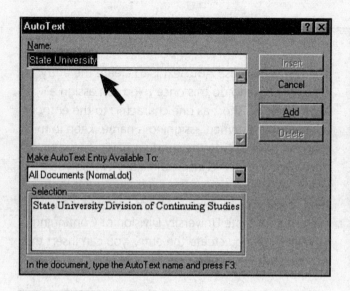

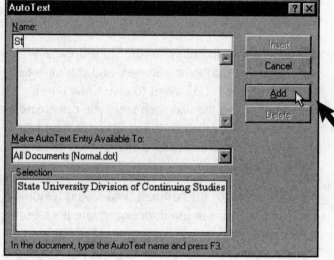

3 You see the AutoText dialog box. The text you have selected appears at the bottom of the dialog box, and Word suggests a name for this entry. If you don't like the name Word has chosen, type a name in the **Name** text box such as **st**.

4 Click the **Add** button. Word creates the AutoText entry and closes the dialog box. On-screen nothing is different.

Begin Guided Tour   Insert an AutoText Entry

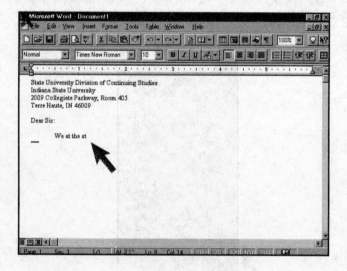

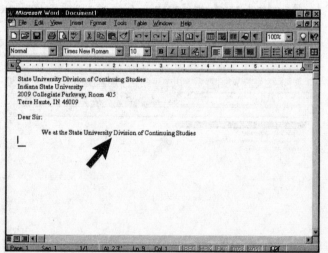

1 Type the entire AutoText name, for example ST, and press **F3**, or open the **Edit** menu again, select **AutoText**, and click on the **Insert** button.

2 Word inserts the entry.

Insert the Date or Time

If you are like me, you may not know today's date off the top of your head. I have to look at a calendar (especially on Mondays). With Word, you can insert the current date quickly without having to do any typing, and you can select from several different formats.

If you insert the date as text, Word inserts the current date but does not update it. Think of this as a date stamp.

In some cases, you may want to update the date, as you work on the document. In this case, you can insert the date as a *field* (a database-related entry in your document), and Word will update it for you when the time comes. For example, suppose that you are working on a project that will probably take you more than two weeks. You want the current date at the top of the document. You can insert the date as a

field and when you finish the document and print it, Word will reflect the current date (not the date when you inserted the field) in the document. Pretty handy!

Because the date is not text, but a field, you cannot delete the date character by character. If you try to, Word beeps. Instead, you must drag across the entire date to select the field. Then press **Delete**.

Word uses the date and time from your system clock. If this date or time is incorrect, you can update it using Windows' Control Panel. Open the **Main** program group and double-click on the **Control Panel** icon. Next, double-click on the **Date/Time** icon. Enter a new date or time in the dialog box and then click **OK**.

Begin Guided Tour Insert a Date or Time

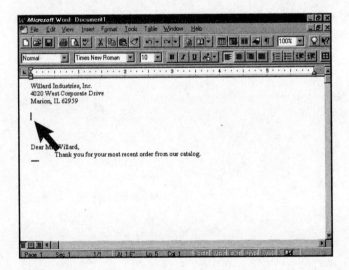

1 Place the insertion point where you want to insert the date.

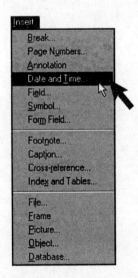

2 Open the **Insert** menu and select the **Date and Time** command.

(continues)

Guided Tour   Insert a Date or Time

(continued)

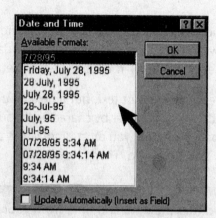

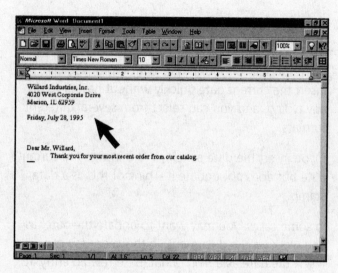

3 You see the Date and Time dialog box. Click on the date or time format you want to use. To insert the entry as a field that will be updated, check the **Update Automatically (Insert as Field)** check box.

4 Click **OK**.

5 Word inserts the date or time in the format you selected.

Check Your Spelling

A typo or misspelling in an otherwise perfect document stands out like a red flag. And speaking of red flags, that's exactly what Word's new spelling feature does. If you see any funny-looking wavy, red lines appear under any words that you type in, don't be alarmed. That's the *Word Spell It* feature kicking in. It automatically checks your spelling while you type, and it's turned on by default. The wavy, red line that you see under a word means one of two things:

> You've misspelled a word

> Or the word you spelled isn't in Word's dictionary.

When you go back and correct the word, the wavy, red line disappears. If you can't tell if the word is misspelled or not, just move your mouse pointer over the word and right-click. Spell It recommends alternative spellings you can use. Select one from the list and the word is corrected.

If you get tired of seeing the wavy, red lines as you type, you can turn the feature off. Open the **Tools** menu; select **Options**. In the Options dialog box, in the Spelling tab, unselect the Automatic Spell Checking option.

> For those of you who never see the wavy, red lines, even when you deliberately misspell something, then the Spell It feature probably isn't turned on. To remedy this, just open the **Tools** menu, select **Options**, click on the **Spelling** tab, and make sure to select the Automatic Spell Checking check box. (Follow these same steps to turn the feature off again.)

The Spell Check Feature

Another way to be sure your document doesn't include any spelling errors is to use Word's Spell Check feature. You can start the Spell Check program at any time, either by clicking on the **Spelling** button on your toolbar, or opening the **Tools** menu and selecting **Spelling**. You can start the Spell Check program anywhere in the document. Word will start checking from the insertion point forward and then go back to the top of the document and check the rest of the document.

If you want to spell check just a passage, you can select the text you want to check and then select the **Spelling** command. Word will check the selection and then ask whether you want to check the rest of the document. Click **No**.

The Spell Check program works by comparing words in the document to words in its dictionary; when it finds a word, it flags it as misspelled. That doesn't necessarily mean the word is misspelled, it just means the speller cannot find the word in its dictionary. For example, the speller may flag proper names and some terminology, although they are spelled correctly. Word will also flag double words such as "the the."

When the speller flags a word, you have several choices, which appear in a dialog box along with the flagged word:

- If the correct word appears in the dialog box, click on it in the **Suggestions** list. Click the **Change** button to change this occurrence. Click the **Change All** button to replace all occurrences of the word with the word in the **Change To** text box.

- If none of the replacements are correct, click in the **Change To** text box and type the correct spelling. Then click the **Change** or **Change All** button.

- If the word is spelled correctly, click the **Ignore** button to skip this occurrence but stop on the next one. To skip all occurrences of this word, click the **Ignore All** button.

- If the word that is flagged is a word that you use often, you can add it to the dictionary by clicking the **Add** button.

- If Word flags a repeated word, click the **Ignore** button to ignore and keep the repeated word. Or click the **Delete** button to delete one of the words.

After you select an option, Word moves to the next word, until it checks all the words.

> You still need to proofread your document. Word only knows whether a word is mis-spelled; it doesn't know whether you have used it correctly. For instance, if you use *there* when you mean *their*, Word won't flag the word. Be sure to proofread your document.

Automatically Correct Common Mistypings or Misspellings

If you ever make a mistake typing and see the mistake corrected automatically, you have seen the magic of *AutoCorrect* at work. Word knows some common typing mistakes such as "teh" for "the." These misspellings are saved as AutoCorrect entries and are corrected automatically.

You can also add new AutoCorrect entries on the fly during a spell check or by manually typing using the **Tools AutoCorrect** command. For example, I often mistype "chapter" as "chatper." When I noticed that I did this consistently, I added the AutoCorrect entry by clicking the **AutoCorrect** button in the Spelling dialog box. Now when I mistype the chatper, Word makes the correction automatically.

> AutoCorrect won't work unless it's turned on. If your AutoCorrect is off, then you need to open the **Tools** menu, choose **AutoCorrect**, and check the **Replace Text as You Type** check box.

Begin Guided Tour   Check Your Document for Spelling Errors

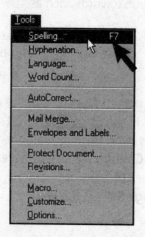

> You can also start the Spell Check feature by clicking on the **Spelling** button on your toolbar.

 Open the **Tools** menu and select the **Spelling** command.

Guided Tour   Check Your Document for Spelling Errors

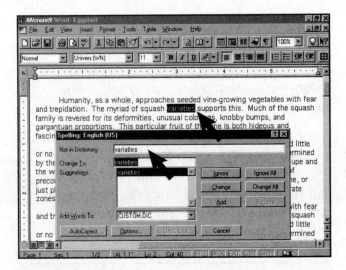

2 Word highlights any words it cannot find and displays the Spelling dialog box. To change the spelling based on Word's suggestion, click the **Change** or **Change All** button. To ignore the spelling, click the **Ignore** or **Ignore All** button.

3 Word highlights the next misspelling or double word. Continue making corrections.

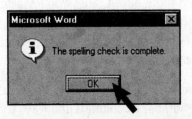

4 When you see the message that the spelling check is complete, click **OK**.

Begin Guided Tour   Add an AutoCorrect Entry

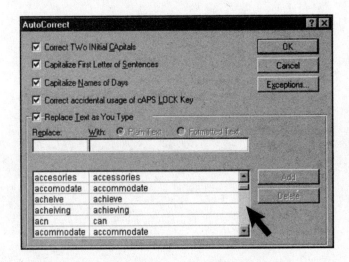

1 Open the **Tools** menu and choose **AutoCorrect**. The AutoCorrect dialog box opens to display a list of programmed misspellings, along with options for adding your own misspellings to the list.

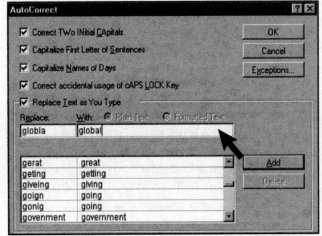

2 Type a word you often misspell into the **Replace** box, type the correct spelling in the **With** box, and then click the **Add** button.

3 Keep repeating these steps to add other common misspellings that you struggle with. When you finish, click **OK** to exit the box. Now anytime you misspell the word, AutoCorrect will come to your rescue and spell it correctly based on your entry in the AutoCorrect dialog box.

Set Up a Table

Forget about using a tabbed list for a grid of information (see the task "Set Tabs" on page 118 to learn more about tabs). You'll waste your time setting up the tabs, pressing Tab again and again, and working hard on aligning the columns just how you want. Instead, set up a table.

A *table* is much more flexible than a tabbed list. You set up the number of columns and rows you want and just type the entries. Word keeps each entry in its cubbyhole, called a *cell*, even if the entry is longer than one line. For longer entries, Word wraps the lines and adjusts the other table entries. You can resize the columns, insert new rows and columns, and make formatting changes (all covered in the next section).

The fastest way to create a table is to use the **Table** button in the Standard toolbar, as described in the Guided Tour. You can create a table this way with up to five columns. You don't have to worry so much about the order of your rows because you can easily add new rows as you create the table.

You type in a table just as you type in a regular document. If you press **Enter**, Word inserts a paragraph break in the cell. You can also make editing changes to the text: delete or copy text, check spelling, and so on.

To move to the next column, press **Tab**. Type that entry and press **Tab** again. To move backward through the cells, press **Shift+Tab**. When you press **Tab** in the last row and column, Word adds a new row. Continue typing until you complete all the entries you want.

If you want more than five columns or you want to set the width of each column to a specific measurement, you can use the **Insert Table** command to create the table. In the Table dialog box you can specify an exact number of columns and rows.

If you have a tabbed list and you want to set the list up as a table, don't redo it. Instead, have Word convert the text to a table. To do so, select the text and then pull down the **Table** menu and select the **Convert Text to Table** command. You see the Convert Text to Table dialog box, which makes a good guess how the table should be set up. Make any changes to the number or columns and then click **OK**.

Begin Guided Tour Add a Table to Your Document

1 Click the **Table** button.

3 x 4 Table

2 You see a drop-down palette. Drag across the number of columns and rows you want to include. Notice that Word displays the dimensions at the bottom of the palette.

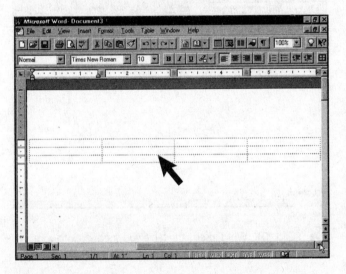

3 When you release the mouse button, Word displays the table on-screen, a grid of columns and rows. The gridlines indicate the columns and rows but will not print when you print the document. The insertion point is within the first cell. Type the entry in the first cell and press **Tab** to move to the next cell. You can also click in the cell you want to move to using the mouse.

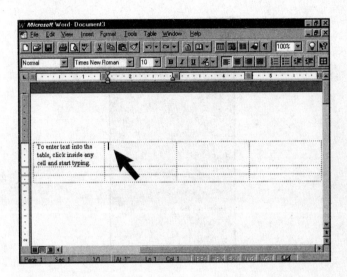

4 You move to the next column. Continue typing entries for the row and pressing **Tab**.

5 When you press **Tab** in the last column, you move to the next row. Complete this row and press **Tab**. When you reach the last row in the table and press **Tab**, Word inserts a new row.

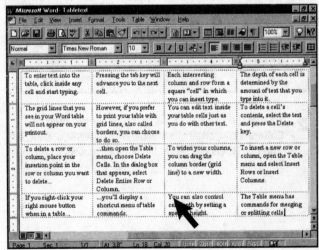

6 Continue entering the table data until you complete all the information you want your table to include (it's okay to leave some cells empty).

Begin Guided Tour Using the Table Dialog Box to Create the Table

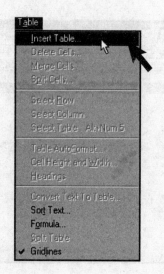

1 Open the **Table** menu and select the **Insert Table** command.

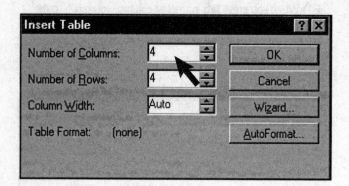

2 You see the Insert Table dialog box. In the **Number of Columns** box, enter the number of columns you want. In the **Number of Rows** box, enter the number of rows you want.

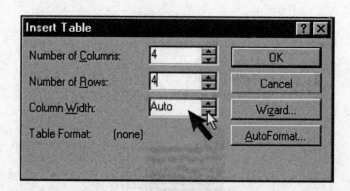

3 In the **Column Width** box, enter the column width you want for each column. If you want Word to create the column width based on the number of columns, leave **Auto** selected.

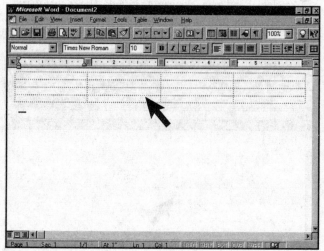

4 Click **OK**. Word inserts the table you specified into your document.

Print Envelopes and Labels

When PCs first became popular, many people kept their typewriters around just for the sole task of typing envelopes. Why? Because setting up and printing an envelope using the older printers and software was more trouble than it was worth. Things have changed considerably, though, and using a laser printer (or dot-matrix or inkjet printer) and Word, you can easily print an envelope. You can also use Word to generate mailing labels.

Note: Your printer probably has a manual feed for envelopes. If your printer can't print envelopes, don't use the envelope feature.

If you have typed a letter and want an envelope to go with it, you'll be amazed at how simple it is to create the envelope. Just select the **Envelopes and Labels** command from the **Tools** menu. Word finds the address and copies it to the Envelopes and Labels dialog box. You simply need to confirm the address, insert the envelope, and click **OK**.

In some cases, you may want to create an envelope in a document without the address. In this case, you can use the Envelopes and Labels command and type the address manually in the dialog box.

If you have a lot of mailings, you can use Word to set up and print mailing labels. This feature makes it easy to send out Christmas cards, catalogs, or other mass mailings. You can select the type of labels that you have; Word recognizes most Avery label types (a popular label company). Word sets up a document with margins, indents, and other settings appropriate for the labels you are using. The resulting document is similar to a big table; you enter the addresses in each cell in the table and then print the document using the labels.

If you aren't sure which way to insert the labels in the printer, mark an **X** on a piece of paper and put it in the paper tray with the **X** up. Print a document. If you see the **X** on the printed document, you know to put the labels in face up. If the **X** is on the back side of the printed page, you know to put the labels in face down.

Begin Guided Tour   Print an Envelope

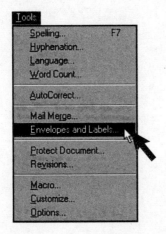

1 Open the **Tools** menu and choose the **Envelopes and Labels** command.

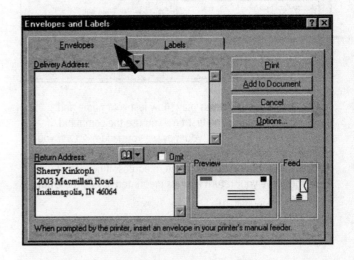

2 The Envelopes and Labels dialog box appears. If necessary, click the **Envelopes** tab to bring it to the front of the dialog box.

(continues)

Guided Tour Print an Envelope

(continued)

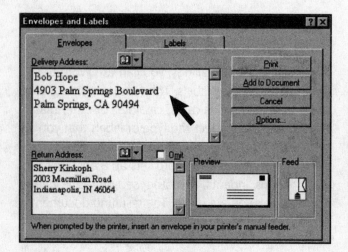

3 If your document contains an address, Word automatically displays it in the **Delivery Address** area. If not, you can enter one into the **Delivery Address** text box or make any corrections to the address that appears there.

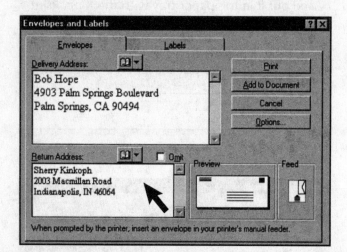

4 The **Return Address** may show just your name and company name the first time you use the command. If you have used this feature, you may see your address. Or if you deleted the address, this area may be blank. In the **Return Address** area, type or edit your return address if needed. If your envelopes have your return address preprinted, check the **Omit** check box.

5 Insert the envelope in the manual feed for your printer.

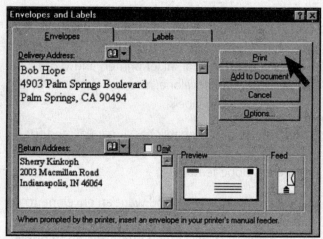

6 Click the **Print** button. Word prints the envelope.

To add the address into your document, click the **Add to Document** button. This inserts the address in your document, which you can then save as part of the document text.

Begin Guided Tour   Create Mailing Labels

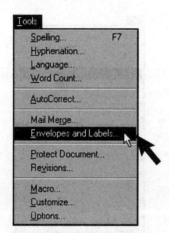

1 Open the **Tools** menu and select the **Envelopes and Labels** command.

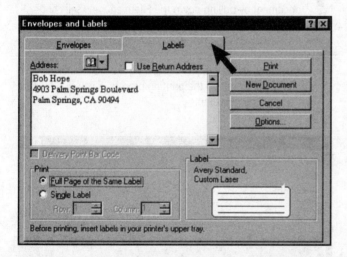

2 You see the Envelopes and Labels dialog box. Click the **Labels** tab to bring it to the front of the box.

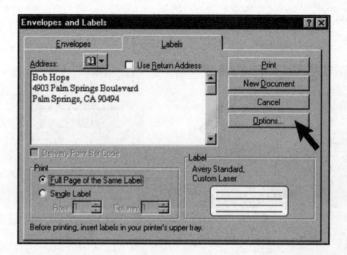

3 To select the type of label you are using, click the **Options** button.

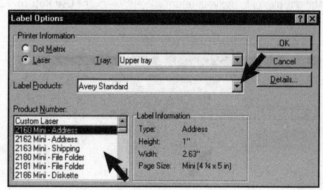

4 Word displays the Label Options dialog box. Click on the down arrow next to **Label Products** and click on the brand of label you are using. Then in the **Product Number** list, click on the product name of the labels you are using. Click **OK** to return to the Envelopes and Labels dialog box.

If you've created a database of addresses with your Schedule+ program (another program in your Office suite), you can use the Address Book drop-down list to select the Schedule+ file to use. Simply click on the **Address Book** icon above the **Delivery Address** box or the **Return Address** box. (Learn more about using Schedule+ to create address lists in the task "Create a Contacts List" on page 331.)

(continues)

Guided Tour Create Mailing Labels

(continued)

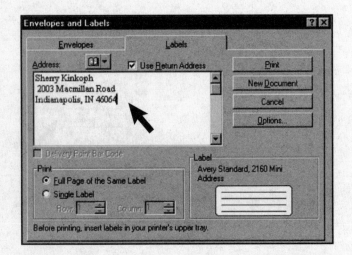

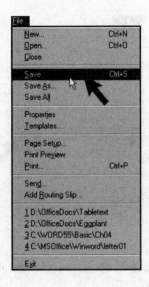

5 If you want to create a sheet of labels, all with the same address, type the address in the **Address** text box. If each label will have a different address as the text on the label, leave the box blank. To use your return address, check the **Use Return Address** check box. Then click on the **New Document** button.

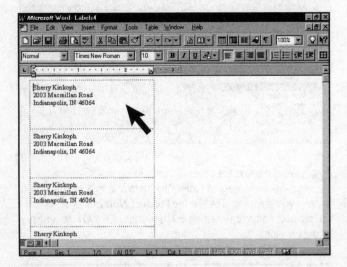

6 Word creates a document formatted into a table. The table is set up to match your selected labels. If you entered an address for step 5, all the labels display this address, and you can skip to step 8. If you did not, the labels are blank. Type the first label, pressing **Enter** to move to the next line in the label. When you complete one label, press **Tab** to go to the next label. Continue to fill in the table labels until you finish.

7 When you finish typing the labels, you can save the document by pulling down the **File** menu and selecting the **Save** command. Even if you think you won't need the labels again, it's a good idea to save the document until after you print the labels. Sometimes, the labels can get jammed. You won't want to go through the process of creating the labels again if something happens during the printing process. If you don't want to save, skip to the next step.

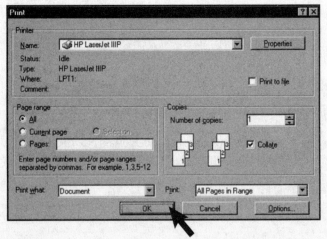

8 Insert the labels into the printer, pull down the **File** menu, select the **Print** command, and click **OK** to print the labels.

HOW TO...

Format a Word Document

I n addition to the many editing features that Word provides, you can also utilize a complete toolbox of formatting features. What is formatting? *Formatting* is changing the appearance of the document. Why change the look? You may want to enhance the appearance of a document for many reasons: to make the document easier to read, to help clarify the meaning, or to make the document more attractive.

In this part of the book, you can find the features and the steps you need to make your document polished and professional looking.

What You Will Find in This Section

Make Text Bold, Italic, or Underline

Take a look at the following sentences:

Sign up for the **free seminar** tomorrow only.

Sign up for the free seminar **tomorrow only**.

Even though the wording of both sentences is identical, notice how the use of formatting changes the emphasis. The sentences read differently because of the font style, that is, the use of bold.

As in this example, you can add emphasis to selected text by using a different font style. The three most common font styles are **bold**, *italic*, and <u>underline</u>. However, Microsoft has added a new formatting option to Word 7.0 that lets you highlight text much like a highlighter pen; the feature is known as *highlight*. You can even select different colors to highlight with. Unfortunately, highlighting your text doesn't do much good unless you have a color printer or are networked to other computer users who can see the color highlighting in the files you send. If you do highlight text and print out to a noncolor printer, you'll still see the highlighting; it will appear as shaded gray.

Before you go wild making all the important words in your document bold, italics, underline, or highlighted, consider these guidelines:

- Use the font styles sparingly. If every other word is bold, how is the reader to know what is *really* important? Too much bold makes the document look messy. Too much italic is difficult to read.

- You can combine the styles. To make text bold and italic, for example, click on the **Bold** button and then click on the **Italic** button.

- Underline is the least "professional" font style and is more of a carryover from the days of typewriters. Instead of underline, consider using italics.

- You can also change the font style using the Font dialog box, as described in the next section.

- Some writers tend to use UPPERCASE letters as a way to emphasize a message. If you use this method, your reader is likely to feel as if you are SCREAMING AT THEM.

Begin Guided Tour   Use Common Formatting Commands

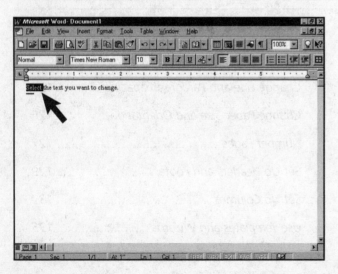

1 Select the text you want to change.

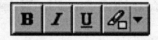

2 The text appears highlighted. Do one of the following:

Click the **Bold** button to make text bold (it looks like a bold capital **B**).

Click the **Italic** button (it looks like an italic capital **I**).

Click the **Underline** button (it looks like an underlined capital **U**).

Click the **Highlight** button (it looks like a highlighter pen).

Guided Tour   Use Common Formatting Commands

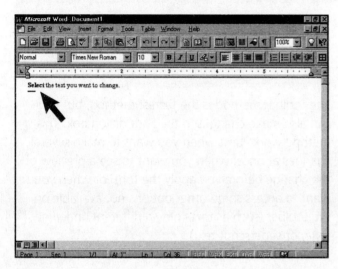

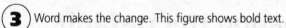

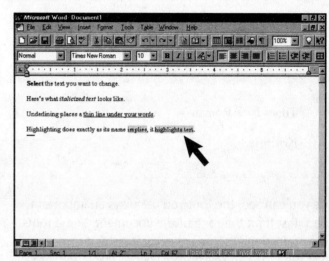

3 Word makes the change. This figure shows bold text.

Prefer to use the keyboard to make formatting changes? Then learn these shortcuts: **Ctrl+B** for bold, **Ctrl+I** for italic, and **Ctrl+U** for underline.

Here you see examples of each of the other styles (italic, underline, highlight).

4 To undo a style change, select the text again and click on the style's button. For example, if you make text bold, you can unbold it by selecting it and clicking on the **Bold** button. Doing so turns off the style.

Change the Font and Font Size

Look at the following font examples.

BluePrint

Times New Roman

Korinna

Shelley Volante BT

As you can see, the font you use plays an important part in setting the tone of the document. Some fonts are professional, some are decorative, and some are just fun. You can select from your available fonts to match the meaning you want for your document.

To use a font, the printer has to know how to print that font. All printers have certain built-in fonts that they know how to print. In a font list, you will see a little printer icon next to printer fonts.

The printer can also get the information about how to print a font from the computer, in the form of a font file. Before the popularity of Windows and the introduction of TrueType fonts, you could find lots of different font formats and lots of methods for using fonts. Now, you'll find mostly TrueType fonts, which are fonts installed through Windows and stored in files on your hard disk. **TT** in the font list indicates TrueType fonts.

Windows 95, as well as some Windows 95 programs, come with TrueType fonts. These fonts install when you install the program(s). You can also purchase and install additional fonts using the Windows 95 Control Panel.

The easiest way to change fonts is to use the Font and Font Size list boxes on the Formatting toolbar, as explained in the Guided Tour. Keep in mind that fonts

are measured in points, and there are 72 points in one inch. The larger the point size, the bigger the font.

The toolbar method is the fastest method, but you can also make changes in the Font dialog box. This method works best when you want to make several changes at once; when you want to see a preview of the change before you apply the font; or when you want to access some other options not available on the toolbar (such as text color, a different underline style, or superscript text).

Change the Default Font

The default font used in all new documents is Times New Roman, 10-point type. If you don't like this font, you don't have to change it over and over again in each new document. Instead, you can select a new default font that will appear in all new documents. For example, I like to use Arial 12-point type because it is clean and easy to read.

To change the default font, follow these steps:

1. Open the **Format** menu and select the **Font** command.

2. You see the Font tab options. In the Font list, click on the font you want to use as the default. In the Font Style area, click on the default style you want. In the Size list, click on the default font size you want.

3. Click the **Default** button.

4. You are prompted to confirm that you want to make the change. Click the **Yes** button.

Begin Guided Tour   Change the Font from the Toolbar

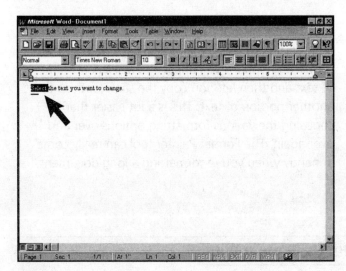

1 Select the text you want to change.

2 With the text selected, click on the down arrow next to the Font list box on the Formatting toolbar.

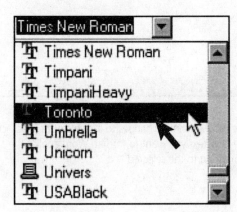

3 You see a list of fonts. Word lists the most recently used fonts at the top of the list. Click on the font you want. You may have to scroll down the list to see the one you want.

4 Word applies the font and closes the list. To change the size of the font, click on the down arrow next to the Font Size list box.

5 You see a list of font sizes. Click on the size you want.

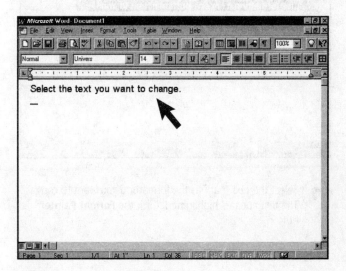

6 Word changes the font size of the selected text and closes the list. Click outside the text to deselect it.

> You can also use the Font dialog box to change a font. Select the font command from the format menu.

Copy Character Formatting

In many cases, you will like the way you formatted a selection of text and want to use the same set of formatting again. For example, suppose that you changed the font, font size, and style of a heading in your document and you want to use this same set of features for another heading. Rather than figure out exactly which commands and which options you selected and repeat them each time, you can simply copy the formatting and use the same options on another selection of text.

You use the Format Painter tool to do this; you'll find it up on the Standard toolbar. It keeps track of the formatting options you applied to a select portion of text and then lets you copy the same options to another portion of text. This is a lot easier than choosing the various formatting options over and over again. The Format Painter tool can really come in handy when you're formatting a long document.

Begin Guided Tour Copy Formatting with the Format Ruler

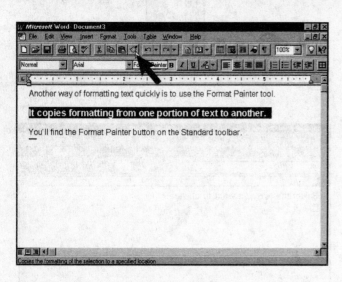

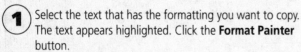

① Select the text that has the formatting you want to copy. The text appears highlighted. Click the **Format Painter** button.

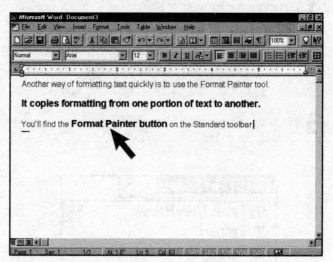

② The mouse pointer changes to a paintbrush. Drag across the new text you want to format. Word applies the formatting to the selected text.

Align Text

When you type in Word, all text is left-aligned, and the right margin appears ragged. For most text, this is the alignment choice that you will use; that's why it's the default. In some instances, though, you will want to choose a different alignment. For example, you may want to center text such as the title of a document, or you may want to right-align text or justify text.

Some formatting features such as alignment apply to the entire paragraph. Keep in mind that a paragraph is any text followed by a hard return (a press of the Enter key). A paragraph can be one line, one word, or several lines of text. You end one paragraph and create a new one by pressing **Enter**. When you press **Enter**, Word inserts a paragraph marker, which is important to formatting. (The paragraph marker is hidden by default, but you can see it if you click on the **Paragraph** button—it looks like a **P**—on the Standard toolbar.) When you make a change to the formatting, the paragraph marker stores the

formatting change—tabs, indents, alignment, and so on. This concept can confuse you in two ways.

First, when you format one paragraph and then press **Enter**, all the formatting continues to the next paragraph. For example, if you center a line and press **Enter**, the next line appears centered, too. You may wonder how this happened. Remember the paragraph formatting continues down.

Second, if you delete a paragraph maker, the paragraph takes on the formatting of the next paragraph. You may wonder what happened to your formatting. Just keep in mind that the paragraph marker stores the formatting.

> Speedy typist? Then remember these alignment keyboard shortcuts: **Ctrl+E** for Center, **Ctrl+L** for Left, **Ctrl+R** for Right, and **Ctrl+J** for Justified.

Begin Guided Tour   Apply Alignment

1 Select the paragraph(s) you want to align. Do one of the following:

 Click the **Align Left** button to left-align text.

 Click the **Center** button to center text.

 Click the **Align Right** button to right-align text.

Click the **Justify** button to justify text.

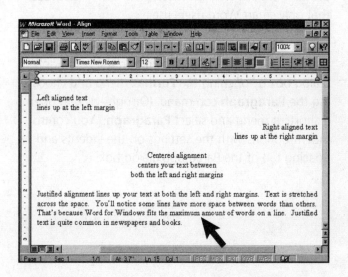

2 In this figure, you can see examples of the other alignment choices. If you change your mind, you can undo the alignment or select the paragraph again and select another alignment option. Unlike the Bold, Italic, and Underline buttons, clicking on a selected button a second time has no effect. You must select another alignment to undo the alignment.

Indent Text

Indents are margins that affect individual paragraphs or lines. For example, when you start a paragraph and press the **Tab** key to scoot the first line over slightly, you're creating an indent. When you set a bulleted text list in the middle of a page, you have created an indent. But why use indents?

If you take a critical look at the layout of documents, you'll spot some of the techniques that the print industry uses to help make text readable and appealing to the eye. For example, when the first line of a paragraph is indented, you can easily spot the beginning of each of the paragraphs; this breaks the document text up into manageable chunks and makes it easy to follow. If a certain passage is set off from the right and left margins, your attention goes to that passage. Those are just some of the many ways indents can help a document.

When it comes to indents, Word offers several paths to choose from. Granted, pressing the **Tab** key is an easy way to indent (see the "Set Tabs" task later in this section for more information about tabs); it's rather mindless, but there are other methods you can use to indent as well—real computer-savvy methods that only smart Word users use.

To indent a block of text in the midst of your page, highlight the text, and then summon the Paragraph dialog box by opening the **Format** menu and choosing the **Paragraph** command. (Or right-click to open a shortcut menu and select **Paragraph**.) You control indent options with the settings on the Indents and Spacing tab of the Paragraph dialog box.

You can choose to set up indents before you type in text or apply indents to text you've already typed in. Remember, if you don't like the indent you apply, you can always set another (or click on the **Undo** button).

Here are some of the options you can apply to your own Word documents:

- You can set *left or right indents* with precise measurements.

- Set a *First Line indent*, an indent that moves the first line of the paragraph over but leaves the remaining text lined up flush with the left margin.

- Set a *Hanging indent*, which leaves the first line flush at the left margin but shifts the remaining lines in the paragraph over to the right.

- For even faster indents, forego the Paragraph dialog box and use the indent buttons on the Formatting toolbar. Click the **Increase Indent** button to indent text by one tab stop. Click the **Decrease Indent** button to undo an indent.

- Also on the toolbar are buttons for creating indents for a bulleted list or numbered list. Use the **Bullet** or **Number** buttons on the Formatting toolbar. (You'll learn more about these types of lists later in this section.)

Note: You can also set indents using the Ruler. See "Use the Ruler" on page 120 for information on using this method.

Begin Guided Tour Indent with the Paragraph Dialog Box

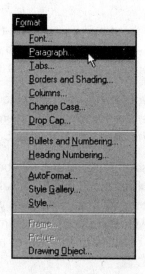

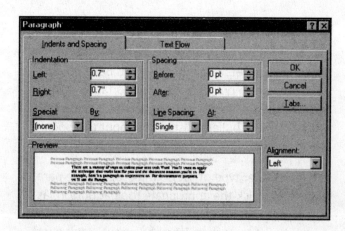

3 You see a sample of how the paragraph will look in the dialog box. Click **OK**.

1 Move the insertion point to the beginning of the paragraph you want to indent. You can also select the entire paragraph you want to indent. Or to indent several paragraphs, select those paragraphs. Open the **Format** menu and select the **Paragraph** command. This opens the Paragraph dialog box.

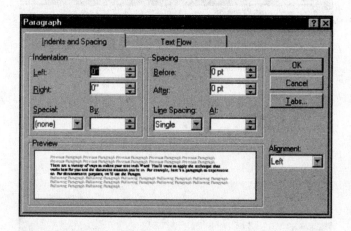

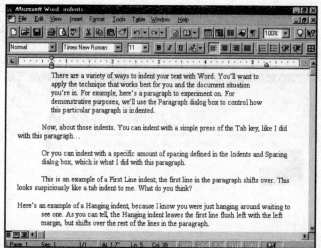

4 Word indents the paragraph per your settings. In this figure, notice the other types of indents you can create.

2 Click the **Indents and Spacing** tab to bring it to the front of the Paragraph dialog box. Then do one of the following:

To indent text from the left, enter the amount you want to indent the text in the **Left** spin box.

To indent text from the right, type the amount or use the spin arrows to enter the amount you want in the **Right** spin box.

To create a first-line or hanging indent, display the **Special** drop-down list and choose the type of indent you want. In the **By** spin box, enter the amount you want to indent.

Create Bulleted and Numbered Lists

Want to summarize the main points in your document? Want to enumerate a process? Then use a bulleted or numbered list. *Bulleted lists* call attention to points of equal importance, such as agenda items or performance goals. You've probably noticed several bulleted lists throughout this book. Use *numbered lists* for a series of steps or directions.

Creating either type of list is simple: select the paragraphs and click the appropriate toolbar button, as described in the Guided Tour. For bulleted lists, Word adds a bullet to each paragraph (except blank ones) and creates a hanging indent. Numbered lists appear similarly, but instead of a bullet, Word adds a number.

The cool thing about numbered lists is that you can delete a paragraph or add a paragraph within the list, and Word automatically renumbers for you.

If you change your mind, you can remove the bullets or numbers the same way you add them: select the text and click the appropriate toolbar button.

You can also assign bulleted and numbered lists by opening the Bullets and Numbering dialog box found on the **Format** menu. This route gives you much more control over the options. For example, you can select the type of bullet or the style of numbering to use.

Begin Guided Tour   Create a Bulleted List

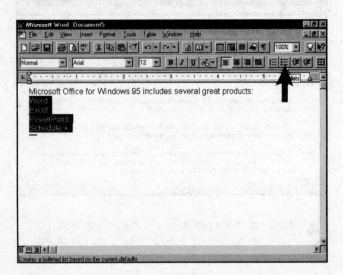

1 Select the text to which you want to add bullets and click the **Bullets** button.

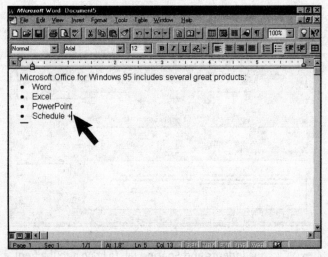

2 Word creates a bulleted list, adding bullets to each paragraph within the selection.

Begin Guided Tour   Create a Numbered List

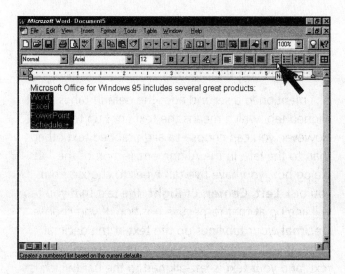

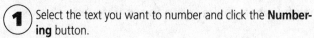

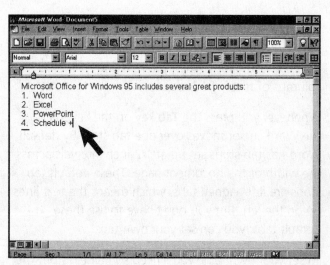

1 Select the text you want to number and click the **Numbering** button.

2 Word creates a numbered list.

Set Tabs

*T*abs provide another way of strategically putting space in your document to make it look nice. Tabs come in handy when you're trying to line up columns of text in your document.

Whenever you press the **Tab** key on the keyboard, the Word cursor moves over one tab stop. By default, Word has tab stops set up at 1/2-inch intervals across the width of the document page. These default tab stops are left-aligned tabs, which means the text lines up on the left. But you don't have to use these default tabs; you can set your own tabs.

To set your own tabs, you'll need some help from the Tabs dialog box. Open the **Format** menu and choose **Tabs**; the Tabs dialog box appears. You can also access the Tabs dialog box via the Paragraph dialog box (just click the **Tabs** button). Wait, there's more! You can also double-click on any tab symbol set on your ruler to open the Tabs dialog box, too. (You'll learn how to use the ruler next.)

If you ever get tired of the 1/2-inch default tabs, you can change them with the Default Tab Stops option in the Tabs dialog box. Click the directional arrows to select a new default setting, or type one in the **Default Tab Stops** text box.

As I mentioned a second ago, the default tab is a left-aligned tab, which means the text lines up to the left. However, you can choose to align tabbed text other than to the left. In the Alignment section of the Tabs dialog box, you have five tab types to choose from. If you pick **Left**, **Center**, or **Right**, the text that you tab will line up at that respective position. If you choose **Decimal**, your tab lines up the text at the decimal point. If you choose **Bar**, a vertical bar appears in your text, and your text is left-aligned to the bar (which is helpful when you're trying to separate tab columns).

The Leader section of the Tabs dialog box enables you to insert dots, dashes, or ruled lines to fill up the empty space between your tab stops. The default option is to have nothing between the stops **(None)**.

Begin Guided Tour   Set a Tab with the Tabs Dialog Box

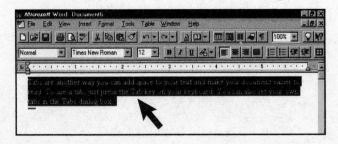

1 Select the paragraph(s) or line for which you want to set tabs.

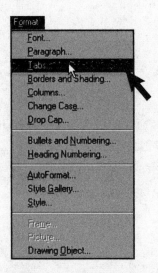

 Open the **Format** menu and select the **Tabs** command.

Guided Tour Set a Tab with the Tabs Dialog Box

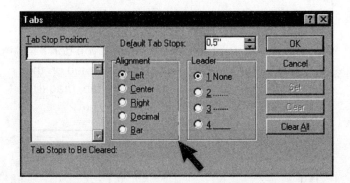

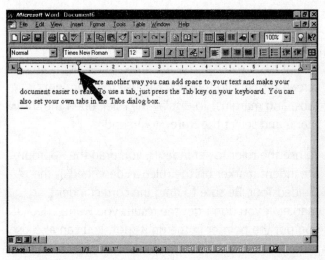

3 You see the Tabs dialog box. In the Tab Stop Position text box, type the position for the tab. Keep in mind that this position is measured in inches and from the left margin.

In the Alignment area, click on the type of alignment you want: Left, Center, Right, Decimal, or Bar.

If you want to use a dot leader for the tab, click on the leader style you want in the Leader area.

4 Click the **Set** button to set the tab position you entered.

6 Word sets up the new tabs. This figure shows a left tab set at the 1.25-inch mark.

The easiest way to create a tabular column of information is to create a *table*. Tables provide a lot of flexibility in formatting and aligning information into columns. See "Set Up a Table" on page 100 in the "How to Create a Word Document" section.

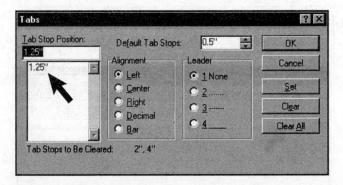

5 Word adds the tab stop to the Tab Stop Position list. Follow steps 2 through 6 for each tab stop you want to create. When finished, click **OK** to exit the box.

Use the Ruler

You may prefer a more visual method for formatting paragraphs (setting tabs and indenting text). In that case, you can use the *Ruler*. The Ruler is an on-screen formatting tool you can use to set indents, tabs, and margins. To display the ruler, open the **View** menu and select the **Ruler** command.

To use the ruler to set indents, you drag the appropriate indent marker on the ruler, as described in the Guided Tour. Be sure to drag the correct indent marker. If you don't get the results you want, check if you put the pointer in the right spot. You can also use the ruler to change the margins. Again, you have to get your pointer in the exact spot: right on the margin in the ruler.

To the far left of the ruler, you'll notice a little button that indicates the current tab type. To set a tab using the ruler, click on this button until you see the tab type that you want. Then click on the ruler on the spot where you want to place the tab. If you don't get it exact, don't worry; you can drag the tab on the ruler to the spot you want. To remove a tab, drag it off the ruler.

Button	Tab Type	What It Does
⌊	Left tab	Text starts on the marker and moves left.
⌋	Right tab	Text starts on the marker and moves right.
⊥	Center tab	Text centers on the marker.
⊥	Decimal tab	Text aligns on the decimal point.

Begin Guided Tour Use the Ruler to Set Indents

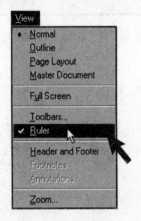

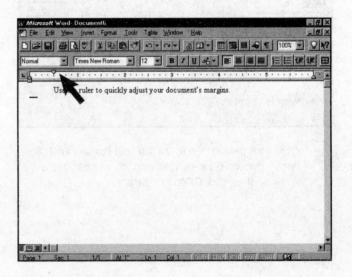

(1) If your ruler doesn't appear on-screen, open the **View** menu and select the **Ruler** command to display it.

(2) Then do one of the following steps:

Drag the indicated indent marker to set a first-line indent.

Guided Tour Use the Ruler to Set Indents

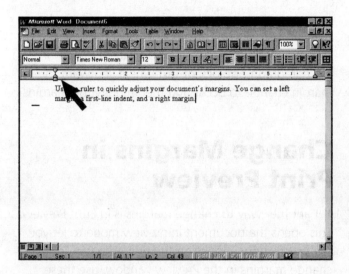

Drag the indicated indent marker to set a left indent.

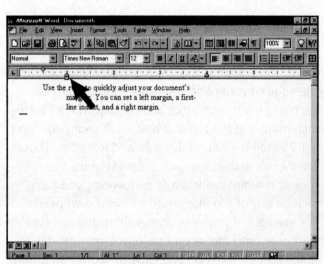

Drag the indicated indent marker to create a hanging indent.

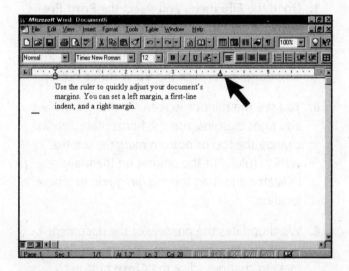

Drag the indicated indent marker to set a right indent.

Change Margins

You learned a little about setting margins with the ruler in the previous task. Time to learn some more. The margin is the space between your text and the edge of your page. There are four margins on each page: left, right, top, and bottom. There's a 1.0-inch margin at the top and bottom of your page, and a 1.25-inch margin on the right and left sides. Those are Word's default margins. For most of us, the default margins work just fine. However, you can change any of the margins to suit your own needs. For example, if you've written a letter that just barely runs over onto the second page, you may be able to make it fit perfectly on one page by slightly adjusting the margins.

You can control the left and right margins using your ruler. To change these margins, simply drag the appropriate margin symbol to a new position on the ruler. (The ruler's margin markers only apply to the paragraph where the insertion marker is parked.)

Alternatively, you can use the Page Setup dialog box to set margins. To access this box, open the **File** menu and choose **Page Setup**. You will find the page margin settings in the Margins tab. You can change any of the four page margin settings and set precise measurements for the settings and even preview how your margins will look in the Preview box.

When you change the margins, you control how much of the document they affect. You can apply the new settings to your entire document, from the location of the insertion point on, or to a block of selected text. It's up to you. Just select the text and modify the margins, or place your cursor directly in the paragraph or block of text where you want the margin change to occur and then modify the margins.

Change Margins in Print Preview

Yet another way to change margins is in Print Preview. This opens the document in preview mode to let you see exactly how it looks on the printed page. To change margins in the Preview window, use these steps:

1. Open the **File** menu and select the **Print Preview** command.

2. You see a preview of the document. If the Ruler is not displayed, click the **View Ruler** button.

3. You see the ruler on-screen. To change the left and right margins, use the horizontal ruler. To change the top or bottom margins, use the vertical ruler. Put the pointer on the margin indicator and drag the margin guide to a new location.

4. Word updates the preview of the document to reflect the new margins. When you finish making changes, click the **Close** button to return to Normal view.

Begin Guided Tour Change the Margins with Page Setup

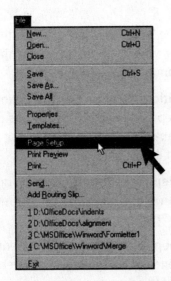

1 Open the **File** menu and select the **Page Setup** command.

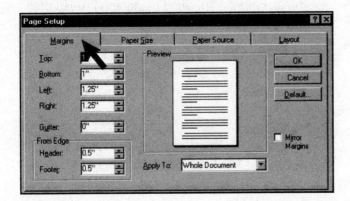

2 The Page Setup dialog box appears. Click the **Margins** tab to bring it to the front of the box. Click in the margin text box you want to change. You can also press **Tab** to move to the margin.

3 Enter the new margin in inches. You can delete or edit the current entry or use the spin arrows to select the value you want. Follow steps 2 and 3 for each margin you want to change. Notice that you can change the top, bottom, left, right, and gutter (space between two side-by-side pages) as well as the margins for headers and footers (see "Set Up Headers and Footers" on page 129).

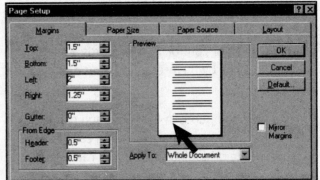

4 The preview in the dialog box shows the effect of the new margins. When you finish making changes, click **OK**. Word makes the change. You won't see the effect of margins in Normal view. You can switch to Page Layout view or preview the document to see the change.

Change Line and Paragraph Spacing

The Paragraph dialog box also contains commands for controlling the space between lines of text and *pagination* (page layout). Paragraph spacing controls the amount of white space above and below a paragraph. Some people will just settle for pressing **Enter** to create white space between paragraphs. However, you can use a better method to adjust spacing. You can use paragraph spacing controls to add a set amount of space after each of your document headings, or control if single words are left floating on a line by themselves at the end of your paragraphs.

The line spacing options in the Paragraph dialog box controls the amount of space between each line, for instance, single or double spaced. You can select single, double, 1 1/2, or a custom value that you enter. To select a custom value, choose **Custom** and then enter the value you want.

The pagination options in the Text Flow tab control how paragraphs and pages flow.

Here's a rundown of what you can do with the spacing commands:

- Use the **Before** and **After** settings (measured in points) to control the amount of space before and after text lines.

- Pull down the **Line Spacing** drop-down list to find such standard line spacing designations as single-space, double-space, and the like.

- Click the **Text Flow** tab to access the text flow options, which you use to control the flow of text from one page to another.

- The **Widow/Orphan Control** option can help you keep single words or small bits of text from being abandoned on the last line of one page or the first line of another.

- The **Keep Lines Together** option prevents the occurrence of a page break in the middle of a selected paragraph.

- The **Keep with Next** option prevents the occurrence of a page break between two designated paragraphs.

- The **Page Break Before** option places a page break before a specified paragraph instead of in the middle of it or after it.

If used effectively, all of the pagination and spacing options can help you create better looking documents that are easier to read, or at least very nicely spaced.

> Press **Ctrl+1** for single spacing, **Ctrl+5** for 1.5 spacing, or **Ctrl+2** for double spacing.

Begin Guided Tour Change Line Spacing and Pagination

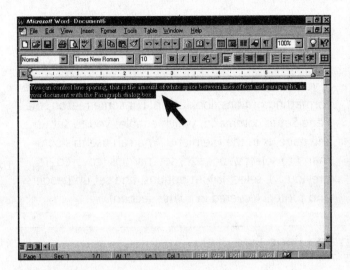

1 Select the paragraph(s) that you want to change.

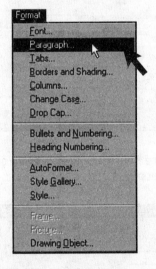

2 Open the **Format** menu and select the **Paragraph** command.

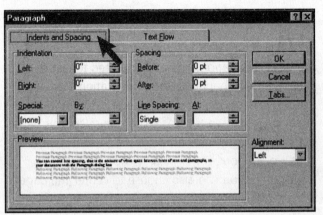

3 Click the **Indents and Spacing** tab to bring the spacing controls to the front of the box. To set spacing between lines, click on the down arrow at the end of the Line Spacing drop-down list box, and choose the line spacing interval you want to use. To add space above and below the paragraph, enter values in the Before or After spin boxes.

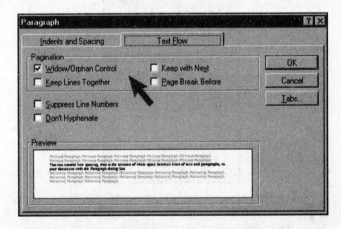

4 Click the **Text Flow** tab to bring the pagination options to the front of the box. Under the Pagination area, select any controls you want to apply to the ends of your paragraphs or pages. You can preview how the pagination options look in the Preview area.

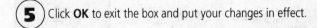

5 Click **OK** to exit the box and put your changes in effect.

Change Paper Size and Orientation

Most documents typically print on the standard size paper (8 1/2-by-11-inch) in *portrait* (vertical) *orientation*. You aren't limited to just this most common paper size and orientation. For example, your printer may be capable of printing on legal size paper; in this case, you can select this paper size. Or you may have a document such as a brochure that would work better in *landscape* (horizontal) *orientation*. You can also choose to center the page to create a special effect for title pages, invitations, or other types of documents.

If you are looking in the Format menu for these page formatting options, look again. For some reason, the Page Setup command, which enables you to set up the page, is in the File menu. You can use this command to select paper size, set margins (covered previously), select layout options, and set up headers and footers (covered in a later section).

Begin Guided Tour Change Orientation and Page Size

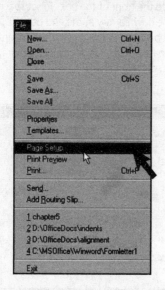

① Open the **File** menu and select the **Page Setup** command. This opens the Page Setup dialog box.

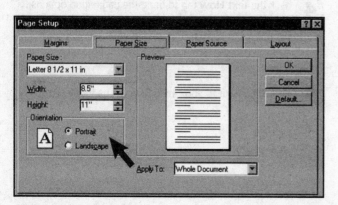

② Click on the **Paper Size** tab. Under Orientation, click on **Portrait** or **Landscape**.

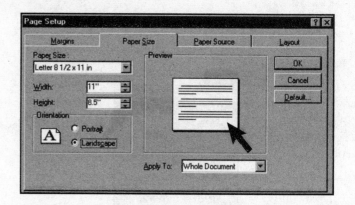

③ Look in the Preview area to see how the orientation will affect your page.

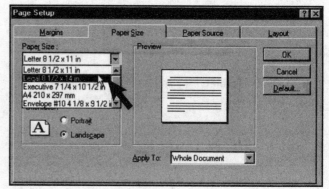

④ To change paper size, display the Paper Size drop-down list. This reveals a list of available paper sizes. If you see the paper type you want, click on it. (You can also enter values in the Width and Height text boxes if your paper size isn't listed.)

⑤ You see a preview of the new paper size in the dialog box. Click **OK** to exit the box and put your changes in effect.

Number Pages

Imagine trying to find page 12 in a 20-page document you printed out if the pages weren't numbered. Imagine trying to put together a 50-page booklet without numbering the pages. Page numbers are a critical element to documents that are longer than one page. Page numbers help the reader and you keep the pages in order.

The great thing about using Word to add page numbers is that you don't have to type them on each page. You can add them once to a header (top of page) or footer (bottom of page) and Word will put them on all pages. You also don't have to worry about making sure the page numbers are correct. If you add or delete a page, Word renumbers all the page numbers.

You can add page numbers while you are creating a header or footer (covered in the next section), or you can add them using the **Page Numbers** command. When you use the command, Word sets up a header or footer automatically.

In addition to selecting to put the page number at the top or bottom of the document, you can select where in the header or footer to place the page number:

Left   Numbers align with the left margin.

Center   Numbers center on the page.

Right   Numbers print flush with the right margin.

Inside   Numbers print on the inside of facing pages (right-aligned on left pages and left-aligned on right pages).

Outside   Numbers print on the outside of facing pages (left-aligned on left pages and right-aligned on right pages).

Format the Page Number

The *page number feature* is a special code which updates automatically. That doesn't mean you can't delete or format the code. You can make the page number bold, italic, change the alignment, and so on by using any of the formatting features. You can also drag across the page number and press **Delete** to delete the page number on the selected page and all other pages.

If you don't like the numbering style used for the page numbers, you can select a different format. To do so, click the **Format** button in the Page Numbers dialog box. Select the format you want. You can also enter a different starting number in this dialog box. For example, you may have broken a long document up into sections. You can start numbering the second half of the document with the appropriate number. Make your changes and click **OK**.

Begin Guided Tour   Add Page Numbers

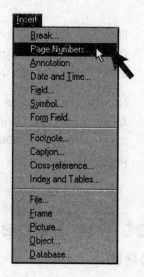

1 Open the **Insert** menu and select the **Page Numbers** command.

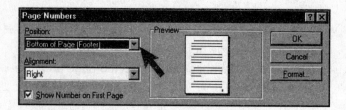

2 You see the Page Numbers dialog box. Click on the down-arrow next to the Position drop-down list box; select **Top of Page (Header)** or **Bottom of Page (Footer)**.

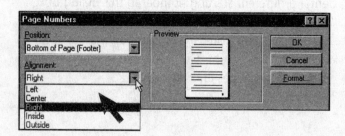

3 Click on the down-arrow next to Alignment. You see a list of different alignment choices; click on the one you want.

4 If you want to skip printing a page number on the first page, uncheck the **Show Number on First Page** check box. (This starts page two with a number 2.)

5 You see a preview of your choices in the dialog box. Click **OK**. Word creates a header or footer and inserts the page number. In Normal view, you won't see the page numbers. You do see the page numbers in Print Preview or in Page Layout view.

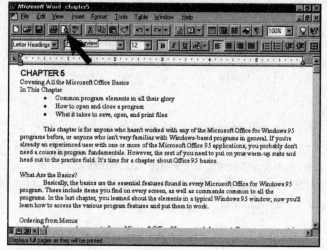

6 Click the **Print Preview** button.

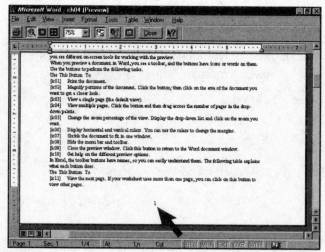

7 You see a preview of the document with the page number in the location you selected. In this figure, Word centered the page number in the footer.

Set Up Headers and Footers

In addition to the page number, you may want to include other identifying information on all pages in your document. For example, if you are submitting the next great thriller to a publisher, you may want to include your last name at the top of each page of the document. If you are creating an annual report, you may want to print the date or the report name at the bottom of each page.

Text that you include at the top of each page is a *header*. Text included on the bottom of each page is a *footer*. With Word, you can easily set up and format headers and footers in your document.

The makers of Word tried to anticipate what you want to do when you use certain features. For example, in a header or footer, it's common to include the page number or the date. Therefore, Word provides some buttons on the Header and Footer toolbar to enable you to insert special information in the header or footer. To use a button, click on it. The following table includes the name and a short description of the buttons you can use.

When you create a header or footer, Word applies the header or footer style to that paragraph. Basically, this style has three tabs: a left tab, a center tab, and a right-aligned tab. That doesn't mean you are stuck with this preset formatting; you can modify any of the paragraph formatting.

You can also format the text, just as you format regular text. For example, to make the header bold, drag across it, and click the **Bold** button. The same thing works for deleting a header or footer. Drag across the text and press **Delete**.

Button	Name	Description
	Switch Between Header and Footer	Lets you switch between the header and footer.
	Show Previous	Shows previous section of document.
	Show Next	Shows next section of document.
	Same As Previous	Creates different header or footer sections in your file.
	Page Numbers	Adds page numbers.
	Date	Adds the date to your header or footer text.
	Time	Adds the current time to your header or footer text.
	Page Setup	Opens the Page Setup dialog box where you can control which pages the header or footer falls on.
	Show/Hide Document Text	Toggles between showing the text on the document page with the header/footer or just the header/footer by itself.
Close	Close	Closes the Header and Footer toolbar.

Begin Guided Tour   Create a Header

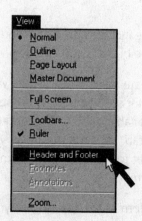

1 Open the **View** menu and select the **Header and Footer** command.

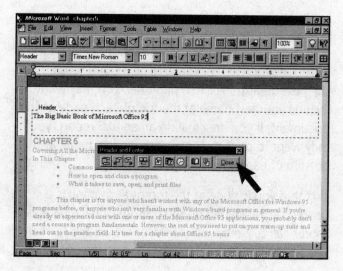

3 When the header is complete, click the **Close** button. Word adds the header to the document. In Page Layout view, you do see the header. In Normal view, you do not.

Word prints the headers and footers 1/2-inch from the top and bottom of the page. To change the margins for the header or footer, see "Change Margins" on page 122.

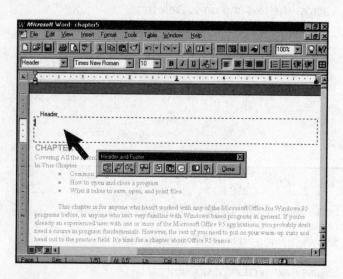

2 You see the Header and Footer toolbar on-screen and a dotted header area at the top of the page. Type the text for the header. Use any of the toolbar buttons to insert special fields such as the page number. Make any formatting changes you want.

Begin Guided Tour   Create a Footer

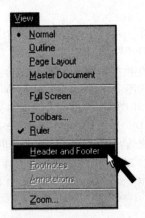

1 Open the **View** menu and select the **Header and Footer** command.

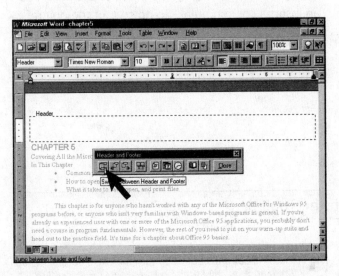

2 You see the Header and Footer toolbar on-screen and a dotted header area at the top of the page. Click the **Switch Between Header and Footer** button.

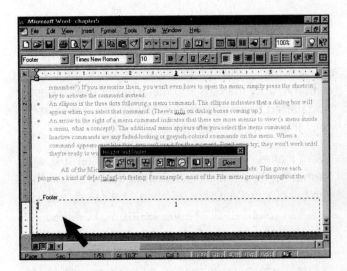

3 Word displays the footer area, with the insertion point inside. Type the text for the footer and make any formatting changes.

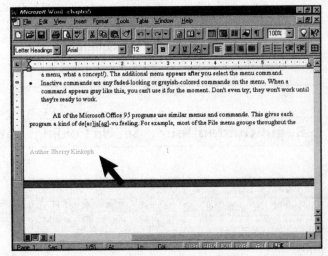

4 When the footer is complete, click the **Close** button. Word adds the footer to the document. In Page Layout view, you do see the footer. In Normal view, you do not.

Set Up Columns

If you are an old-timer, you may remember the manual method of creating a newsletter. For my grade school paper, for example, we typed the text within narrow margins and then cut out the articles and pasted them into the semblance of a "newsletter." If only we had Word then... .

Word makes it easy to set up columns, enter text, and format the columns. The easiest method is to use the toolbar button. With this method, you can select up to seven columns, all of equal width. You can also set up columns using the **Columns** command. With this method, you can select different widths for the columns, create more than seven columns, and select options such as adding a line between the columns. The Guided Tour covers both methods.

> You can also create the columns using the toolbar button and then modify the formatting or column width using the **Columns** command.

You can set up your columns and then type the text for the document. Or do the reverse: type the text and then change the formatting for columns. When you type in Normal view, your text will wrap within the margins for that column, but you won't see the columns side by side. This is the fastest method for typing because Word won't continually have to adjust the line breaks and redraw the screen. If you want to see the columns side by side, you can switch to Page Layout view.

If you turn on columns and then type, Word will fill up one column and move to the next. If you want to manually end one column and move to the next, you can insert a column break. To do so, put the pointer where you want the break. Then open the **Insert** menu, choose the **Break** command, select the **Column** break option, and click **OK**.

Begin Guided Tour Set Up Columns with the Toolbar

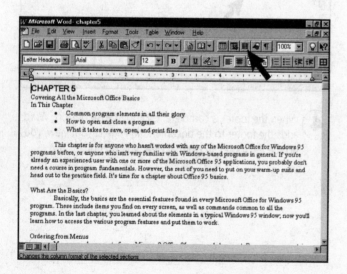

1 Click the **Columns** button to turn the entire document into columns. If you prefer to just turn existing portions into columns, first position the insertion point where the columns should begin; then highlight the text included.

2 You see a drop-down palette of columns. Click on the number of columns you want.

Guided Tour Set Up Columns with the Toolbar

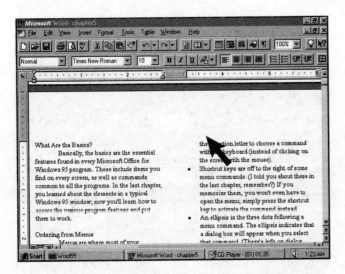

3 If you have already typed the document and are in Page Layout view, Word reformats the text into columns, as shown here.

If you haven't typed the text, just type as you do in a one-column document. As you type, notice that the text does not wrap across the entire screen, but wraps in columns. Type all the text you want to include, inserting any column breaks you need.

Begin Guided Tour Use the Columns Command

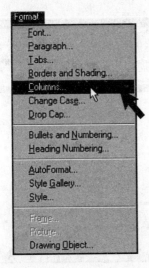

1 Open the **Format** menu and select the **Columns** command.

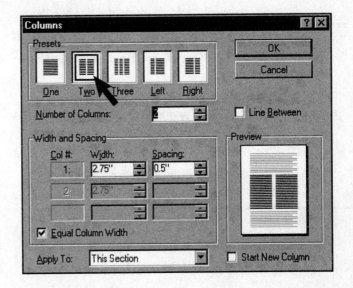

2 You see the Columns dialog box. To use one of the preset column formats, click on the one you want in the Preset area: **One**, **Two**, **Three**, **Left**, **Right**.

(continues)

Guided Tour Use the Columns Command

(continued)

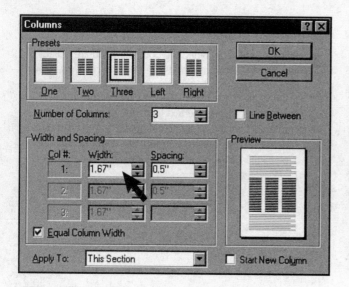

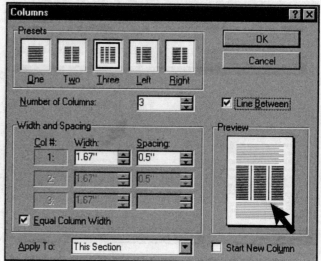

3 To set the number of columns manually, enter the number of columns you want in the Number of Columns spin box.

Word displays a preview of the document in the dialog box. Word also updates the Width and Spacing area to reflect the number of columns you have selected. To change the width of all columns, enter a new width in the Width spin box. Word uses this width for all columns.

To create columns of unequal widths, uncheck the Equal Column Width check box. Click in the **Width** spin box for the column you want to change and enter a new width. Do this for each column width you want to change.

4 To change the spacing between columns, click in the **Spacing** text box for the column spacing you want to change. Then enter a new width. Do this for each column you want to change.

5 If you want to include a line between the columns, check the **Line Between** check box.

6 You see a preview of how the columns will look. When you finish making changes, click **OK**.

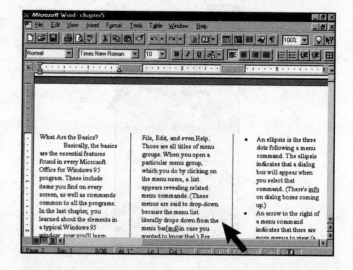

7 Word reformats the document into the number of columns you have selected with the column width and spacing as you entered it.

Use Templates and Wizards

If you don't want to spend your time setting up a document and messing with formatting, you may want to investigate some of Word's "auto" documents, that is, the *templates* and *wizards* provided with Word.

Both templates and wizards are preformatted, designed layouts for common document types, such as reports, press releases, memos, faxes (although wizards are processes for building documents and not exactly documents in and of themselves). You select the one you want, and Word sets up the formatting. Most templates and wizards also include some text. For example, in the memo templates and wizards, the headings (MEMO, TO, FROM, and so on) are already entered.

The difference between a template and a wizard is the level of automation. If you select a wizard, Word leads you through the process of creating the document step by step. You make the selections you want

and when you finish, you have a completed document. If you select a template, you basically just open a new document that includes appropriate formatting and text.

Create Your Own Template

If none of the predefined templates are what you want, you can create your own template. The template can be any type of document you choose and can include any text and formatting you want.

Remember that all new documents based on this template will include all the formatting and text you include. Therefore, include in the template only the elements you want in all documents based on this template.

Begin Guided Tour   Use a Template or Wizard

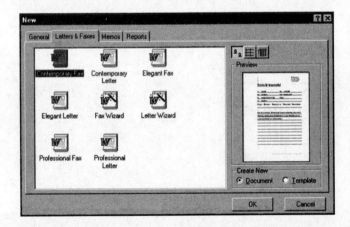

1 Open the **File** menu and select the **New** command. Word displays the New dialog box. Click on the template or wizard you want to use and click **OK**.

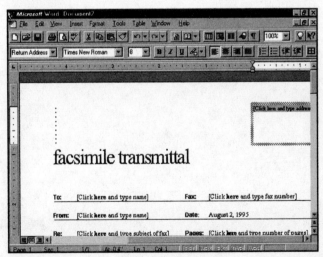

2 Word displays the document or wizard on-screen, here's a fax form template. In many of the documents, Word inserts filler text—for example, Your Company Name.

3 Replace or add text, as needed, to complete your document.

HOW TO...

Build an Excel Worksheet

The second most popular program included in Microsoft Office is Excel. To start Excel, click the **Start** button on the Windows 95 taskbar; select **Programs** and **Microsoft Excel**. With Excel, you can create worksheets, for example, to total sales for your company or to track your personal expenses. You can use Excel to set up a budget or to create an invoice. You can also use Excel as a simple database program (as covered in "Create an Excel Database" on page 217) and to create charts (see "Create an Excel Chart" on page 197).

To set up a worksheet, you enter text, numbers, dates, and formulas into the grid of columns and rows in the worksheet. Excel provides many shortcuts for setting up the worksheet, as covered in this part of the book.

What You Will Find in This Section

Move Around the Worksheet

When you start Excel, you see a blank worksheet on-screen. In Excel, each individual spreadsheet is called a *worksheet*. The worksheet is a grid of rows (16,000 of them!) and columns (256). Within each worksheet page in Excel, you can enter data, perform calculations, organize information, and more. Worksheets look like grids, with intersecting columns and rows that form little boxes, called *cells*.

You can move around an Excel worksheet using the mouse or the keyboard. As you move your mouse pointer around on-screen, you'll notice it changes shape. Sometimes, it's the arrow pointer you've come to know and love, and other times, it's a strange-looking, giant plus symbol. When the mouse pointer is inside the worksheet area of your screen, it takes the shape of a plus sign, but it's still the same old mouse pointer you use to select and point at things. Anytime you move the mouse pointer outside the worksheet area, it becomes the old pointer arrow shape again.

To move from cell to cell, simply click on the cell to which you want to move. The cell you click on becomes highlighted, or *selected*. A dark line, called a *selector*, always surrounds a selected cell. When you select a cell, it is active and ready to accept any numbers or text you type.

You can also select more than one cell at a time. To do this, click on the first cell you want to select, hold down the left mouse button, and drag over the other cells you want to select. This highlights the cells you drag over. Let go of the mouse button and they're selected.

Sometimes, you can get lost in the vast forest of worksheet cells, so one of the first things you need to learn is how to read cell names, called *references* or *addresses*. Excel worksheets are laid out like grids, and each cell in the grid has a name or reference based on which row and column it's in.

Excel labels columns with alphabet letters, and rows with numbers. Cell names always reference the column letter first, and then the row number. For example, the cell in the top left corner in a worksheet is A1. If you become confused about which cell you're in, look at the reference area below the menu bar, called the Name or Reference box. This is kind of like a "you-are-here" marker; it will always show you which cell you're in. (You can also use the scroll bars to see other parts of the worksheet.) Here's a helpful chart of key combinations you can use.

Press	To Move
→	Right one cell
←	Left one cell
↓	Down one cell
↑	Up one cell
Ctrl+→	To right edge of current region
Ctrl+←	To left edge of current region
Ctrl+↓	To bottom edge of current region

Press	To Move
Ctrl+↑	To top edge of current region
Home	First cell in the row
Ctrl+Home	First cell in the worksheet
Ctrl+End	Lower right cell in the worksheet
PgDn	Down one screen
PgUp	Up one screen
Alt+PgDn	Right one screen
Alt+PgUp	Left one screen
Ctrl+PgDn	Next sheet
Ctrl+PgUp	Previous sheet
F5	Display the Go To dialog box

You can move to a specific cell in the worksheet by selecting the **Go To** command from the **Edit** menu. In the **Reference** text box, type the name of the cell to which you want to move, and click **OK** or press **Enter**. If you've designed a particularly complex worksheet utilizing zillions of rows and columns, you'll find the Go To dialog box helpful in zipping around a vast worksheet.

Begin Guided Tour   Select a Cell

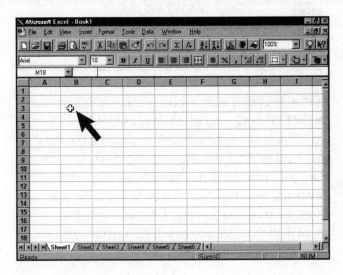

1 Point to the cell you want to select. The pointer should look like a fat plus sign.

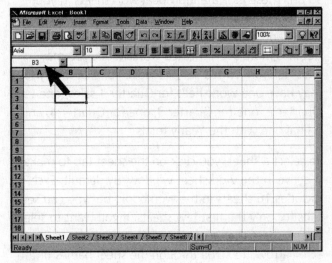

3 The cell's address appears in the reference area of the Formula Bar.

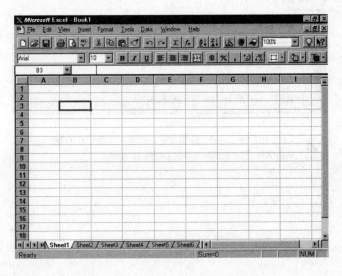

2 Click the mouse button, and Excel selects that cell. You see a thick black border around the cell.

When you first open Excel, you may see an extra toolbar on your screen, called the **WorkGroup toolbar**. This toolbar includes buttons for performing tasks in a network environment, including sending and receiving e-mail. Unless you use a networked computer, you probably don't need the toolbar on your screen. To remove it, open the **View** menu, select **Toolbars**, then unselect the WorkGroup check box.

Work with Worksheets

The grid of columns and rows that you see on-screen is a *worksheet*. In addition to the first sheet you see, you have more sheets available. Basically, you have a pad of workbook paper. Excel stores all the worksheets together in one file, called a *workbook*. An Excel workbook can hold as many as 256 worksheets.

If you look at the bottom of the worksheet screen, you'll notice little tabs named **Sheet1**, **Sheet2**, and so on. These indicate individual worksheets in your workbook. In many cases, you'll use only the first sheet, and the others will remain blank. When you get into more sophisticated worksheets, you may want to work with a set of sheets. For example, you may have one worksheet for Quarter 1 sales, one for Quarter 2, one for Quarter 3, one for Quarter 4, and a final one with the Yearly totals.

To select a sheet, you click on the sheet tab to make it active in the worksheet window. By default, Excel includes 16 sheets in the workbook, but you can see tabs for only the first few sheets. If you want to select a worksheet that is not on-screen, you can use the scroll arrows to scroll through the sheet names until

the one you want appears. Then click on the sheet you want.

Click This Button	To
◄◄	Scroll to the first sheet in the workbook.
◄	Scroll to the previous sheet.
►	Scroll to the next sheet.
►►	Scroll to the last sheet in the workbook.

As I've described, each worksheet has a default name, **Sheet1**, **Sheet2**, and so on. You can rename your worksheets at any time to better describe the data they contain. You can also add and delete worksheets from your workbook file. Remember that Excel will delete not only the sheet but all the data on that sheet. Be sure that you don't delete sheets that contain information you need. Also remember that you can't undo a worksheet deletion.

Begin Guided Tour Move to a Different Sheet

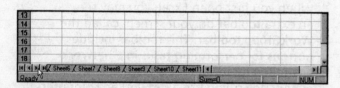

1 Scroll until you see the sheet tab you want to move to.

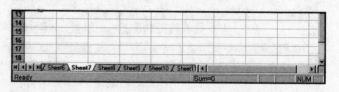

2 Click on the sheet tab at the bottom of the workbook window. The active tab appears in white.

Begin Guided Tour   Rename a Sheet

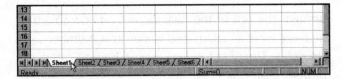

1 Double-click on the sheet tab of the sheet you want to rename.

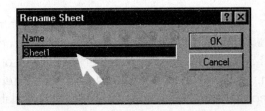

2 You see the Rename Sheet dialog box. Type a name for the sheet. You can include spaces in the name and type up to 31 characters, including spaces. Click **OK** to exit the box and name the sheet.

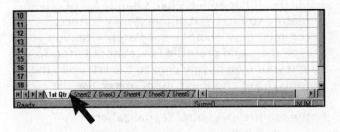

3 Excel displays the new name on the worksheet tab.

Begin Guided Tour   Delete a Sheet

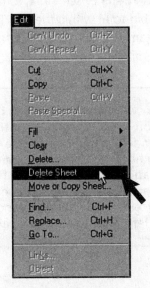

1 Select the sheet you want to delete. Open the **Edit** menu and select the **Delete Sheet** command.

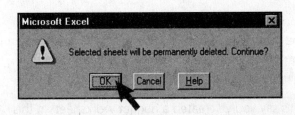

2 You are prompted to confirm the deletion. Click **OK**. Excel deletes the worksheet and all its data. Excel does not automatically renumber existing sheet names.

Another way to delete a sheet is to right-click on the sheet and choose the **Delete** command from the shortcut menu.

Enter Text and Numbers

A worksheet contains three basic types of entries: *labels*, *values*, and *formulas*. You can type up to 255 characters in a cell, whether they're text or numbers. Excel refers to text data as a *label*; Excel cannot perform calculations on entries that are labels. For example, if you type the word **February** into a cell, you won't be able to perform a mathematical function or calculation with it—it's just a word.

> Microsoft has added Word's handy AutoCorrect feature to Excel 7. It automatically corrects common misspellings immediately after you type them and press the **Spacebar** or **Enter**. To add your own misspellings to the list, open the **Tools** menu and select **AutoCorrect**; use the AutoCorrect dialog box to add words, turn off the feature, or control capitalization.

Excel refers to numerical data as a *value*. Excel *can* calculate value entries. Values include numbers, dates, and times. For example, if you type the number **1024**, you can do something with that, such as multiply or add.

The third type of data is a *formula*, which is simply an entry that tells Excel to perform calculations on the values in a cell or group of cells.

Let's say you've created a budget worksheet. In this type of worksheet, you may include a worksheet title, column labels for each month, and row labels for each expense category. All of these entries would be text. Within the columns for each month, you may enter the expenses for that category. These entries would be numbers. For each month, you may want to calculate the total expenses. This entry would be a

formula. The rest of this task focuses on how to enter the basic types of labels and values: text, numbers, and dates. The next task will explain how to create a formula.

Excel displays different data types in different positions in your worksheet cells. A text entry always lines up to the left side of the cell it's in. However, you can change the alignment (see the "Change the Alignment of Entries" task in the next section). If the text entry is too long, it will spill over to the cells next to it, unless those cells contain data. If those cells contain data, the displayed entry will be truncated; the actual entry is still intact, you just can't see it. You need to widen the column (also covered in the next part).

Numbers always line up to the right of the cell. By default, numbers appear in the *General number format* (no specific number format). You can change how the numbers appear (change the alignment, use a number format such as currency, make entries bold, and more). Learn about formatting in the next section. If you enter a number and see something strange such as **1E+09** or see **####**, it means the number is too big to fit within the cell. To fix this problem, you can change the number format or widen the column.

> What if you want your numbers to be treated like text? You know, say you want to use numbers for a ZIP code instead of a value. To do this, you have to precede your entry with a single quotation mark (') as in '90210. The single quotation mark is an alignment prefix that tells Excel to treat the following characters as text and left-align them in the cell.

Enter a Date or Time

Another type of value you can include in a worksheet are dates and times. For example, you can use dates to keep track of when you incur an expense, when you complete a project, when you received a bill, and so on.

Excel keeps track of dates by assigning each date a *serial number*, starting with the first day in the century. No matter how the date appears in the cell, Excel thinks of the date as this serial number. With this tracking method, you can use a date in a calculation. For example, you can figure out how many days a bill is past due.

Excel keeps track of times by storing them as a fractional part of 24 hours. Again, this tracking method enables you to create calculations with times.

To enter the date, use one of the following formats:

4/4/95

4-Apr-95

4-Apr (assumes current year)

Apr-4 (assumes current year)

To enter a time, type the time using one of these formats:

9:45 PM

9:45:55 PM

21:45

21:45:55

Use these steps to enter a date or time:

1. Select the cell you want.

2. To enter a date, type the date using one of the formats described in the text.

3. Press **Enter**.

4. Excel enters the date or time.

To enter the current date in a cell, press **Ctrl+;**.
To enter the current time, press **Ctrl+Shift+:**.

Use the Formula Bar

When you start typing data into a selected cell, the data immediately appears in that cell and also in the Formula Bar above the worksheet window. (You see the Formula Bar to the right of the Reference or Name box.) Three new buttons appear in the Formula Bar as you enter data:

- The left button is the **Cancel** button. It's easy to identify because it has a red **X** in it. Click on it to cancel your entry.

- The middle button (with the green check mark) is the **Enter** button. Click on it to confirm that you want to enter your data into the cell.

- The third button with the funny **fx** symbol in it is the **Function Wizard** button. (Learn about this in the "Use Functions" task later in this section on page 152.)

When you finish typing in data, press **Enter** or click on the **Enter** button (the button with a check mark) on the Formula Bar. You can also click in the next cell in which you want to enter data.

Begin Guided Tour   Enter Text

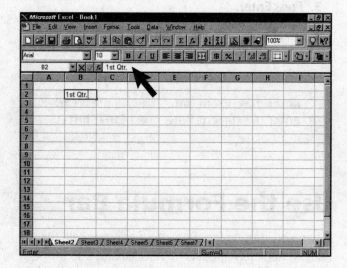

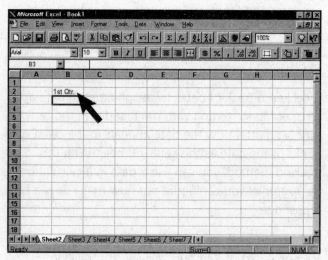

1 Select the cell you want and type the text. As you type, Excel displays an **X** and a check mark next to the entry in the Formula Bar. Click the check mark or press **Enter** to accept the entry. Click the **X** or press **Esc** to cancel the entry.

2 Excel enters the text and moves to the next cell. You can also press any arrow key to make the entry and move the cell pointer to the next cell in that direction.

Begin Guided Tour   Enter Numbers

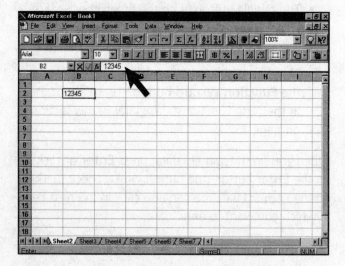

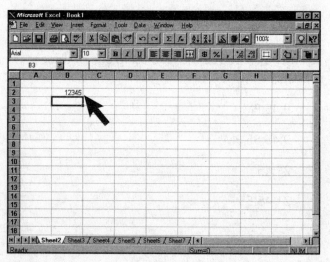

1 Select the cell you want and type the number. (To type a negative number, precede the number with a minus sign or enclose the number in parentheses.) As you type the entry, Excel displays an **X** and a check mark next to the entry in the Formula Bar. Click the check mark or press **Enter** to accept the entry. Click the **X** or press **Esc** to cancel the entry.

2 Excel enters the number and moves to the next cell.

Work with Ranges

A *range* is a rectangular group of connected cells that you can connect in a column, a row, or a combination of columns and rows or even an entire worksheet. You can connect them in a number of ways, but they always have to be *contiguous* (next to each other in a sequence) and they must form a rectangle.

Why use ranges? Well, you can select a range and use it to format a group of cells with one simple step. You can use a range to print only a selected group of cells. Ranges are also handy when you use them with formulas (which I'll explain later in the "Enter Formulas" task on page 148).

You can use the mouse (easiest way) to select a range (explained in the Guided Tour), or if you are a fast typist, you might prefer to use the keyboard. To use the keyboard to select a range, move to the first cell. Then hold down the **Shift** key and use any of the arrow or movement keys to highlight the range. To deselect a range, click outside the selected range or press any arrow key.

Excel indicates a range with a *range reference* (name), which refers to its specific anchor points: the top left corner and the lower right corner. A range with more than one cell uses a colon to separate the anchor points. For example, range A1:B3 would include cells A1, A2, A3, B1, B2, and B3.

You can give a range name to a single cell or a large group of cells. Once you define the name, you can use it in formulas. Range names appear in the Reference box at the top of your worksheet. When you have more than one range name in a worksheet, you can click on the Reference box drop-down list to see a list of ranges and make your selection from the list.

You can also use the **Go To** command to quickly move to and select a named range. To make it easier to create and understand formulas, you can create a range name. For example, the formula INCOME-EXPENSE is easier to understand than B8:B24–C8:C24.

When working with ranges, there are some shortcuts you can use to select them. The following table describes the mouse and keyboard shortcuts for selecting ranges.

To Select	*Mouse Shortcut*	*Keyboard Shortcut*
A column	Click on the column letter.	Press **Ctrl+Spacebar**.
A row	Click on the row number.	Press **Shift+Spacebar**.
The entire worksheet	Click on the **Select All** button (the blank spot above the row numbers and to the left of the column letters).	Press **Ctrl+Shift+Spacebar**.

Begin Guided Tour   Select a Range with the Mouse

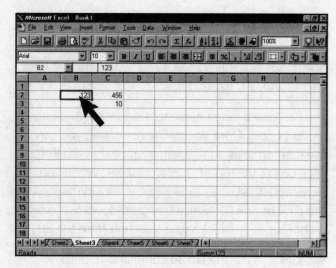

1 Click on the first cell in the range.

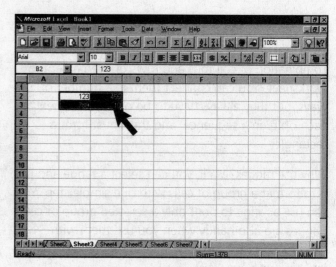

3 The range appears highlighted on-screen. When you have selected the range you want, release the mouse button.

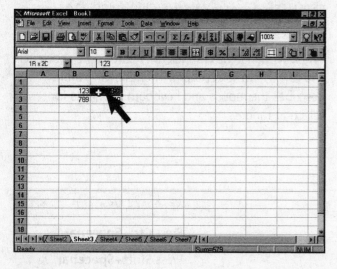

2 Hold down the mouse button and drag across the cells you want to include.

Begin Guided Tour Naming a Range

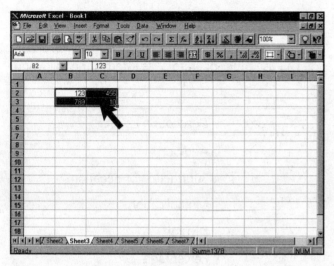

1 Select the cell or range you want to name.

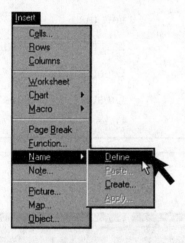

2 Open the **Insert** menu and select the **Name Define** command.

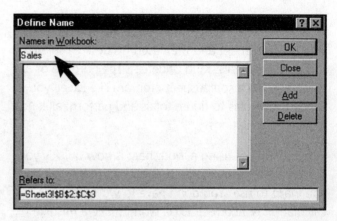

3 You see the Define Name dialog box. Type the range name you want to use. You can type up to 255 characters. Be sure not to type a name that looks like a number or cell reference. Also, you must start the name with a letter, underscore (_), or backslash (\).

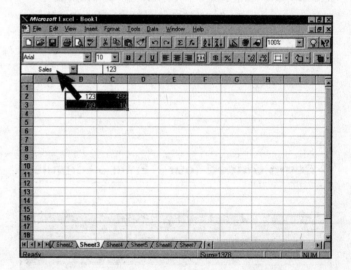

4 Click **OK**. You have named the range, and the name appears in the Reference box at the top of your worksheet.

Enter Formulas

I once knew someone that entered all the numbers in his worksheet and then used his desk calculator to figure the totals. Kind of defeats the purpose of a worksheet. In a spreadsheet program like Excel, you can use formulas to figure totals and perform all kinds of other calculations.

The real thrill of using a worksheet is how quickly you can create a formula. You simply point to the values you want to use. You don't have to worry that the calculation is incorrect; Excel won't make a mistake. Also, you can change any of the values included in the formula, and Excel will update the formula automatically. Pretty cool.

A formula consists of these key elements: the equal sign (=), the values or cell references you want to calculate, and the operators (mathematical operations such as addition and multiplication). Take a look at this simple formula:

=A1+A2

This formula takes the value in cell A1 and adds it to A2. You can include more than two references, and you can use other operators, as listed in the following table.

Operator	Description
+	Addition
-	Subtraction or negation
*	Multiplication
/	Division
%	Percentage
^	Exponentiation
=	Equal
<	Less than
<=	Less than or equal to
>	Greater than
>=	Greater than or equal to
<>	Not

Begin Guided Tour Enter a Formula

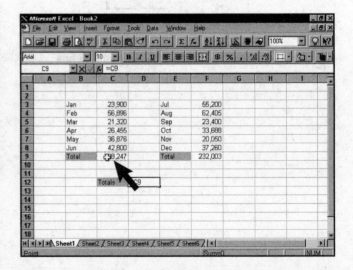

1 Select the cell that will contain the formula. Type an equal (=) sign. That tells Excel you are about to enter a formula.

2 Point to the first cell you want to include in the formula. (You can also directly type in the cell reference.) The cell reference appears in the active cell and in the Formula Bar.

Guided Tour Enter a Formula

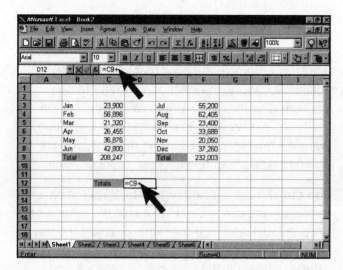

3 Type an operator such as the + sign.

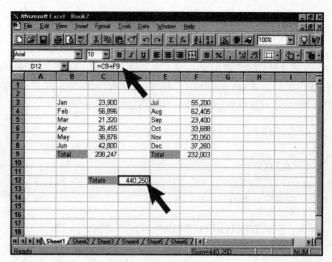

5 When you complete the formula, press **Enter**. In the Formula Bar, you see the actual formula. The cell displays the results of the formula.

In some formulas, you may want to perform two calculations. To make sure you get the results you want, use parentheses to surround the part of the formula you want to calculate first. Compare these two formulas: (10*3)+5=35 and 10*(3+5)=80.

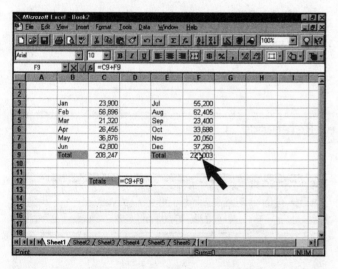

4 Point to the next cell you want. Continue typing operators and selecting cells until you complete the formula.

Use Absolute Addresses in Formulas

To make it easy to copy and move formulas, Excel uses a concept that is known as *relative addressing*. Excel doesn't think of the cells you include in the formula as a set location. Instead, Excel thinks of the cells as a relative location. Here's an example:

A150

A2100

A3=A1+A2

When you create this formula, Excel doesn't think "Go to A1." Instead, it identifies the first cell in the formula as two above the current one. Basically, Excel thinks this: "Go up two cells, get this value, go up one cell, get this value, and add the two." Now if you move or copy the formula, the same set of instructions work. If you copied this formula to B3, you'd get =B1+B2. This type of referencing saves you from having to create the same formula over and over again. You can just copy it.

In some formulas, however, you may want to refer to a specific cell, that is, you don't want the formula to adjust. For example, suppose that you have several columns of pricing information that refer to one discount rate, in cell A1. When you create this formula, you always want to refer to cell A1; you don't want the references to adjust. In this case, you use a different type of cell reference: an *absolute reference*.

You can also use a *mixed reference*. With this type of reference, you can tell Excel to adjust the column but keep the row reference the same, or adjust the row but keep the column reference the same. To change a reference from relative to absolute, type a **$** sign before the part you want to make absolute. Here are some examples:

$A1   Refers always to row A, column will vary.

A$1   Refers always to column 1, row will vary.

A1   Refers always to cell A1.

Begin Guided Tour   Enter an Absolute Cell Reference

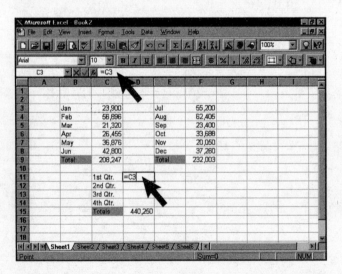

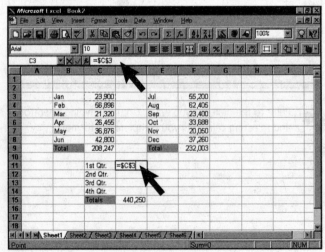

1 Select the cell that will contain the formula. Type an equal (=) sign, type or point to the cell reference, and type the operator.

2 After you enter the reference that you want to make absolute, press **F4**. Excel enters dollar signs before the column letter and row number.

3 Continue building the formula until it is complete. Press **Enter**. Excel creates the formula. When you copy a formula with an absolute reference, Excel will not update the reference.

Sum Numbers

The most common calculation used in worksheets is summing a group of numbers. To make it quick and easy to create this type of formula, use the **AutoSum** button on the toolbar. When you click on this button, Excel looks around the formula cell and guesses what you want to sum.

Excel bases its guess on what you want to sum by looking up and suggesting the range above the selected cell, if those cells contain values. If the cells above the formula cell do not contain values, Excel looks to the left and suggests the range to the left of the selected cell. In many cases, Excel guesses right, but even if it doesn't, you can simply drag across the range you want to sum. Press **Enter** and you have a sum formula.

The formula that Excel creates looks something like this: =SUM(A1:B5). (The numbers inside the parentheses reflect the selected range to sum.) This formula is actually a *function*, a prebuilt formula. In addition to

the SUM function, Excel includes more than 100 other special functions. The next section covers using a function.

> **Press Alt+= to create a SUM formula.**

Excel 7 has a new *AutoCalculate* feature that automatically sums a range of cells and displays the figure on your status bar. To see it work, just highlight a cell or range of cells containing data you want summed up; then look down on your status bar for a running total. This is handy if you want to quickly see the total of your cells without entering a formula or using a function.

If you right-click on the status bar, you can access a shortcut menu for viewing the average of the selected cells, or you can get a count of the selected items.

Begin Guided Tour Use the AutoSum Tool

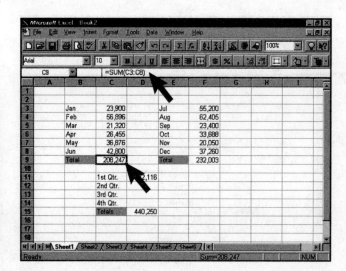

1 Select the cell that you want to contain the sum formula. Click the **AutoSum** button.

2 Excel guesses which cells you want to sum, surrounds them with a faint line, and enters them in the Formula Bar and cell. Check that the correct range is selected. If that range is correct, skip to the next step. Otherwise, select the correct range you want to sum.

3 Press **Enter**. Excel enters the function into the cell. In the cell, you see the results of the function. When the cell is selected, you see the actual function in the Formula Bar.

Use Functions

Excel provides many calculation functions for you so that you don't have to get out your slide rule and old trigonometry books. You can calculate a loan payment, find the square root of a number, calculate an average, count items in a list, and much more using one of the hundred or more Excel functions. (Part IV of this book has a list of the most common functions and what they do.)

Functions are a shorthand way for entering complex formulas. For example, the AVERAGE function condenses a longer formula into a shorthand version. Rather than have this formula

=(A1+A2+A3+A4+A5)/5

You can use this function

=AVERAGE(A1:A5)

Like a formula, the function starts with an equal (=) sign. The next part is the function name: usually a short, abbreviated word that indicates what the function does. After the function name, you see a set of parentheses, and inside the parentheses, you see the *arguments*—the values used in the calculation. Arguments can be a single value, a single cell reference, a series of cell references or values, or a range. Different functions require different arguments. Some arguments are mandatory; some are optional. You can look up the specific format or syntax for the function in online Help or in your Excel manual.

For the function to work properly, you must enter the parts in the correct order and format. You can type the function and hope you remember the right order for the arguments, or you can have Excel build the function for you using the *Function Wizard*—the preferred method. This method leads you through the steps to create the function.

Begin Guided Tour   Enter a Function with Function Wizard

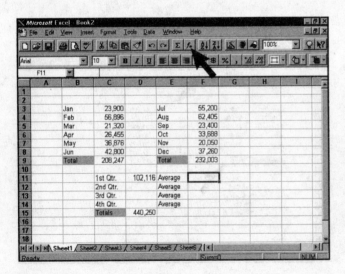

1 Select the cell you want to contain the function, and click the **Function Wizard** button.

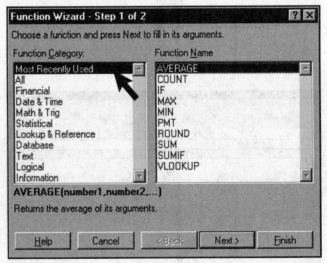

2 You see step 1 of the Function Wizard. This dialog box lists the most recently used functions. Other categories appear in the Function Category list. Click on the function category you want.

Guided Tour Enter a Function with Function Wizard

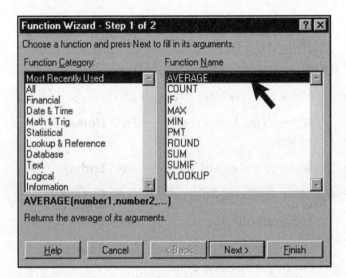

③ The Function Name list box lists the functions in that category. Click on the function you want.

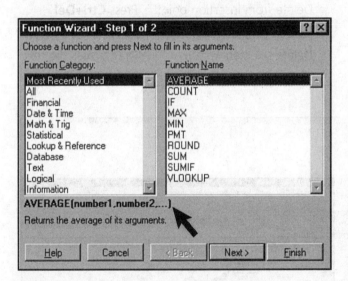

④ Excel lists the function format and a short description at the bottom of the dialog box. Click the **Next** button.

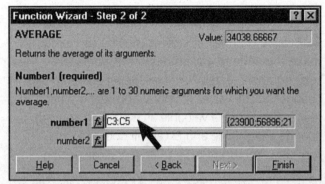

⑤ Excel displays step 2 of the Function Wizard. Here you enter the arguments for the function.

The insertion point is in the first argument text box. Enter a value for this argument. You can click on a cell in the worksheet or drag across a range. You can also type the cell reference, range reference, or value directly in the argument text box. Excel enters the argument in the dialog box.

Click in the next argument text box if necessary and enter the value for this argument. Do this for each mandatory argument and any optional arguments you want to use. Remember, if the text box is bold, you have to enter a value to complete the function.

⑥ After you enter all the arguments, press **Enter** or click the **Finish** button.

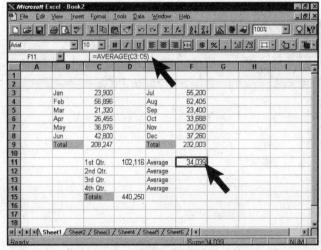

⑦ Excel creates the function. Here the AVG function averages each month's sales totals in a quarter.

Edit and Delete Entries

Did you enter a number incorrectly? Or did a value change? In either case, you can easily make a change to any entries in the worksheet—text, numbers, dates, formulas. Being able to make changes to the values in your worksheet is what makes Excel such a valuable analysis tool. You can change a key value and Excel will update all the formulas. You don't have to do any recalculating.

With Excel 7.0, you can now edit the entry directly in the cell as described in the Guided Tour. You can also edit directly in the Formula Bar by selecting the cell you want to edit, pressing **F2** or clicking in the Formula Bar, making the change, and pressing **Enter**.

When you are editing an entry, you need to move the insertion point (the flashing vertical pointer) to the spot you want. You can use the following key and key combination to move the insertion point and make changes:

To	Do This
Move one character right	Press →
Move one character left	Press ←
Move to the beginning of line	Press **Home**
Move to the end of line	Press **End**
Move right one word	Press **Ctrl+→**
Move left one word	Press **Ctrl+←**
Delete the character to the left of the insertion point	Press **Backspace**
Delete the character to the right of the insertion point	Press **Delete**
Delete from insertion point to end of line	Press **Ctrl+Del**
Delete selected text	Drag across the text and press **Del**

Begin Guided Tour Edit Data

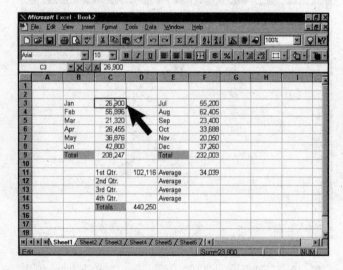

1 Double-click on the cell you want to edit. The insertion point appears within the current cell. Use the arrow keys to move to the spot you want to make the change. Then make any changes and press **Enter**.

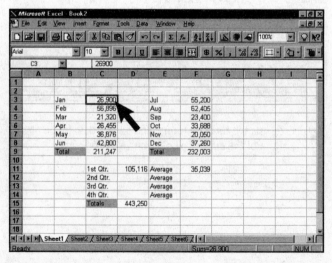

2 Excel updates the entry.

Begin Guided Tour   Delete Data

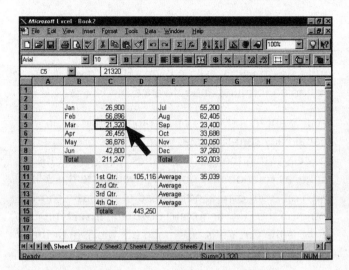

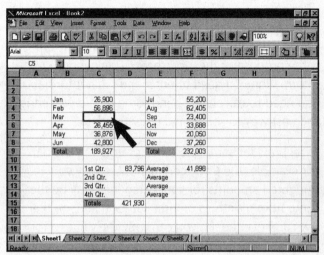

1 Select the cell or range you want to delete and press the **Del** key.

2 Excel deletes the selected cell or range. If any of the selected cells are referenced in a formula, the formula is updated, also.

Just as you can edit data, you can also delete data. When you delete a value referenced in a formula, Excel updates that formula. If you accidentally delete a selected cell or range, immediately open the **Edit** menu and select the **Undo** command; or click on the **Undo** button.

Move and Copy Data

When you create a new worksheet, you should spend some time planning the layout. What is the purpose of the worksheet? Think about what information you need to enter and what information you need to calculate. Spend some time considering the best way to set up and enter the data.

Excel provides some shortcuts for entering the data, for example, the Copy command. Let's say your budgeted amounts for your categories may be the same from month to month. Rather than type them over and over again, you can copy the values. (You can also fill data as a shortcut for entering information. Check out the next task.)

If you don't get things in the right spot, you can move them. You may want to move something over to make room for something else, for instance. (You can also insert new rows and columns, as covered in "Insert and Delete Rows and Columns" on page 163.)

To copy or move information, use the **Cut**, **Copy**, and **Paste** commands. These commands work the same from application to application and they all use the Windows Clipboard. When you cut or copy something, it is placed on the Clipboard. You can then use the Paste command to paste the item in the same document, in another document, or even in another application.

> Like to use keyboard shortcuts? Press **Ctrl+C** for Copy, **Ctrl+X** for Cut, or **Ctrl+V** for Paste.

Note that when you move or copy values, the values are pasted identically. Formulas are handled differently, though. What happens to the formula when you move or copy depends on the type of reference.

Excel adjusts all relative references. All absolute references stay the same. (See "Use Absolute Addresses in Formulas" on page 150 for more information on formulas and references.)

If you want to move or copy a range within an area that already contains data, you can have Excel insert the cells within the existing entries. Copy or cut the range, as you normally do. When you paste the cells, use a different command. Instead of the Paste command on the Edit menu, pull down the **Insert** menu and use the **Cut Cells** command (for moving) or the **Copied Cells** command (for copying).

Use the Drag-and-Drop Technique

If you want to move or copy a selected range just a short distance, you can drag and drop it. To use this method, you have to get the mouse pointer in just the right spot, which can make it frustrating for beginners. You then have to drag the range to the new location. With a little practice, you can master the technique in no time.

Use these steps to drag-and-drop data:

1. Select the cell or range you want to move or copy.

2. Move the mouse pointer over the selection's border. The mouse pointer should change to an arrow.

3. To copy the range, hold down the **Ctrl** key. To move a range, you don't need to press any keys.

4. Drag the border. As you drag, you see an outline of the selected data. When the data is in the spot you want, release the mouse button.

Begin Guided Tour   Move Data

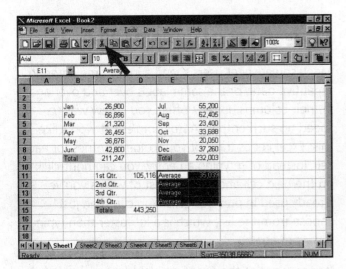

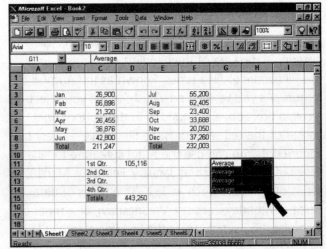

1 Select the cell or range you want to move, and click the **Cut** button.

2 A message at the bottom of the screen prompts you to select a destination. Select the cell at the upper-left corner of where you want the pasted cells. Keep in mind that Excel will overwrite any cells in the destination area.

3 Click the **Paste** button. Excel moves the selected cell or range.

Begin Guided Tour   Copy Data

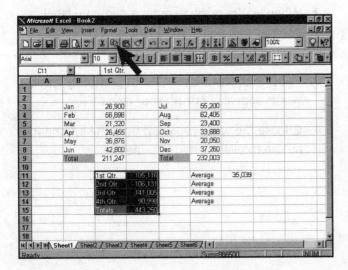

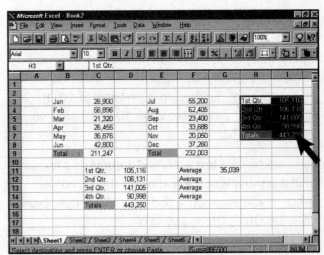

1 Select the cell or range you want to copy, and click the **Copy** button.

2 The status bar prompts you to select a destination. Select the cell at the upper-left corner of where you want the pasted cells.

3 Press **Enter**, open the **Edit** menu, and select the **Paste** command; or click the **Paste** button. Excel copies the selected cell or range.

Fill in Data

To make it as quick as possible to create a worksheet, Excel provides some shortcuts for entering data. One of the handiest shortcuts is using the *fill handle* to fill a series, known as the *AutoFill* feature. As you've seen previously, when you select a cell, a box appears around it. In the bottom right corner of the cell selector is the fill handle—a very tiny square dot. You can use the AutoFill feature to fill a series of months (such as January, February, March), a series of numbers (such as 1, 2, 3), a series of dates (such as Monday, Tuesday, Wednesday), or a series of formulas. You simply enter the first value and let Excel fill the rest. If you're using a series of dates, all you have to type is one date to start the series. But if you're using numbers, you'll need to enter two variables to start the fill series.

The starting value determines how the fill works. If you start with a date that Excel recognizes and then drag the fill handle to extend the series, Excel fills in the cells you dragged over with a series of dates. If you start with a formula or value and then fill, Excel simply copies the formula or value.

To fill a series of numbers, you have to enter the first two values to show Excel the pattern that you want. For example, to fill a series of numbers 1, 2, 3, you would enter 1 and 2 in adjacent cells and then fill. To enter a series of numbers in increments of 10 (10, 20, 30, and so on), you would enter 10 and 20 in two cells and then fill.

If you are filling a text entry and it contains a number, Excel will increment the number in the fill. For instance, if you enter Qtr 1 and then fill a range, Excel will enter Qtr 2, Qtr 3, and so on.

Use AutoComplete

Many spreadsheet users spend a lot of time entering repetitive data, or the same labels over and over again in their columns. Excel 7 offers you a new way to speed up such entries: *AutoComplete*. It works like this: Excel keeps track of your column entries for each cell. Instead of retyping an entry, you can right-click on the next cell and display a list of words you've already used in previous cells. You can then just choose from the list, which is a lot faster than typing the word again.

You may notice the AutoComplete feature kicking in while you enter text. If you repeat the first few letters of a previous entry, AutoComplete guesses that you're typing in repeat information and finishes your word for you. If it's not the correct word, however, just keep typing and ignore AutoComplete.

To use the AutoComplete feature, follow these steps:

1. Type the labels in the first cells of the column.

2. When you're ready to enter a duplicate label in another cell, right-click on the empty cell to open a shortcut menu.

3. Select **Pick from List**. A list of previously typed words appears beneath your cell.

4. Choose the word you want from the list and it's automatically inserted into the cell.

Begin Guided Tour   Use the AutoFill Feature

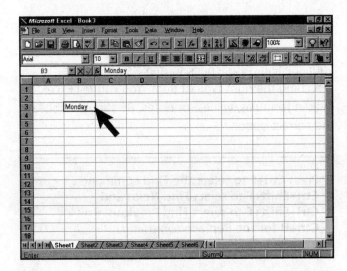

1 Type the entry into the first cell. If you want to use a series, enter the first two values in two cells next to each other. Then select the cell or cells that contain the entry.

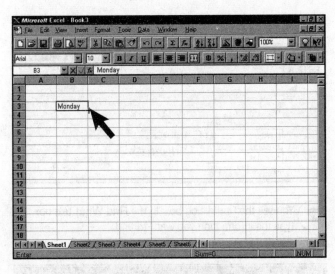

2 Put the mouse pointer on the fill handle in the lower right corner of the cell. The pointer should look like a small cross.

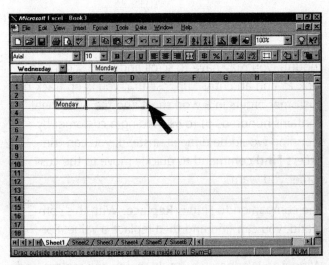

3 Drag across the range you want to fill. As you drag, you see an outline, shown in the example.

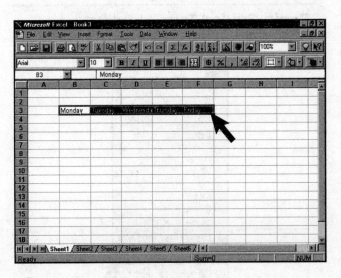

4 Release the mouse button and Excel fills the series in.

Find and Replace Data

If you have a worksheet that fits on one screen, you can quickly spot an entry. In a bigger worksheet, though, you may have to scroll and look, scroll and look to find an entry. Suppose that you keep track of customer orders in a worksheet and the worksheet contains hundreds of rows. Finding a customer by scanning would be difficult. Instead, you can use Excel's **Find** command to quickly move to the customer you want.

The companion to Find is **Replace**. With this command, you can find and then replace a value. For example, if you changed a product name from Widget to Wadget, you could search and replace and make the changes automatically.

If Excel can't find a match, you see a message saying so. You can try the command again and double-check your spelling. Also, check to make sure you are searching the right type of item. You can tell Excel to look in formulas, values, or notes. Be sure to choose the correct option.

Press **Ctrl+F** to select the **Find** command, **Ctrl+Shift+F** to select **Find Next**, and **Ctrl+Shift+E** to select **Find Previous**. Press **Ctrl+H** for the **Replace** command.

Begin Guided Tour Find Data

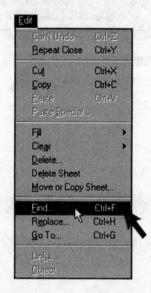

1 Open the **Edit** menu and select the **Find** command.

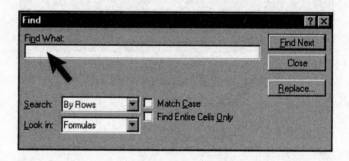

2 You see the Find dialog box. In the **Find What** text box, type the information you want to find.

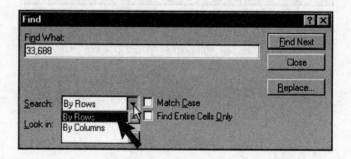

3 Select how to search by displaying the **Search** drop-down list and then choosing **By Rows** or **By Columns**.

Guided Tour   Find Data

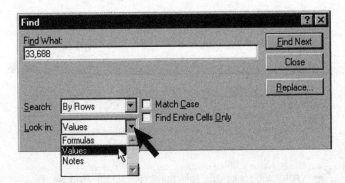

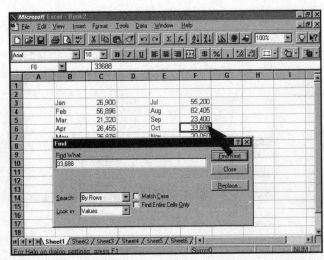

(4) Select where to look by displaying the **Look in** drop-down list and clicking on one of the following: **Formulas**, **Values**, or **Notes**.

(5) If you want Excel to match the case as you've typed it, check the **Match Case** check box. If you want to find only entire entries (not partial entries), check the **Find Entire Cells Only** check box.

(7) Excel moves to and highlights the first matching entry. Continue clicking **Find Next** until you find the entry you want. Then click the **Close** button to close the dialog box.

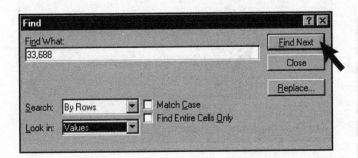

(6) After you enter the text to find and select any search options, click the **Find Next** button to find the first matching entry.

Begin Guided Tour Replace Data

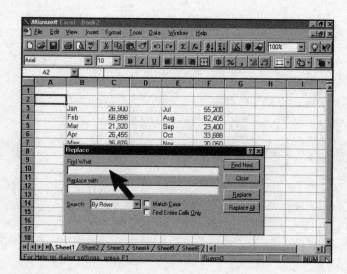

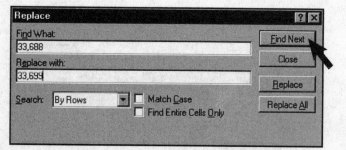

5 After you make your selections, click on the **Find Next** button to find the first matching entry.

1 Open the **Edit** menu and select the **Replace** command. You see the Replace dialog box. In the **Find What** text box, type the information you want to find.

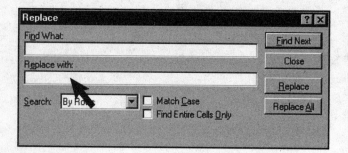

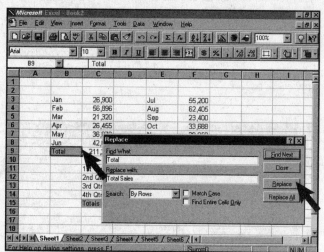

6 Excel moves to the first match; the Replace dialog box remains open. Do one of the following:

Click **Replace** to replace this occurrence and move to the next.

Click **Find Next** to skip this occurrence and move to the next.

Click **Replace All** to replace all occurrences.

2 In the **Replace with** text box, type the entry you want to use as the replacement.

3 Select how to search by displaying the **Search** drop-down list and then choosing **By Rows** or **By Columns**.

4 If you want Excel to match the case as you've typed it, check the **Match Case** check box. If you want to find only entire entries (not partial entries), check the **Find Entire Cells Only** check box.

7 When all the replacements you want are made, click the **Close** button to close the dialog box.

Insert and Delete Rows and Columns

Imagine using the old paper-and-pencil method of tallying up numbers. Your budget is perfect, with all 50 categories and the totals exactly right. Then your boss asks you to add a new expense category right in the middle of the worksheet, or your boss wants you to delete an expense category. Arghhh!!! You'd have to re-enter all the data. Not with Excel. In Excel, you can easily insert and delete rows or columns.

To delete a row or column, you select the row or column that you want by clicking on the row number or column letter. You can delete multiple rows or columns by dragging across them (in the number or letter area). Remember that you are not only removing the row or column from the worksheet, you are also removing all the data in that row. Be sure that's what you intend. If you make a mistake, immediately undo the deletion.

If you forget to include something in the worksheet, you can easily add a new row or column, and Excel

will move existing rows down or columns over to make room. You can easily rearrange your worksheet until you include all the data you need.

Just as with deleting, you start by selecting the column or row. If you want to insert more than one row or column, select the number you want to insert.

One thing to remember when you insert a row or column is that the new row or column does not include any formatting (styles, font sizes, and so on) you may have applied to the rows or columns in which the new row appears. You'll need to format the new row or column. (You can learn more about formatting in Excel in the next section.)

> Press **Ctrl+–** to select the **Delete** command.
> Press **Ctrl++** to select the **Insert** command.

Begin Guided Tour   Delete a Column or Row

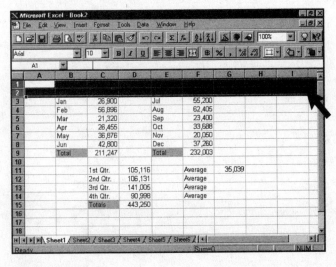

1 Select the column(s) or row(s) you want to delete.

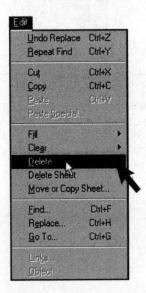

2 Then open the **Edit** menu and select the **Delete** command. Excel deletes the column(s) or row(s) and shifts the remaining cells over.

Begin Guided Tour   Insert a Column or Row

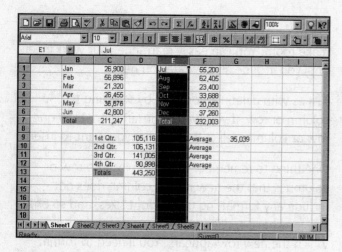

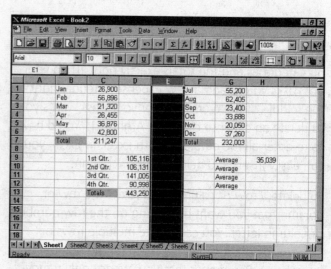

1 Select the row or column. Excel inserts new rows above the selected row. Excel inserts new columns to the left of the selected column.

3 Excel inserts the row or column and shifts the existing cells over.

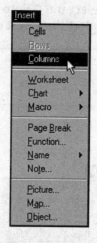

2 Open the **Insert** menu and select the **Rows** command to insert a row. Select the **Columns** command to insert a column.

HOW TO...

Format an Excel Worksheet

The first task in creating a worksheet is entering the appropriate data, which is the focus of the previous chapter. Once you enter the data, you will probably want to spend some time enhancing the appearance of the data to make sure that the worksheet is easy to read and understand. Ask yourself these questions: Do you need to point out key factors? Do you need to clarify the numbers?

If so, you can use bold, italic, and underline to call attention to data. You can also add a border to data, shade a certain area, or change the color of a worksheet element. You can change the number format so it is clear what the numbers represent (currency, units, or percents, for example).

Take a moment to examine how the worksheet looks on the page. Do the headings align over the columns of data or do you need to make adjustments? Does the data fit on the page or do you need to adjust the margins or the orientation? If so, you can make these changes as well.

This part of the book covers all these formatting options you can use with Excel. Use this section to make your worksheet picture perfect.

What You Will Find in This Section

Make Entries Bold, Italic, and Underline

Your worksheet is going to be a mix of information, numbers, and text. Usually, each set of numbers has a row and column heading that identifies what the data means. To make it easy to spot these headings, you may want to add emphasis; you can make them **bold**, *italic*, or underline, or apply all three styles.

You may also want to use these font styles to call attention to other data in the worksheet. For example, you may want to boldface the totals so that they are easy to see on the page, or you may want to italicize the worksheet title. Formatting is the key to making your spreadsheet data look good. Excel makes it easy to select any of these formatting styles using the toolbar.

Excel's Formatting toolbar holds many of the same buttons as the Formatting toolbar in Word, such as Bold or Italics. To use any of the buttons, simply click on the formatting you want to apply. You can also control formatting through the Format Cells dialog box. Open the **Format** menu and select **Cells** to open the dialog box. You can easily change many of the formatting features for your data by clicking on the appropriate tabs in this dialog box.

If you don't know how to format your spreadsheet, let Excel's *AutoFormat* feature give you some professional help. Simply select the data you want to format (or the whole worksheet); then open the **Format** menu and choose **AutoFormat**. A dialog box appears with options you can try. Look through the **Table Format** list to find a formatting style you want to use, and look at the sample to see if you like it. Click **OK** and Excel formats your data accordingly.

Excel provides over 15 different autoformats to choose from. The formats include preset number, border, font, patterns, alignment, column width, color, and row height selections. You simply select a style that you like, and Excel will make all the formatting changes at once.

> Like to use the keyboard? Then learn these shortcuts: **Ctrl+B** for Bold, **Ctrl+I** for Italic, and **Ctrl+U** for Underline.

Copy Formatting with the Format Painter Tool

In many cases, you will make several formatting changes to the same cell or range. For example, you may change the number format (see 175 for tips about number formats) for your totals and make them bold. Once you get the range formatted how you want, you may like the look so much that you want to use it on other cells or ranges in the worksheet. Do you need to go through all the same formatting steps? No. With Excel, you can copy the formatting with the Format Painter button on the Standard toolbar.

1. Select the cell or cells that contain the formatting you want to copy. Then click the **Format Painter** button on the toolbar (it's the one with a paint brush on the button).

2. The mouse pointer displays a little paintbrush next to the cross. Select the cells that you want to format with the same options.

3. When you release the mouse button, Excel applies the formatting to the selected range.

Begin Guided Tour   Format Data with the Toolbar

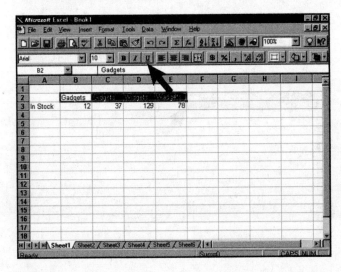

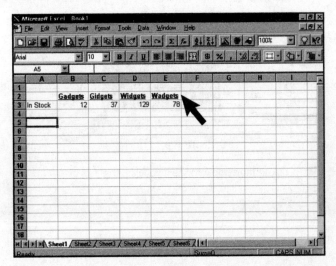

1 Select the cell or range you want to change and do any of the following:

Click on the **Bold** button in the toolbar (it looks like a capital **B**) to make the entries bold.

Click on the **Italic** button in the toolbar (it looks like a capital **I**) to make the entries italic.

Click on the **Underline** button in the toolbar (it looks like a capital **U**) to underline the text in the cells.

2 Excel formats the selected range accordingly. You can turn off bold, italic, and underline by selecting the range and then clicking the appropriate button again.

Begin Guided Tour   Use AutoFormat

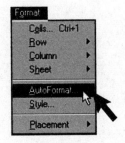

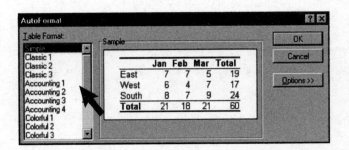

1 Click inside the range, open the **Format** menu and choose **AutoFormat**.

2 The AutoFormat dialog box appears with options you can try. Look through the **Table Format** list to find a formatting style you want to use. Select a style from the list.

(continues)

Guided Tour   Use AutoFormat

(continued)

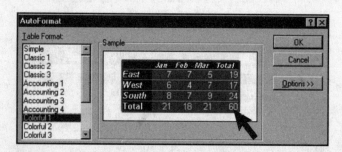

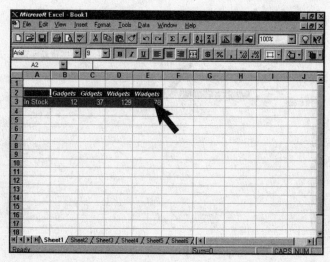

3 Look at the sample to see if you like it.

4 Click **OK** to exit the box, and Excel formats your data accordingly.

Change the Font

When you create a new worksheet and enter data, Excel uses the default font and font size (Arial 10-point type). With this formatting, all the data has the same emphasis and looks the same. If you find this font is too small or if you prefer a different font, you can make a change. For example, you may want to use a large, more decorative font for your title. You may want to use a larger point size for all the entries.

With Excel, you can change the font for the entire worksheet or for only a selected cell or range. The fastest way to change the font is by using the Formatting toolbar. With this method, you can only make one change at a time, and you can't see a preview of the change. If you want to make several changes (for example, change the font, use a different size, and use bold), you can use the Format Cells dialog box. The *Guided Tour* covers both methods.

If you make a change and realize immediately that you don't like it, you can undo it with the **Edit Undo** command. If you didn't undo the command immediately, you can clear formatting by selecting the cell or range. Open the **Edit** menu and select the **Clear Formats** command. Excel clears all the applied formatting.

Change the Default Font

If you don't like the default font for new worksheets, you can change the font each time you create a new worksheet, or you can change the default. When you change the default, Excel will use the new font for all new worksheets, which will save you time.

1. Open the **Tools** menu and select the **Options** command. Click on the **General** tab.

2. You see the General tab of the Options dialog box. Click on the down arrow next to the **Standard Font** drop-down list. Click on the font you want. Click on the down arrow next to the **Size** drop-down list. Click on the size you want.

3. Click **OK** twice. All new worksheets will use the font you selected.

Begin Guided Tour   Use the Toolbar

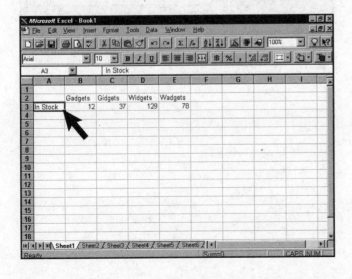

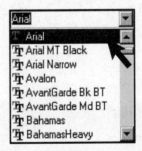

1 Select the cell or range you want to change (you can also select the entire worksheet). In this figure, a single cell is selected for change. Then click on the down arrow next to the **Font** list.

2 You see a drop-down list of font choices. Click on the font you want. Excel makes the font change.

(continues)

Guided Tour Use the Toolbar

(continued)

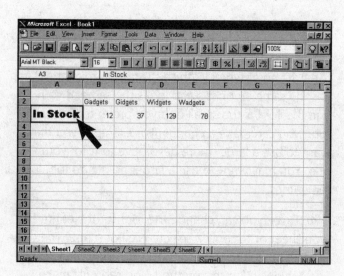

3 To change the size of the font, click on the down arrow next to the **Size** list to see a list of font sizes. Click on the size you want.

4 Excel formats the range with the new size (here 16-point type). If necessary, Excel also adjusts the row height.

Begin Guided Tour Use the Format Cells Dialog Box

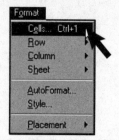

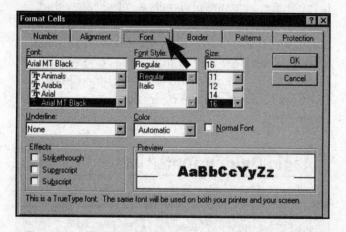

1 Select the cell or range you want to change. Then open the **Format** menu and select the **Cells** command. (You can also press **Ctrl+1**.)

2 If necessary, click the **Font** tab of the Format Cells dialog box to bring it to the front.

Guided Tour Use the Format Cells Dialog Box

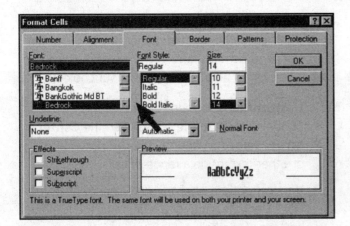

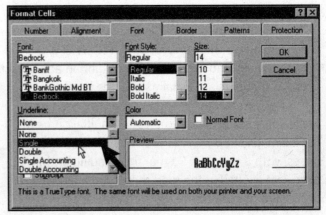

3 In the **Font** list, click on the font you want. Click on the size you want in the **Size** list. Select a style from the **Font Style** list.

5 If you want to use a different type of underline, display the **Underline** drop-down list and click on the underline style you want.

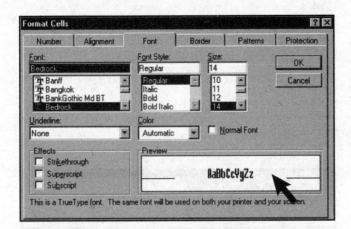

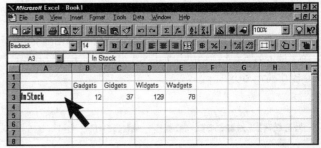

6 When you finish making changes, click **OK**. Excel formats the selected range with the options you selected.

4 Look in the Preview area to see what the selected formatting will look like. If you want any special effects, check the check box for any of these special effects: **Strikethrough**, **Superscript**, **Subscript**.

For more information on understanding fonts and figuring out what fonts you have, see "Change the Font" on page 169.

Change the Alignment of Entries

By default, Excel automatically aligns data, depending on what type of data it is. Excel aligns text on the left and numbers on the right. In addition, text and numbers are initially set at the bottom of the cell. After you make the entries, you may need to make some adjustments to these default alignments. For example, suppose that you have a column of prices, with a heading. So that the heading and the prices are aligned in the worksheet, you may want to right-align the column heading.

In addition to making adjustments to column headings, you may want to center your worksheet title over the worksheet. You can fake a centered title by placing the title in about the center of the column, or you can have Excel center the title perfectly.

The easiest way to make any alignment changes is to use the toolbar buttons. You can also use the Format Cells dialog box.

The Alignment tab in the Format Cells dialog box has plenty of alignment options to choose from. Take a look at this list to help you decipher your choices:

- **Horizontal** options enable you to specify a left/right alignment in the cell(s). With the **Center across selection** option, you can center a title or other text inside a range of cells.

- **Vertical** options enable you to specify how you want the data aligned in relation to the top and bottom of the cell(s).

- **Orientation** options let you flip the text sideways or print it from top to bottom (as opposed to left to right).

- The **Wrap Text** check box tells Excel to wrap long lines of text within a cell. (Normally, Excel displays all text in a cell on one line.)

Begin Guided Tour   Aligning Entries with the Toolbar

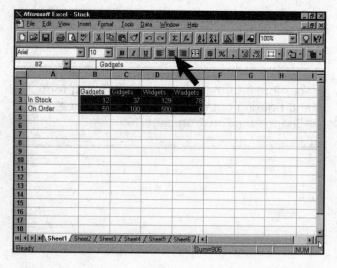

1 Select the cell or range you want to change and do one of the following:

To left-align the entry, click the **Align Left** button.
To center the entry, click the **Center** button.
To right-align the entry, click the **Align Right** button.

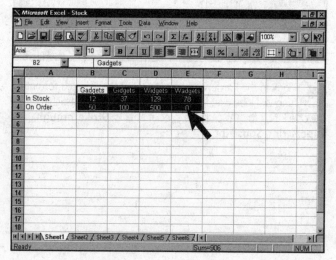

2 Excel changes the alignment of the selected cell or range. In this example, Excel centers all the text inside the range.

Begin Guided Tour   Center a Heading

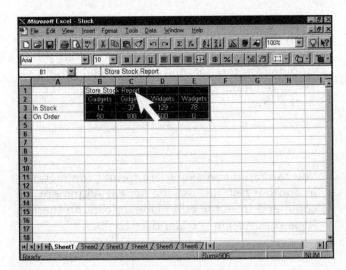

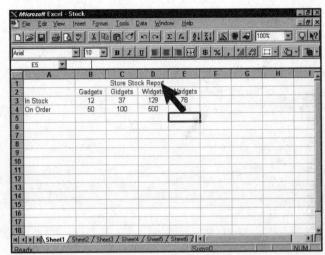

1 Select the range that contains the heading and the range that you want to center across. If you just select the cell with the entry, this feature won't work properly. Then click on the **Center Across Columns** button.

2 Excel centers the headings across the selected columns.

Begin Guided Tour   Align Entries with the Format Cells Dialog Box

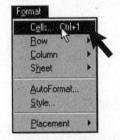

1 Select the cell or range you want to change; then open the **Format** menu and choose **Cells**.

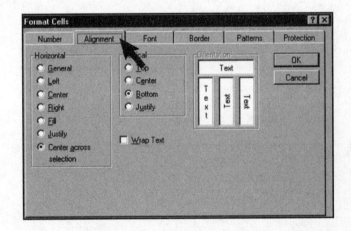

2 This opens the Format Cells dialog box. Click the **Alignment** tab to bring it to the front. Make your alignment changes under the following areas:

To change horizontal alignment, choose an option under the **Horizontal** area.

To change vertical alignment, select an option from the **Vertical** area.

To change data orientation in the cell, use the **Orientation** options.

To wrap text onto other lines inside your cell, select the **Wrap Text** check box.

(continues)

Guided Tour   Align Entries with the Format Cells Dialog Box

(continued)

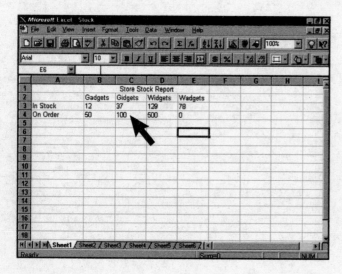

Even though a centered title looks as if it is in a different cell, it is still in the same cell that you originally entered it in. If you try to edit the cell and it looks blank, try selecting the first cell in the row.

You can repeat an alignment format command in another cell. Just use the **Repeat Alignment** command from the **Edit** menu, or click on the **Repeat** button in the Standard toolbar.

3 Click **OK** to exit the box and implement your alignment changes.

Change the Number Format

When you enter a number in Excel, it's entered as a plain number—**25**, for instance. But that number can mean different things. For example, does 25 mean $25, .25, or 25%? As you can see, the way you format a number changes its meaning. In your worksheet, you need to apply the appropriate number format so that the meaning of the numbers is clear.

The formatting of a number is called a *style*, and Excel provides many number styles to choose from. The three most common are available as toolbar buttons (Currency, Comma, and Percent). You can also use the **Format Cells** command to select from other available styles. The *Guided Tour* covers both methods.

If none of the predefined formats fits your needs, you can create your own custom format. Elect a format that's close to what you want and then edit its code to match the custom format you want to create. To apply a custom format to other cells or ranges, display the **Number** tab and click on **Custom** in the Category list. The format code you defined will be listed with this category. Click on it and click **OK**.

> If you see number signs (######) in a cell or range after formatting, you know the number with the new formatting is too wide to appear within the current column width. "Resize Columns and Rows" on page 182 covers how to change the column width.

Decode the Format Codes

If you use the **Format Cells** command to select a style, you'll notice that the styles aren't named, but are represented by codes. The easiest way to figure out the codes is to select a style and view the sample in the dialog box.

If you are curious or if you want to create a custom code, you can take a closer look at the parts of a number format. You can include up to four parts: a positive number format, a negative number format, a format for zeroes, and a format for text. Each part is separated by a semicolon. Within each part, a code represents digits. The following table explains the most common digits used in a style:

#	Placeholder for digits. If the digit is a nonsignificant zero, it does not appear.
0	Placeholder for digits. Zeroes appear. (For example, 9.5 in the format #.00 would display as 9.50.)
?	Placeholder for digits. Uses a space for nonsignificant zeroes.
.	Decimal point.
,	Thousands separator.
%	Percent sign. Excel multiplies entry by 100.
;	Separates positive number format from negative number format.
Underline	Skips the width of the next character. Use this to align positive numbers and negative numbers displayed in parentheses.

Begin Guided Tour   Use a Number Style Button

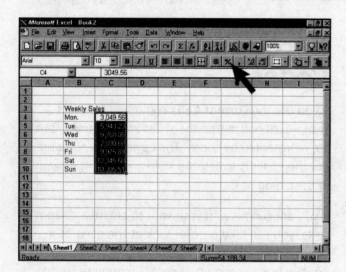

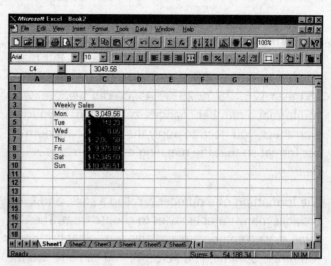

1 Select the cell or range you want to change and do one of the following:

To use currency style, click the **Currency Style** button (it has a dollar sign on it).

To use percent style, click the **Percent Style** button (it has a percent sign on it).

To use comma style, click the **Comma Style** button (it has a comma on it).

2 Excel applies the style. In this example, the **Currency** style was selected; Excel added number signs to the numbers. If necessary, change the number of decimals that appear by clicking the **Increase Decimal** or **Decrease Decimal** buttons on the toolbar.

Begin Guided Tour   Use the Format Cells Number Tab

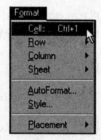

1 Select the cell or range you want to change; open the **Format** menu and select the **Cells** command.

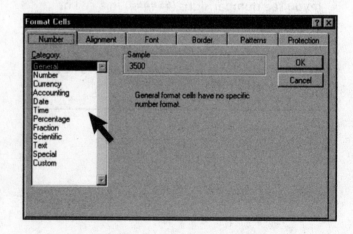

2 Click the **Number** tab to bring it to the front. In the **Category** list, click on the category you want.

Guided Tour Use the Format Cells Number Tab

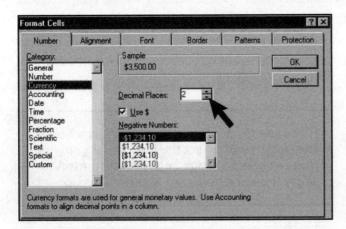

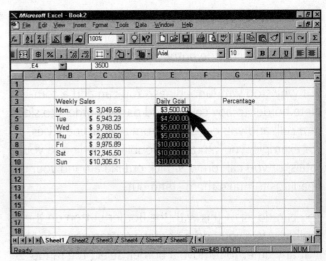

3 Excel displays the styles and options for this category. Select the type of number format or decimal points you want to apply.

5 Click **OK** to exit the box and Excel makes the change.

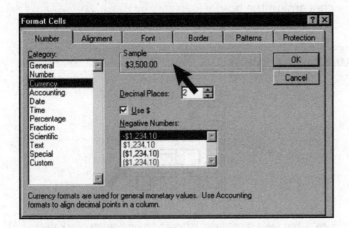

4 Excel displays a sample of the selected style in the dialog box.

Add Borders

You can use the **Underline** button in the toolbar to underline the entries, but if you want to underline the entire cell, you need to use a border. But why stop with underlines? You can add a complete border to any cell, or add partial borders to sides of a cell; and you can select from several line styles. For example, you can add a double-underline to your totals, or you can draw a thick outline around your headings to make them stand out.

You can do all of this with the Border button on the toolbar. After you add a border, you can easily delete it at any time. To remove a border, select the range again. Click the **Border** button and click the **None** option. Excel removes the border. Remember that a cell can contain a border to the left or right and top

or bottom. If you can't find the border to turn off, try selecting the cell next to, above, or below the cell you *think* has the border.

> If you use the toolbar button to select a border, the button will reflect the last border you used. You can select a range and click the button to apply the same border to another selection.

If the Border button doesn't include the line style you want, you can use a different method to add a border: use the Border tab of the Format Cells dialog box. The Border tab lets you control more details concerning the border.

Begin Guided Tour Change the Border with the Toolbar

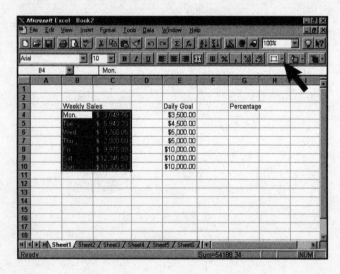

1 Select the range that you want to add a border to and click the **Border** button.

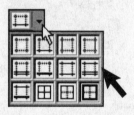

2 You see a drop-down list of common borders. Click the button that represents both the side you want to border and the line style you want to use.

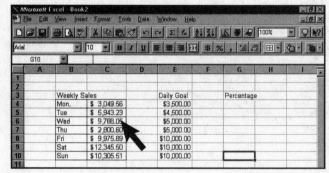

3 Excel applies the border to the selected cells.

Begin Guided Tour Use the Border Tab

1 Select the cell or range you want to change; open the **Format** menu and select the **Cells** command.

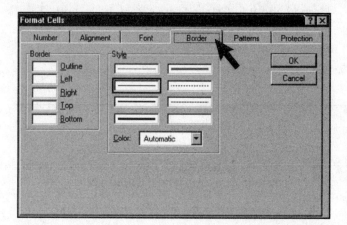

2 The Format Cells dialog box appears. Click the **Border** tab.

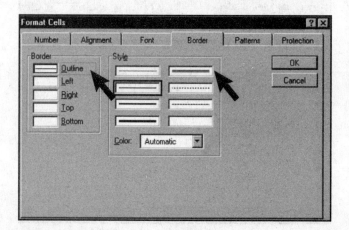

3 Click the border you want: **Outline** (all sides), **Top**, **Left**, **Right**, **Bottom**. Click a border style in the **Style** list.

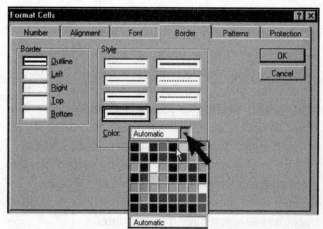

4 If you want to change the line color, click on the down arrow next to the **Color** list. Then click on the color you want.

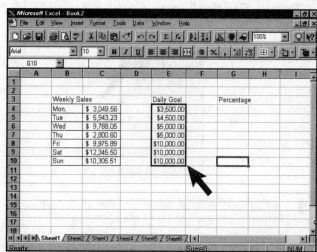

5 Click **OK** to exit the dialog box, and Excel applies the border.

Add Patterns and Change Colors

Suppose that you are creating a worksheet of your sales performance and your Quarter 4 sales were superior. Or suppose that a certain division or product did extremely well. You can rely on your audience to spot these highlights, or you can call attention to them. One way to highlight data is to use a border, as covered in the previous section. You can also add a pattern or change the color. You can change both the color of the cell background or the cell contents. Keep in mind that data that appears in color will print in color only if you have a color printer.

If you don't have a color printer, you'll still be able to see a difference in background and pattern; however, it will print out as shades of gray. Use caution when assigning backgrounds and colors to your spreadsheet data. You still want the data to be readable, and if you choose too dark a color or too busy a pattern, the data may become illegible.

It's important to note that colors and backgrounds can greatly enhance the presentation of your data. You'll even find colors and backgrounds recommended by Excel's AutoFormat feature, which you learned about in "Make Entries Bold, Italic, and Underline" on page 166.

Begin Guided Tour   Add a Pattern

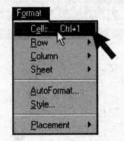

1 Select the cell or range you want to change; open the **Format** menu and select the **Cells** command.

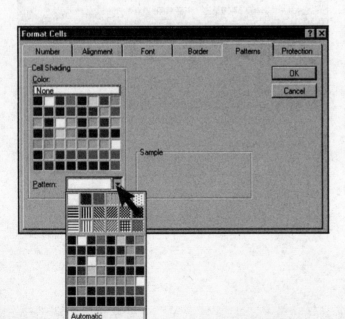

2 Click on the **Pattern** tab. Click on the down arrow next to the **Pattern** drop-down list and click on a pattern.

3 You see a sample of the selected pattern; click **OK**.

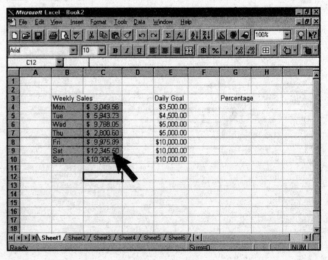

4 Excel applies the pattern to the selected cells.

Begin Guided Tour Change the Background Color

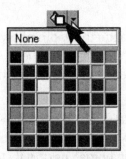

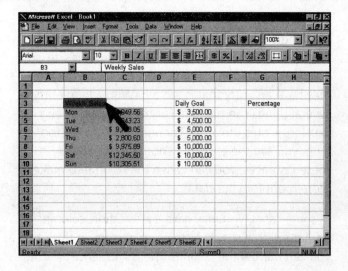

1 Select the cell or range you want to change and click on the down arrow next to the **Color** button.

2 Click on a color in the palette. Excel applies the background color.

Begin Guided Tour Change the Text Color

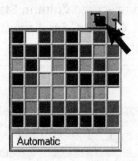

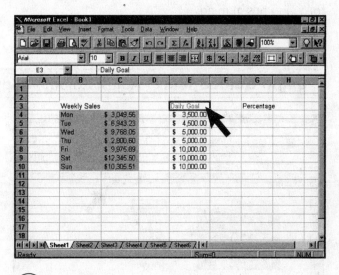

1 Select the cell or range you want to change, and click on the down arrow next to the **Font Color** button. You see a palette of colors.

2 Click on the color you want. Excel changes the text color.

Resize Columns and Rows

In a new worksheet, all the columns are the same size. As you enter data, you'll find that this size isn't going to work for all your entries. For example, you may have an entry that is too big. With a long entry, several things can happen. For text that is too long, Excel truncates the entry. For numbers that are too long, you see the entry with nothing but #####. In these instances, you can widen the column to make more room for your data.

In some cases, you may have a really short column, perhaps with just two or three characters. In this case, you can narrow the column. There's no sense wasting the space.

Resizing Tips

When you are resizing columns and rows, keep the following tips in mind:

- You can change the width of several columns or rows at once by selecting the ones you want to change. Then drag one border to change them all.

- To have Excel adjust the column width to fit the largest entry in that column, double-click the right column border, next to the column letter.

- If you want to enter an exact value for the column width, start in the column you want to change. Then open the **Format** menu and select the **Column Width** command. Type a value and click **OK**.

- You can hide a column by dragging the right border past the left. Hide a row by dragging the bottom border past the top.

- If you change the column width and then want to return to the default width, open the **Format** menu and select the **Column Standard Width** command. Click **OK**. Excel adjusts all columns in the worksheet.

Begin Guided Tour   Adjust Column Width

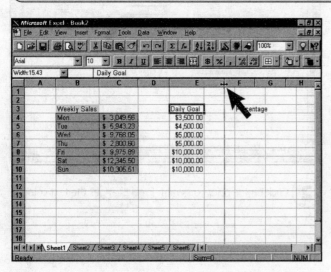

(1) Point to the right column heading border. The pointer will change to a thick line with arrows on either side of it. This indicates the pointer is in the right spot. Hold down the mouse button and drag to a new width. As you drag, you see an outline of the column border. A measurement of the width also appears in the reference area of the formula bar. When the column is as wide as you want, release the mouse button.

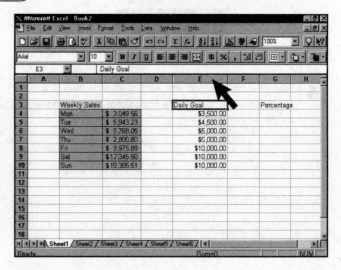

(2) Excel adjusts the width.

Begin Guided Tour   Change the Row Height

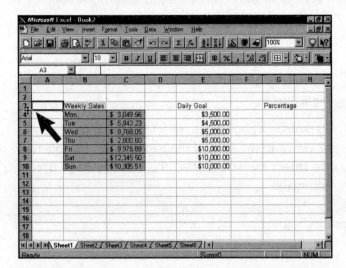

1 Point to the border below the row number that you want to change. The pointer will change to a thick vertical line with arrows on either side of it. This indicates the pointer is in the right spot.

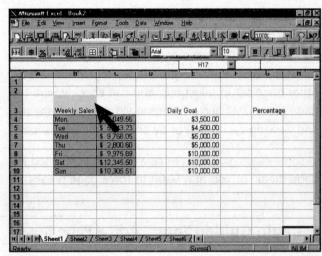

3 Excel adjusts the row.

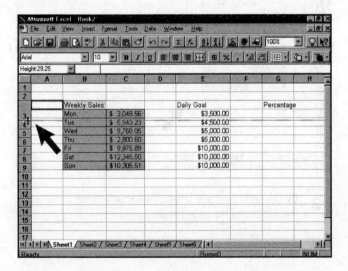

2 Drag up or down to change the height. As you drag, you see an outline of the row border. The row height appears in the reference area of the formula bar.

Insert Page Breaks

When you print a worksheet, Excel breaks up the pages based on the margins you have selected, the column width, the scaling options, and other page setup selections. You can check where the page breaks will occur by previewing the worksheet and viewing each page or by printing the worksheet.

In some cases, you won't like where Excel inserted a page break, or you may want to force page breaks.

For example, if you had a worksheet with sales for each division, you could print each division on a separate page. In both cases, you can insert a *hard page break*.

To remove a page break, select the cell immediately below or to the right of the page break. Then open the **Insert** menu and select the **Remove Page Break** command.

Begin Guided Tour   Add a Page Break

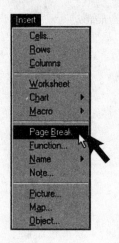

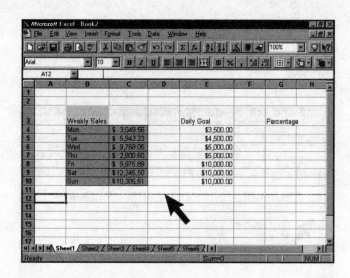

1 Select the cell where you want to insert the page break. The page break will appear above and to the left of the selected cell. Then open the **Insert** menu and select the **Page Break** command.

2 Excel inserts the page break. On-screen you see a dotted line indicating the page break.

Set Margins

By default, Excel uses a 1-inch top and bottom margin and a .75-inch left and right margin. Headers and footers have a .5-inch margin. For your worksheet, you may want to use bigger or smaller margins. In that case, you can change any of the margins using the Page Setup dialog box. If you prefer to see the effects of the change as you make them, you can change the margins in Print Preview. The *Guided Tour* covers both methods.

The Page Setup dialog box contains all kinds of options you can select to controlling how your page layout appears.

If you can't get your printout to look right on the page, try centering it. Check the **Horizontally** check box in the Page Setup dialog box to center the page horizontally (across). Check the **Vertically** check box to center the page vertically (up and down). You can use both methods on a single page.

Begin Guided Tour   Change Margins in the Page Setup Dialog Box

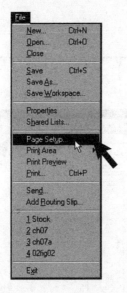

1 Open the **File** menu and select the **Page Setup** command.

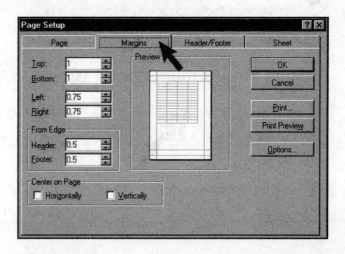

2 You see the Page Setup dialog box. Click the **Margins** tab.

(continues)

Guided Tour   Change Margins in the Page Setup Dialog Box   *(continued)*

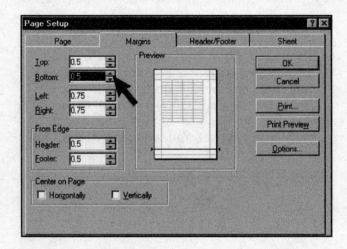

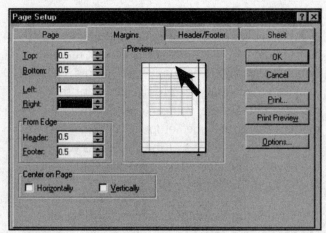

3 Click in the margin text box you want to change: **Top**, **Bottom**, **Left**, or **Right**. Delete and retype the entry, or edit the existing entry.

4 If you want to change the header or footer margin, click in the **Header** or **Footer** text box in the From Edge area. Delete and retype the entry, or edit the existing entry.

5 You see a preview of the page. Click **OK**. Excel makes the changes. In the worksheet, you won't notice the changes, but you can preview the worksheet to see the changes.

Begin Guided Tour   Change Margins in Print Preview

1 Click the **Print Preview** button.

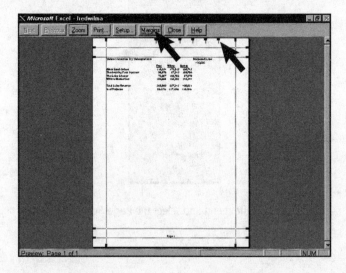

2 Excel displays a preview of the worksheet. Click the **Margins** button.

Guided Tour Change Margins in Print Preview

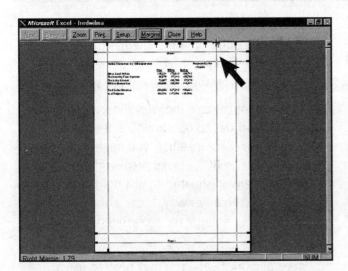

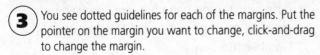

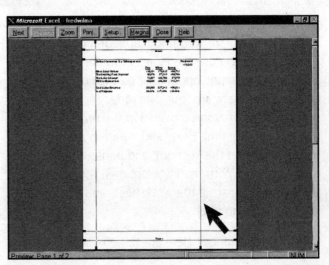

3 You see dotted guidelines for each of the margins. Put the pointer on the margin you want to change, click-and-drag to change the margin.

4 Excel uses the new margin.

Set Up the Page

When you are setting the appearance of the page, you use the Page Setup dialog box. Excel provides many options for controlling the look of the page; there are four categories for the various page options: margins (covered in the preceding task), sheet (covered in the next task), headers and footers (covered later in this section), and page. What are the page options? With the page options, you can select the orientation, scale the worksheet, and set the starting page number.

Why make a change? Here are some reasons:

- If your worksheet has many columns, you may want to switch to *landscape orientation*, printing your data across the long side of the page. (By default, your page is set up to print in portrait orientation, that is, 8 1/2-by-11-inch.)

- If you want to squeeze the worksheet so that it fits on a certain number of pages, you can use

the **Fit to page** option and enter the dimensions of the pages (1 by 1, for instance). Excel will fit the worksheet within those specifications.

- If you want to scale the worksheet a percentage, use the **Adjust to** option and enter a percentage to scale. For instance, you might scale the worksheet by 80%. Experiment with the value to get the worksheet to fit just right. You can also scale the other way; enter a number larger than 100 to enlarge the worksheet.

- If you are creating a report with data from several worksheets, you may need to use a different starting page number. You can enter the starting page number in the First Page Number text box.

- You can also change the paper size or print quality.

Begin Guided Tour   Change the Page Setup

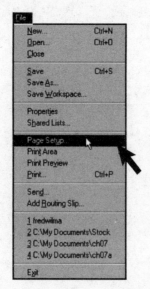

 Open the **File** menu and select the **Page Setup** command.

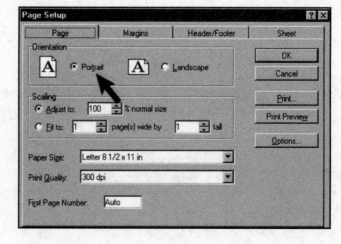

② You see the Page Setup dialog box. Click the **Page** tab. Click on an orientation: **Portrait** or **Landscape**.

Guided Tour   Change the Page Setup

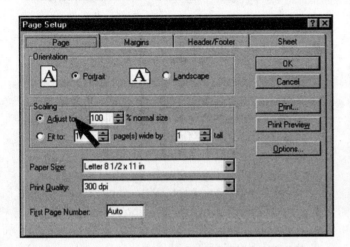

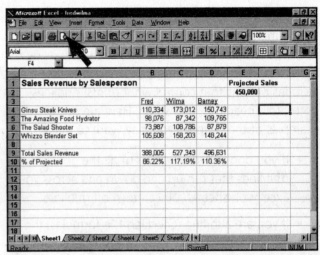

3 If you want to scale the page, click the **Adjust to** option and enter a percentage to scale. Or click the **Fit to** page option and enter the dimensions of the pages (1 by 1, for instance).

4 If you want to change the paper size, display the **Paper Size** drop-down list and select the size you want. If you want to change the print quality, display the **Print Quality** drop-down list and select the quality you want.

7 You won't notice any changes on-screen. To see the changes, click the **Print Preview** button.

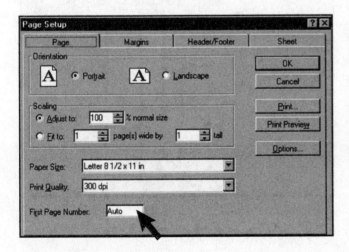

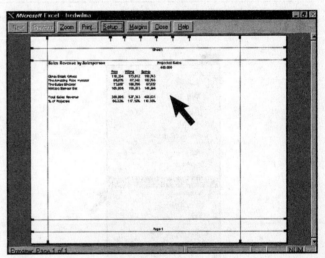

5 If you want to start numbering pages with a different number, enter the number you want to use in the First Page Number text box.

6 Click **OK**.

8 Excel shows the page with the setup options you selected. Here you see a worksheet in landscape orientation.

Set Up the Sheet

As mentioned, Excel breaks up the page layout options into different groups, each with its own tab in the Page Setup dialog box. The Sheet tab includes options that control what prints: gridlines, notes, row headings, and so on. Here are some examples of the changes you may want to make:

- If you don't like the clutter of all the gridlines (the lines that run up and down and across your Excel worksheet), you can turn off gridlines.

- If you are auditing (checking the formulas) the worksheet, you may want to print the column letters and row headings so you can check formula references.

- You may want to repeat row or column headings on worksheets that span two pages because the second page might not make sense without proper headings. For example, you may have a worksheet that lists monthly sales for all your products. The first page includes the product names, but sheet 2 doesn't. You can repeat the column with the product names on sheet 2. For worksheets with many columns, you can repeat the column headings on all pages. For worksheets with many rows, you can repeat the row headings on all pages.

- If you want to print only part of the worksheet, you can enter the print range in the Sheet tab.

Begin Guided Tour   Change the Sheet Setup

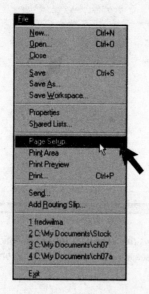

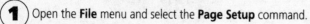

1 Open the **File** menu and select the **Page Setup** command.

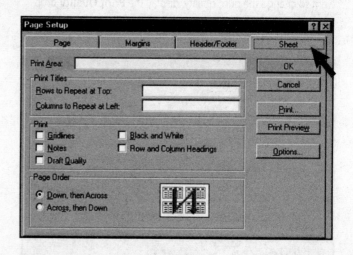

2 You see the Page Setup dialog box. Click the **Sheet** tab to bring it to the front of the box.

Guided Tour Change the Sheet Setup

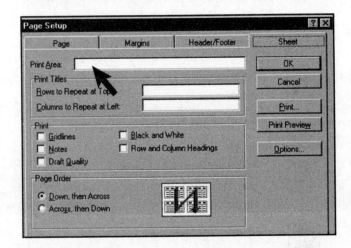

3 If you want to print just a range, enter the range in the Print Area text box.

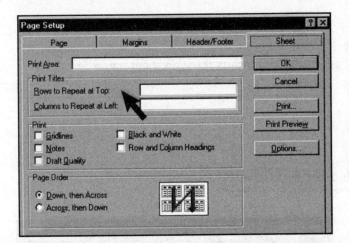

4 If you want to print titles, click in the **Rows to Repeat at Top** and/or the **Columns to Repeat at Left** text boxes. Then click on the worksheet row or column you want to repeat. Excel enters a row or column reference—for instance, $A:$A indicates column A will be repeated.

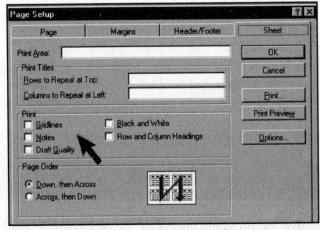

5 Check which elements to print: **Gridlines, Notes, Draft Quality, Black and White, Row and Column Headings**.

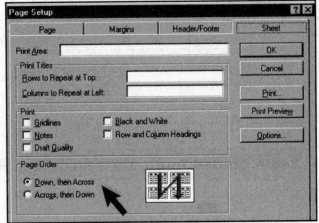

6 Click on a page order: **Down, then Across** or **Across, then Down**.

7 Click **OK** to exit the dialog box.

8 You won't notice any changes on-screen. To see the changes, click the **Print Preview** button and Excel shows a preview of the worksheet with the selected changes.

Add Headers and Footers

If you print a worksheet, you may wonder why the sheet name and page number appear at the top and bottom of the worksheet. These are the default header and footer and print on all worksheets, unless you change them. You may want to use different information such as the date, the worksheet title, or your name; or you may not want to use any headers or footers. You can select to use another predefined header or footer, turn off the header or footer, or create a custom header or footer.

Before you go to the trouble of creating a custom header or footer, check some of the ones Excel has set up for you. Excel provides many combinations of the key data you are likely to want to include: your name, page number, sheet name, company name, workbook name, and date.

If none of the predefined headers or footers is what you need, you can create your own, as explained in the *Quick Tour*. Excel provides some buttons that enable you to quickly insert the special information, such as the page number, as explained here.

Button	Description
A	Changes the font
#	Inserts page number
⊞	Inserts number of pages (for instance, you can print Page 1 of 12 using this button and the preceding button)
📅	Inserts the date
🕐	Inserts the time
📄	Inserts the file name
📋	Inserts the worksheet name

Begin Guided Tour   Use a Predefined Header or Footer

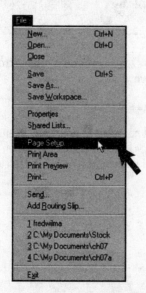

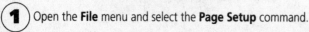

1 Open the **File** menu and select the **Page Setup** command.

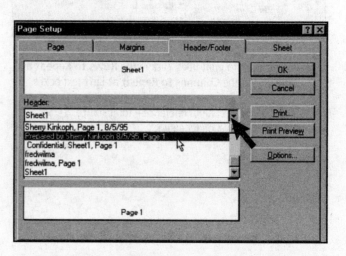

2 You see the Page Setup dialog box. Click the **Header/Footer** tab. To use a predefined header, click on the down arrow next to the Header drop-down list box. You see a list of predefined headers. Click on the one you want.

Guided Tour   Use a Predefined Header or Footer

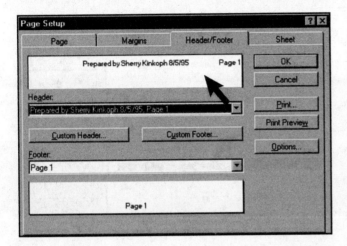

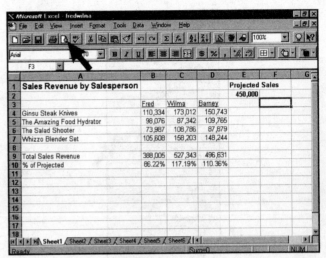

3 Excel displays a preview of the header in the dialog box. If you only want to add a header, skip to step 6.

6 In the worksheet, the headers and footers aren't displayed. To see them, click the **Print Preview** button.

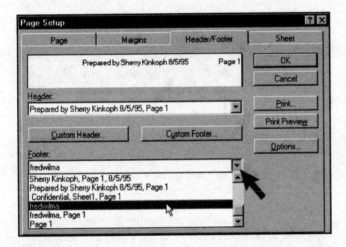

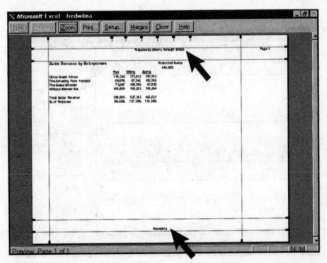

4 If you want to change the footer, click on the down arrow next to the **Footer** drop-down list box; then click on a predefined footer. Excel displays a preview of the footer in the dialog box.

5 Click **OK** to exit the box.

7 Excel displays a preview of the worksheet with the headers and footers you selected.

Headers are printed 1/2-inch from the top of the page, and footers 1/2-inch from the bottom. You can change these margins, if you want. (See "Set Margins" on page 185)

Begin Guided Tour   Create a Custom Header or Footer

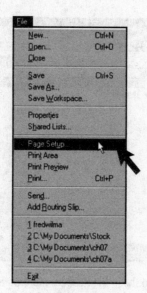

1 Open the **File** menu and select the **Page Setup** command.

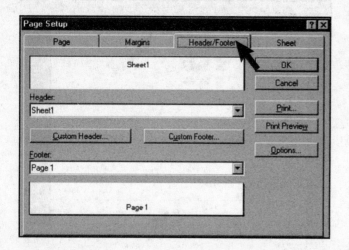

2 You see the Page Setup dialog box. Click the **Header/Footer** tab.

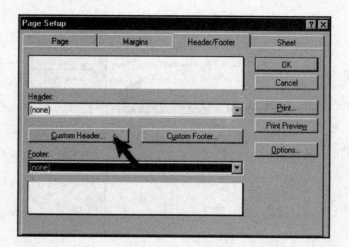

3 To create a custom header, click the **Custom Header** button.

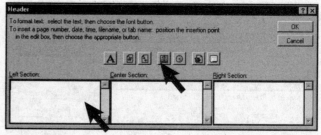

4 You see the Header dialog box, which has three sections: left, center, and right (these represent parts of the header, not the alignment of text). You also see buttons which enable you to insert special codes for the page number, date, worksheet name, and so on in the header or footer. Move to the section in which you want to enter text. Enter the text and codes you want. To insert a code, click on the buttons that appear in the dialog box.

5 When you complete the header or footer, click the **OK** button. You return to the Page Setup dialog box. If you only want a custom header and are finished, skip to step 8. If you want to create a custom footer, click the **Custom Footer** button to create a customized footer.

Guided Tour Create a Custom Header or Footer

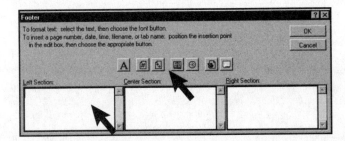

6 You see the Footer dialog box. Enter the text and codes you want for the footer. When the footer is complete, click **OK**.

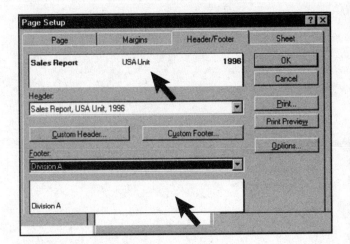

7 You return to the Page Setup dialog, which shows your custom header and footers. Click **OK** to exit the dialog box.

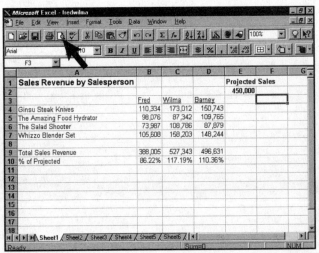

8 You return to the worksheet. To view your custom header or footer, click the **Print Preview** button.

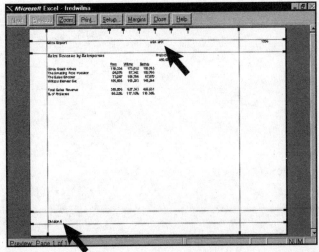

9 Excel displays the worksheet with the custom header or footer.

HOW TO...

Create an Excel Chart

f you just look at the numbers in a worksheet, you may find it hard to spot trends or patterns. Also, the relationship of the numbers may not be readily apparent. To visually show trends, patterns, and relationships, you can create a *chart*.

Excel makes it easy to quickly create a chart from your worksheet data, and you can select from one of many different chart types to convey your message. For example, if fourth-quarter sales peak dramatically, you may want to create a bar chart. To compare product sales, you may want to create a pie chart. Interested in showing a trend over time, such as your household spending? Consider a line chart.

In addition to the features for creating a chart, Excel also provides a complete set of tools for formatting and editing a chart, as covered in this section.

What You will Find in This Section

Create a Chart

A chart takes your data and represents it visually. You can think of a chart as a snapshot picture of your data. With this picture, you or your intended audience can more easily see the relationship among the data. For example, if you chart sales by division, you can see, at a glance, which division leads in sales. If you create a pie chart of household spending, you can easily see which area has the biggest slice of the pie. You not only can visually see the relationship, but you can see patterns and trends, and you can quickly summarize data in a chart.

To make it easy to chart your data, Excel includes the ChartWizard. This feature leads you step by step through the process of creating a chart. You can choose to add a chart on the worksheet or as a separate sheet in the workbook. If you create a chart on the same sheet as your data, Excel prints it side-by-side with your worksheet data. If you create a chart on a separate worksheet, you can print it separately. Both types of charts link to the worksheet data that they represent, so when you change the data, Excel automatically updates the chart.

Excel also offers you great flexibility when it comes to types of charts (there are a total of 15 chart types you can apply). After you select the data to chart, Excel will prompt you to select the type of chart you want to create. What's the difference among the chart types? Each has a specific purpose; you can select the chart type that best conveys your message. Excel provides 14 chart types to choose from, and each chart has several subtypes, or styles, of each chart. The table on the following page explains each chart type.

If you change your mind while working through the ChartWizard, click the **Back** button to go back a step. Also, if you don't like the chart type that you selected, you can change it. See "Change the Chart Type" on Page 207.

As you're working with charts, you may come across charting terms that you're unfamiliar with. Here's a list of explanations for the various chart terms you'll encounter:

Data Series A collection of related data that you want to plot on a chart. For example, if you're charting your monthly household spending, the data series would include the values (amounts) of your spending categories.

Axis One side of an Excel chart. If you're building a two-dimensional chart, the horizontal axis is the X-axis, and the vertical axis is the Y-axis.

Legend An information box inside the chart that defines the chart elements.

Chart Title A name for the chart, usually describing what the chart illustrates.

Example	Chart Type	Description
Area	Area	Use this chart when you want to show change in volume or magnitude over time. This chart type is similar to a line chart, but an area chart emphasizes the amount of change. You can select a 2-D or 3-D version of this chart.
Bar	Bar	Select this chart type when you want to compare items, emphasizing the comparison rather than time. The values are plotted horizontally (as opposed to a column chart where the values are plotted vertically). You can select a 3-D or 2-D chart. You can also create a stacked bar chart (values are stacked on each other) and 100% stacked (the percentage of each value is stacked).
Column	Column	This is the default chart type and is useful when you want to compare items but emphasize change over time. The values are charted vertically. You can select a 2-D, 3-D, stacked, or 100% column chart.
Line	Line	Use this chart type when you want to show trends or emphasize change over time. You can choose to create a 2-D or 3-D line chart. You can also choose a high-low-close-open chart that is useful for charting stock prices.
Pie	Pie	Use this chart when you want to show the relationship of the values to the whole. Select a 2-D or 3-D chart style.
Doughnut	Doughnut	Use this chart when you want to show more than one data series and show the relationship of the values to the whole.
Radar	Radar	Use this chart when you want to show changes relative to a center point.
XY (Scatter)	XY Scatter	This chart type is useful for charting scientific data and shows the relationship of values in several chart data series.
3-D Surface	3-D Surface	Similar to a topographical map, this chart type is useful for finding relationships that may be otherwise difficult to see.
Combination	Combination	One of the data series is charted using a different chart type. For instance, the first three series are charted as a column chart, and the fourth series is charted as a line chart.

Begin Guided Tour   Make a Chart

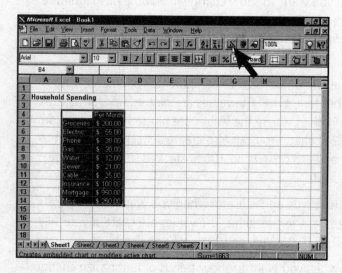

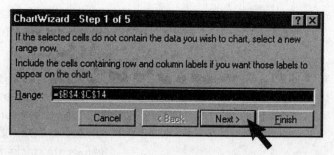

3 When you release the mouse button, you see the ChartWizard - Step 1 of 5 box. Here you are prompted to confirm the selected range. If the right range is selected, click the **Next** button. Or select a different range and then click **Next**.

1 Select the range that you want to chart. (Keep in mind that the type of data you select effects how your chart appears.) If you want to insert the chart on this worksheet, click the **ChartWizard** button. To insert the chart on a new sheet, select the **Insert Chart** command. Then select **As New Sheet**. If you inserted the chart as a new sheet, skip to step 3.

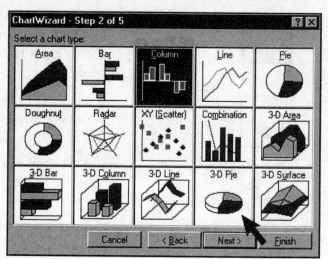

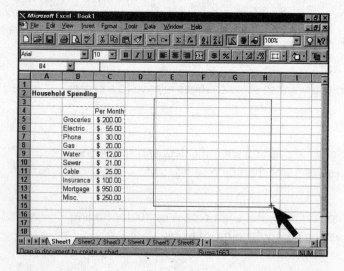

4 You see the ChartWizard - Step 2 of 5 box, which displays a selection of chart types. Click on the chart type you want to use and then click **Next**.

2 The mouse pointer looks like a cross with a little chart beneath it. In the worksheet, drag across a blank area to tell Excel where to place the chart.

Guided Tour   Make a Chart

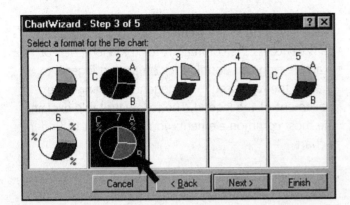

5 You see the ChartWizard - Step 3 of 5 box, which displays different styles or formats of the selected chart type. Click on a chart format and then click **Next**.

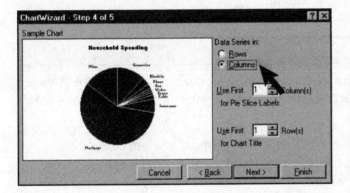

6 You see the ChartWizard - Step 4 of 5 box, which displays a preview of the chart. If necessary, make changes to how the data series is charted (in rows or in columns), select which row/column to use as the X-axis labels, and select which row/column to use for the legend. Click **Next**.

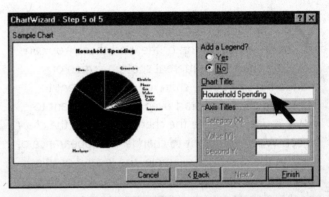

7 You see the ChartWizard - Step 5 of 5 box. For this step, select whether you want to include a legend. If you want a chart title, type the title in the Chart Title text box. Finally, type any axis titles you want to include in the Category and Value text boxes. Click **Finish**.

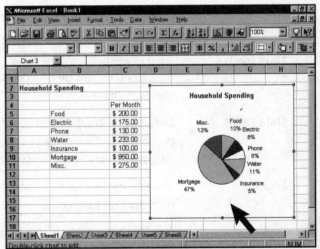

8 Excel creates the chart, here a pie chart.

Work with the Chart Object

You can think of the chart as an object—a Post-it note—stuck on top of the worksheet. You can move the chart to a different spot on-screen or change the size of the chart, or you may want to delete the chart and start over. When you want to move, resize, or delete the chart, you select the *chart object*. When you want to change the appearance of items in the chart (for example, the legend or titles), you need to open the chart for editing. Once you select the chart, you can access any of the chart commands and change any of the elements in the chart.

The elements in a chart vary depending on the chart type and the options you select. When you want to make a change to the element, you can double-click on it to access the commands for that element. For example, you can double-click on a chart legend to change the font used in the legend or change the placement of the legend. The following table explains the most common elements you can expect to find in a chart.

If you inserted the chart as a new sheet in the workbook, you can work on the chart by simply selecting the sheet tab named **Chart1**. (You can rename the sheet with a more descriptive name by double-clicking on the sheet tab, typing a new name, and pressing **Enter**.) The remaining parts of this section cover formatting.

Chart Element	Description
Data point	Each individual charted value. For example, if you chart product sales for three years, a data point would be one product's sale for one year. Think of a data point as one cell in the worksheet.
Data series	Data points are grouped together into a series. For example, you can chart one product's sale for three years as one series. In a worksheet, a series is either a row or column of data (you can select which).
Legend	The key to the chart. For some charts (such as a pie chart), the legend is often redundant and isn't included.
Axis	A 2-D chart is plotted along two axes: the Y-axis (vertical) and X-axis (horizontal). A 3-D chart has an X-, Y-, and Z-axis. The axes usually include tick marks and labels.
Plot area	The grid against which the chart is plotted. In a 3-D floor, the wall and floor provide the background for the charted data.
Title	You can include a chart title or titles for the X-axis or Y-axis.

Begin Guided Tour   Select the Chart Object

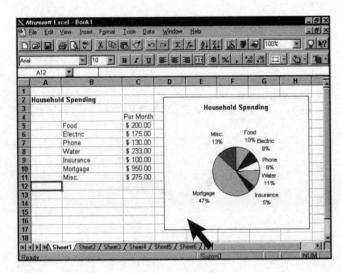

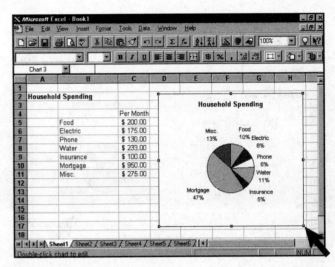

1 Point to the chart object and click once.

2 The chart object is selected. You see black selection handles around the border of the object.

Begin Guided Tour   Move a Chart

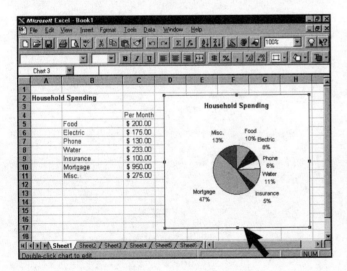

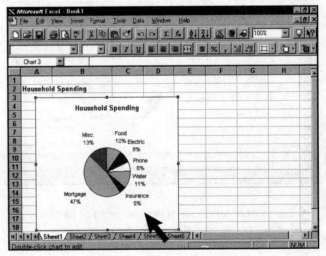

1 Click once on the chart to select it. Then drag the chart to a new location on the worksheet.

2 Release the mouse button and Excel moves the chart object.

Begin Guided Tour   Resize a Chart

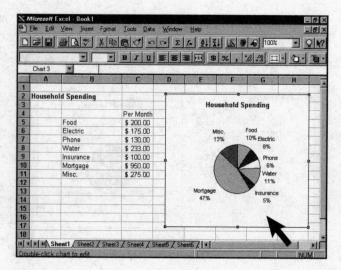

1 Click once on the chart to select it.

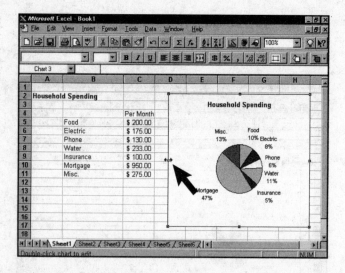

2 Put the pointer on one of the black selection handles. The mouse pointer should look like a two-headed arrow. While still holding the mouse button down, drag to resize the chart.

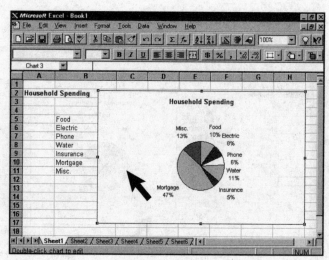

3 Excel resizes the chart.

Begin Guided Tour Delete a Chart

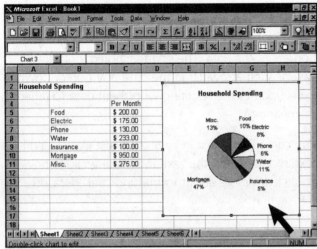

1 Click once on the chart to select it and press the **Delete** key.

2 Excel deletes the chart object.

Begin Guided Tour Select a Chart for Editing

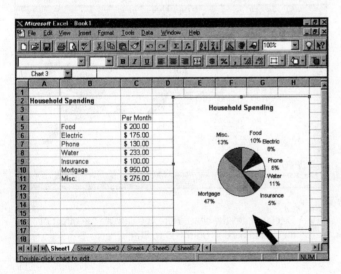

1 Double-click on the chart.

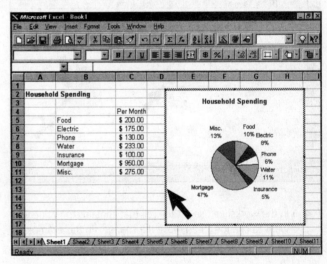

2 You should see a shaded border around the chart. Now, you're all set to edit the chart.

Edit the Chart Data

Just like you can change a value and update a formula automatically, you can change a charted value, and the chart automatically updates to reflect the new value. The chart and worksheet data are linked. (For more information on linking, see the "Use Data Together from Different Office Applications" section on page 345.) You can edit or delete data as necessary.

You can also do the reverse: change the chart and update the worksheet value. First, double-click on the chart to select it; then click on the data point you want to change. When you select a single data point on a chart, black selection handles appear along the borders of the area. The pointer should look like a two-headed arrow. Drag the data point up or down. Excel updates the resulting worksheet data to reflect the change.

You can edit the text in your chart just like you edit text in cells. Select the text and make your changes. You'll learn more about formatting chart data later in this section.

Begin Guided Tour   Update a Chart

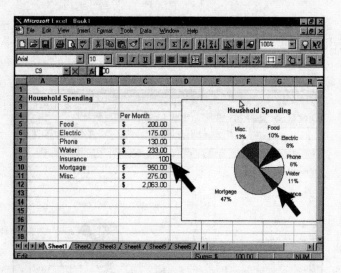

1 In the worksheet, select the cell that contains the value you want to change. Then make the change. (In this example, I'm changing 100 to 500.)

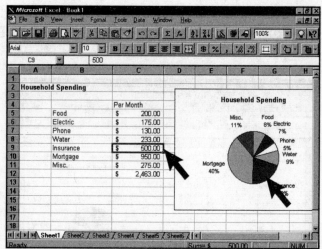

2 Excel updates the chart. Here you can see the effect of increasing a value from 100 to 500.

Change the Chart Type

When you first start working with the charting features of Excel, you may not really know which chart type works best for your data. When you create the chart, you select the one you think will do, but if that type doesn't seem to work, you can select another chart type—without recreating the chart.

The easiest way to change the chart type is to use the Chart toolbar. To display the Chart toolbar, move your mouse pointer over a blank area on any of the Excel toolbars and right-click to open a toolbar menu listing the various toolbars available. Select the Chart toolbar, and a floating Chart toolbar appears on your screen. The Guided Tour covers how to change the chart type using the toolbar.

The toolbar displays only the most common chart formats. If you want to select from the entire palette of chart types, you need to use a command to change the chart type. Follow these steps:

1. Double-click on the chart.

2. Open the **Format** menu and select the **Chart Type** command.

3. You see the Chart Type dialog box. Select a chart dimension: 2-D or 3-D.

4. Excel displays the available chart choices. Click on the chart type you want. Then click **OK**.

Begin Guided Tour Change the Chart Type

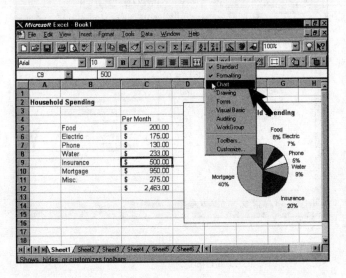

1 Move your mouse pointer over a blank area on a toolbar and right-click. This displays a menu of available toolbars.

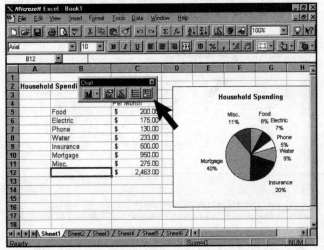

2 Select the **Chart toolbar**, and the Chart toolbar appears on your screen.

(continues)

Guided Tour Change the Chart Type

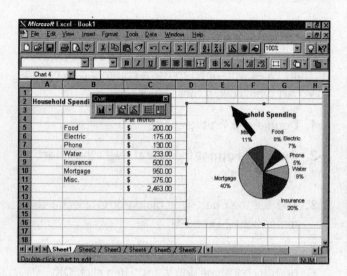

3 When you're ready to change the chart type, click once on the chart to select it. Black handles appear around the chart.

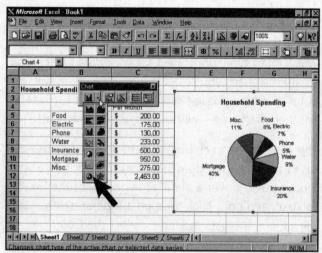

5 You see a drop-down list of chart types. Click on the new chart type you want.

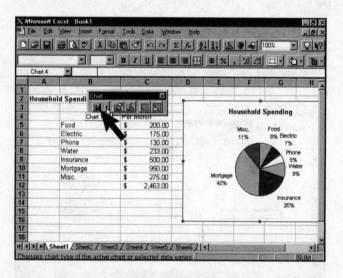

4 Click on the drop-down arrow next to the **Chart Type** button on the floating Chart toolbar.

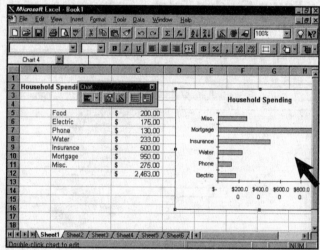

6 Excel changes the chart type. In this figure, the pie chart changed to a bar chart.

Format Chart Series

Excel groups each set of data points into a series, which will appear in the chart with a predefined pattern. For instance, if you chart quarterly sales by division, division 1 sales are one series, division 2 are another series, and so on.

By default, Excel assigns a certain pattern and color to each series and a certain width between each series. Excel charts the series in the order they appear in the worksheet. You can make changes to any of these series options. For example, if you don't like the color used, you can select a different color or pattern. Or you may want to rearrange the series so the series appears from smallest to largest. Finally, you may want to add more or less space between each series. You can easily make these changes.

When you make any change to a chart, make sure to select the right element. You can recognize the selected element by looking for the black boxes on or around the selected object. For series, select the entire series (not just one point), and click once on the series to select it. Then open the **Format** menu and select the **Selected Series** command.

The chart includes a lot of information that explains the meaning of the numbers. The Y-axis usually displays the values, so you can see what each charted point represents numerically. The X-axis usually displays the category or series names so that you know what the values represent, and the legend gives you the color pattern code for each data point in the series.

In addition to these elements that Excel includes by default, you may choose to include additional explanatory text. For example, you may want to add text to each series to show its value or overall percentage. Pie charts often include the percentages and label names to identify the pie slices rather than using a legend. The Guided Tour also explains how to add labels to series.

Begin Guided Tour   Change the Series Pattern

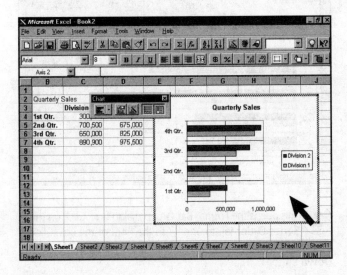

1 Double-click on the chart. Then double-click the series you want to edit.

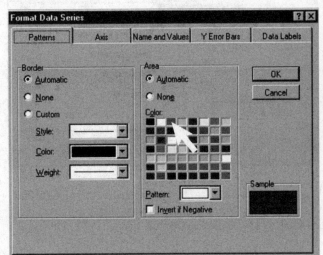

2 You see the Patterns tab of the Format Data Series dialog box. Click on the color you want to use. Then click on the down arrow next to the Pattern list; click on the pattern you want to use.

(continues)

Guided Tour   Change the Series Pattern

(continued)

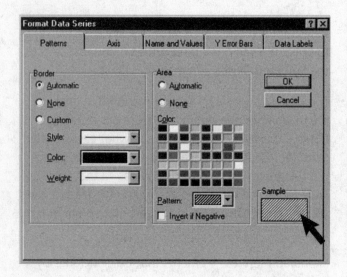

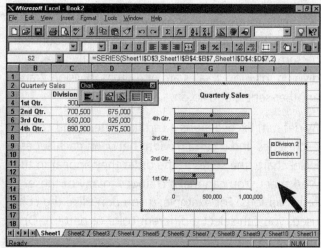

3 Excel displays a sample of the new color and pattern in the dialog box. Click **OK**.

4 Excel formats the selected series with the new color and pattern.

Begin Guided Tour   Rearrange the Series

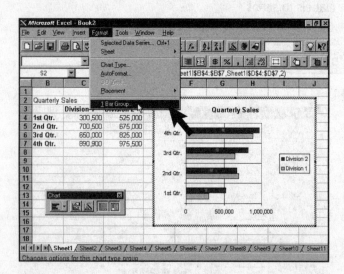

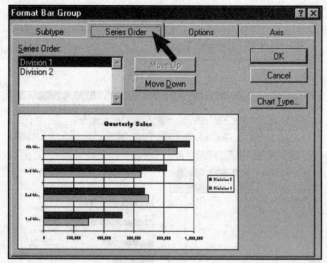

1 Double-click on the chart to edit it. Then open the **Format** menu and select the **1** *Bar* **Group** command. The word in italic will vary depending on the chart type.

2 This opens the Format Bar Group dialog box. Click on the **Series Order** tab to bring it to the front of the box. Click on the series you want to move; click the **Move Up** or **Move Down** buttons.

Guided Tour   Rearrange the Series

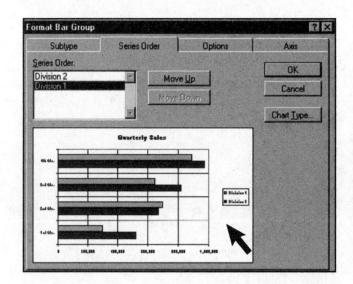

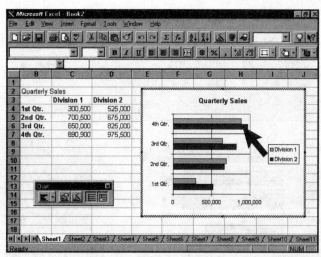

3 You see a sample of the chart using the new series order. Click **OK**.

4 Excel rearranges the series.

Begin Guided Tour   Overlap Series and Change the Gap Width

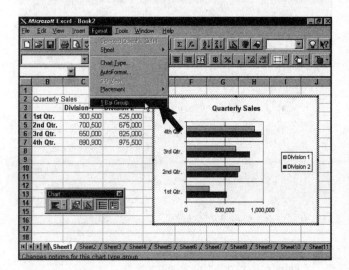

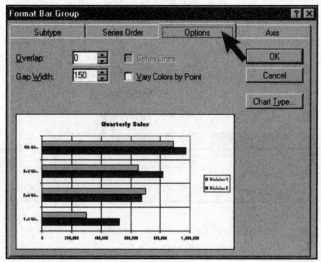

1 Double-click on the chart to edit it. Then open the **Format** menu and select the **1 *Bar* Group** command. The word in italic will vary depending on the chart type.

2 This displays the Format Bar Group dialog box. Click the **Options** tab to bring it to the front. If you want to overlap the series, type a value in the **Overlap** text box. Or use the spin arrows to select a value.

If you want to change the width between the data series, click in the **Gap Width** text box and type a value. Or use the spin arrows to select a value.

(continues)

Guided Tour Overlap Series and Change the Gap Width

(continued)

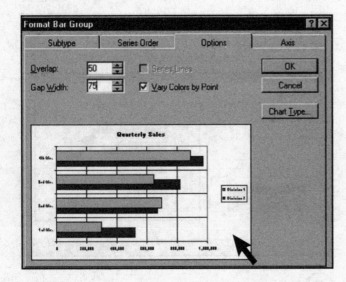

3 You see a sample of the chart using the new gap width and overlap. This example uses a 50 overlap and 75 gap width. Click **OK**. Excel formats the series accordingly.

Begin Guided Tour Add Series Labels

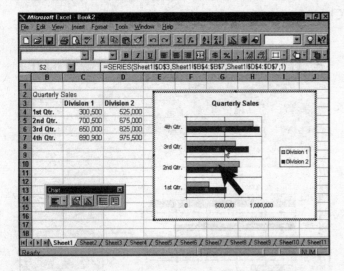

1 Double-click on the chart. Then double-click on the chart series you want to add labels to.

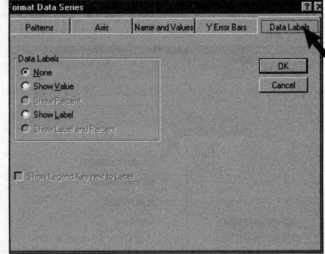

2 You see the Format Data Series dialog box. Click the **Data Labels** tab to bring it to the front.

3 Select what you want to show: value, percent, label, and percent. (Depending on the chart type, some of the options may not be available.) If you want to show a small legend key next to the values, check the **Show Legend Key next to Label** check box.

4 Click **OK** to exit the box, and Excel adds the labels to the selected series.

Add and Format Chart Titles

Without explanatory text, your reader won't know what the data in your chart represents. Quarterly sales? Yearly sales? Product sales? To explain the data as clearly as possible, you will most likely want to include a chart title.

The Y-axis (usually the value axis) will include the appropriate values, and the X-axis (usually the category axis) will include labels for the series. You can add additional titles. For example, you can include a title that says "in thousands" or "unit sales" along the Y-axis to clarify the meaning of the values. You can add a title that further explains your series or categories along the X-axis.

You can add these titles in the ChartWizard when you create the chart. If you forget to add them then, you can easily add them later.

You can also format the titles so they are attractive. For example, you may want to use a larger, more distinctive font. Or you may want to add a border around the title or change the alignment of the text. You can change these options using the Format Titles dialog box.

> If you open a menu and the chart commands are not available, it means that you have not selected the chart for editing. Double-click the chart first; then the commands should be available.

Begin Guided Tour   Add a Chart Title

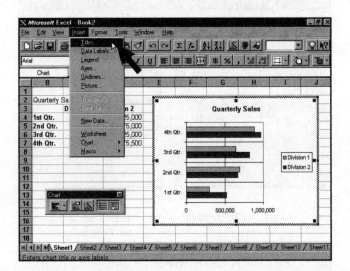

(1) Double-click on the chart. Then open the **Insert** menu and select the **Titles** command.

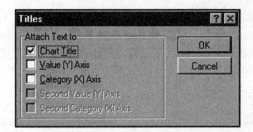

(2) You see the Titles dialog box. Check the kind of title you want displayed: Chart Title, Value (Y) Axis, Category X Axis. (Depending on the chart type, you may have more or fewer options for the axes.) Click **OK**.

(continues)

Guided Tour   Add a Chart Title   (continued)

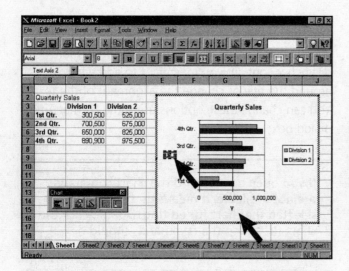

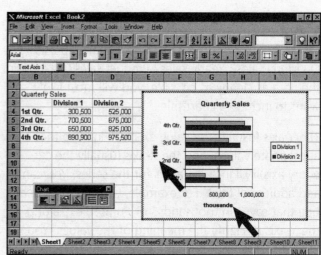

3 Excel adds a title and displays filler text. To fill in each title separately, click on the title and enter the appropriate text you want; then press **Enter**.

4 Excel adds the title to the chart.

Begin Guided Tour   Format a Title

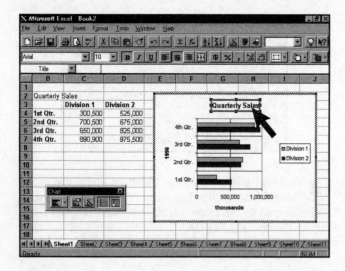

1 Double-click on the chart. Then double-click on the chart title you want to format.

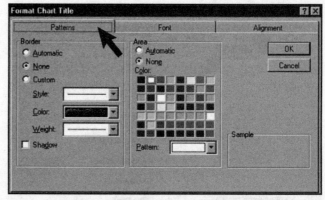

2 You see the **Patterns** tab of the Format Chart Title dialog box. To use a different border, click the **Custom** button and select a style from the **Style** drop-down list, a color from the color palette, and a weight from the **Weight** drop-down list. If you want to use a drop shadow, check the **Shadow** check box.

To use a different pattern, click on a color for the background from the color palette. Then display the **Pattern** palette and click on a pattern.

Guided Tour   Format a Title

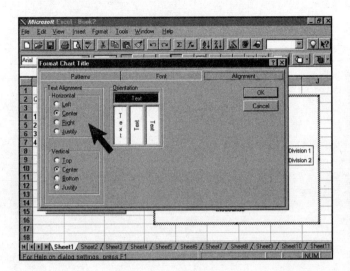

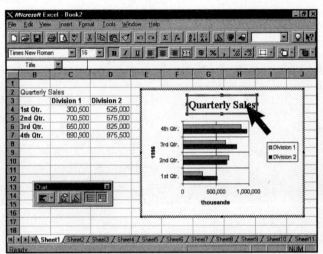

3 To change the alignment of the text, click on the **Alignment** tab and make your selections from the alignment options.

5 Click **OK** to exit the box, and Excel formats the title with the options you selected. Here the font changed to 16-point Times New Roman, bold.

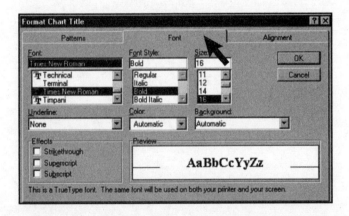

4 To make changes to the font, click the **Font** tab. Select the font, style, size, and color you want to use for the text.

HOW TO...

Create an Excel Database

n addition to keeping track of numerical data such as budgets or expenses, you can also use Excel to keep track of lists of data. You can use Excel as a simple data management program to store information about clients, products, sales, or other information. Excel provides many tools that make it easy to enter and work with the data in a list.

Once you create an Excel database, you can easily update it as necessary. For example, if you build a database containing names, addresses and phone numbers, it will probably require you to make changes as people move or change phone numbers.

What You Will Find in This Section

Create an Excel Database

To use any program to keep track of data, you need to have an understanding of the structure of a database. Basically, a *database* is a set of related information about a particular person, place, item, transaction, or event. For instance, you can keep a list of your clients with names, addresses, and phone information. Or you can keep your household inventory in an Excel database and include the item name, value, warranties, and so on in the list. One of the easiest databases to create is a Christmas card mailing list that contains all the names and addresses of people you send holiday cards to.

Excel stores each set of related information together in one worksheet. The categories of data you include are known as *fields*. For example, in a Christmas card database, you can have fields for the last name, first name, address, city, state, and ZIP code. You set up each field in a column and at the top of the column you include the name of the field.

One set of fields for one person or item in the database is a *record*. For example, if you have a relative named Jacob Cannon, the information (name, address, city, and so on) for this person forms one record. Excel stores each record as a row in the worksheet.

You don't have to do anything special to set up a database in Excel. Basically, you enter the field names in columns—one field name for each field you want to include. This row of field names is the *header row*

and enables Excel to separate the field names from the data.

Before you start typing away, spend some time thinking about the data you want to store and then plan your fields accordingly. For example, what fields do you need? Think about each individual piece of data you need to store and then set up fields for each. For example, you can put the address, city, and state all in one field, but then you couldn't sort by state. Instead, put each in a separate field.

Also, think about the best order to enter the data and use this order to structure the fields. For instance, think about entering a Christmas card list where the fields were in this order: City, ZIP, State, Phone, Last Name, First Name. Of course, another order would make more sense! If you are entering data from a hard copy list (an existing list you printed on paper), consider setting up the database to match the order used on the hard copy.

Finally, be sure to use unique names for each column. If you use the same name in more than one column, you will confuse Excel.

Format your headings so they stand out. You can make them bold, add a border, or add shading. Doing so separates the headings from the data.

Begin Guided Tour   Build a Database

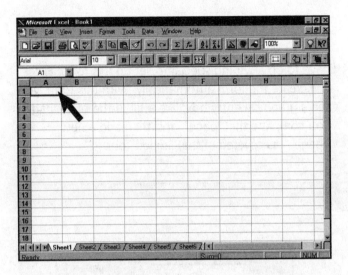

1 Start with a blank worksheet. You can include a database as part of another worksheet, but it's best to put the database on its own sheet.

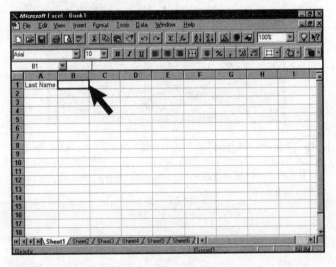

2 Type the first field name and press **Tab**. Excel enters the first field name and moves to the next column. Continue entering each field name you want to include.

3 You can format the headings so they stand out. You may also want to adjust the column widths, as necessary.

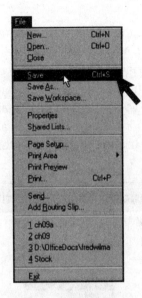

4 When you finish setting up the database, save the worksheet by opening the **File** menu and selecting the **Save** command.

Enter Data in an Excel Database

Remember: the Excel database is just a regular worksheet. You can select any cell you want and enter data or make changes. You can create formulas, make formatting changes, insert new rows, and so on. Therefore, you enter data in a database just like you do in a worksheet: select the cell and type the entry. You can use this method to enter your records.

If you prefer to concentrate on one record at a time, you can use Excel's *data form* to enter data. You don't have to do anything special to set up this form; Excel will create the form automatically. With this form, you see a graphical entry box, like a fill-in-the-blank page. You complete the "page" and then add a new "page," as covered in the Guided Tour.

Begin Guided Tour   Use the Data Form

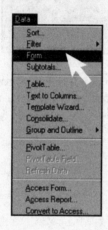

1 Open the **Data** menu and select the **Form** command.

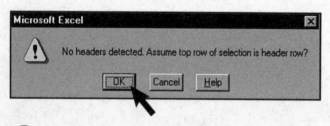

2 You may see a prompt asking whether the first row is the header row. Click **OK**.

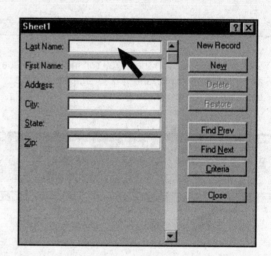

3 You see the data form on-screen. Type the entry for the first field and press **Tab**. You can type more information than the size of the field in the data form. As you type, the information scrolls to the left.

Guided Tour   Use the Data Form

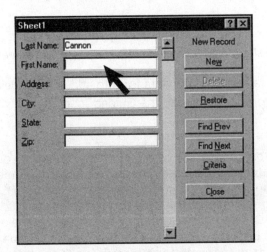

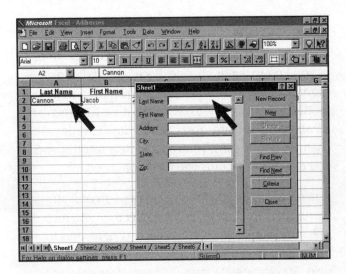

4 The insertion point moves to the next field. Type the entry for the next field and press **Tab**. Complete all the fields in the record.

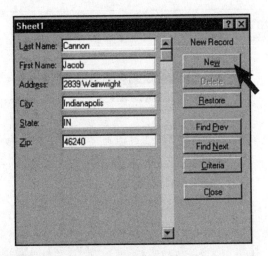

5 When the record is complete, click **New**.

6 Excel adds the record to the worksheet and displays a blank form. Continue completing and adding records until you've added the ones you want.

7 Click **Close** when you finish.

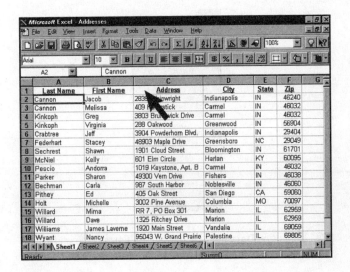

8 You see the records (rows) added to the worksheet.

Add, Edit, and Delete Records

If you are going to use the data in your database effectively, the information must be current. And, as you know, things change. Prices go up. People move. Companies discontinue products and add new products. Fortunately, Excel makes it easy to keep any database up-to-date. You can edit data to reflect any changes or mistakes, you can add new records, and you can delete records you no longer need.

Again, remember that the database is an ordinary worksheet. You can edit a field directly in the record row and field column. You can insert new rows to add a new record or insert new columns to add a new field. You can delete rows (and therefore delete the record). You can copy and paste similar data. All the

features you use when creating and entering a regular worksheet are available with a database worksheet.

You can also use the data form to add, edit, or delete a record, as covered in the Guided Tour.

> Excel keeps track of the number of records you enter in a database. The current record number and total record number appear in the upper right corner of the data form—for instance, 2 of 3. This information may help you find the record you want. You can also use the **Criteria** button to search for a record. See "Search the Database" on page 226.

Begin Guided Tour   Add a Record with the Data Form

1 Open the **Data** menu and select the **Form** command.

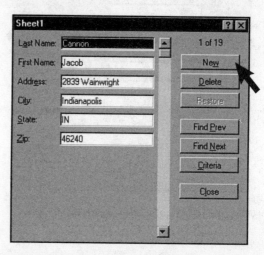

2 You see the first record in the database. Click the **New** button.

Guided Tour   Add a Record with the Data Form

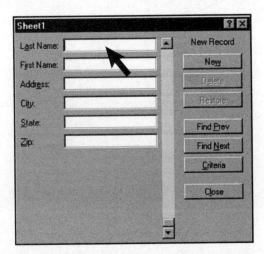

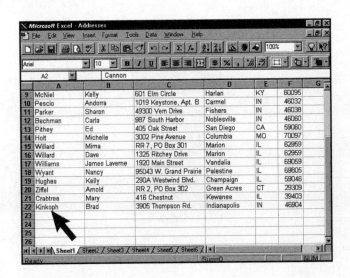

3 Excel displays a blank record. Complete the information for the new record.

5 Excel adds the new record(s) to the database at the end of the list.

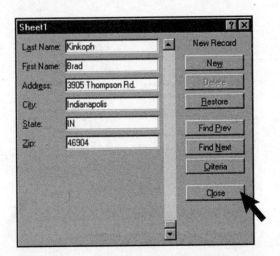

4 When the information is complete, click **New** to add another record, or click the **Close** button to close the dialog box.

Begin Guided Tour   Edit a Record

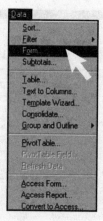

1 Open the **Data** menu and select the **Form** command.

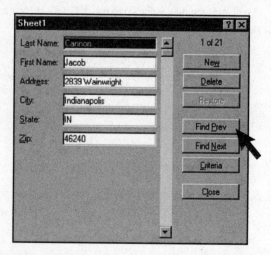

2 You see the first record in the database. Click on the scroll arrows to display the record you want to change. Or click on the **Find Prev** or **Find Next** buttons until the record you want appears.

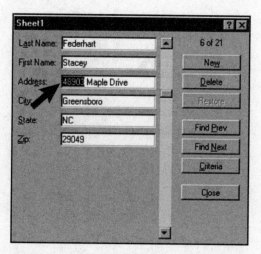

3 When the record you want appears, click in the field you want to change and make any changes.

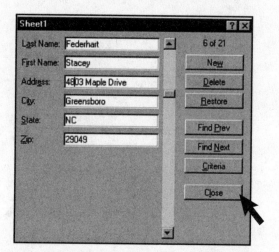

4 When the changes are complete, click **Close** to save the changes and close the data form.

Begin Guided Tour   Delete a Record

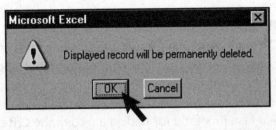

1 Open the **Data** menu and select the **Form** command. You see the first record in the database.

2 Use the scroll arrows or **Find** buttons until you display the record you want to delete.

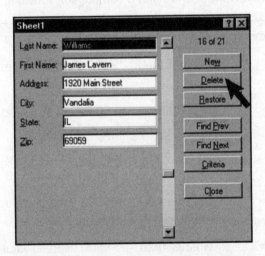

3 With the record displayed, click the **Delete** button.

4 Excel prompts you to confirm the deletion. Click **OK**. Excel deletes the record.

5 Click **Close** to close the data form.

Search the Database

As you continue to build your database, you'll add more and more records, possibly hundreds of records. When you are looking for information about a particular record, you can scan through the columns and rows until you see the one you want, or you can use a faster method for finding a record: the **Criteria** button.

With this button, you can quickly move to a record of interest. You can also use this command to search for and display a range of records. Clicking this button displays a form in which you enter the values you want to search for. These items are the *criteria*.

When you type the search criteria, you can type all or part of the value. For example, if you were searching for the name Wagner in your list and you weren't sure whether the client spelled the name Wagner or Waggoner, you could type **Wag** and search. When you type a value, Excel finds all entries that contain that value.

> If you want to display a certain group of re-cords at once, use the **Filter** command, covered later in this section.

If Excel can't find a match, you'll hear a beep, and Excel will return to the data form. Check your spelling. Rather than typing the entire value, type a partial value or use a comparison formula.

Use Comparison Formulas

In some cases, you may want to find a range of entries in a database. For example, suppose that you want to display all sales over $500. In this example, you don't want to search for a particular value. Instead, you want to find a range of values. To do this, you create a *comparison formula,* like the following:

>= 500

This formula tells Excel to find all records that have 500 or a greater value in the Sales field. You can use the following operators in a comparison formula:

Operator	Meaning	Example
>	Greater than	>500 (Find all values greater than 500)
<	Less than	<500 (Find all values less than 500)
=	Equal to	=500 (Find all values that are exactly 500)
<=	Less than or equal to	<=500 (Find all values that are 500 or less)
>=	Greater than or equal to	>=500 (Find all values that are 500 or more)
<>	Not	<>500 (Find all values that are not 500)

Begin Guided Tour   Search for a Particular Value

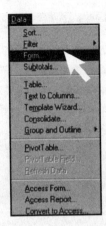

1 Open the **Data** menu and select the **Form** command.

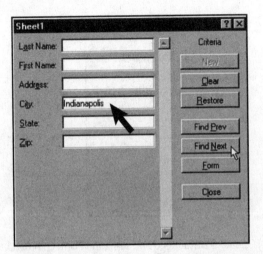

3 Excel displays a blank record on-screen. Here you enter the criteria you want to match. Click in the field on which you want to search. For instance, if you are searching for a city in an address database, click in the City field. Type the entry you want to find. You can type all or part of the entry. You can use more than one criteria in your search

4 After you complete the criteria, click the **Find Next** button.

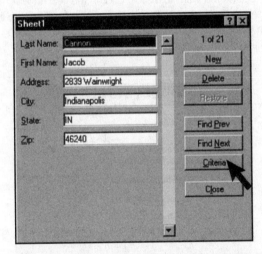

2 You see the first record in the database. Click the **Criteria** button.

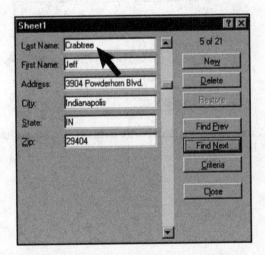

5 Excel displays the first matching record. Continue clicking the **Find Next** button until the record you want appears. Then click **Close**.

Begin Guided Tour   Search for a Range of Values

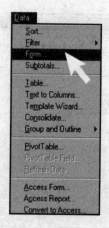

1 Open the **Data** menu and select the **Form** command.

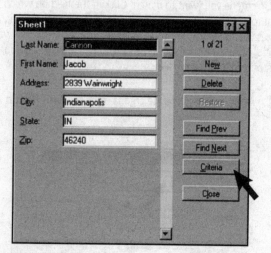

2 You see the first record in the database. Click the **Criteria** button.

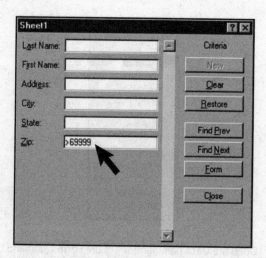

3 Excel displays a blank record on-screen. Here you enter the criteria you want to match. Click in the field on which you want search. For instance, if you are searching for ZIP codes in a certain range, click in the ZIP code field. Type the comparison formula using the operators in the table in the text.

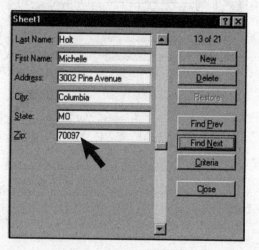

4 Click the **Find Next** button and Excel displays the first matching record. Continue clicking the **Find Next** button until the record you want appears. Then click **Close**.

Sort an Excel Database

One of the benefits of taking the time to enter all your data is you can easily manipulate the data. For example, if you had a paper copy of a data list, the list would be confined to one order: the order you used to enter the records. With Excel, you can select to arrange the database in different orders by *sorting*. For example, in an address database, you could sort by last name, by state, or by ZIP code.

You can do a simple sort on one field or you can sort by multiple fields. For example, you may want to sort by last name and then first name. Using the Sort dialog box, you can select up to three sort fields. You can also choose to sort in *ascending* or *descending* order. When you sort fields in ascending order, the data appears alphabetically or numerically in order from top to bottom in your list (1–100 or A–Z). With descending order, the opposite occurs. Excel's sorting feature is flexible and fast.

> You can also use the **Sort Ascending** or **Sort Descending** buttons in the toolbar to quickly sort on the current field.

Begin Guided Tour   Perform a Sort with the Sort Dialog Box

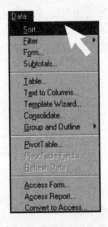

1 Open the **Data** menu and select the **Sort** command.

2 You see the Sort dialog box. If you select the **Header Row** option button, Excel uses the column headings as choices in the sort drop-down lists; Excel will not include this header row in the sort. If you don't have column headings, Excel will display the first value in the column in the drop-down list. In this case, click the **Header Row** option button so that Excel will not include the first row.

(continues)

Begin Guided Tour Perform a Sort with the Sort Dialog Box

(continued)

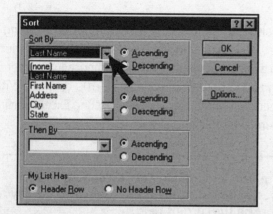

3 Display the **Sort By** drop-down list and click on the column name that you want to sort by first. For instance, if you were sorting by last names, you'd select **Last Name** from this list.

4 Click on **Ascending** or **Descending** order.

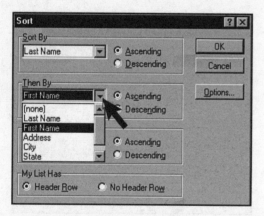

5 To sort on a second field, display the **Then By** drop-down list, click on the column, and then click on a sort order.

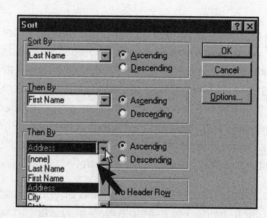

6 To sort on a third field, display the **Then By** drop-down list, click on the column, and then click on a sort order.

7 When you have selected all the sort fields, click **OK**.

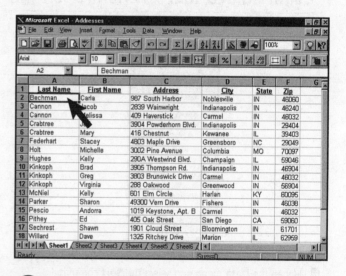

8 Excel sorts the database in the order you selected. In this example, the address database was sorted alphabetically by last names.

For a quick sort, use the sort buttons on the toolbar. You can sort by ascending or descending order.

How to Create and Edit a PowerPoint Presentation

f you need to make a presentation to an audience, utilize the presentation package included as part of Microsoft Office 95—*PowerPoint*. With this program, you can create and combine slides (similar to document pages) into a visual presentation to effectively communicate your message. With PowerPoint, you can also create overheads, audience handouts, and speaker notes that help convey your thoughts and ideas in a visual way.

For example, you may want to give an overview of sales performance to your sales department, or you may have been drafted to give a speech to your local civic organization. Perhaps you are giving a seminar and want to use a slide show. Using PowerPoint, you can create a visual presentation for any goal or purpose.

To start PowerPoint, click on **the** Start menu; select **Programs** and **Microsoft PowerPoint**.

This section covers how to create a presentation and includes the following topics. For information on formatting (changing the look of the presentation), see "Format and Print a PowerPoint Presentation" on page 253.

What You will Find in This Section

Create a New Presentation

When you start PowerPoint, you see the initial PowerPoint dialog box. From this dialog box, you can choose to create a new presentation using one of several methods, or you can open an existing presentation.

Before you start PowerPoint, you should spend some time thinking about the goal of the presentation you want to create. Do you want to inform the audience? Persuade the audience? Teach the audience? Sell something? Recommend some course of action or product? You need to determine what you intend to accomplish with the presentation.

Next, think about your audience and how you can reach the audience (prove your point, sell your product, whatever the goal). Think about the kind of information you will need to convey. Do you need simple text slides? Or do you need to convey some financial or other numerical data in the form of a graph? Do you need to show the organizational structure of the company? PowerPoint includes several different types of slides that you can select and add to your presentation. You'll be better pre-pared to work through the presentation if you first think about the types of slides you want to include.

Once you know the type of information you need to include, think about what data you need to create the slides. For example, if you want to graph the sales results for the last four years, you need to have that data available.

Finally, once you establish a goal and a plan to achieve the goal, start building the presentation. You can create a new presentation using one of three methods.

Here's a brief description of the three presentation options:

AutoContent Wizard   Leads you through the process of building a presentation by asking you pertinent questions about how you're going to use the presentation. Once AutoContent Wizard asks all the important questions, it formats your responses, turning them into a slide program outline in which you enter the specific text you want to present. If you want PowerPoint to do most of the work, this option is for you.

Template   Gives you a model slide on which to build a presentation. You enter the content, and PowerPoint plugs it into a predesigned format.

Blank Presentation   Enables you to create a presentation from scratch, designing and filling in your own information. This option is for those of you who boldly go where no presentation-planner has gone before, or for those of you who like to do things your own way.

Depending on which option you choose, PowerPoint will lead you through a variety of dialog boxes to create the presentation.

You can use data from the other Office pro-grams in your PowerPoint presentation. For example, if your numerical or financial data is stored in Excel, you don't have to enter the data twice. You can use your Excel data in a PowerPoint presentation. See the "Use Data Together from Different Office Applications" section on page [15TBD] for information on using other program data in a presentation.

Begin Guided Tour Start a Blank Presentation

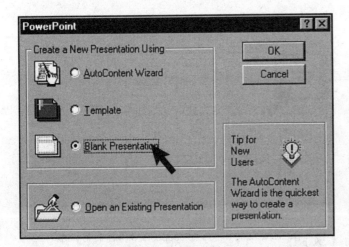

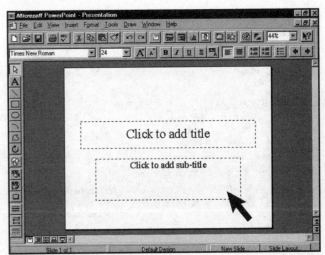

1 Start PowerPoint. You should see the PowerPoint dialog box on-screen. To build a presentation from scratch, select the **Blank Presentation** option and click **OK**.

3 PowerPoint creates the presentation and adds the first slide. You see text placeholders for a title and sub-title. You can then add text to the slide, as covered in the "Add Text to a Slide" task on page 238.

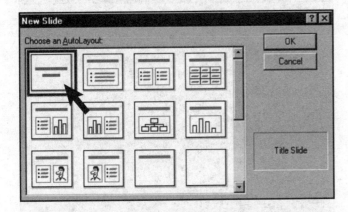

2 You see the New Slide dialog box. In this dialog box, you select the first slide you want to include in the presentation. Most presentations start with a title slide, which is the type that is selected. Click **OK**.

Begin Guided Tour Build a Presentation with the Template Option

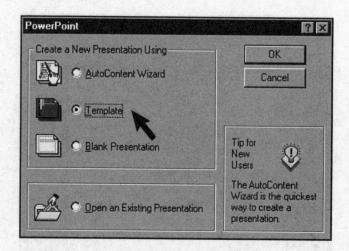

1 After you start PowerPoint, the PowerPoint dialog box appears. To base your presentation on a template (premade design), select the **Template** option and click **OK**.

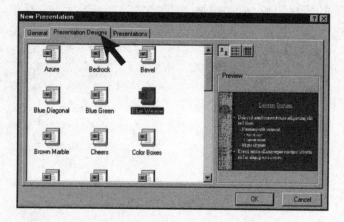

2 The New Presentation dialog box appears with three tabs. Each tab holds templates you can use to build your slide show. Select a template from the available choices; then look at the Preview area to see what the design will look like. To select the design, click **OK**.

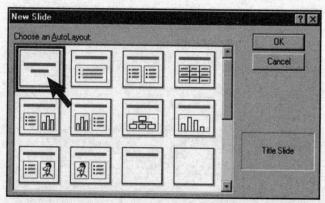

3 The New Slide dialog box appears. In this dialog box, you select the layout of the first slide you want to include in the presentation. Most presentations start with a title slide, which is the default layout selection. Click **OK**.

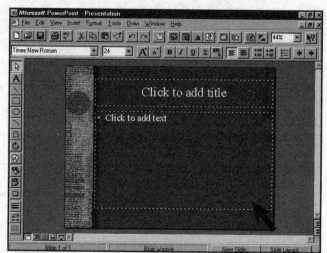

4 PowerPoint starts the presentation and adds the first slide. You see text placeholders for a title and subtitle. You can then fill in text, as covered in the "Add Text to a Slide" task on page 238.

Create a Presentation with AutoContent Wizard

With AutoContent Wizard, PowerPoint makes you tell it what your presentation topic is and what kind of presentation you want to create. In turn, it builds a presentation for you, complete with individual slides and a design. What you type into the slides becomes your presentation. How things look isn't really a priority with AutoContent Wizard; Microsoft designed it to help you organize your content.

When you select the **AutoContent Wizard** option button, a series of Wizard dialog boxes appear on your screen to lead you through the steps for building a slide show. The first box is merely introductory, but the other Wizard dialog boxes instruct you to fill in specific information. (You can always change the information you enter at a later time, so don't think your input is written in stone.)

AutoContent Wizard asks you what you're going to talk about in your presentation and what kind of

information you're going to display. If you're not too sure, you need to stop and sort out what exactly it is that you're presenting. You see, PowerPoint can only help you with the visuals; you'll have to come up with the actual content.

As part of AutoContent Wizard, you'll need to choose what kind of presentation you want to create. You can select a variety of types, such as strategy, training, reporting, and so on. If that's not enough types for you, then click the **Other** button (when applicable) and choose from the PowerPoint templates.

You'll also have the opportunity to choose a visual style and length for your presentation, as well as what type of presentation output you're creating. *Output* includes an on-screen slide show, overheads, or actual slides, and audience handouts. When you're done jumping through wizard dialog box hoops, your presentation appears on-screen and you can start filling in the content.

Begin Guided Tour   Use the AutoConnect Wizard

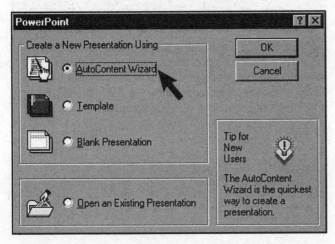

1 From the PowerPoint dialog box that appears when you first start PowerPoint, select the **AutoContent Wizard** option. Then click **OK**.

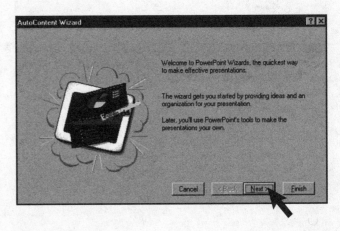

2 The first Wizard dialog box appears. Click the **Next** button to continue.

(continues)

Guided Tour Use the AutoConnect Wizard *(continued)*

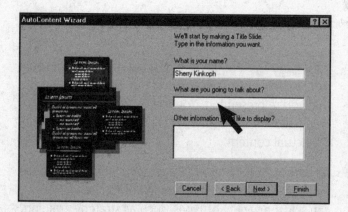

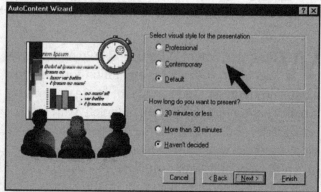

3 AutoContent Wizard prompts you to create a title slide. Type in your name (if you want it to appear in the first slide); then type in the topic you're going to present. In the final text box, you can add any additional information you'd like on the presentation slides. Click **Next** to continue.

5 In the next Wizard box, select a visual style for your presentation, and determine how long the presentation will be. After making your selections, click **Next**.

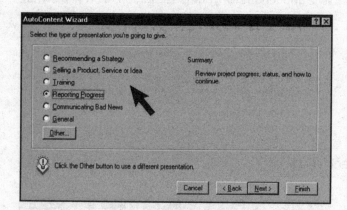

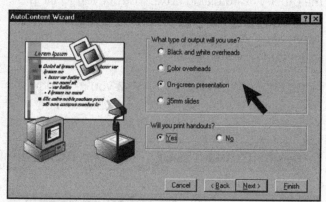

4 The next Wizard box lets you choose the type of presentation you want to give. Select an option from the list. (If you can't find a type listed that's suitable, click the **Other** button to choose from a longer list of presentation types.) Click the **Next** button to continue.

6 Choose the output you want your presentation to take. For example, if you're creating an on-screen slide show, select the **On-screen presentation** option. If you plan on using handouts based on your presentation, make sure you select **Yes** under the handout options. Click the **Next** button to continue.

Guided Tour   Use the AutoConnect Wizard

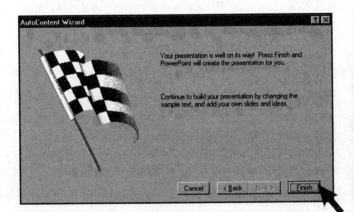

7 The final Wizard box instructs you on how to build your presentation. Click **Finish** to exit AutoContent Wizard.

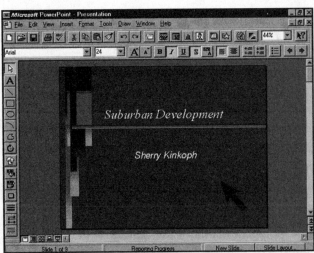

8 PowerPoint opens the presentation to the first slide. You see text placeholders for a title and subtitle. You can then fill in text, as covered in the next task.

If you change your mind about any of the selections you make in the wizard boxes, you can click the **Back** button to move back to the previous dialog boxes and make any changes.

Add Text to a Slide

When you add a new slide to a presentation, you'll see *placeholders* for text and/or objects. Two things determine what text PowerPoint includes on the slide and how that text appears.

The AutoLayout determines the number and placement of the text objects. For example, the title slide includes two text placeholders: one for a title and one for a subtitle. Different slide layouts include other areas for text; a bullet slide, for instance, includes a text area formatted with bullets.

The template sets the formatting for the master slide, and the *master slide* controls the typeface and alignment used for the text objects. Each template has a slide master that works in the background to control slide structure and design, such as background color or layout. This gives each slide in your presentation a

consistent look. You can make changes to the master slide or to the individual text objects. The next section covers formatting text.

To add text to any type of slide, you simply click the placeholder and type the new text. As you type, you can press **Enter** to insert a paragraph break. (If you are creating a bullet slide, pressing **Enter** ends the paragraph and inserts a new bullet.) For help on making editing changes, see the next task.

> You can use more than just the default text placeholders. You can use the **Text** tool to draw and add text to any spot on the slide.

Begin Guided Tour   Enter Text

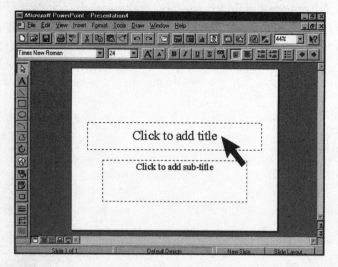

1 Click the text placeholder to select it.

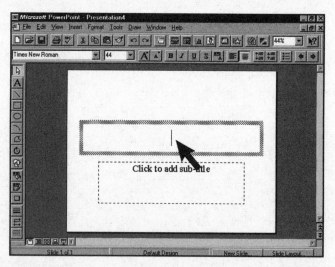

2 The filler text disappears, and the insertion point appears in the text box. Type the text.

Guided Tour   Enter Text

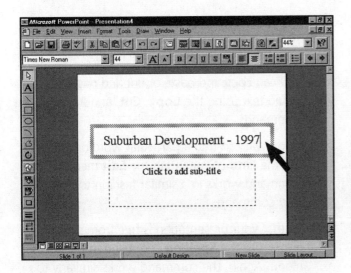

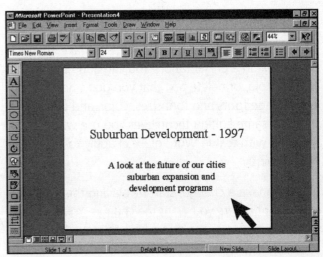

3 You see the new text in the text box. The font style and alignment of the text are determined by the master slide (preset format). Click the next text box and repeat step 2.

4 Fill in each text box on the slide. When you finish typing the text, click outside of the text box and PowerPoint displays the slide with all of your text added.

To add a new text block to the slide, click on the **Text** tool on the Drawing toolbar. Next, click inside the slide where you want the new block to go and start typing in the text.

Edit Text

Just like you can make changes to any type of electronic document, you can easily make changes to the text in a presentation. You can add new text, for example, or delete text that you don't need. You can change fonts and font sizes, color, and positioning. The same editing techniques you use when working with text in Word or Excel apply to PowerPoint:

- To make a change, start by placing the insertion point where you want the change. You can use the mouse or the arrow keys to move the insertion point.

- To delete text to the left of the insertion point, press **Backspace**. To delete text to the right of the insertion point, press **Del**. If you have a lot of text to delete, drag across the text to select it and then press **Del**.

- To add text, just start typing. PowerPoint moves the existing text over to make room.

- You can copy and paste or cut and paste selected text using the **Copy**, **Cut**, and **Paste** commands.

- If you want to find a particular word or phrase, use the **Find** command in the **Edit** menu. This command works in a similar fashion to Word's Find command.

- So that your presentation is free from spelling errors, use the **Spelling** command in the **Tools** menu. Again, the command works similarly to Word's spell check feature.

Begin Guided Tour   Make Changes to Slide Text

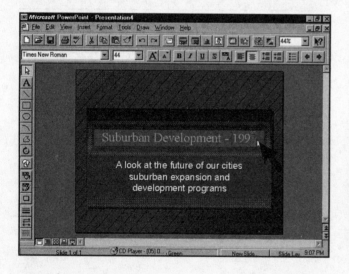

1 Click in the text box you want to edit. PowerPoint displays a shaded box around the text, indicating it is selected. The insertion point appears at the point in the text where you clicked. Move the insertion point to where you want to make the change and then make the change.

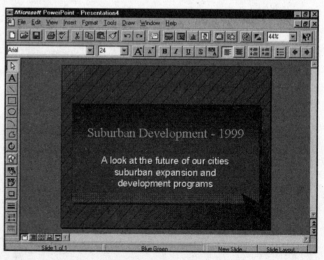

2 PowerPoint updates the text. Click outside the text box to complete the editing. PowerPoint updates the slide.

Add a Slide

When you create a new presentation, you start with one slide and add text or objects. Then you add another slide, add text or objects to that slide, add another slide, and so on until you have a collection of several slides. You can add slides any place in the presentation, and you can select from several layouts.

> If you've created a presentation with AutoContent Wizard, PowerPoint has already added slides for you complete with layouts. To move to the next slide, click the **Next Slide** button (the one with two downward pointing arrows) on the vertical scroll bar.

When you add a new slide, you are prompted to select a slide type from the dialog box. Rather than name the slide types, you see a visual representation of the slide type, called an *AutoLayout*. Nearly all of the slides have a slide title along the top of the slide. The "body" of the slide can be in a one- or two-column format and can include any of the following: bulleted list, graph, picture, text, or table.

From the selection, you pick the one that best matches the format you want, and PowerPoint then creates the slide, with the appropriate placeholders. You then replace the objects as described in other tasks in this section and the next section.

> Press **Ctrl+M** to insert a new slide. You can also use the **Insert New Slide** button in the toolbar, the **New Slide** button on the status bar, or the **New Slide** command in the **Insert** menu.

Begin Guided Tour   Insert a New Slide

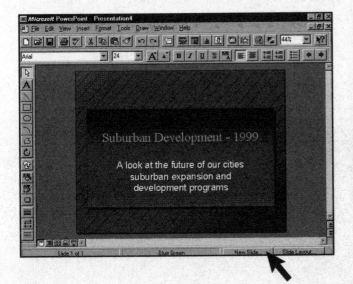

1 Click the **New Slide** button in the status bar.

2 PowerPoint displays the New Slide dialog box. Click on the slide type that you want to add. You can see additional layouts by clicking on the scroll arrows in the dialog box. Click **OK** to exit the dialog box.

3 PowerPoint adds the slide to the presentation. Replace the filler text with the text you want to include on the slide.

Create a Graph

In many cases, you will want to include visual elements such as graphs on your slide. For example, you may want to show a bar graph of quarterly sales, or you may want to include a line chart that shows the past years' sales performance. You may want to include a column chart that compares income to expenses. For these types of slides, you use the mini-application (called *Graph*) included with Office 95. (You can also use charts created in Excel, as covered in "Use Data Together from Different Office Applications," starting on page 345.)

To add a graph object, you simply select a slide AutoLayout that includes a graph in the location you want. You can then double-click the graph object to create and edit the graph.

To enter data using Graph, you use a *datasheet*, which is similar to a simple worksheet. The datasheet, like a worksheet, is a grid of rows and columns, and the intersection of a row and column is a *cell*. This datasheet appears with sample data when you double-click on the graph object the first time. You replace the sample column and row headings with the data you want to graph. You also replace the numerical data with the data appropriate for your graph.

To select a cell for editing, you can click on it or use the arrow keys (just like moving around in Excel). Type the new entry and press **Enter** to replace the current entry. If the graph you want to create includes more columns or headings than the sample data, simply enter the data in the appropriate row and column. If the graph contains less data, be sure to delete the sample data that isn't appropriate. To delete data, select the range (drag across the cells to highlight them) and press **Del**.

Once you add the graph to the slide, it is like any other slide object; you can move it around on the slide, resize it, make formatting changes, and so on. To edit the graph itself, though, you have to switch back to **Graph**. To do so, simply double-click on the graph. The graph should have a gray, lined border, and you should see Graph commands in the menus.

Once you select the graph for editing, you can display the datasheet and change the data to be graphed. Or you can use the **Format** menu to change the chart type or make other changes to the appearance of the graph. For example, PowerPoint uses a 3-D column chart for the graph. If this chart type isn't appropriate for your slide, you can select a different chart type. You can select, for instance, a line chart to show trends, or you may want to use a horizontal bar chart. (For more information on chart types, see the section on Excel charts, starting on page 197.)

You can also use the **Insert Microsoft Graph** command or button to insert a graph to an existing slide.

Begin Guided Tour Add a Graph Slide

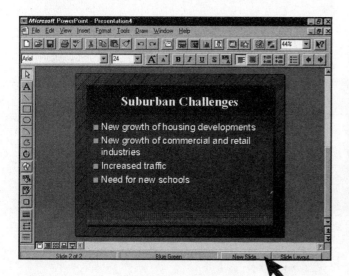

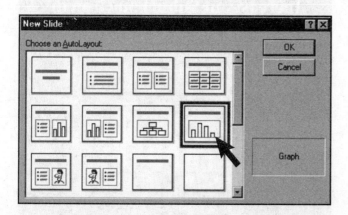

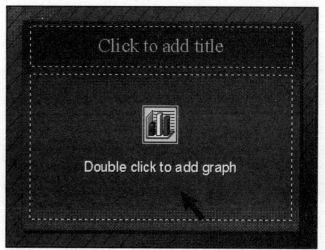

1 Move to the location in the presentation where you want to add the graph slide. PowerPoint adds new slides after the current one. Click the **New Slide** button.

2 PowerPoint displays the New Slide dialog box. Click on a layout that includes a graph as one of its objects.

3 PowerPoint adds the slide after the current one and displays placeholders. Here you see a placeholder for the slide title and one for the graph.

4 Replace any text placeholders with the text you want.

Begin Guided Tour   Create the Graph

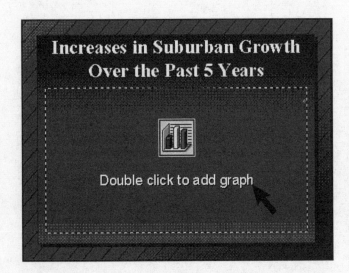

1 Double-click the graph object to start the Microsoft Graph feature.

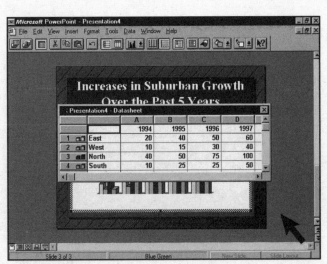

4 When the data is complete, click anywhere outside of the datasheet.

2 You see the datasheet on-screen with sample data. Click in the cell you want to replace.

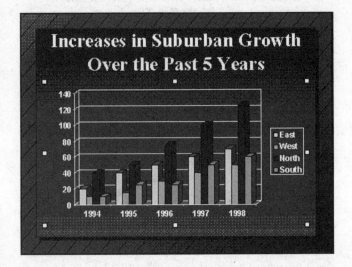

5 PowerPoint closes the datasheet and adds the graph object to the slide using the data you entered.

3 You should see a black rectangle around the current cell. Type the new entry and press **Enter**. PowerPoint moves to the next cell. Continue replacing the sample data with your data until the chart is complete.

Begin Guided Tour   Edit the Graph

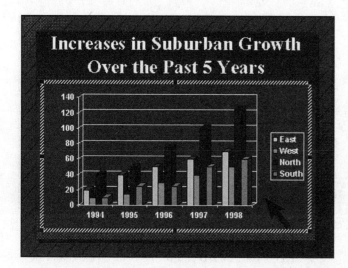

1 Double-click the graph object. You should see a gray selection border around the graph, indicating it is selected. (If you don't see this, the object isn't selected, and you won't be able to access the Graph commands.)

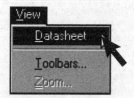

2 Then open the **View** menu and select the **Datasheet** command.

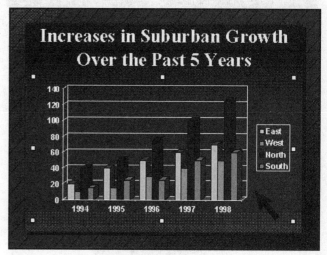

3 PowerPoint redisplays the datasheet you used to enter the data for the graph. Click in the cell you want to change and make the change. Do this for any of the entries you need to change or add. When you finish making changes, click back on the slide.

4 PowerPoint updates the slide.

Begin Guided Tour Change the Graph Type

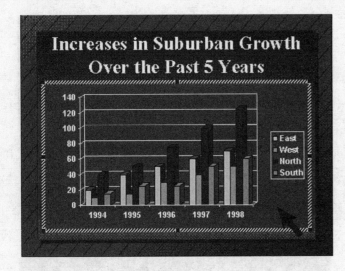

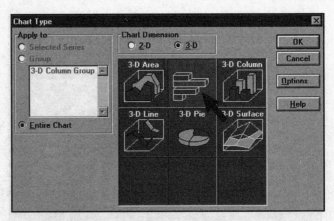

3 PowerPoint displays the Chart Type dialog box. Select the chart dimension: **2-D** or **3-D**. Then click on the chart type you want to use. Click **OK**.

1 Double-click the graph object. You should see a gray selection border around the graph, indicating it is selected. (If you don't see this, the object isn't selected, and you won't be able to access the Graph commands.)

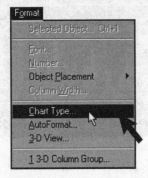

2 Open the **Format** menu and select the **Chart Type** command.

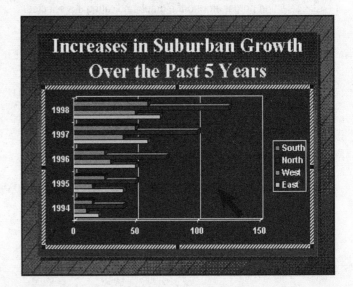

4 PowerPoint changes to the new chart type.

Create an Organization Chart

Another type of chart that you may want to include in a presentation is an organization chart. You can show the top-level managers in your company, or perhaps just show the organizational structure for one department. With an organization chart, you can show any type of hierarchy of people or ideas.

When you create an organization chart, PowerPoint uses a separate application called *Microsoft Organizational Chart*. Like other chart types, you select an **AutoLayout** with an organization chart object, double-click the object, and then replace the filler text with text that is appropriate for your presentation.

Keep the following tips in mind when creating or editing an organization chart:

- Use the **Styles** menu to select how you want the boxes in the organization chart arranged and connected. When you display this menu, you see a visual representation of different styles. Click on the one you want.

- Use the **Text** menu to change the font or alignment of the text in the text boxes.

- If you want to change the color, border, or line thickness of the boxes in the organization chart, use the commands in the **Boxes** menu.

- To add a box, click on the appropriate toolbar button (subordinate, coworker, manager, or assistant). Type the name and position for the new box.

Begin Guided Tour   Insert an Organizational Chart

1 Move to the location in the presentation where you want to add the organization chart. PowerPoint adds new slides after the current one. Click the **New Slide** button.

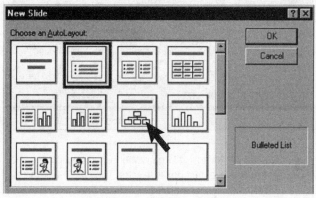

2 PowerPoint displays the New Slide dialog box. Click on a layout that includes an organization chart as one of its objects.

(continues)

Guided Tour   Insert an Organizational Chart   *(continued)*

3 PowerPoint adds the slide after the current one and displays placeholders. To create the organization chart, double-click on the org chart object.

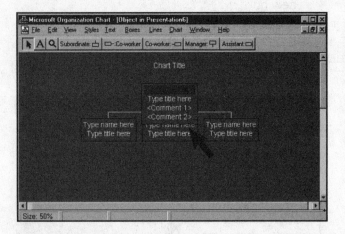

4 You see the Microsoft Organization Chart application. The first or top-level text box is selected. Type the name, press **Enter**, and then type the title.

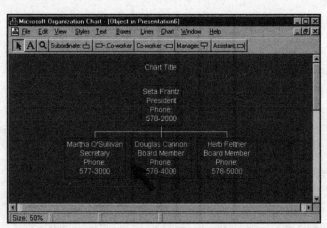

5 Click on the next text box. Type the name, press **Enter**, and then type the title. Do this for each text box included in the organization chart.

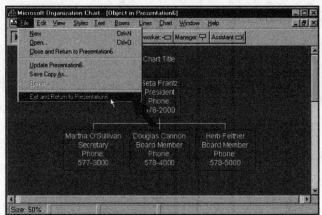

6 When you complete the data for the org chart, open the **File** menu and select **Exit and Return to Presentation**. (Depending on whether you've named the file yet, your Exit command may list the actual name of the file rather then the default name.)

Guided Tour Insert an Organizational Chart

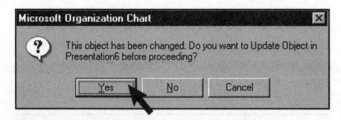

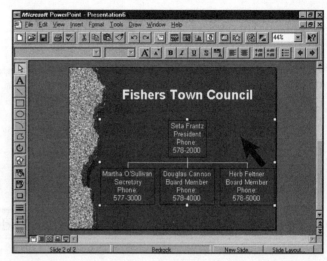

7 Click on the **Yes** button.

8 PowerPoint adds the organization chart to the slide.

Move Around in Slide View

PowerPoint displays only one slide at a time in Slide View (the view you use to create each slide). When you want to make an editing or formatting change, you first display the slide you want to work on. You can move from one slide to the next using the vertical scroll arrows.

If you click the arrow once, you move one slide in that direction. You can also drag the scroll box. As you

drag, you see a pop-up box next to the scroll bar indicating the current slide. Drag until you see the slide number you want; then release the mouse button. PowerPoint displays that slide.

> Press **PgDn** to move to the next slide. Press **PgUp** to move to the previous slide.

Begin Guided Tour   Move Between Slides

Click the **Next Slide** button to display the next slide in the presentation.

Click the **Previous Slide** button to display the previous slide in the presentation.

Use the Slide Sorter

Y ou mostly work on one slide at a time when you are first building the presentation. This view, called *Slide View*, is the default view for PowerPoint. You can also change to other views. For example, to check and make changes to the order of the slides in a presentation, you can use **Slide Sorter View**.

In Slide Sorter View, you can make changes to the overall presentation. For example, you may prefer a different order for the slides, or you may want to delete a slide you no longer need or that doesn't seem to fit.

Note that you don't have to be in Slide Sorter View to delete a slide. You can also delete a slide from **Slide View**. Open the **Edit** menu and select the **Delete Slide** command. PowerPoint deletes the slide.

Begin Guided Tour   Change to Slide Sorter View

1 From **Slide View**, click the **Slide Sorter View** button in the status bar.

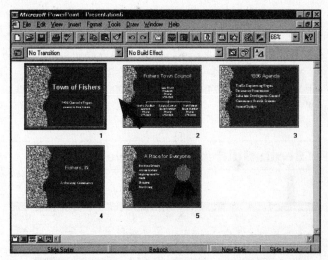

2 PowerPoint displays a small *thumbnail* (miniature slide) of each slide. The slides are numbered, and the current slide has a black box around it. You can use the scroll arrows to scroll through all the slides in the presentation.

Begin Guided Tour Rearrange Slides

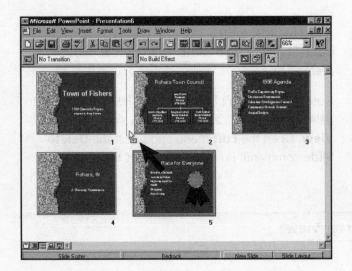

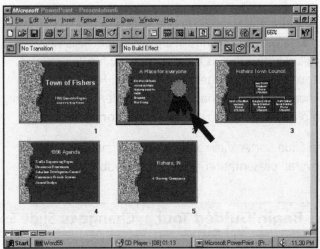

1 Click on the slide you want to move. You should see a black box around the selected slide. Hold down the mouse button and drag the slide to the new location. As you drag, you see a line and small slide icon indicating where the current slide will appear. In this example, the slide will appear in between slides 1 and 2.

2 When you release the mouse button, PowerPoint rearranges the slides in the presentation.

Begin Guided Tour Delete Slides

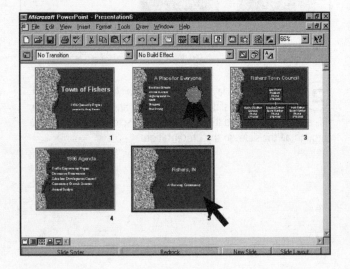

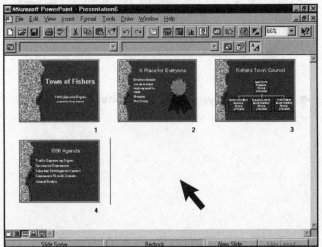

1 Click on the slide you want to delete. You should see a black box around the selected slide. Press the **Delete** key.

2 PowerPoint deletes the slide.

HOW TO...

Format and Print a PowerPoint Presentation

Part of the process of creating any document is getting the content right. The content conveys the message to the reader or audience of the document. If content is half of document creation, then formatting is the second half. *Formatting* is changing the appearance so the reader can more easily understand the message.

After you create a PowerPoint presentation, you can spend some time improving the look of the presentation. For example, you can change the font of selected text, change the color scheme, apply a template, and much more. Look to this part for help on adding the finishing touches to your presentation.

What You Will Find in This Section

Change the Look of Text

When you add text to a slide, the *master slide* you are using determines the style, size, and alignment of the text. The master slide is the underlying settings for the design and default formatting of the slide. PowerPoint selects readable, well-placed text so that you don't have to spend so much time making changes. However, if you don't like the selected font, you can always make changes.

The fastest way to change the font, font size, and font styles is to use the toolbar. (For more information on fonts, see "Change the Font and Font Size" on page 110 under the Word coverage.)

Consider the following other ways to make formatting changes:

- You can combine the font styles (bold, italic, underline, and shadow), but don't overdo it!

- If you like keyboard shortcuts, try the following: Press **Ctrl+B** for bold, **Ctrl+I** for italic, **Ctrl+U** for underline.

- To make selected text larger or smaller, use the **Increase Font Size** and **Decrease Font Size** buttons in the toolbar.

- If you want to make several changes at once, use the **Font** command in the **Format** menu. When you select this command, you see the Font dialog box, where you can select the font, size, style, and any special effects all at once.

- If you want more control over the type and color of the text shadow, use the **Shadow** command in the **Format** menu. From the dialog box that appears, select a color and offset; then click **OK**.

Begin Guided Tour   Change the Font and Font Size

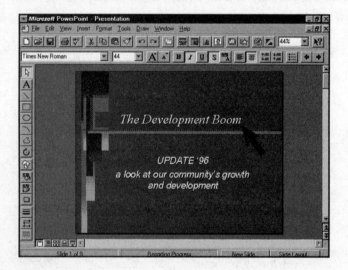

1 Move to the slide that contains the text you want to change. Select the text you want to change. If you select the entire text box, you should see a gray border and selection handles around the text box, as shown in this figure. If you select just some of the text, the text will appear highlighted.

2 Click the down arrow next to the **Font** list box in the toolbar. You see a drop-down list of font selections. You can use the scroll arrows to scroll through the list until you see the one you want. Click on the font you want.

Guided Tour Change the Font and Font Size

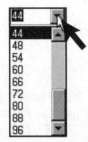

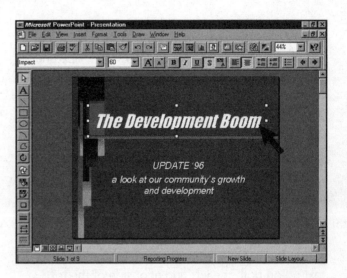

3 If you want to adjust the size of the font, click the down arrow next to the **Font Size** box in the toolbar. You see a list of font sizes. Click on the font size you want.

4 PowerPoint formats the selected text. Click outside the text box to deselect it.

Begin Guided Tour Change Text to Bold, Italic, Underline, or Shadow

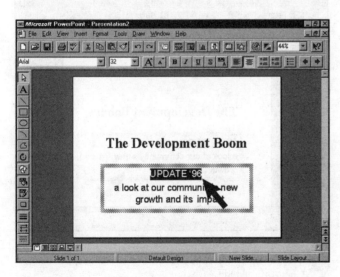

1 Select the text you want to change. You can select the entire text box or just part of the text.

2 Then click the **Bold** (it looks like a capital **B**), **Italic** (it looks like a capital **I**), **Underline** (it looks like a capital **U**), or **Text Shadow** (it looks like a capital **S**) button in the toolbar.

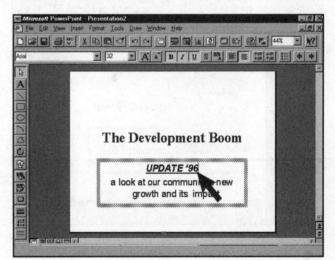

3 PowerPoint formats the selected text.

Change the Alignment of Text

Where the text appears within the text box or alignment depends on the master slide and the AutoLayout you select. Just like most other options, if you don't like the placement of the text, you can change the alignment. You can choose left, center, right, or justified (aligned on both sides).

Alignment controls where the text appears within a text block. For example, *left alignment* lines up the words on the left side of the text block. *Right alignment* lines up all the words on the right side of the text block, and center alignment centers the words within the text block. *Justified alignment* lines your text up on both the left and right side of the text

block, and spreads out the words and characters to stretch between.

Only left-alignment and center have buttons on the toolbar. To select right or justified, you have to use a menu command. Open the **Format** menu and choose **Alignment**. This opens a submenu where you can choose from all four alignment controls.

Note: Keep in mind that you can also move the text object around on the slide. For example, you may want to put the subtitle before the title. For help on moving an object, see "Move and Resize an Object" on page 260.

Begin Guided Tour Set a New Alignment

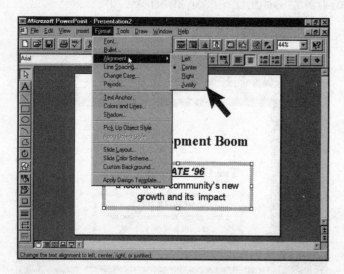

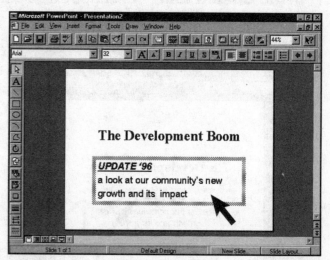

1 Put the insertion point in the paragraph you want to change. Then click the **Center Alignment** button to center text, or click the **Left Alignment** button to left-align text.

Or

Open the **Format** menu, choose the **Alignment** command, and choose the alignment you want from the submenu.

2 PowerPoint makes the change. In this example, the text is now left-aligned.

Draw on a Slide

Along the left edge of the Slide View window, you see the Drawing toolbar, which includes a collection of drawing tools. You can use these tools to draw objects on the slide. For example, you may want to add another text box, or you may want to create a logo using the available shapes. The following table identifies and explains how to use each tool.

If you don't get the object in the right spot or the right size, you can move and resize it. You can also delete it and start over. See "Move and Resize Objects" on page 260 for help on working with slide objects.

Tool	Name	Description
	Selection Tool	Enables you to select an object so that you can move, delete, resize, or format it.
	Text Tool	Use this button to draw a text box on-screen. After you drag to draw the text box, type the text within the box.
	Line Tool	Use this button to draw a line. To draw a straight line, hold down the **Shift** key as you drag.
	Rectangle Tool	Use this tool to draw a rectangle. To draw a perfect square, hold down the **Shift** key as you draw.
	Ellipse Tool	Use this tool to draw a circle or oval. Press the **Shift** key as you drag to draw a circle.
	Arc Tool	Use this tool to draw curved lines (an arc).
	Freeform Tool	Draws as if you were dragging a pencil on the screen. Click to start the drawing and then drag. To draw a polygon with this tool, click where you want to place the first point. Point to where you want the next point and click. Continue doing this until you get the shape you want. Click next to the first point to finish the polygon.
	Free Rotate Tool	Use this tool to rotate an object.
	AutoShapes	Click this button to display a palette of autoshapes. Click on the shape you want and then drag on the slide to draw the shape.
	Fill Color	Click this button to fill the selected object with the default fill (a color or pattern).
	Line Color	Click this button to change the color of the selected line.

(continues)

Tool	Name	Description
	Shadow On/Off	Click this button to apply a shadow to the selected object.
	Line Style	Click this button to change line styles.
	Arrowheads	Use this tool to add arrowheads to the ends of lines.
	Dashed Lines	Use this tool to set dashed lines in your slide.

Begin Guided Tour   Use the Drawing Tools

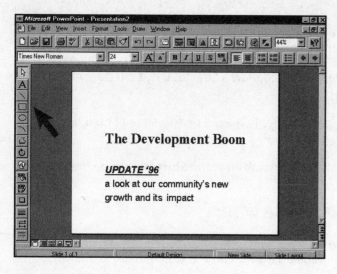

1 Display the slide you want to add the object to, and click on the tool that you want to use.

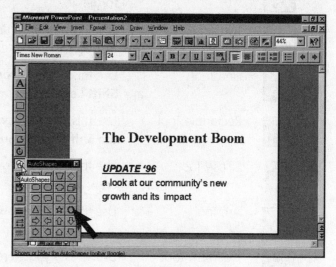

2 If you select AutoShapes, you see the AutoShapes toolbar. Click on the shape you want to draw. If you select a tool other than Autoshapes, skip to step 3.

Guided Tour   Use the Drawing Tools

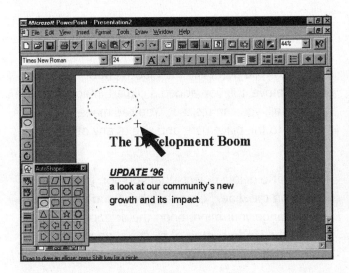

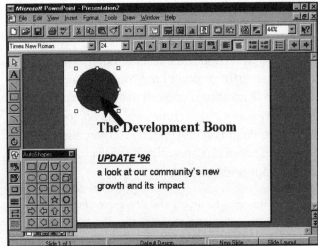

3 Move the pointer into the slide area. The pointer appears as a small crosshair. Hold down the mouse button and drag to draw the shape.

4 Let go of the mouse button and PowerPoint adds the shape to the slide.

To close the AutoShapes toolbar, click on its **Close (X)** button.

Add Clip Art Graphics

If you are worried about using the drawing tools and combining the various shapes until you get some kind of recognizable picture, don't. If you aren't much of an artist or don't have the time to create your own illustrations, you can use *clip art* (predrawn art). Many applications come with clip art these days, and PowerPoint is no exception. You can also purchase additional clip art and add these images to any slide in your presentation.

When you select to insert clip art, PowerPoint starts the ClipArt Gallery and displays the clip art in the gallery. You simply select the image you want to add.

Move and Resize Objects

As mentioned previously, a slide is actually made up of different objects. You can have a text object, a drawn object, a clip art object, a graph object, and so

on. You can think of each object as a cut and pasted item that you can easily move around on the slide. For example, if you don't like the placement of the title, you can move it. If you added a clip art image and it is too small, you can resize it. You can make any changes to the placement and size of any of the objects.

You can also delete objects that you don't want to include on the slide. Select the object and press **Del**. If you change your mind, undo the deletion by clicking the **Undo** button or by choosing the **Undo** command in the **Edit** menu.

PowerPoint gives you great flexibility in the ability to move and resize objects. Simply select the object you want to work with, regardless of whether it's a text block or a piece of clip art; then you can move it around the slide or resize it. To move it, you drag it to a new location on the slide. To resize the selected object, you must drag on one of the object's handles, depending on what size or direction you want it to go.

Begin Guided Tour Insert Clip Art

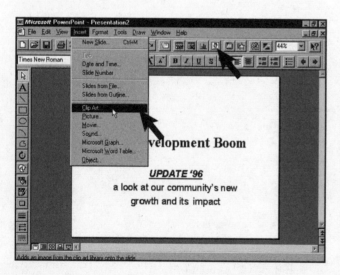

1 Display the slide to which you want to add the clip art. Then open the **Insert** menu and select the **Clip Art** command; or click the **Insert Clip Art** button in the toolbar.

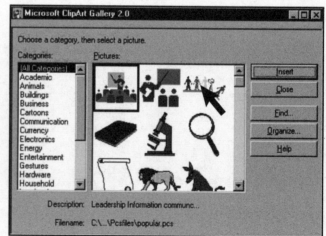

2 You see the Microsoft ClipArt Gallery dialog box. This dialog box displays all the available clip art images in the ClipArt gallery. Click on the scroll arrows until you see the image you want to add. Then click on the image.

Guided Tour — Insert Clip Art

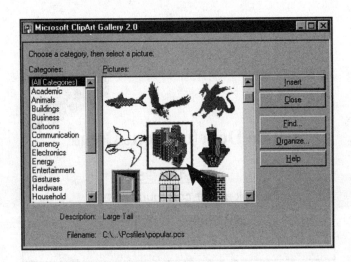

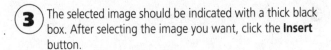

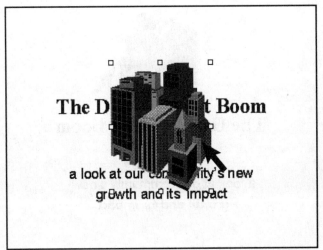

3 The selected image should be indicated with a thick black box. After selecting the image you want, click the **Insert** button.

4 PowerPoint adds the object to the slide. You can move and resize the object, as needed. In this example, the art needs to be moved and resized to fit on the slide. See the next task for instructions.

Begin Guided Tour — Resize an Object

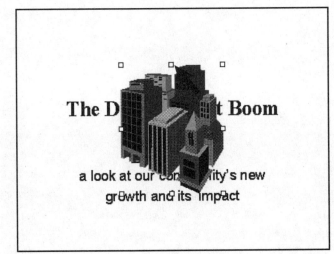

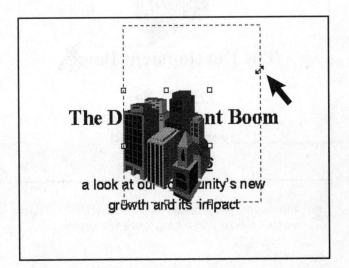

1 Click the object once to select it. Selection handles (little squares) surround the object.

2 Put the mouse pointer on a selection handle (the handles around an object allow you to resize the object). The pointer should look like a two-headed arrow. Drag the object to resize. PowerPoint makes the adjustment to the size.

Begin Guided Tour Move an Object

(1) Click the object once to select it. You should see selection handles around the border of the object.

(2) Then put the mouse pointer within the object, but not on a selection handle. Drag the object to a new location.

(3) PowerPoint moves the object to a new location.

Change the Color Scheme

PowerPoint comes with a variety of presentation designs and colors. A typical design uses one color for the background, one for the text, a set of colors for any graphs, and so on. The collection of the eight basic colors used in a presentation is the *color scheme*.

If you don't like the colors of your chosen presentation design, you can change each individually, but you may spend a lot of time looking for and selecting complementary colors. You may end up with a hodgepodge of colors.

An easier way is to let PowerPoint select appropriate colors. You select two colors that you like: one for the

background and one for the text, and PowerPoint selects other colors that work well with the two you selected. PowerPoint selects colors that not only look well together but that contrast well enough to make the presentation readable.

> If you don't like the new color scheme after you apply it, undo the change using the **Edit Undo** command or the **Undo** button on the toolbar.

Begin Guided Tour   Select a New Color Scheme

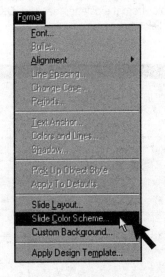

1 If you want to change the background color of just one slide, display that slide. Then open the **Format** menu and select the **Slide Color Scheme** command.

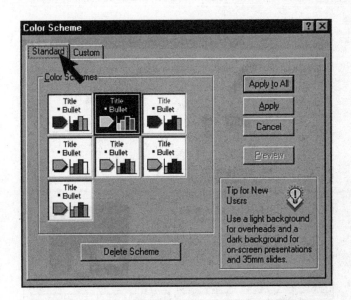

2 PowerPoint displays the Slide Color Scheme dialog box. Click on the **Standard** tab to bring it to the front of the box. The Standard tab shows examples of complementary colors that would go well with the presentation. Each example shows colors for shadows, background, text and lines, fills, and graphs. To select a color scheme, click on the example.

(continues)

Guided Tour Select a New Color Scheme

(continued)

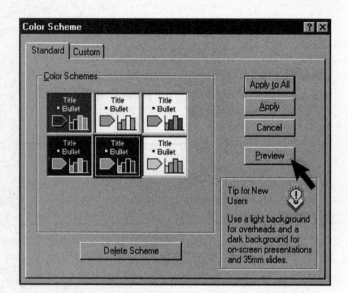

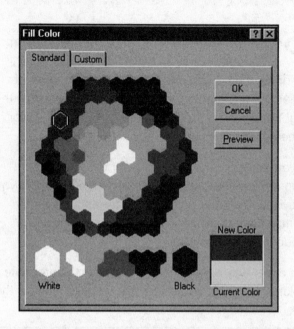

3 To preview the color scheme, click the **Preview** button and look on your slide screen to see the colors (you may have to move the dialog box out of your way to see the slide). Once you find the color scheme you want to use, proceed to step 5.

5 A color dialog box appears. Depending on what slide item you choose, the color dialog boxes will appear differently. However, they all let you pick a new color to apply to the item. Select a new color from the palette; then click **OK** to return to the Color Scheme dialog box.

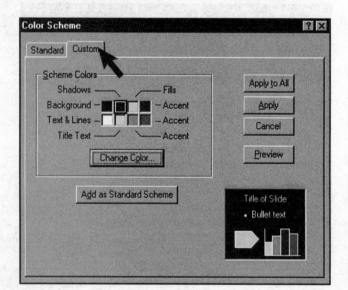

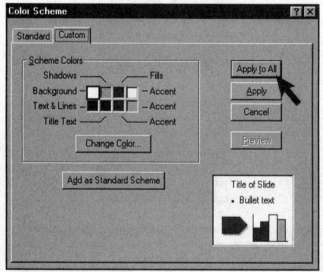

4 You can also customize the color scheme if you don't like any of the examples shown. Click the **Custom** tab and select your own colors for the slide items. You can even add the new color scheme to the list of standard color schemes by clicking the **Add as Standard Scheme** button. To change an item's color, select the current color; then click the **Change Color** button.

6 To apply the color scheme to your slide, click the **Apply** button. To apply the scheme to your entire presentation, click the **Apply All** button.

7 PowerPoint updates the slide(s).

Customize the Background

If you use the blank presentation style, the background of the slide is pretty bland—black text on a plain white background. This style will work okay for presentations that you print on a black-and-white printer, but for a color presentation, you might want a more exciting background.

Although PowerPoint comes with many background designs, you can make changes to the individual backgrounds of your slide presentation. To do so, you must open the Custom Background dialog box. In this box, you can customize background colors and patterns; you can even choose from some special backgrounds that will give your presentation a professional look. For example, you can choose a background that looks like marble or wood. There are a variety of backgrounds you can create with the Custom Background box.

If you want to change your entire presentation's design, check out all the PowerPoint templates. You'll learn how to change templates in the next task.

Begin Guided Tour   Customize the Background

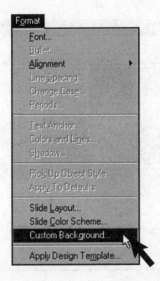

1 Display the slide with the background you want to change; then open the **Format** menu and select the **Custom Background** command.

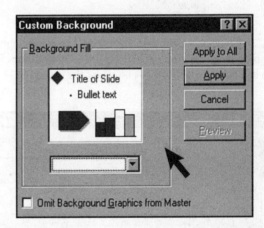

2 You see the Custom Background dialog box. From this dialog box, you can select background colors, a shade style, a pattern, or a texture. Click the drop-down arrow to see the background options.

(continues)

Guided Tour Customize the Background

(continued)

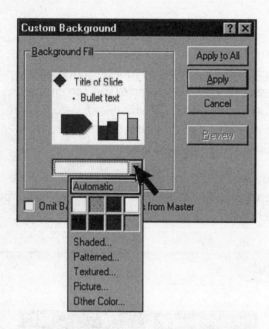

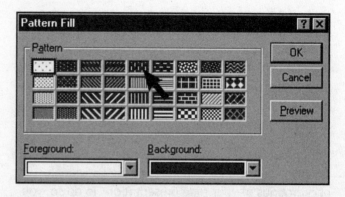

5 To change the background's pattern, select **Patterned** from the drop-down list to open the Pattern Fill dialog box. Select a pattern to use in your background. You can also choose the pattern's color. Click **OK** to return to the Custom Background box; then skip to step 7 to finish.

3 To change background colors, click on a new color in the drop-down list. (You can also select the **Other Color** option and choose a different color from a color dialog box.)

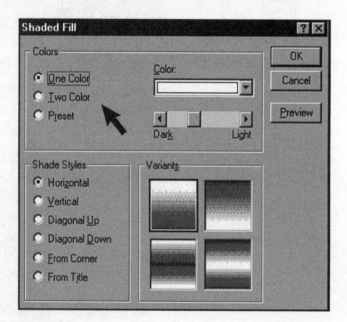

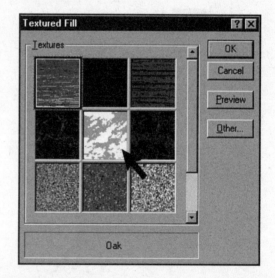

6 To select a texture for the background, choose **Textured** from the drop-down list. This opens the Textured Fill dialog box, which has a variety of textures such as wood, marble, granite, and more. Select a texture; then click **OK** to return to the Custom Background dialog box.

4 To change your background's shading, select **Shaded** from the drop-down list to open the Shaded Fill dialog box. In this box, select a shade color, style, and variant. You can even choose how light or dark the shading will appear. Click **OK** to return to the Custom Background dialog box. Skip to step 7 to finish.

Guided Tour Customize the Background

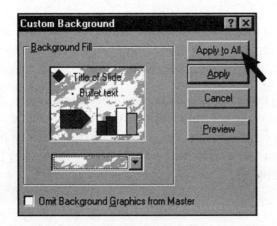

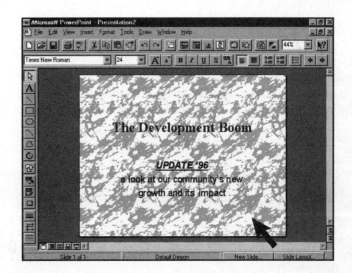

7 To apply the custom background to just the current slide, click the **Apply** button. To apply the background to all slides in the presentation, click the **Apply All** button.

8 PowerPoint formats the presentation with the new background.

Apply a Template

W hen you create a new presentation, you can build it using the default template, or you can select a different template. If you don't like the template that you select, you aren't stuck with it. You also don't have to make the individual formatting changes. Instead, you can apply a different template and make several formatting changes at once.

The template affects the typestyle used, the color scheme, the location/alignment of the slide objects, and other formatting options. When you apply a new template, PowerPoint updates all of these elements for the entire presentation.

To use a new template, open the **Format** menu and choose the **Apply Design Template** command. This opens the Apply Design Template dialog box where you can choose from among PowerPoint's many templates.

Begin Guided Tour   Use a New Template Design

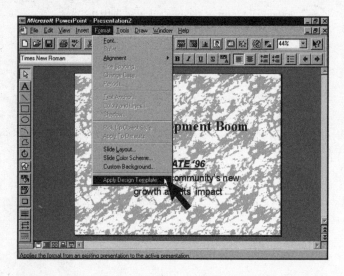

1 With the presentation on-screen and any slide displayed, open the **Format** menu and select the **Apply Design Template** command. Or click the **Apply Design Template** button in the status bar.

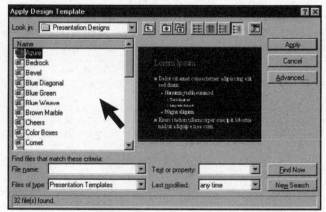

2 You see the Apply Design Template dialog box. Select the template design you want to use from the Presentation Designs folder.

3 PowerPoint lets you preview the selected template in the Preview box. (Make sure you click the **Preview** button to do so.) Click **Apply**.

4 PowerPoint updates all the slides in the presentation.

Create Speaker Notes

When you make a presentation, you may want to make *speaker notes* for each slide. For example, you can include more details that better explain the slide. You may want to explain the source of financial data or be sure to emphasize a key point. You may want to remind yourself to pass out handouts or to take a break. Think of the notes as your script.

If you want notes, you can set them up and print them using PowerPoint. The notes will include a small thumbnail (miniature slide) of the slide, along with your notes. You can add notes to any or all of the slides in the presentation. (For the steps to print these notes, see "Print a Presentation" on page 273.) Speaker notes do not show up in your actual slide presentation. They are just a tool to help you prepare and give your presentation.

Begin Guided Tour Create Speaker Notes

1 Open the **View** menu and click the **Notes Pages** command. Or click the **Notes Pages View** button in the status bar (it's the fourth button to the right of the Slide View button).

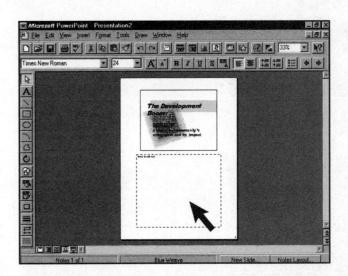

2 PowerPoint displays the slide and adds an area for notes. The view may be too small, so the first thing you will want to do is zoom the view. Click the Zoom Control list box in the toolbar and select a larger number to zoom the notes.

(continues)

Guided Tour   Create Speaker Notes

(continued)

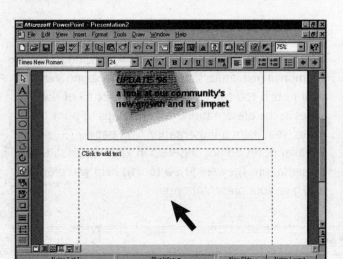

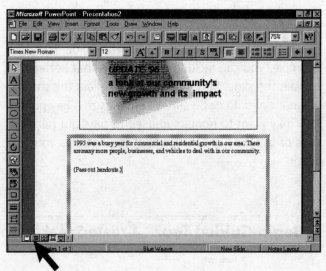

3 When the notes are big enough for you to see and work with, click the text placeholder and type the notes text for this slide.

4 When you complete the text for the slide, you can go to the next slide by clicking the **Next Slide** button and continue adding notes. When you finish adding notes, click the **Slide View** button to return to Slide View.

To print out your speakers notes, follow the steps in the "Print a Presentation" is on page 273.

Set Up Handouts

In addition to speaker notes, you can create *handouts* from the slides in your presentation. You can pass these out to your audience so they can follow along, take notes, and have something to take with them after the presentation. The handouts will include a picture of the slide, a place for notes, and any other text or graphics you want to include.

To add text or graphics to the handouts, you edit the *master page*. The slide and speaker notes also have a master page. Basically, any text or graphics that you add to a master page are added to all pages. You may want to add your company logo, the current date, your name, the page number, or other information.

> You can use the **Date**, **Time**, and **Page Number** commands in the **Insert** menu to add the date, time, or page number to each page.

Begin Guided Tour   Create Handouts

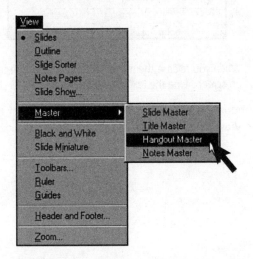

1 Open the **View** menu and select the **Master** command. From the submenu, select **Handout Master**.

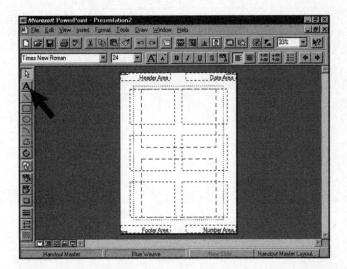

2 PowerPoint displays the master for the handouts. The lines indicate where the slides will print (you select how many slides to print on the handouts when you print the presentation). Add any text or graphics you want to the master. For example, to add a title, click the **Text** tool and move the pointer to the master.

(continues)

Guided Tour Create Handouts

(continued)

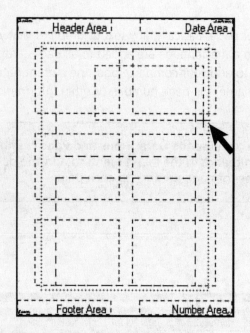

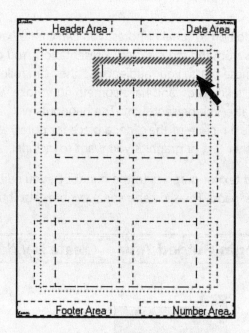

3 The pointer should look like a line with a cross at the bottom. Click and drag to draw the text box.

4 When you release the mouse button, you see the text box on-screen. Type the text you want to use.

5 After you add the text and objects you want, click the **Slide View** button in the status bar to return to the Slide View.

Print a Presentation

With PowerPoint, you can print not only the presentation, but also your speaker notes, handouts, or an outline of your presentation. When you are preparing to give the presentation, you may need to print each of these elements: the presentation and outline to check the order, the notes to use as your script, and the handouts for your audience.

In addition to selecting what to print, you can also select the number of copies to print, the range of slides to print, and other options. For example, if you

are having your presentation turned into slides, you will probably be using a service bureau (a printing company that can print slides and other high-quality documents). Rather than print to the printer, you can create a file that you can then give to the service bureau to create the slides. You can find all of the printer options in the Print dialog box.

Press **Ctrl+P** to display the Print dialog box.

Begin Guided Tour   Use the Print Command

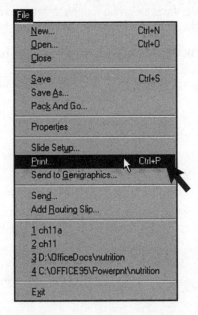

1 Open the **File** menu and select the **Print** command.

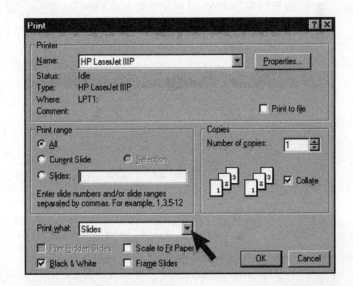

2 You see the Print dialog box. By default, PowerPoint expects to print the presentation, but you can use this same dialog box to print speaker notes or handouts. Click on the down arrow next to **Print what**.

(continues)

Guided Tour   **Use the Print Command**   *(continued)*

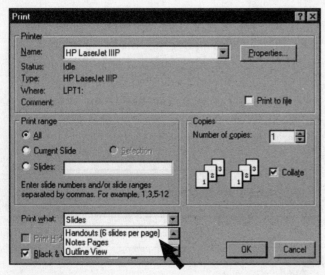

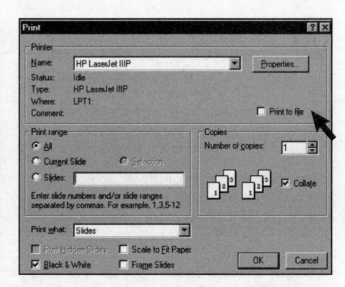

3 You see a drop-down list of choices. Notice that you can print notes, slides, various layouts for handouts, and an outline. Click on what you want to print.

5 Make changes to any of the other print options. For example, if you are giving your presentation to a service bureau to make slides, check the **Print to file** check box.

6 Click **OK**. PowerPoint prints the presentation, notes, or handouts.

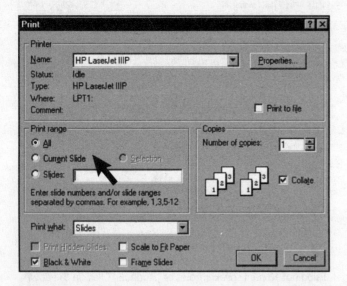

4 Select which slides you want to print: **All**, **Current Slide**, or certain slides (enter the range in the **Slides** text box).

View the Slide Show

There are several ways you can display your presentation. You can print transparencies and use an overhead to give the presentation, or you can create slides and use a slide projector. You can hand out a printed copy of the presentation and go over the slides without a visual display. However, one of the best methods for giving the presentation is to use your own computer. You can display your presentation on your monitor, or you can use special equipment and the PC to display your presentation as a slide show on a larger screen.

Any presentation you run on your computer is, in effect, a slide show. You don't need to do anything special to create this slide show. When you have your show in order, take it for a spin. Starting from the first slide in the presentation, click the **Slide Show** view button. (You can also start the presentation by opening the **View** menu; then select **Slide Show** and click on the **Show** button.)

Your first slide fills the screen, obscuring all the toolbars and window features. This first slide stays on-screen until you click a mouse button or press a key. The following table explains how to move from slide to slide in a slide show.

To	Do This
Display the next slide	Click anywhere on the screen or press the right arrow or down arrow on the keyboard.
Display the last slide	Press **End**.
Display the first slide	Press **Home**.
Stop the Slide show	Press **Esc**.
Display a menu of slide show controls	Click the button in the lower left corner of the screen.

Begin Guided Tour   Start a Slide Show

1 Open the **View** menu and select the **Slide Show** command. You see the Slide Show dialog box. If you want to display only certain slides, select **From** and then enter the first slide number in the **From** text box and the last slide number in the **To** text box.

The Advance options control how your slide show moves from one slide to the next. (Learn more about the Pen option in the next task.)

2 Click the **Show** button.

3 PowerPoint displays the first slide in the presentation. Click the mouse right button, or press the **Spacebar** to move through each of the slides in the presentation.

Use the Slide Show Controls

When you start a slide show presentation, you'll notice a button in the lower left corner of your slide screen. You can open a menu of slide show controls by clicking on this control button. The menu lists controls for moving to the next slide, turning the arrow pointer into a pen that writes on-screen, and even ending the show.

You'll find plenty of options among the slide show controls to help you work with the presentation. For example, you can use the **Slide Meter** option to help you time your presentation and gauge how long it takes you to move from slide to slide and present your material. All of the slide show controls can help you with your presentation, work with the audience, and communicate effectively during the course of your show.

Here's what each menu item controls:

Next   Takes you to the next slide or the next build effect.

Previous   Takes you back to the previous slide or build effect.

Go To   Opens a submenu for accessing the Slide Navigator box (a dialog box for specifying which slide you want to see next) or a hidden slide.

Meeting Minder   A new feature that lets you stop your slide show and compose notes, comments, and other observations made by your audience.

Slide Meter   Opens a dialog box for timing your slide show.

Arrow   Lets you use the mouse pointer arrow to navigate the screen.

Pen   Turns your mouse pointer into a pen that you can then use to scribble on the slides that you show. PowerPoint does not save the scribbles as part of your presentation; however, the effect is kind of like using an electronic chalkboard.

Pointer Options   Lets you hide the mouse pointer altogether or change your pen's color.

Screen   Opens a submenu for blacking out your current slide, pausing the show, or erasing your pen scribbles.

End Show   Puts a stop to your slide show.

Use the Pen Feature

One of the options on the slide show control menu is a *pen* feature. Use it to turn your mouse pointer into a writing pen during your show. You can then use it to underline points that you make or to add scribbles or notes to an on-screen slide. This turns your slides into interactive screens where you and the audience can use them like a chalkboard.

To turn your pointer into a pen during the presentation, click on the slide show control button to open the menu, and then select **Pen**. (If you want to change back to an arrow pointer later, open the menu again and choose **Arrow**.) To write on the slide, move your pen (mouse pointer) to the place you want to "write," and hold down the left mouse button and drag. Practice this technique to get the hang of it before actually doing this during an important presentation.

You can change your pen color at any time by opening the slide show control menu again; this time select **Pointer Options**, **Pen Color**, and choose a specific color.

Take Notes Meeting Minder

Microsoft added a feature for recording notes, meeting minutes, and action items that may occur during the course of your slide show: *Meeting Minder*. You can access it anytime during your slide show. Click on the slide show control button, select **Meeting Minder**, and the Meeting Minder dialog box appears.

The following options are available in the Meeting Minder dialog box:

> **Notes Pages tab**   Lets you view your own Notes Pages.

Meeting Minutes tab   Lets you type in notes to turn into meeting minutes.

Action Items tab   Lets you enter text for becoming action points after the presentation.

Choose any of the tabs, enter your information, and then you can save it along with your program and export it to create meeting minutes. You may find this very helpful when presenting a program that requires audience feedback. By opening the Meeting Minder, you can immediately start typing in audience responses. Of course, it helps to be a fast typist and to have practiced with this feature before using it during your presentation.

To see your Meeting Minder information later, open the **Tool** menu and select **Meeting Minder**.

Begin Guided Tour   Turn the Mouse Pointer into a Pen

1 When the first slide in the show appears on-screen, click on the slide show control button to open the menu, and then select **Pen**.

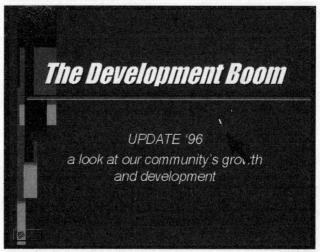

2 To write on the slide, move your pen to the place you want to write on-screen, and hold down the left mouse button and drag.

(continues)

Guided Tour Turn the Mouse Pointer into a Pen *(continued)*

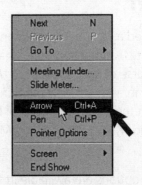

④ To turn the pen off, open the slide show control menu again by clicking on the button; then choose **Arrow**.

③ The pen immediately writes on-screen.

Begin Guided Tour Use the Meeting Minder Function

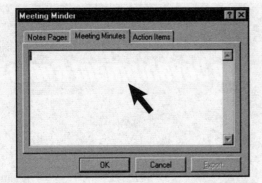

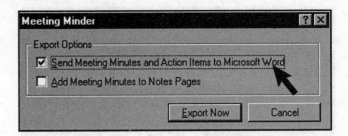

③ If you want to use your meeting notes to make a document, click the **Export** button. Select **Send Meeting Minutes and Action Items to Microsoft Word**; then click the **Export Now** button. This immediately opens Microsoft Word and creates a document from the slide presentation and the notes you added with Meeting Minder. You can then save the file and return to the presentation.

① Click on the slide show control button to open the menu, and then select **Meeting Minder**. The Meeting Minder dialog box appears. Click the **Meeting Minutes** tab to bring it to the front. Type in any notes pertaining to the slide.

Use the **Notes Pages** tab to add comments to your slide's notes pages.

Use the **Action Items** tab to insert a new slide and place the typed information into bullet points.

② To return to the slide show, click **OK** to exit the box. If you want to export the notes, continue to step 4.

Add Special Effects

PowerPoint 7.0 comes with some new *animation effects* you can use to liven up your slide shows. Animation effects control the transition of your slides from one to another during the course of the slide show, and how your slide items appear on-screen. The effect of having your slide items appear at different times and in different ways on-screen is called a *build*.

There are many different builds you can use with PowerPoint, such as bulleted items appearing one bullet at a time when you click on the slide, or a graphic flying in from the side of the screen. If you click the **Animation Effects** button (the one with a yellow star on it) on your Standard toolbar, you'll display the Animation Effects toolbar on your screen. When it comes to having precise control over the effects you assign to your slide items, the Animation Effects toolbar is the easiest way to go.

You can select from these effects to create such animations as making your slide text appear on-screen as if being typed by a typewriter, accompanied by the sound of a typewriter clicking. Or how about making your slide title drop down from the top of the slide? Or maybe you'd like to add a flash of text or art? There's lots to try, but start by looking at this table to see your choices.

Button	Name	Description
	Animate Title	Causes the slide's title to drop down into the slide.
	Build Slide Text	Inserts slide text one sentence at a time.
	Drive-in Effect	Inserts object into slide like a speeding car, complete with sound effect.
	Flying Effect	Object flies into slide.
	Camera Effect	Inserts object into slide with the sound of a camera click.
	Flash Once	Flashes object onto slide, then off again.
	Laser Text Effect	Writes text onto slide with a laser-like effect and sound.
	Typewriter Text Effect	Inserts slide text one character at a time, like a typewriter complete with typewriter sounds.
	Reverse Text Build	Builds your text block from bottom up.
	Drop-in Text Effect	Drops in each word one at a time.

You can use the Animation Effects toolbar in Slide Sorter view or Slide view. If you're assigning effects to individual elements on your slide, you'll want to switch to Slide view and open the Animation Effects toolbar.

You can also add animation effects in Slide Sorter view, using the same Animation Effects toolbar and the Slide Sorter toolbar. You won't be able to apply effects to individual elements in the slide (use Slide view to do that), but you can apply effects to how slides appear and disappear in your presentation. You can also open the **Tools** menu, select **Slide Transition**, and use the **Slide Transition** box to assign transition effects to your show.

When you're ready to run your slide show, the assigned slide effects will appear on your screen on command. Click on-screen when you're ready for the next effect to appear.

Add Effects with the Animation Settings Box

Another way to add effects is with the Animation Settings dialog box. You'll find options for controlling how text appears (builds), as well as sound and visual effects. You can access the Animation Settings box by clicking on the **Animation Settings** button on the Animation Effects toolbar, clicking the **Animation Settings** button on the Slide Sorter toolbar, or by opening the **Tools** menu and selecting **Animation Settings**.

> You can also select an object on your slide (in Slide view) and right-click to view a shortcut menu; then choose **Animation Settings** from the menu.

When you open the Animation Settings box, you'll find the following options:

Build options   Control how slide text appears on-screen.

Effects options (described previously)   Let you add visual and sound effects to the slide. Use the drop-down lists to choose from the available effects.

Build this object drop-down list   Helps you select the order that items appear on-screen and when.

After Build Step drop-down box   Lets you change the color of your build text after it appears on-screen.

The new PowerPoint comes with a small collection of sound effects you can add, but you may have some other sound files (WAV files) available. If you do, you can add them to your presentation, too. You can add music, prerecorded messages, sound clips, and more. Of course, your computer has to be capable of recording sounds (with a sound board such as SoundBlaster Pro).

You can also use the **Insert Object** command to place sound wave files into your slides. In the Insert Object dialog box, you can select from wave sounds or other such sources. You can even record new sounds to insert (such as someone talking) or sounds from CDs, and so on.

Sounds aren't the only dynamic effects you can add. You can also insert movie or video clips (if you're using a multimedia computer equipped with such things). You'll find this option also available on your **Insert** menu.

Begin Guided Tour   Add a Transition

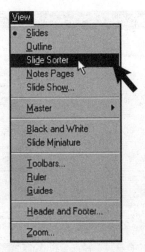

1 Open the **View** menu and select **Slide Sorter**; or click on the **Slide Sorter** button at the bottom of your screen.

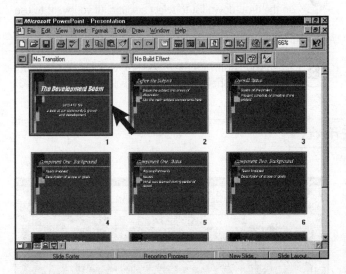

2 To set up a controlled transition for one specific slide, select the slide. To select them all, hold down the **Shift** key and click on each slide; or open the **Edit** menu and choose **Select All**.

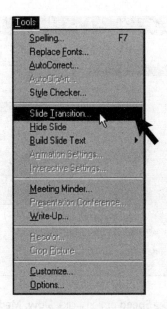

3 Then open the **Tools** menu and choose **Slide Transition**. (You can also click the **Slide Transition** button in the Slide Sorter toolbar.) The Transition dialog box appears.

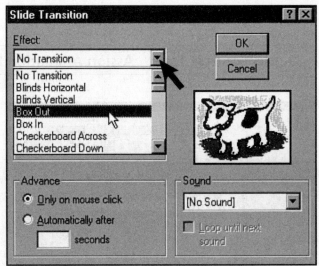

4 Open the **Effect** drop-down list and pick a transition option. Look in the preview area (below the command buttons) to see a demonstration of the transition.

(continues)

Guided Tour Add a Transition

(continued)

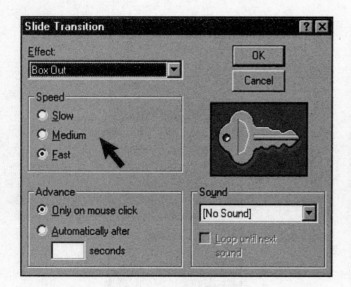

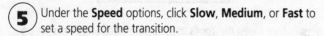

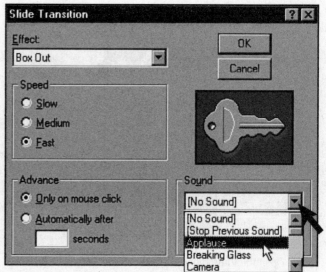

5 Under the **Speed** options, click **Slow**, **Medium**, or **Fast** to set a speed for the transition.

6 In the **Advance** area, specify whether you want PowerPoint to advance the slides for you. If you do, click on **Automatically after** and fill in how many seconds you want the slide to remain on-screen.

7 To add a sound to your slide, use the **Sound** options. Click on the drop-down list to select a sound. (If you want to use a sound not found on the list, select **Other Sounds** and locate the sound file you want to use.)

8 When you finish with the dialog box, click **OK**. When you run your slide show, the transitions will appear as assigned.

Begin Guided Tour Assign Animation Effects

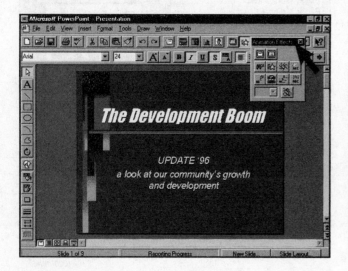

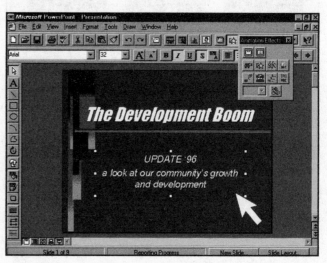

1 Open the first slide of your presentation in Slide view, or open the slide in which you want to assign an effect. Click the **Animation Effects** button to display the Animation Effects toolbar.

2 If you want to apply an effect to a specific slide element, such as a title or art, select the item on the slide. Next, click on the effect you want to assign to the element from the Animation Effects toolbar. To close the Animation Effects toolbar, click the **Animation Effects** button again. The assigned slide effects will appear when you run your slide show.

HOW TO...

Use Schedule+

Microsoft Office 95 comes with a handy program to help you keep track of your busy schedule. *Schedule+* is a *Personal Information Management* application, or PIM for short. PIMs help you keep your daily life organized by assisting you with appointments, lists, and more.

Schedule+ resembles a personal organizer, a time-management tool popular these days in the business community, but useful at home as well. Most organizers include sections arranged in a three-ring binder; each section helps you organize a particular part of your daily life. Schedule+ comes with sections, too. Each feature in the program can help you balance appointments and meetings, manage tasks and projects, organize names and addresses, and much more.

In this part of the book, you'll learn how to use Schedule+ to set up appointments, events, and even audible reminders to prompt you when you need to be somewhere.

What You Will Find in This Section

Log On with the Logon Box

The first thing you see when you start Schedule+ is a logon box. This is a little different than what you encounter with the other Office 95 programs. You'll see a logon box every time you open Schedule+. Depending on whether you're networked (connected to other computers) or not, your computer may show different logon boxes. If you're networked (and you share e-mail on the network with other users), you'll use a *group-enabled mode* box. If you're not connected to a computer network, you'll use a *stand-alone mode* box.

Why go to the trouble of using a logon box? Because the things you keep in your personal Schedule+ program may be personal or private, and you might not want everyone to have access to your schedule. Logons and passwords will help you keep your data safe. Logon boxes are also useful if several people are using the same computer. For example, if you're using Schedule+ at home, other members of your family can set up their own schedules and open them up through the logon box.

If you've logged onto Schedule+ previously and created a schedule, your user name may already appear in the logon box when you log on again.

The first time you create a schedule, the Schedule+ welcome box appears. (This box may also appear when the program cannot find a schedule you previously created.) To create a new schedule, select the **I want to create a new schedule file** option in the welcome box; then click **OK**. To use a previously made schedule, select the **I want to use an existing schedule file** option; then click **OK**. Either method opens the Select Local Schedule box. You can use this second box to locate previously made schedules or to simply confirm your new schedule and its location.

Begin Guided Tour   Use the Schedule+ Welcome Box

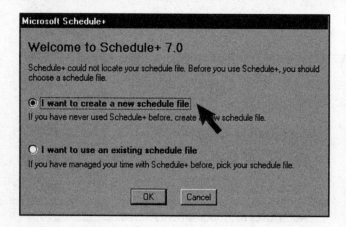

1 The first time you logon to Schedule+, you may see the welcome box.

If you want to create a new schedule, select the **I want to create a new schedule file** option.

To use a previously made schedule, select the **I want to use an existing schedule file** option.

2 Click **OK** to exit the box and open the Select Local Schedule box.

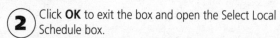
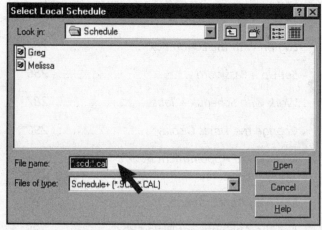

3 Type in a name for your schedule in the **File name** text box; then confirm the new schedule you're creating by clicking the **Open** button.

Guided Tour Use the Schedule+ Welcome Box

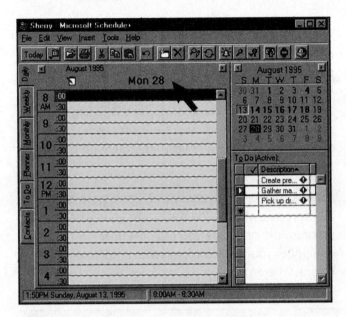

If you want to save the schedule in another location, select a folder from the **Look in** drop-down box. To look for an existing schedule, use the Look in drop-down box to locate the folder containing the schedule. Once you find the schedule, select it and click the **Open** button.

4 Schedule+ opens the schedule you selected or named.

Begin Guided Tour Log On with Logon Box

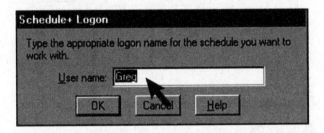

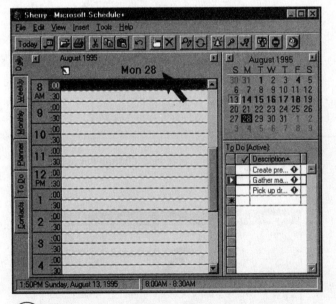

1 Open Schedule+ and the Schedule+ Logon box appears. If you're using group-enabled mode, the logon box may appear differently than the one in this figure.

2 Type your name in the **User** name box and click **OK**. If you didn't set a password, you don't have to worry about typing one in; proceed to step 4.

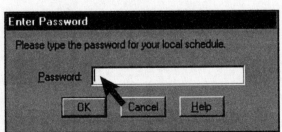

4 The Schedule+ program opens up onto your screen.

3 Type in your password (if applicable) and click **OK**.

Set Up a Password

Passwords are a common element with many computers and computer programs today that help keep your data safe by only allowing certain users to log onto your files—especially when more than one person uses the computer (such as in a home environment). You can set up passwords for everyone who uses your Schedule+ program. If you're using Schedule+ in a network environment, your network administrator may have already assigned you a password, but you can change it at any time. It's a good idea to change your password every few weeks to keep your data secure.

You can use the Change Password dialog box to change your password at any time. As you type your password into the text boxes, you won't be able to see the characters that you type. Instead, you'll see asterisks. Don't be alarmed, you're still typing in characters even though you can't see them. Because of this, make sure you're very accurate with the keys that you press.

After you enter a new password, you'll have to use the new password to log back onto your Schedule+ program the next time you use Schedule+. Be sure to remember your password, or write it down and keep it somewhere safe.

Begin Guided Tour   Change a Password

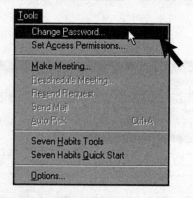

1 Open the **Tools** menu and select **Change Password**.

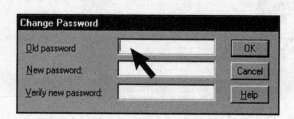

2 In the Change Password dialog box, type in a password for yourself in the **New password** text box. If you're changing an old password, type the old password in the **Old password** box.

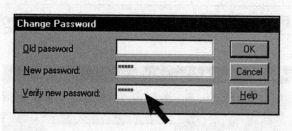

3 Confirm the new password by retyping it in the **Verify new password** box.

4 Click **OK**; Schedule+ sets up your password.

Work with Schedule+ Tabs

There are six tabs along the left side of your Schedule+ screen. Each of them lets you use and view a specific Schedule+ feature. By default, Schedule+ opens to the Daily tab view so you can see the day's schedule of activities. However, you can open any tab by simply clicking on its name.

> By default, Schedule+ does not make full use of your monitor screen. You can maximize the Schedule+ program window by clicking on its Maximize button.

Here's a description of each tab and the feature it displays:

Daily Click on this tab to view your daily schedule. You can quickly see your appointments and meetings arranged by times.

Weekly Use the Weekly tab to view your schedule by week, showing five consecutive days.

Monthly To see your schedule by month, much like a calendar, click on the Monthly tab. This lets you see several weeks of your schedule at a time.

Planner To see your schedule in blocks of busy and free times, use the Planner view. With this tab, you can also see other time blocks of other users that are networked with you.

To Do Use this feature to help track and manage tasks and projects that go along with your schedule. Such tasks can be as simple as a note to pick up the dry cleaning or a grocery list, or you can list complex project steps that must be completed.

Contacts With Schedule+, you can compile a database of people you contact the most. You can keep an address book of clients, friends, and family, including names, addresses, phone numbers, and more.

Using the Daily View Tab

By default, Schedule+ always opens to the Daily view tab where you can see your day's appointments at a glance. There are several distinct parts of your Daily tab. Three of them stand out in particular:

The **Appointment Book** (the biggest part of your screen with all the times and lines in it) shows your daily schedule. You can use it to note appointments, meetings, and other items.

Use the **Date Navigator** (the month displayed in the upper right corner) to change dates displayed in the Appointment Book.

Use the **To Do list** (right underneath the Date Navigator) to display a list of what you're supposed to do on the date displayed.

An important part of using the Daily view tab is the ability to change the date displayed on the schedule. Use the two tiny buttons with arrows on them at the top of Appointment Book area to move backward and forward in your schedule. Another way to change dates fast is by using the *Date Navigator calendar*. You simply click on a date on the calendar and it appears in the Appointment Book. Like the Appointment Book area, the Date Navigator has two arrow buttons at the top that let you view previous or future months.

> You can also open a calendar quickly by clicking the **Go To Date** button on the toolbar. When you click on this button, a calendar drops down from which you can select other dates to display.

Begin Guided Tour   Change Dates in the Appointment Book

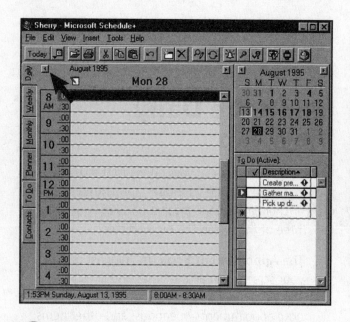

1 A click on the left arrow button moves your schedule back one page to the previous date.

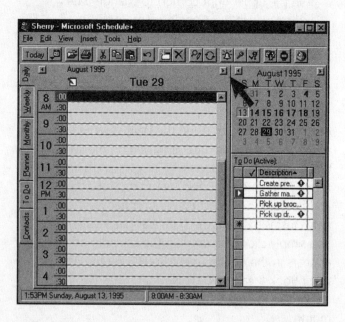

2 A click on the right arrow button moves your schedule forward one page to the next date.

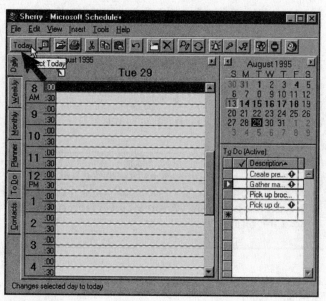

3 To quickly return to the current date, click the **Today** button on the toolbar.

If you notice that clicking on the **Today** button on the toolbar gives you the wrong date on your schedule, then your computer's date is wrong, too. To fix it, you'll need to open the Windows 95 Control Panel and select the Date/Time icon.

Begin Guided Tour Change Dates in the Appointment Book

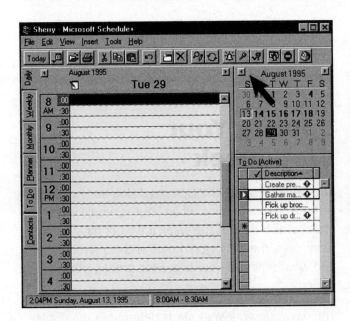

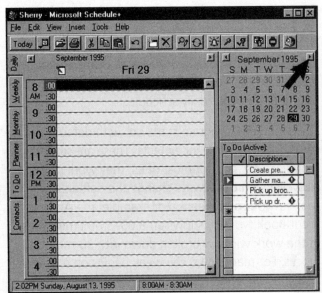

1 Click on the left arrow button to display the previous month.

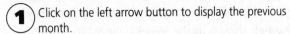

Click on either arrow button and hold your mouse button down to speed through your schedule pages forward and backward.

2 Click on the right arrow button to view the next month.

3 To shuffle quickly through the months in either direction, hover your mouse pointer over the appropriate arrow; then hold down the left mouse button as the calendar months shuffle. Let go of the mouse button when you reach the month you're looking for.

Change the Times Display

Not only can you change the days that appear in the Appointment Book, but you can also change the times. The scroll bar at the right of the Appointment Book lets you scroll through the increments of time found in your daily schedule.

The Schedule+ program starts out with default settings for the time increments. These are set for typical usage, and for most of us, they work just fine. However, you can always change the default settings to meet your own needs. For example, the Appointment Book typically shows an 8:00–5:00 time frame in the work window broken down into 30-minute blocks. For many folks, the week begins on a Sunday and ends on a Saturday, and the workday runs from 8:00 a.m. to 5:00 p.m. These happen to be your default settings, but you can change them to your own hours using the Options dialog box. When you open the box, you can zip around the four tabs to adjust settings for your schedule, screen display, and even reset your time zone.

The following descriptions tell what each Options tab contains:

General tab   Controls your workweek's start day, work and non-work hours, and even options for using the reminder feature (learn more about this feature in the "Set Appointment Reminders" task later in this section).

Defaults tab   Contains default settings for appointments, tasks, and contacts.

Display tab   Holds settings for controlling the colors and backgrounds of the Schedule+ features. (Learn more about changing background colors in the next task.)

Time Zone tab   Lets you select a time zone for your schedule. (You'll learn how to change the time zone in the Guided Tour to come.)

Synchronize tab   Helps you to synchronize your schedule on your computer and your schedule posted on the network, if you're using Schedule+ in a network situation.

Specify Your Workweek

The **General** tab in the Options dialog box holds settings that determine when your schedule week starts, which days of the week are work days or non-work days, the daily work hours and non-work hours, and what time increments appear, among other options.

The day your workweek starts determines the display of days in the Date Navigator calendar and the days of the week shown in the Weekly view tab. The workdays and hours determine the background colors of your schedule. As you may have noticed, the workweek appears in a brighter shade of color on the schedule, and non-work days and non-work hours appear in a darker shade.

Not everybody uses the same workdays and work hours, so you can adjust these settings on Schedule+ to help you tailor the program to your situation. To change the settings for workweeks and workdays, you use the Options dialog box. To change what day of the week your workweek starts on, and what work hours you want to focus on, follow these steps:

1. With the **General** tab displayed in the Options dialog box, locate the **Week starts on** option.

2. To change the day, click on the drop-down arrow and select the appropriate day.

3. To change your work hours and non-work hours, change the settings in the **Day starts at** and **Day ends at** boxes.

4. To exit the box and put the settings in effect, click **OK**.

Begin Guided Tour Change the Time Increments Display

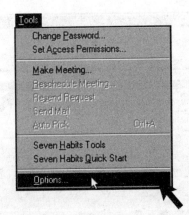

1 Open the **Tools** menu and select **Options**.

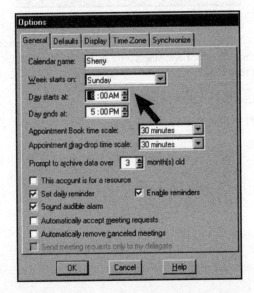

2 The Options dialog box appears on your screen. Click the **General** tab to bring the time controls to the front of the box. To change what time the day display begins, set another time in the **Day starts at** box.

3 To change what time the day display ends, set a time in the **Day ends at** box.

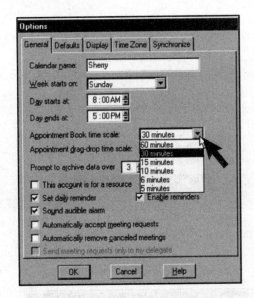

4 To change how the minute increments appear, click on the drop-down list in the **Appointment Book time scale** box and select a new increment.

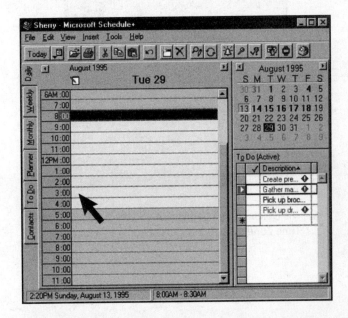

5 Click **OK** to save your changes and exit the box. The changes now appear in your daily schedule. In this figure, I changed the time increments to 60 minutes.

Begin Guided Tour   Change the Time Zone

1 Open the **Tools** menu and select **Options**.

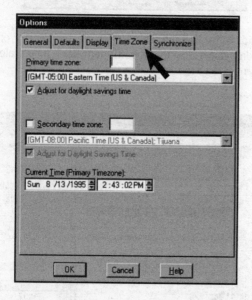

2 The Options dialog box appears on your screen. Click the **Time Zone** tab to bring it to the front of the box.

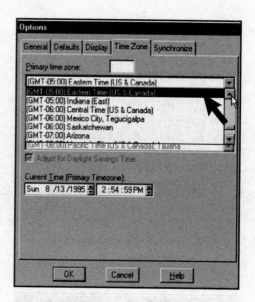

3 To change the time zone, click the **Primary time zone** drop-down list and select a time zone for your Appointment Book.

4 Click **OK** to close the box.

Change the Appointment Book's Appearance

You can also control how your Appointment Book looks with the Display options in the Options dialog box. You can change the background color of the daily schedule and change the point size of the data you enter into the schedule. If you're having trouble reading what you type into the Appointment Book portion of your screen, you should definitely enlarge the font size of the text.

Not only can you change backgrounds and font sizes, but when you're using the Daily view tab, you can alter how the three features appear. You can change the size of the Appointment Book, the Date Navigator, and the To Do list. You can change the proportions of all three of these parts by moving the lines that separate them. Move your mouse pointer over any line separating the features, and click-and-drag to change the feature's size.

Begin Guided Tour   Change the Appointment Book Background

1 Open the **Tools** menu and select **Options**.

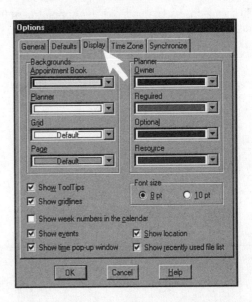

2 The Options dialog box appears on your screen. Click the **Display** tab to bring it to the front of the box.

(continues)

Guided Tour Change the Appointment Book Background *(continued)*

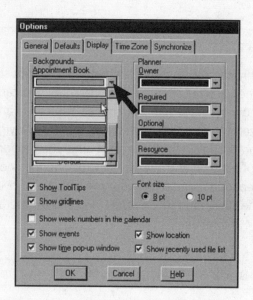

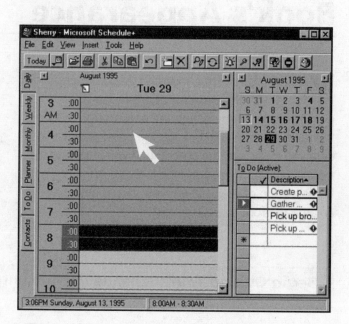

3 To change the background, click the **Appointment Book** drop-down list under the **Backgrounds** options and select a color.

5 Click **OK** to close the box and your changes take effect.

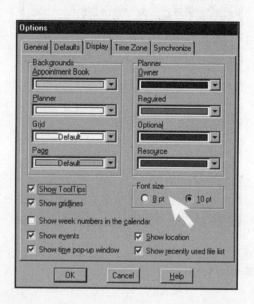

4 To change font size for the appointment text (which you'll learn to enter in the next task), click the **Font size** option button you want to use.

Begin Guided Tour   Resize the Daily View Features

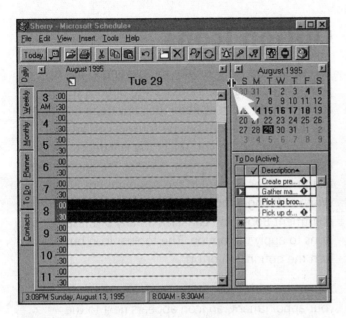

1 Move your mouse pointer over any line between the Appointment Book, Date Navigator, or To Do list until the pointer becomes a double-headed arrow.

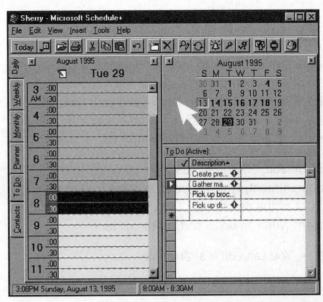

3 When you've moved the border to a new location, release the mouse button and the screen area is resized.

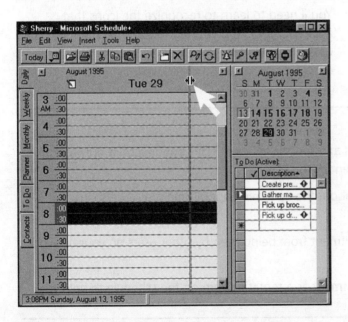

2 Hold down the left mouse button and drag the pointer to resize the screen items.

Make an Appointment

Are you ready to start filling in your daily appointments? You can select any time slot in your Appointment Book to enter an appointment. Use the scroll arrows on the right side of the Appointment Book to move back and forth along your time schedule. (There are more hours than the typical 8:00–5:00; scroll up and down to find them.)

By default, Schedule+ assigns a reminder to the appointment, which appears as a bell icon at the front of the description. Once you enter an appointment, you can do all sorts of things to it:

- You can edit it at any time.

- You can move it to another date or copy it.

- You can delete it.

- You can view it in weekly or monthly views.

- You can set it up so it reminds you when the appointment time gets close. (This feature is on by default.)

Option Icons

You'll also find icons on the toolbar and in the Appointment dialog box for assigning options to your appointments, such as Reminder, Private, and Tentative. Each of these options performs a certain function. For example, if you select the Private icon and assign it to an appointment, it keeps the appointment text private (or hidden) in the Appointment Book. When entering appointments directly into the Appointment Book, you can click on any of these option icons to apply the option. The toolbar icon buttons turn the options on or off.

When you assign an option (such as a reminder) to your appointment, an icon appears next to the description in your daily schedule. By default, Schedule+ assigns a reminder option to any appointment you type directly into your Appointment Book.

You'll need to learn to recognize the icons that appear in your Appointment Book and remember what they stand for. Here's a handy table to help you out.

Icon	Name	Description
🏠	Location	Indicates the appointment is at a specific location. (This option icon is only assignable through the Appointment dialog box.)
🔔	Reminder	Schedule+ will remind you about the upcoming appointment as it gets closer.
🔑	Private	Schedule+ keeps the appointment from being seen by other users on your network (if you're networked).
🔑	Tentative	Schedule+ notes the appointment as a tentative item on the schedule to help you easily spot the time slot.

Begin Guided Tour Enter an Appointment

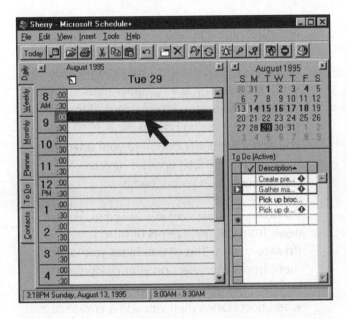

1 Click on a time slot that you want to insert an appointment into, highlighting the selection.

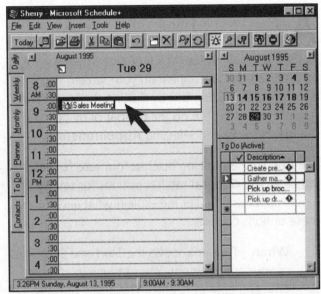

2 Type in a description of the appointment. (If you type an exceptionally long description, you may not be able to see it all in the Appointment Book frame, unless you maximize the program window.) When you finish, click anywhere outside of the slot. The appointment is set.

Begin Guided Tour Increase an Appointment's Time Length

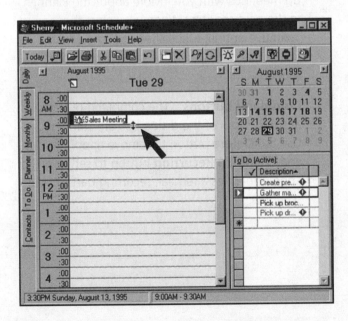

1 Click on the first slot where the appointment starts; then move your mouse pointer over the bottom of the appointment border until it becomes a two-headed arrow.

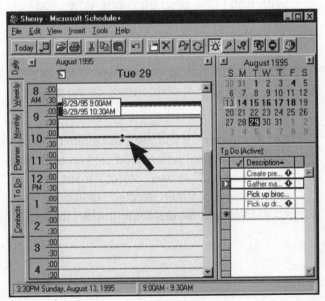

2 Hold down the left mouse button and drag to the ending time slot. Release the mouse button. You can now type in your appointment's description, and Schedule+ sets the appointment in your Appointment Book.

Use the Appointment Dialog Box

Another route to entering more detailed appointments is to open the Appointment dialog box. To do this, double-click on a time slot. The Appointment dialog box will appear on your screen. You can also access this dialog box by clicking the **Insert New Appointment** button on the toolbar or by opening the **Insert** menu and selecting **Appointment**.

The Appointment dialog box has four tabs for entering data. The **General** tab has options for setting up a new appointment. Let me explain what each one of these options controls:

When   This area shows the Start and End times of your appointment. You can type in another time and date as needed. The arrow buttons next to the times let you scroll through other hours. The drop-down arrows next to the dates let you view a monthly calendar to select a new date.

Description   This box is where you type in details about your appointment. For example, let's say you're entering your lunch date with Bob in your daily schedule. You can type **Lunch with Bob** in the description box. When you close the Appointment box, the description appears in your daily schedule.

Where   This option lets you type in the location where your appointment is taking place (if applicable).

Set Reminder   If you want to be reminded of your appointment beforehand with an on-screen box and an audible beep, select the **Set Reminder** option. When selected, additional controls appear for designating when the

reminder message is to appear. (The message that appears is simply a dialog box telling you about your appointment.) For example, you can set it up to send you a reminder message fifteen minutes before your appointment. (More about the Reminder dialog box on page 301.) When you add a Reminder option to your appointment, a tiny bell icon appears next to the description in your schedule.

Private   To keep your appointment description away from the prying eyes of others, use the **Private** option. This option hides your appointment from other users on your computer network, but you can still see it in your schedule when necessary. When you add a Private option, a tiny key icon appears next to your appointment description.

Tentative   If your appointment is tentative, and not concrete, use the **Tentative** option. This keeps the appointment time from appearing as untouchable in your Planner feature, especially if you're networked and people are trying to set up meetings with you. (More about the Planner in the next chapter.) When you select the Tentative option, a tiny check-question mark icon appears next to the description in your schedule.

Command buttons   The command buttons at the bottom of the dialog box are standard. Use the **Delete** button to remove appointments and the **Make Recurring** button to set up an appointment as a regular, recurring part of your schedule.

The Other Appointment Box Tabs

There are some other things you can do in the Appointment dialog box besides set appointments. If you're networked, the other tabs in the Appointment box can give you more information.

> Use the **Attendees** tab to view a list of people who are attending the appointment with you.

> Use the **Notes** tab to create notes about your meeting, or type up a meeting agenda for distribution among the attendees. (See page 287 to learn how to use the **Notes** tab.)

Use the **Planner** tab, a miniaturized Planner feature that you'll learn about in the next section, to view everyone's schedule times to help you pick a free time for all. The **Auto-Pick** button helps you locate the first free time available among the attendees.

Print out a copy of your schedule at any time. Open the **File** menu and select **Print**. In the Print dialog box, you can select which portion of your Schedule+ program you want to print.

Begin Guided Tour   Set an Appointment with the Appointment Dialog Box

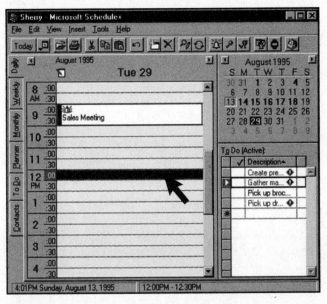

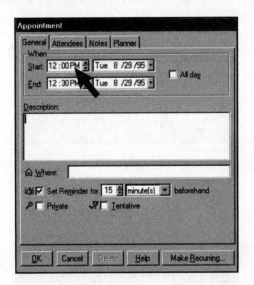

1 Double-click on any time slot in your daily schedule. This will open the Appointment dialog box. Click the **General** tab to bring its options to the front of the box.

2 Set a specific time and date in the **Start** and **End** boxes. (By default, these boxes show the current date and the time you double-clicked on in your schedule.)

(continues)

Guided Tour   Set an Appointment with the Appointment Dialog Box   *(continued)*

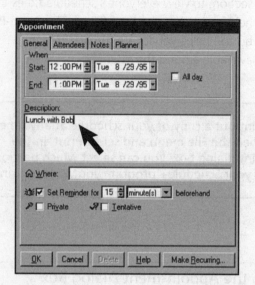

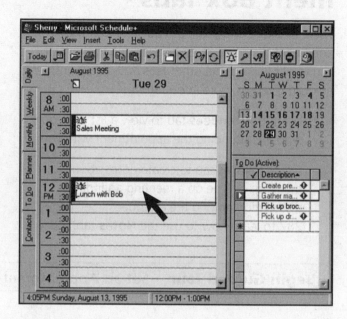

3 Type a description of your appointment in the **Description** box.

5 When you finish, click **OK** and Schedule+ sets your appointment. It will now appear on your schedule.

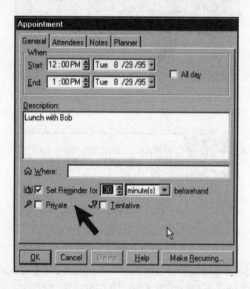

4 You can add any additional options, such as a reminder or a recurring appointment, by selecting those options now.

Set a Reminder

Do you have any pressing appointments that you can't possibly miss? Then the *Reminder* feature can really help you remember them. You've already learned a little about inserting a reminder icon into your appointment in the previous tasks. A reminder icon resembles a tiny bell that appears in front of your appointment description.

By default, Schedule+ inserts a reminder icon whenever you type in a description in the daily schedule. You can also insert a reminder using the Appointment dialog box.

After setting a reminder, you won't be reminded about your appointment until it draws closer. In order for the reminder to work, however, you must have your Schedule+ program open or minimized.

Use the Reminder Box

But when does the Reminder feature get around to reminding you? It depends. What advance time did you set? You can set the Reminder feature when you open the Appointment dialog box. The **Set Reminder** check box, when selected, lets you choose what time the Reminder feature calls your attention to the appointment. Fifteen minutes beforehand is a typical setting.

When your appointment nears, the Reminder box will pop up on your screen (depending on when you set it to appear). When the Reminder box appears, you'll hear an audible beep and the box suddenly interrupts what you were doing. The box itself describes your appointment and its time. The catch to using this Reminder feature, however, is you need to have your computer on, Schedule+ running (or minimized), and you need to be in the same room with your computer or you won't hear the beep or notice the Reminder box on your screen.

This title bar of the Reminder box tells you your appointment time. Inside the box, you'll see a description of the appointment and where your appointment is to take place (if you entered that data earlier). With the options at the bottom of the box, you can choose to remind yourself again as the appointment gets even closer.

- Click the **Notify me again** option if you want another reminder before the appointment, and select a time for it.

- If you don't need another reminder, select the **Don't notify me again** option.

- When you finish with the box, click **OK** to exit.

By default, Schedule+ is set to show reminder boxes along with an audible beep. However, if you turned these settings off, you may be missing all of your reminder boxes. To check, open your **Tools** menu, select **Options**, and click on the **General** tab. Make sure to select the **Set daily reminder**, **Set audible alarm**, and **Enable reminders** check boxes. Click **OK** to exit and your reminder boxes should now work.

Begin Guided Tour   Set a Reminder Using the Appointment Dialog Box

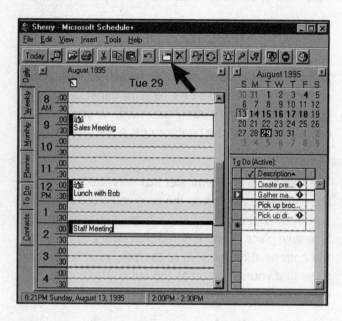

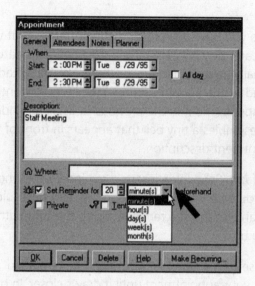

1 Double-click on the appointment in the Appointment Book, or click the **Insert New Appointment** button on the toolbar to add a new appointment to your schedule.

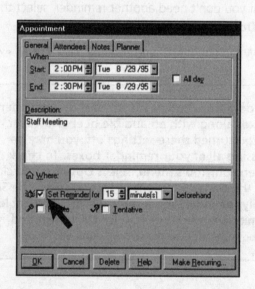

2 The Appointment dialog box appears on-screen. Make sure to select the **Set Reminder** check box. When selected, additional options appear in the dialog box.

3 Choose an advance time for the reminder. This will cause a reminder box to appear on-screen when the appointment draws near. You can set a time in the time box, and you can also click on the drop-down arrow to set other measurements of time.

4 After you set a time, you're ready to exit the box. Click **OK** and the reminder is set.

To quickly insert a reminder icon in an existing appointment, select the appointment and click the **Reminder** button on the toolbar.

Begin Guided Tour   Use the Reminder Box

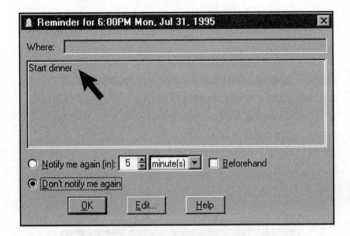

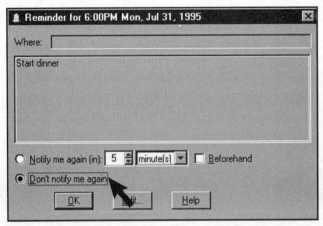

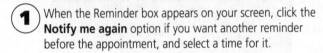

1 When the Reminder box appears on your screen, click the **Notify me again** option if you want another reminder before the appointment, and select a time for it.

2 If you don't need another reminder, select the **Don't notify me again** option.

3 When you finish with the box, click **OK** to exit.

Begin Guided Tour   Turn Off the Default Reminder Setting

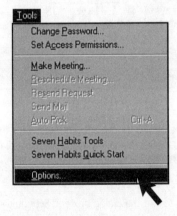

1 Open the **Tools** menu and select **Options**.

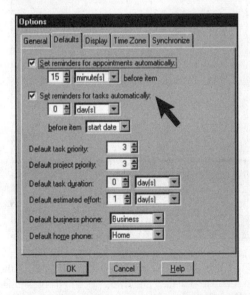

2 In the Options dialog box, click the **Defaults** tab.

3 Unselect the **Set reminders for appointments automatically** check box. Click **OK** to exit the box.

Set Recurring Appointments

Some of your appointments might happen every week or every day, such as a weekly staff meeting or a daily car pool. Rather than typing these appointments in over and over again in your schedule, use the *Recurring* option. You'll find the Recurring option available all over the place. It's on your toolbar, in your Insert menu, and even in the Appointment dialog box.

A recurring appointment always appears with a circular icon in your Appointment Book. You can set recurring appointments daily, weekly, monthly, and yearly with Schedule+.

Begin Guided Tour Set a Recurring Appointment

1 Select the appointment on your schedule and click the **Recurring** button on your toolbar.

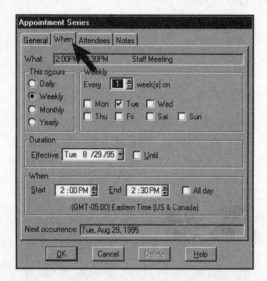

2 This opens the Appointment Series dialog box. Use the tabs to set up information about your recurring appointment. Click the **When** tab to designate when the appointment occurs (daily, weekly, monthly, or yearly) and what day it falls on. You can also set the exact time of the meeting. Make your adjustments to the **Start** and **End** settings under the **When** area.

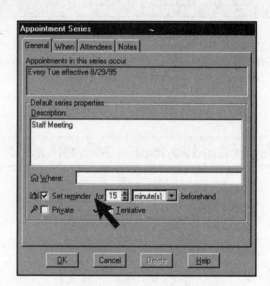

3 To set a reminder for the appointment, click the **General** tab, which looks just like the Appointment dialog box. Use the **Set Reminder** option to add a reminder to the recurring appointment.

4 Click **OK** to exit the dialog box and Schedule+ sets your recurring appointment. The dates of your recurring appointments will appear bolded on the Date Navigator calendar.

Edit Your Appointments

In the previous tasks, you learned how to enter appointments and add options to them. So, what if you want to change an appointment; how are you going to do that? In the world of paper organizers, you can make changes to things you've written down by simply scribbling them out, or erasing them and scribbling them somewhere else in your schedule. In your electronic organizer, you can scribble things out too, but it works a little differently, and you won't have to worry about smudging your schedule or creating a giant ink blob on the screen.

There are several different ways to edit your scheduled appointments. You can use toolbar buttons, menu commands, or take a more direct approach. One of the easiest ways to change an appointment is to make an edit directly to an appointment as it appears in the Appointment Book. You can also make edits by selecting the appointment and opening the Appointment dialog box.

To add a new appointment to your schedule with the Appointment dialog box, double-click on the time slot where it's to appear; or click the **Insert New Appointment** button on the toolbar.

> To delete an appointment, click the **Delete** button on the toolbar or press the **Delete** key.

Begin Guided Tour   Edit an Appointment in the Appointment Book

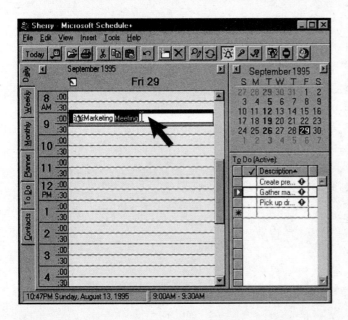

1 Click inside the time slot. You can edit the description text just like you edit text in a word processing program. You can delete characters, insert new words, and so on.

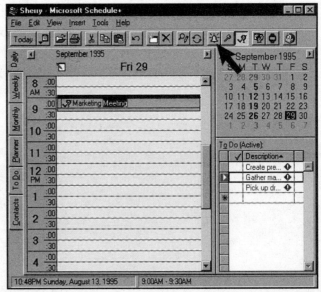

2 To turn appointment options on or off, click the appropriate toolbar buttons. For example, to add a reminder to the appointment, click the **Reminder** button.

3 When you finish with the edits, click anywhere outside the time slot.

Begin Guided Tour Edit with the Appointment Dialog Box

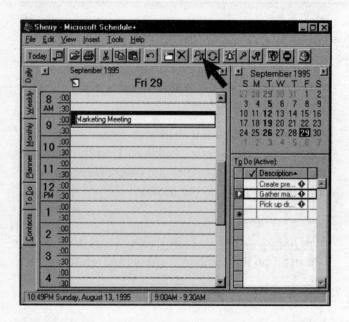

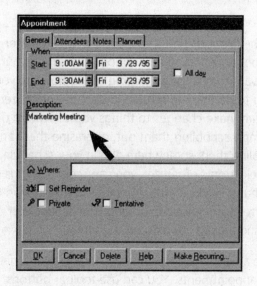

1 Select the appointment in the Appointment Book; then click the **Edit** button on the toolbar (or double-click on the appointment's time slot). This opens the Appointment dialog box containing the appointment's details.

2 Make your changes to the options in the dialog box. Click **OK** to exit the box and put your edits in effect.

Move an Appointment

If you want to move the appointment to another time slot on your daily schedule, you can drag it there with the mouse. Move your mouse pointer over the top border or left border and it becomes a four-sided arrow. You can then use this arrow to drag the appointment to a new location on your daily schedule.

An even simpler way to move an appointment is with the Move Appointment dialog box. Open the **Edit** menu and select **Move Appt**. This opens a box where you can designate a new time slot and date for the appointment.

If you want to reschedule the appointment for a future date, use the *Date Navigator*: the calendar in the upper right corner of the Daily view tab. Click on the appropriate date on the calendar, and your Appointment book turns to the date's schedule page. The tiny arrow buttons at the top of the Date Navigator let you move back and forth between months to select other dates.

You can also use the Cut, Copy, and Paste commands to move your appointments around. Any appointment you select and apply the Cut or Copy command to is placed in the Windows Clipboard, a temporary holding area. When you're ready to place the appointment in a new location, use the **Paste** command.

Begin Guided Tour   Move Appointments in the Appointment Book

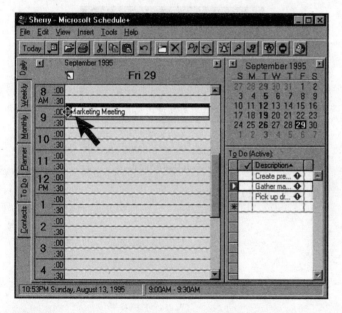

1 Move your mouse pointer over the left edge of the appointment that you want to relocate. The mouse pointer takes the shape of a four-sided arrow.

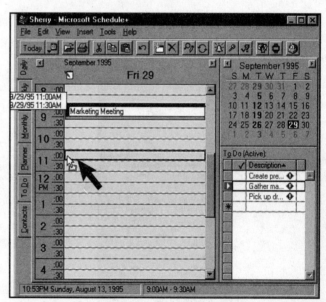

2 Hold down the left mouse button and drag the appointment to a new time slot. Notice that only the appointment's frame moves with the dragging motion.

(continues)

Guided Tour   Move Appointments in the Appointment Book   *(continued)*

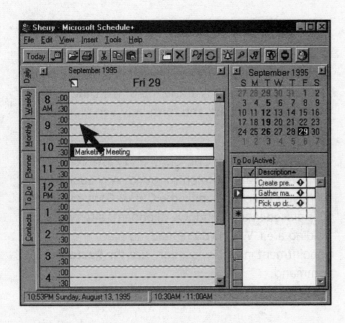

3 Release the mouse button and Schedule+ moves the appointment.

Begin Guided Tour   Move an Appointment with the Move Appointment Box

1 Select the appointment you want to move.

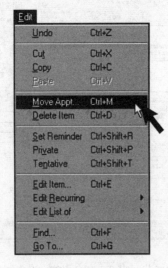

2 Open the **Edit** menu and choose **Move Appt**.

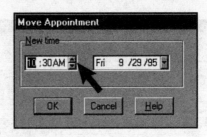

3 When the Move Appointment dialog appears, select a new time and date for the appointment.

4 Click **OK** to exit the box.

Begin Guided Tour   Move an Appointment with the Date Navigator

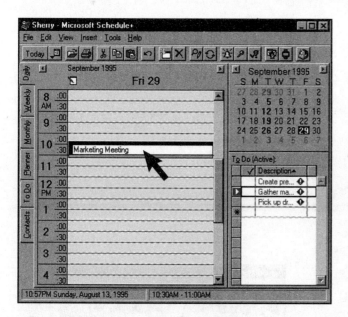

1 Select the appointment you want to move.

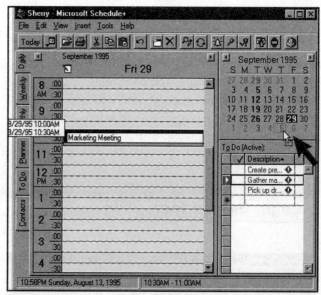

2 Hold down the left mouse button, and drag the appointment over to the Date Navigator calendar to the new date. Let go of your mouse button and the appointment will now appear in the other date's daily schedule.

Begin Guided Tour   Cut, Copy and Paste

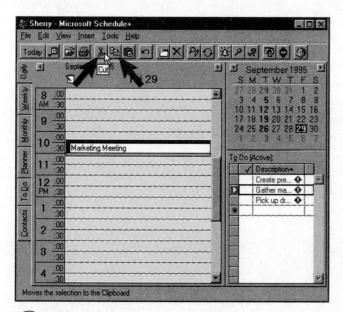

1 Select the appointment you want to move or copy. Click the **Cut** or **Copy** button on the toolbar.

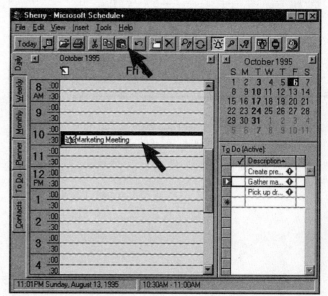

2 Move your schedule to the new date where you want to place the appointment.

3 Click the **Paste** button on the toolbar and Schedule+ adds the item.

Add Notes to Appointments

With paper organizers, it's easy to add notes to your schedule. All you have to do is scribble them down. You can also add notes to help you with your electronic schedule. You can create detailed notes along with any appointment you set on Schedule+. The notes won't appear in the daily schedule, but they're readily available in the Appointment dialog box.

You can add notes to any appointment by opening the Appointment dialog box and clicking the **Notes** tab. Just type in your notes and they're saved as part of the appointment.

To see the notes regarding the appointment, just open the Appointment dialog box again and click the **Notes** tab to read them.

Begin Guided Tour Add Notes

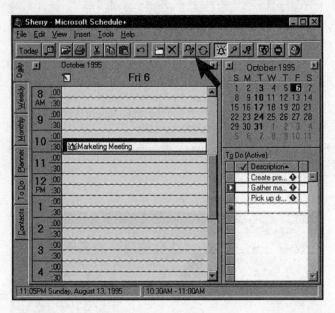

1 Select the appointment you want to add notes to; then click the **Edit** button in the toolbar to open the Appointment dialog box.

2 Click the **Notes** tab to bring it to the front of the box. In the empty text box, you can type in all kinds of notes, jot down thoughts, and so on.

3 To exit the box, click **OK**.

Use the Event Scheduler

Need to schedule a big event or an annual event on your busy calendar? Use the *Event scheduler* to help you. Events show up a little differently on your schedule than appointments do. Events show up at the top of your daily schedule, right under the day and date that they're associated with. They don't affect the time slots in your schedule. For example, if you set up your schedule to show your 50th wedding anniversary as an event, it will appear at the top of your schedule. (If you switch over to Weekly view, which you'll learn about on page 315, events appear at the top of the day of the week in which they occur.)

When you set an event into your schedule, the Event icon at the top of your daily schedule looks like it has writing on it. That's one way you can tell you've planned an event. An event day also appears bolded on the Date Navigator calendar. The event appears on your schedule as a heading at the top of the event day's column.

What constitutes a big event? I consider my vacation to be a very big event, so I'm always trying to work it into my busy schedule. Other events might include out-of-town conferences or trade show conventions, weddings, training classes, seminars, company trips, and more. Events can be a one-day thing, span days and weeks, or even months. With Schedule+, you can set recurring events so that they show up each week, month, or year (such as birthdays or anniversaries).

Here's a list of events you may have a use for in your own schedule:

- Conferences and conventions
- Classes and seminars
- Vacations and holidays
- Birthdays
- Weddings and anniversaries
- Retirements
- Promotional events (such as End-of-Month Sale)
- Office events (such as Staff Recognition Day)

Be sure to set up your friends' and family's birthdays as events in your calendar. That way, you'll spot them right away. If you set them up as recurring events, they'll appear on your schedule every year!

You can edit an event by opening the Event dialog box. One way to open the box is through the Insert menu. Open the **Insert** menu and select **Event** to display the Event dialog box. There you can make edits to the event.

You can also see all of the events on your schedule compiled in a list. Open the **Edit** menu and select **Edit List of**. This displays a list of all the events you've set. This is especially helpful when you want to edit events that do not appear on the current day in your schedule.

To reschedule or move an event, you can open up the **Events** list box again and change the date by editing the event.

You can easily delete an event from the Events list by selecting it and clicking the **Delete** button.

Begin Guided Tour   Adding Events

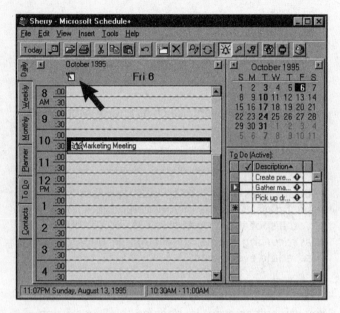

1 Click the **Event** icon at the top of your schedule.

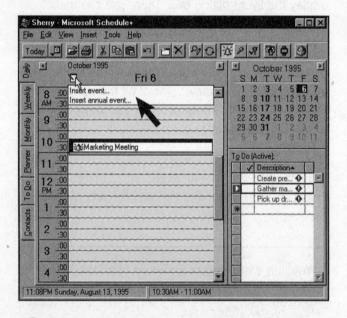

2 When you click the **Event** icon, a submenu appears with the option of selecting **Insert event** or **Insert annual event**. (If you select **Insert annual event**, you'll make the event a recurring part of your schedule.) From the submenu, choose the appropriate type of event you want to add. The Event dialog box or the Annual Event dialog box appears on your screen.

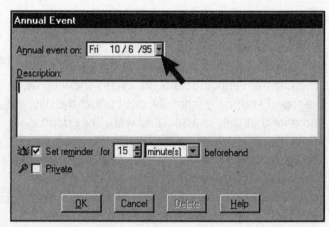

3 In the Event or Annual Event dialog box, choose the event start date. If you're setting an event, you should also select an end date. You can use the arrow buttons next to the dates to choose other dates, or you can type in the dates you want.

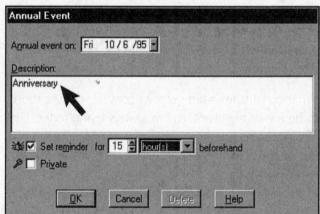

4 Click in the **Description** box and type in a description of the event.

5 Add any additional options, such as a reminder or a private icon.

Guided Tour Adding Events

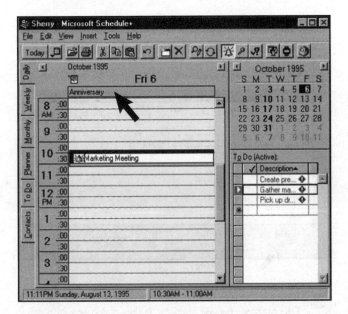

6 Click **OK** to exit the box, and Schedule+ adds the event to your schedule.

Begin Guided Tour Edit and Reschedule Events

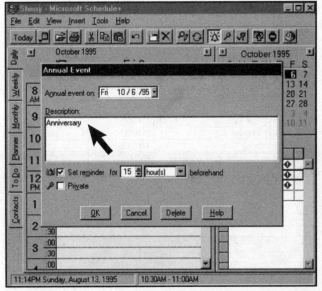

1 Click the **Event** icon; this time, your event's description appears in the submenu. You can also directly click on the event description at the top of your daily schedule to view the submenu.

2 Double-click on the event's description in the submenu to open the Event dialog box.

3 Make your changes in the dialog box. For example, to change to the description, edit the description text. To edit any options, simply turn the option check boxes on or off.

4 Click **OK** to exit the box.

Begin Guided Tour   Listing Events

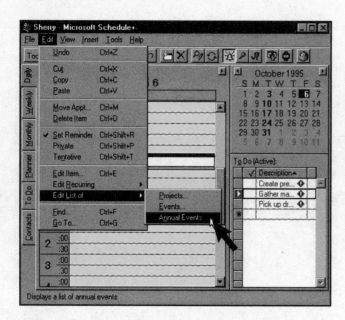

1 Open the **Edit** menu and select **Edit List of**. This displays a submenu. From the submenu, select **Events** or **Annual Events**, depending on which type of event you want to edit.

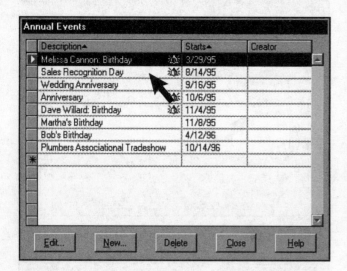

2 Depending on which event type you select, an Events or Annual Events list box opens up, listing all of the events you scheduled and their start dates.

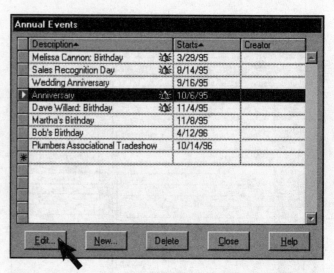

3 To make changes to a specific event, select it and click the **Edit** button. This will open the Events dialog box. You can make your edits to the event and then click **OK**.

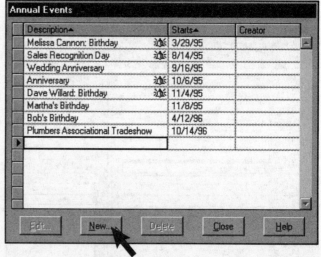

4 To add a new event to the list, click the **New** button. This opens a new Events dialog box where you can enter detailed information about the event.

5 To exit the Events list box, click the **Close** button.

View Appointments with the Weekly Tab

It's time to switch views. How about looking at your busy schedule in a weekly format? You'll need to click on the **Weekly** tab. When you do, your screen will display your Appointment Book in a slightly different view.

By default, Schedule+ shows you five days of the week in Weekly view. You no longer see the Date Navigator or the To Do list. Your screen looks a little crowded in Weekly view, and some of your appointments may not fit completely into your weekly columns and will look cut off. Don't forget, you can enlarge the Schedule+ screen by clicking the **Maximize** button.

The schedule you see in the Weekly view is the same as the schedule in Daily view; however, you see more days of the week in the Weekly view. You can perform the same functions in your Weekly view as in Daily view. The scroll bar at the far right side of the

box lets you scroll through the time slots on the schedule.

At the top of the Weekly view tab are two arrow buttons, one on the left and one on the right. Like the arrow buttons in Daily view, you can use these to move your Weekly view back a week or forward a week.

You can insert appointments, events, move items, delete items, and edit items in Weekly view just like you can in Daily view. The only difference is in how you view the items on the daily schedule. You have a better picture of how busy your schedule is for any given week when you switch over to Weekly view.

You can use the same methods for adding appointments to the Weekly view tab as you did in Daily view. You can insert appointments with the **Insert New Appointment** button on the toolbar, or you can add them directly to your schedule.

Begin Guided Tour　　View Another Week

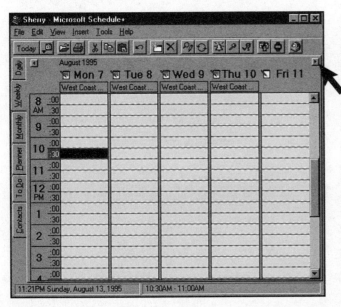

1 To move forward to the next week, click once on the right arrow button.

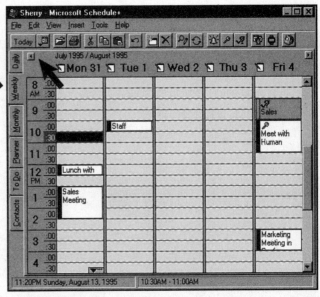

2 To move back to the previous week, click once on the left arrow button.

Begin Guided Tour   Change the Day Display

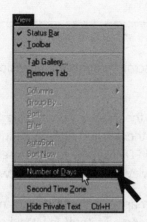

1 Open the **View** menu and select **Number of Days**.

If you hold down your mouse button while selecting the arrow buttons, you'll move quickly through the weeks of the month.

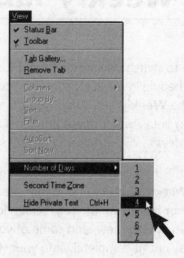

2 In the submenu that appears, choose the number of days you want displayed in the Weekly view tab. The Weekly view changes to reflect the selection you made in the Number of Days submenu.

View Your Schedule by Month

Want to see your entire month's worth of appointments? Switch over to Monthly view by clicking the **Monthly** tab. Your screen opens and you can view the entire month.

Things look a little crowded when in Monthly view. If you want to see details about any appointment listed in your schedule from Monthly view, double-click on the appointment. This will open the Appointment dialog box where you can see details about the appointment. If it's an event you want to see, double-click on it to open the Event dialog box to view the details.

You can edit schedule items in Weekly view at any time; however, it's a little harder to see everything on-screen, so you're better off switching to Daily or Weekly view to make edits.

At the top of the Monthly view tab, you'll find two arrow buttons, one on the left and one on the right. Like the arrow buttons in Daily and Weekly view, you can use these to move your schedule view back a month or forward a month.

Another way to move to the next month is to click anywhere on the shaded days or weeks that appear in Monthly view.

> If you hold down your mouse button while selecting the arrow buttons, you'll move quickly through the months of the year.

Begin Guided Tour   Change Months

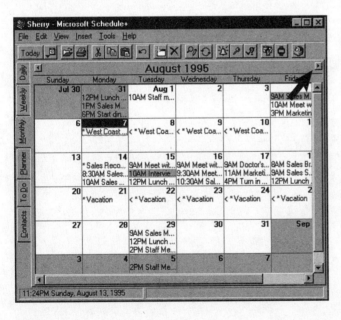

1 To move forward to the next month, click once on the right arrow button.

2 To move back to the previous month, click once on the left arrow button.

Set Up Tasks and Contacts Lists with Schedule+

Scheduling appointments isn't the only thing you can do with Schedule+. You can also use the program to help you manage tasks and projects you need to accomplish; plus you can organize names and phone numbers of the people you contact the most. In this part of the book, you'll learn how to do each of these things, and you'll also learn how to use the Planner tab to gauge how much free time and busy time is on your daily schedule.

What You Will Find in This Section

Use the To Do List

Use Schedule+'s To Do list to enter, manage, and track tasks and projects that are important to the various dates and appointments on your schedule. With the To Do list, you can assemble lists of daily things you need to do, items that you must work on to complete a project, and even a compilation of groceries you need to pick up on the way home. You can use the To Do list in all kinds of ways, but its main purpose is to help you keep track of things you need to do.

To display the To Do list, click the **To Do** tab. This will open the screen to a To Do list format. You've already seen the To Do list in smaller scale on the Daily view tab. (Flip back to Daily view to see the To Do list in the bottom right corner.) That particular list relates to the date displayed on your Appointment Book schedule. It lists the tasks you need to complete that day, or any held-over tasks that you didn't complete from the previous days. The To Do list shown in your To Do tab is the entire list of all your tasks you're keeping track of.

After you enter some tasks and associate them with a particular date on your schedule, switch back to Daily view (click the **Daily** tab). The To Do list will reflect tasks that pertain to that particular date on your schedule. This can help you keep track of things you have to do each day, besides appointments to attend.

Tables such as the one shown in the Schedule+ To Do list consist of intersecting columns and rows that form *cells*. Each row and column represents a *heading/ entry* or *field/record*. In databases, which is what you're working with in the To Do list, each column is a field and each row is a record.

The following Guided Tour shows you how to read a To Do list.

Begin Guided Tour   Read Your To Do List

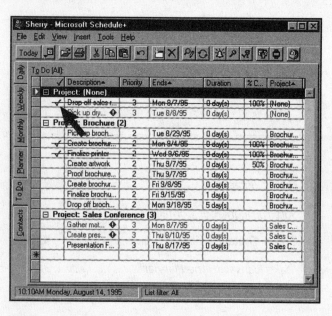

1 Completed tasks appear with a line through them and a check mark in the Completed column.

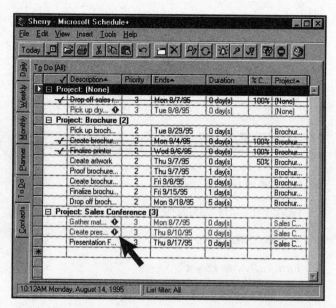

2 Any tasks not completed by their specified end dates will appear with an overdue symbol and their dates are marked in red so you can't miss them.

Guided Tour   Read Your To Do List

3 If you're viewing the To Do list in the Daily view tab, note that uncompleted tasks from the previous day or days are held-over and appear in your next day's To Do list, marked in red.

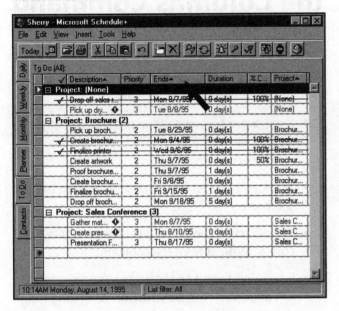

4 If you sort your tasks (which you'll learn to do in "Group Tasks" on page 330), you'll see an arrow next to the heading indicating which direction the sorting occurred. An up arrow means Schedule+ sorted in ascending order, and a down arrow means it sorted in a descending order.

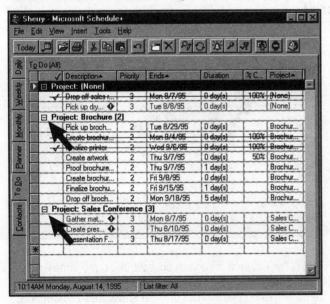

5 You can group your tasks under project headings (more about this in "Group Tasks" on page 330). The symbols in front (plus or minus signs) of the project heading let you hide or display the tasks related to the project. The figure shown has a minus sign next to the project heading, which means all the tasks are listed.

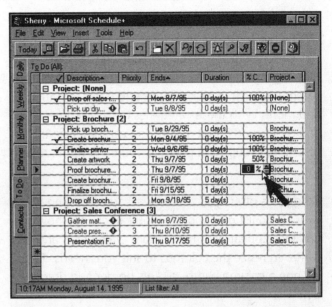

6 Some categories in your To Do list, when selected, open boxes for changing dates or percentages. These come in handy when you're editing your task's progress and status.

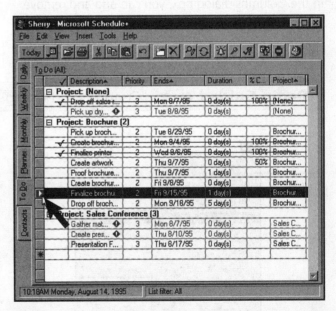

7 Use the **Row Selection** button to select an entire row.

Work with Task Categories

The big To Do list appears as a grid, and the more tasks you add, the bigger your grid gets. Schedule+ organizes the tasks into columns that represent categories such as task priority, end dates, duration, and more. With these categories (also called *fields*), and others you might assign, you can organize the tasks into groups and projects; you can even filter and sort your tasks.

Schedule+ offers you several ways to control how your To Do list grid appears. You can change how the gridlines appear with the Options dialog box, and you can even resize the columns to suit your needs. To change a column width, click its border and drag it to a new size.

By default, Schedule+ shows several column categories that might relate to the tasks you want to list. However, you can change the categories at any time. In the Columns dialog box, you can add and remove the column categories that will appear on your grid.

Change Columns with the Columns Command

For a faster change of your To Do list columns, use the Columns submenu. Open the **View** menu and select **Columns**. In the submenu that appears, you have several category options to use:

- If you want to show all the possible column categories in your grid, select **All** from the submenu that appears.

- To show a limited few, choose **Few** from the submenu.

- To go back to the original categories display, choose **Typical** from the submenu.

- If you don't want to see any additional categories at all, click the **Description** command from the submenu. This leaves you with just the Completed and Description columns shown in the To Do list.

Begin Guided Tour   Change Grid Categories

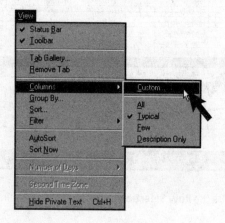

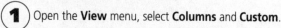

1 Open the **View** menu, select **Columns** and **Custom**.

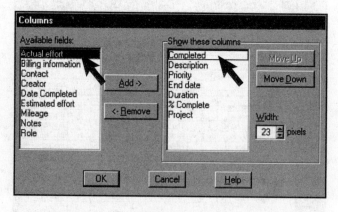

2 The Columns dialog box appears. You can change which categories appear. The **Available fields** list box shows remaining categories you can use. The **Show these columns** list box shows what categories currently appear in your grid.

Guided Tour   Change Grid Categories

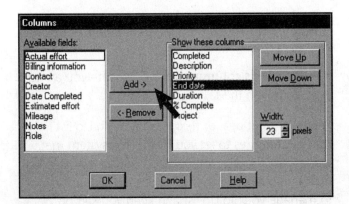

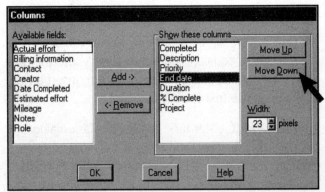

3 To add a category to the **Show these columns** list, click the category on the left, and click the **Add** button. To remove a category from the **Show these columns** list, select the category; then click the **Remove** button.

4 To change the order of the categories, select the category to move. Then click the **Move Up** or **Move Down** buttons until the category is in the desired location.

5 To exit the dialog box and get back to your To Do list grid, click **OK**.

Begin Guided Tour   Changing the Grid Display

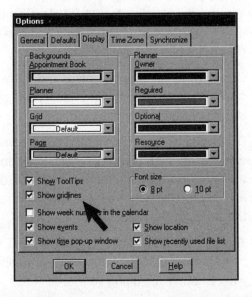

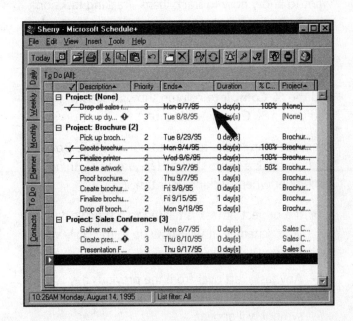

1 Open the **Tools** menu and choose **Options**. This opens the Options dialog box. Click the **Display** tab to bring it to the front of the box. Unselect the Show gridlines check box.

2 Click **OK** to exit the dialog box and the To Do list shows no gridlines.

Add Tasks to the To Do List

Time to start adding your own tasks to the To Do list. A *task* can be any item you want to accomplish or track. You can add a task directly into the grid by typing it in. Click the row you want to insert a task, and type in the text for each column.

Another way to enter tasks is with the Task dialog box. This box lets you add more details to your task. You can use the same options found in the Appointment dialog box with tasks. For example, you can set up your task with a reminder. When the day arrives for you to complete the task, a reminder box will greet you when you log on to Schedule+, reminding you to complete the task.

Tracking Tasks

Once you assemble several tasks on your list, you'll want to know how to track them. Tracking tasks on your To Do list is straightforward. When you complete a task, click the **Completed** column (the column with a check mark at the top). This places a check mark in front of your task, strikes through the task with a line, and the **% Complete** column shows 100% (if your grid uses a % Complete category).

There are many ways for you to utilize the To Do list's fields to track a task's status. Here are a few things to remember when tracking your tasks:

- If a project or task is related to a specific date on your schedule, it will show up in the Daily view tab on the To Do list.

- Any tasks left over from the previous day will appear in red on the To Do list; an overdue symbol will appear.

- The **% Complete column** lets you log in a percentage that indicates how much of the task you have completed.

- The **Priority column** lets you prioritize the tasks based on a number scale.

- The **Ends column** specifies the date you are to complete the task by.

There's a great deal of flexibility in the To Do list's tracking features to let you maintain a system that works best for you. Although Schedule+ will help you with reminders and overdue icons, it's still up to you to manage your To Do list and keep yourself on schedule.

Editing Tasks

After you compile a task in your list, you can easily go back and make changes to it. There are all kinds of ways you can edit the tasks displayed in your To Do list. Here are a few:

- You can double-click the **Row Selection** button next to the task you want to edit and make your changes in the Task dialog box.

- Or you can select the task fields and make your changes directly into the individual parts of your task displayed in the list.

- Depending on the column, additional controls will appear when you click a field. You can use the controls to set different percentages, dates, and so on. These controls are helpful in tracking the status of the tasks.

- You can also right-click your selected task to open a shortcut menu with more commands you can apply to editing your task.

- To delete a task, select it and press the **Delete** key.

- Don't forget about those handy Cut, Copy, and Paste commands. You can select them from your toolbar or the **Edit** menu.

- To change your column headings (fields), open the **View** menu and select **Column**; then select **Custom**. This opens the Column dialog box where you can edit which columns appear in your list.

- To display more or less columns, open the **View** menu, select **Column**, and select the amount of columns you want displayed on your grid.

- To adjust any column width, move your mouse pointer up to the border between two column headings; the mouse pointer becomes a two-headed pointer. Drag the pointer to a new width to change column size.

- To insert a new row onto your grid, select the row where you want the new row to appear before. Open the **Insert** menu and choose **Row**.

- You easily can turn a task into an appointment on your schedule. Select the task, right-click to display the shortcut menu, and select **Appt. from Task**. This opens the Appointment dialog box that you can use to assign the task as an appointment.

> Another way to open the Task dialog box is to right-click the grid and select **New Task**.

Begin Guided Tour   Add a Task

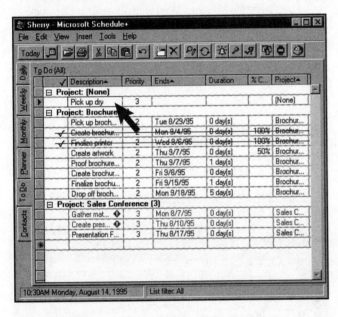

1 Choose a row to start your task in. Then click the **Description** column and type in a description for your task.

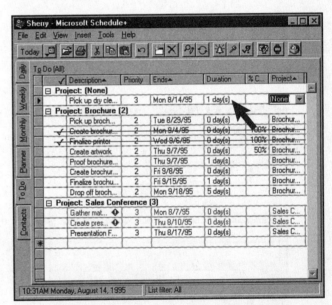

2 Continue adding information in each category/column for the task row you've selected until you have filled in everything that's relevant. (You can press the **Tab** key to advance to each category in the row, or you can click the cells using your mouse.) Use the category boxes to help you enter information.

Begin Guided Tour   Add Tasks with the Task Dialog Box

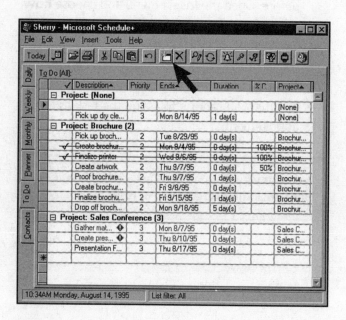

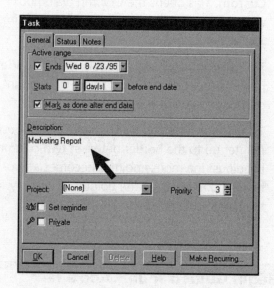

1 There are two ways to open the Task dialog box; you can double-click the **Row Selection** button in front of the task, or you can click the **Insert New Task** button on your toolbar. Either method opens the Task dialog box.

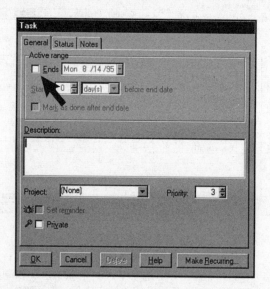

2 In the **General** tab, enter an ending date in the **Active range** area associated with the task, or select a date with the drop-down arrows. You can also specify a starting date, which helps you track the duration of the task.

3 Use the **Mark as done after end date** check box to automatically mark the task when completed. By the way, this feature marks the tasks as completed after a period of time regardless of whether you remember to or not.

4 Type a description of your task in the **Description** box. If you want the task associated with a specific project, type the project's name in the **Project** box. (Learn more about projects on page 327.)

5 If you want to prioritize the task, especially when dealing with project tasks, mark a priority rating with the **Priority** box.

6 If you need a reminder to help you with your task, set one with the **Set Reminder** check box, and specify when the reminder should appear. If you don't want anyone else viewing your task, click the **Private** option.

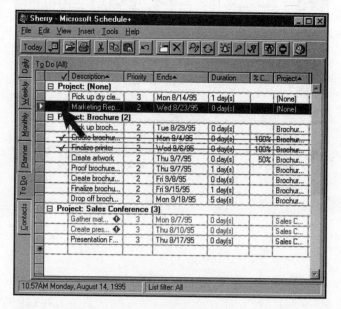

7 Click **OK** to exit the dialog box and return to the To Do list; your new task appears on the grid.

Turn Tasks into Projects

With Schedule+, you can group your tasks under a particular project name to help you organize the things you need to do. Let's say your boss put you in charge of creating a company brochure highlighting products or services. To accomplish a project like this, you would have to complete many individual tasks such as writing the materials to include inside the brochure, coming up with a design, creating artwork, proofing the material, and having the brochure printed by a professional printer.

Schedule+ can help you keep track of these various tasks with the To Do list. By organizing them under one project name, you'll make it easier to locate, track, and see the tasks accomplished.

If you have existing tasks displayed in your To Do list, you easily can list them under project headings, too. To do so, simply select the task by clicking on the **Row Selection** button (at the front of each task) and drag it under the appropriate project heading. You

can also reopen the Task dialog box (by double-clicking on the task) and assign a project heading to the task from the Project drop-down list.

Displaying Projects and Related Tasks

When you have several projects on your To Do list, you can choose to list all the tasks under each project or to hide the tasks. The tiny boxes (symbols) in front of the project heading can turn your project task list on or off. A minus sign means all your tasks appear (also referred to as *expanded*) under the project; a plus sign means the tasks are hidden (or *collapsed*) in the list.

To hide the tasks under a project heading, click the project heading box. This changes the minus sign to a plus sign. To display the tasks, click the tiny box again.

Begin Guided Tour Create a Project Heading

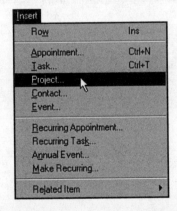

1 Open the **Insert** menu and select **Project**; or right-click anywhere on the grid to open the shortcut menu and select **New Project**.

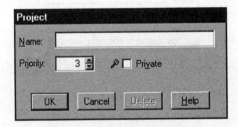

2 The Project dialog box opens. Type a name for your project.

3 You can prioritize your project with the **Priority** box. Simply type in a priority assignment, or use the up and down arrows to set a different number.

(continues)

Guided Tour   Create a Project Heading

(continued)

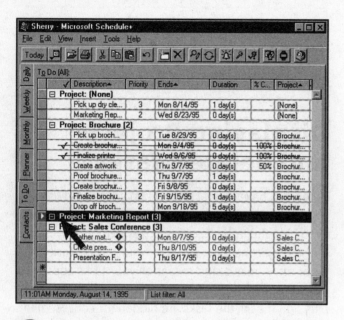

4 Click **OK** to exit the dialog box. The project heading appears in the To Do list.

Begin Guided Tour   Add Tasks to Your Project

1 To add new tasks to the project heading, open the **Insert** menu and select **Task**.

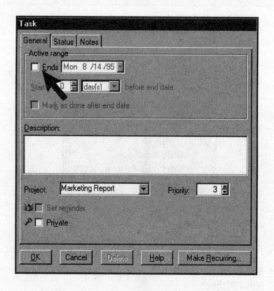

2 In the Task dialog box, type in information pertaining to the task, such as an end date and a task description.

Guided Tour Add Tasks to Your Project

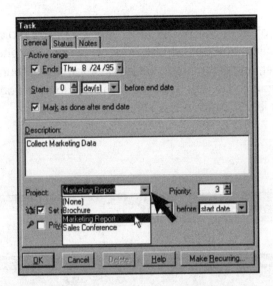

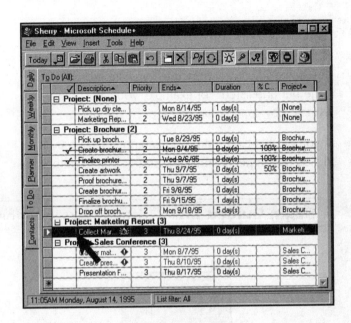

3 To place the task under a project, click the **Project** drop-down list. Choose a project heading from the list.

4 To exit the dialog box and add the task under the project heading, click **OK**.

Group Tasks

Not only can you control how projects and tasks appear on your To Do list (hidden or displayed), you can also control how the items are grouped together and listed. For example, you can choose to list tasks by completion dates, or by priority.

If you double-click a project heading, a Group By dialog box appears. You can use this box to determine

the order in which your tasks appear under a project heading. You can list tasks in ascending or descending order, and list the tasks based on information found in your To Do list's categories. The Group by dialog box lets you group tasks in up to three tiers.

Begin Guided Tour   Group Tasks with the Group By Dialog Box

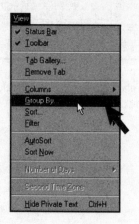

1 Double-click the project heading, or open the **View** menu and select **Group by**.

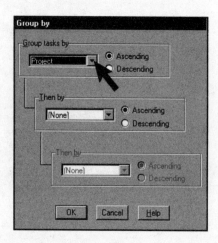

2 The Group by dialog box appears. Make your grouping selections from the drop-down lists, and select to show the list in ascending or descending order.

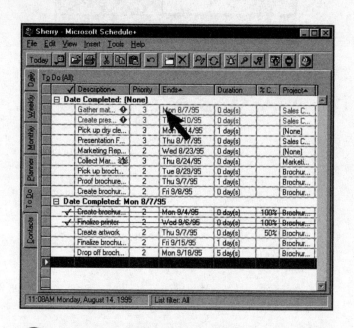

3 Click **OK** to exit the dialog box; Schedule+ rearranges the tasks as determined by your selections.

Create a Contacts List

Y ou can use the Contacts tab to compile information about people you contact the most, such as business associates, sales leads, friends and neighbors, whoever. Once you complete your Contacts list, you can keep updating it, and use it to make appointments. You can even list each contact's birthday or other special events so they appear on your schedule. If you're using Schedule+ on a network, you can share your Contacts list with other users. Regardless of how you use it, you'll quickly find the Contacts feature to be an important part of your Schedule+ program.

The Contacts list that you build in Schedule+ is actually a database. A *database* is a collection of

information that you can store, organize, and retrieve quickly. The information you store for each person is a *record* in the database. The individual parts of the record such as the name or address are *fields*.

You can use the names, addresses, and phone numbers from your Contacts database to create mailing lists, call up other computers (with a modem), and more. It's kind of like having an electronic Rolodex.

To display the Contacts List, click the **Contacts** tab in your Schedule+ window. As you look around the Contacts tab, you'll see a grid listing contacts on the left and a card format for entering data on the right. After you have started a list of contacts, you can then sort and group them.

╭───╮
│ **Begin Guided Tour**   Use the Contacts Tab │
╰───╯

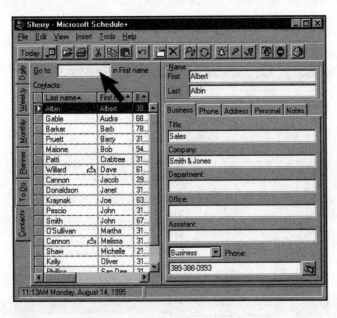

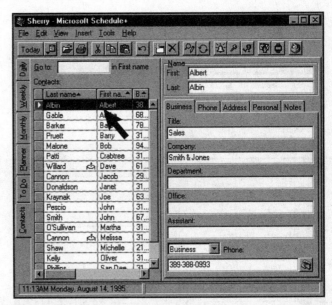

1 Use the **Go to** box to quickly locate names in your database. Type in the name you're looking for, and the name appears highlighted in your list. (You can use the box to locate any fields in your list.)

2 The **Contacts** portion of the tab displays a grid list of your database names and fields.

3 The **Name** area (card format) displays a form in which you can enter information pertaining to your contact, such as name, business, phone, and address.

Enter Contacts

You might as well jump right in and start compiling your own list of contacts. Remember, a contact can be anybody you know or do business with. Contacts can include friends, relatives, co-workers, business associates, vendors, and more. You can enter information about your contacts directly into the grid list, or you can use the card format of tabs and fields.

If you don't like the direct approach to contact list-building, you can use the Contact dialog box. It neatly displays similar fields from the form on the Contacts tab, but puts them in a larger dialog box. To open the Contact dialog box, follow one of these methods:

- Open the **Insert** menu and select **Contact**.

- Right-click to display the shortcut menu and select **New Contact**.

- Double-click an empty row's **Row Selection** button.

- Click the **Insert New Contact** button on your toolbar.

All of these methods open the Contact dialog box. The dialog box looks like the card format on your Contact tab, only wider and arranged differently. If you want to enter personal information about the contact, you'll need to do so back on the Contacts tab. The Contacts dialog box does not include fields for birthdays or anniversaries. To use the Contacts dialog box, proceed to fill in each field in the tabs that you have information for. When you finish, click **OK** and you return to the Contacts tab.

You can edit your contacts at any time; you can make edits directly to the information on the grid list or in the form on the right. You can also edit in the Contact dialog box.

Begin Guided Tour   Add a Contact

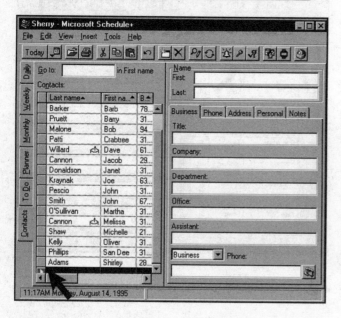

1 Click a **Row Selection** button in front of the row you want to enter your contact into, preferably an empty row. You can also open the **Insert** menu and select **Row**. This will display a blank form on the right side of your screen.

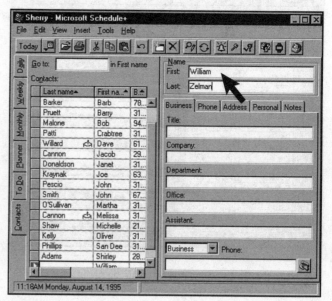

2 In the **Name** area, start typing in new information into each field as necessary. For example, to enter a name, click inside the **First** box and type a first name.

Guided Tour Add a Contact

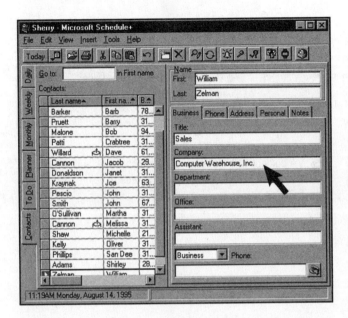

3 Next, start filling in the **Business** tab fields. Click inside each box (field) to fill in its related information. Keep in mind that not every box needs to be filled in, only the ones you will use the most.

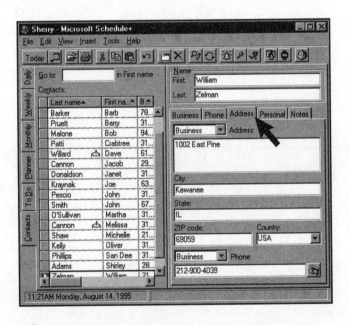

4 Click the other card tabs to enter in more details such as other phone numbers and the contact's address.

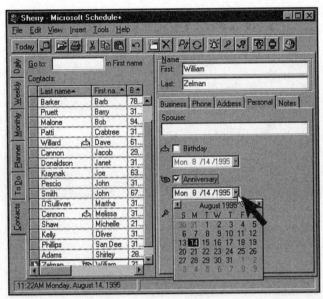

5 To enter birthday or anniversary information about the contact, click the **Personal** tab and set the date. When you enter personal information about a contact (such as a birthday), a symbol (such as a birthday cake) appears in your contact grid.

6 When you finish with the contact information, click inside the grid area and your entry appears as a contact on the list.

Use the Phone Dialer button to use your computer modem to call your contact. You can use the little phone symbols that appear next to phone numbers to dial up your contacts. Just click the **Phone Dialer** button, and your computer starts dialing for you. Your phone must be hooked up to a modem to make this work for you.

Begin Guided Tour Delete a Contact

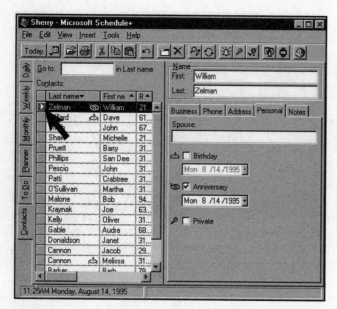

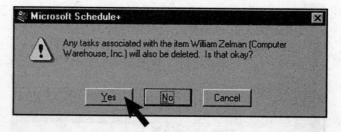

3 A box appears warning you the record will be deleted. Click **Yes**, and Schedule+ removes the record.

1 Select the record you want to remove.

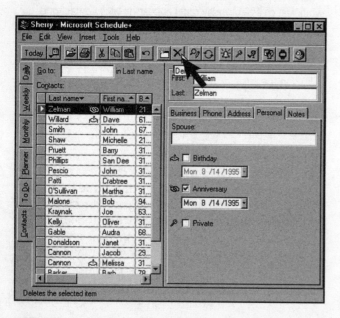

2 Click the **Delete** button on the toolbar. (You can also press the **Delete** key on your keyboard.)

Begin Guided Tour Turn a Contact into an Appointment

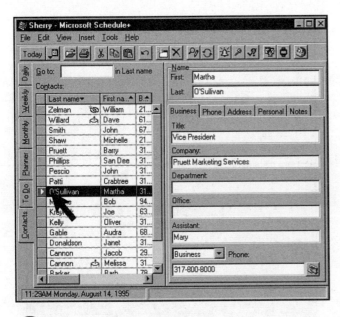

① Select the contact you want to turn into an appointment.

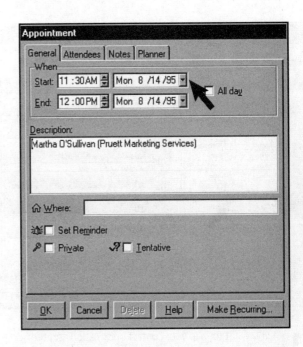

③ The Appointment dialog box appears on-screen. The Description box shows your contact's name and company. Set a time and date for the appointment. Click **OK** to exit the box, and Schedule+ adds the appointment to your schedule.

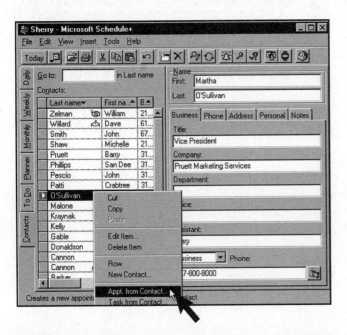

② Right-click to open the shortcut menu and choose **Appt. from Contact**.

Begin Guided Tour   Turn a Contact into a Task

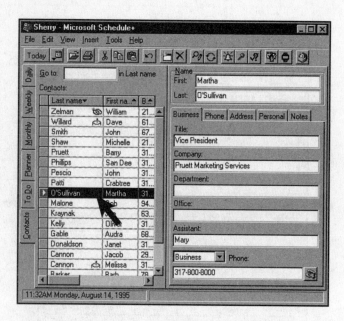

1 If you want to take your contact information and use it in a task, you can do so. Select the contact containing the information you want to turn into a task on your To Do list.

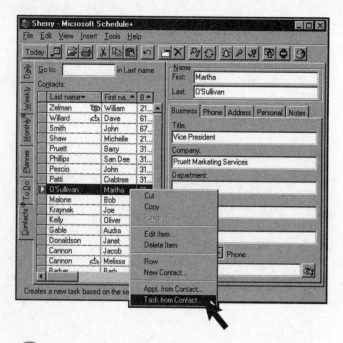

2 Right-click to open the shortcut menu and choose **Task from Contact**.

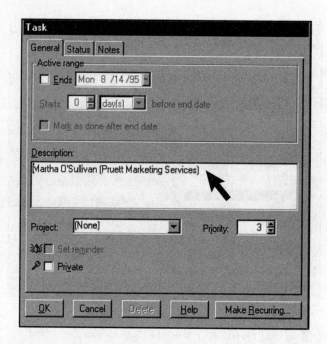

3 The Task dialog box appears on-screen, and its Description box shows your contact's name and company. Add any options you'd like to include in the task, such as an end date or reminder. If the task relates to a specific project, identify that project heading with the Project drop-down list. Click **OK** to exit the box, and Schedule+ adds the task to your To Do list.

Sort Through Your Contacts List

After you compile a list of contacts, you'll need to sort through the list, especially if it's a long list. When you perform a sort, you look through the database for specific records, fields, and common elements. You can then display those records in a particular order.

There are several ways to sort your contacts. Let's start out with a simple sort directly in your Contacts grid. Click any of the column headings in your grid list to perform an immediate sort of data in ascending order in that column (field). For example, if you click the First name column heading, Schedule+ immediately sorts the data alphabetically by first names and the records appear in ascending order (A's at the top of the list and Z's at the bottom).

The up arrow on the column heading means the selected column sorted in ascending order. To sort in descending order (Z to A), press the **Ctrl** key while clicking on the column heading. When you do this, Schedule+ sorts your list in descending order. You determine the column headings that appear in your grid with the Group by settings command, which you'll learn about later in this task.

There are a couple of other ways you can sort. If you want to sort new entries immediately after you enter them, use the AutoSort command. Open the **View** menu and select **AutoSort**. Any time you type in a contact, it will be automatically sorted as soon as you finish entering it. Yet another way you can sort data is with the Sort dialog box.

Sort with the Sort Dialog Box

When you sort with the Sort dialog box, you have the option of sorting by three levels and by several categories. To display the box, open the **View** menu and choose **Sort**. In addition to these options, you can choose to view the sort in ascending or descending order. In each level, you can click the drop-down arrow to reveal which category you want to conduct the sort by.

All of the categories displayed in the drop-down list are actually fields from your Contacts tab. The Sort feature lets you choose to sort by any field available on the Contacts tab or Contacts dialog box.

You can use the Sort dialog box to be very specific about how your contacts appear in the grid list. For example, perhaps you want to sort your Contacts list by ZIP code (called *postal code* in Schedule+). In the Sort box drop-down lists, you have the choice of sorting by business address postal codes or home address postal codes. You'll find a great deal of flexibility in Schedule+'s sorting capabilities.

Also on the **View** menu is a **Sort Now** command, which immediately sorts your list based on specifications set in the Sort dialog box.

Begin Guided Tour Perform a Sort with the Sort Dialog Box

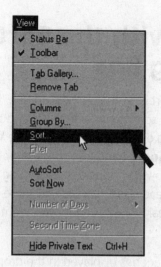

1 Open the **View** menu and select **Sort**.

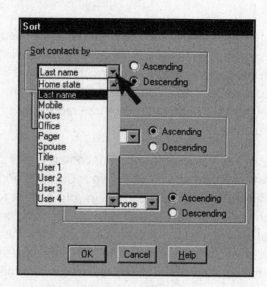

3 Click the drop-down arrow to display a list of sort categories; then choose a category from the list. You can use the scroll bar to view the different categories in the list.

4 (Optional) Continue choosing other levels and categories to narrow your sort.

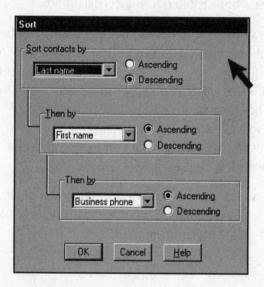

2 This opens the Sort dialog box for determining how you want the list arranged. You can sort your Contacts list using up to three different levels. Select the first sort level.

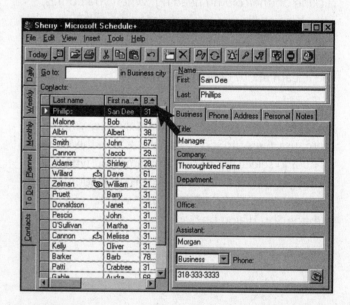

5 Click **OK** to exit the box and perform the sort on your list. In this example, the names are sorted by business phone.

Group Contacts

Do many of your contacts have the same information, such as phone numbers or departments? Another thing you can do with your list is to group your contacts. For instance, because some of the people on your list work for the same company, or same industry, you can group them together. The Schedule+ grouping feature lets you group items in a variety of categories and into subgroups.

Once you group your contacts, the grid list displays the specified groups. The group name appears bold and above each group of contacts on the list. You can expand or collapse the list in a group by clicking on the group symbol (a tiny box) in front of the group name.

A minus sign in front of the group name means every contact appears. A plus sign means all of the contacts pertaining to the group name are hidden (collapsed). Click the plus or minus sign to hide or show contacts listed under the group name.

To ungroup your Contacts list, open the Group By dialog box again, this time selecting **None** for each group by category.

The categories that you choose to group by in your list also determine which columns appear on the grid.

Begin Guided Tour   Group Items in the Contact List

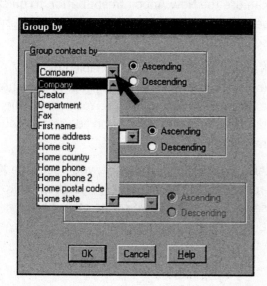

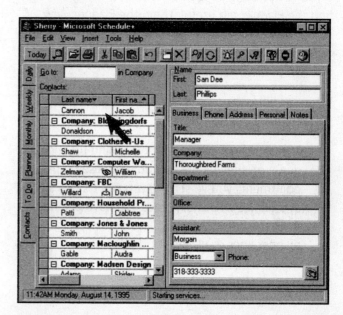

1 Open the **View** menu and select **Group By**. This opens the Group By dialog box. Open the first level's drop-down list and select a category to group by. The categories are based on fields in your Contacts tab.

2 Choose ascending or descending order for each grouping you select.

3 Click **OK** to exit the box and display your groups.

Make Plans with the Planner

For a different perspective of your busy schedule, take a look at the Planner view. Click the **Planner** tab to open your schedule into Planner view. The Planner lets you see your schedule in chunks of time, graphically displayed; this graphical depiction of your schedule is the *free/busy display*.

Aside from the Planner display, your screen also shows the Date Navigator (which you'll recognize from the Daily view tab), and an Attendees box, which lists other networked users that you've invited to the meetings you've scheduled. The Planner's real functionality comes into play when you're using Schedule+ on a network. In a network situation, you can view other users' schedules when you're trying to set up a meeting and see when they are free or busy. This is helpful when you're trying to coordinate meeting times.

If you're not using Schedule+ on a network, you'll still find the Planner tab useful. Using the Planner view, it's a lot easier to look at your schedule with it spread out in blocks of time over several days. You can easily discover available time blocks.

What are you supposed to do with the Planner view? Check these things out:

- The blue lines, called bars, extending up and down on the Planner schedule represent appointments you've set. So, you can quickly see at a glance what busy times you have planned. (If you're networked, you'll see other users' planner lines displayed in other colors.)

- The vertical gaps between the blue bars represent open chunks of time that you've not set aside for appointments. This lets you see when you're available.

- To move your Daily or Weekly view, click the arrow buttons at the top of the Planner screen. The left arrow takes you back and the right arrow takes you forward, date by date.

- To see other days in a glance, click the appropriate date on the Date Navigator calendar.

- To see the details concerning a particular appointment, double-click the blue bar. This reveals whose appointment it is. Click the name to reveal details about the appointment.

- If you're working in stand-alone mode (not connected to other computer users), your screen also shows a **New Appointment** button. You can use the New Appointment button to quickly set another appointment on your already busy schedule.

- If you're working in group-enabled mode (networked with other users), your screen shows a **Request Meeting** button. You can use the button to invite other networked users to your meetings.

- Also in group-enabled mode, you'll see little **X**'s appear in the Attendees box if you happen to select a time slot in which the other person is busy.

Begin Guided Tour   Change the Planner View

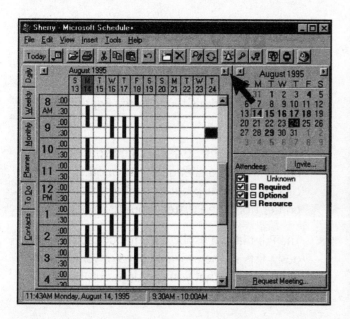

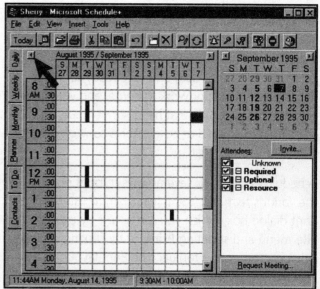

1 To move forward in your Planner view and view another set of days, click on the right arrow button.

2 To move back to the previous display, click on the left arrow button.

If you hold down your mouse button while selecting the arrow buttons, you'll move quickly through the weeks of the month.

Print Your Schedule

Being able to print out portions of your schedule is an important part of using Schedule+. There are times when you won't always be sitting in front of your computer with your daily schedule ready to use. You may have to travel, or work at home, and you'll need a copy of your schedule at hand. Or perhaps, you need to give a friend or co-worker a copy of your To Do list or Contacts list.

Schedule+ offers you several ways to print portions of the various features. You'll find them all listed in the Print dialog box, which you can access by opening the **File** menu and selecting **Print**, or by clicking on the **Print** button on the toolbar. The Print layout list box displays the parts of your Schedule+ program selectable for printing. Simply highlight the layout you want to print; then click **OK** to print it out. By default, the dialog box is setup to print a full page of the selected item in its current date.

Depending on what layout you select, your printout may show different elements and page orientation. You may be quite surprised with the professional-look of the printout. In the top-left corner of every page, you see the schedule name (usually your name, if that's the schedule you chose to print). At the very bottom of the printed page, you'll find a footer (text line) indicating when the page printed, complete with date and time.

> One way you can see what your printout will look like before you print it is to use the **Preview** button in the Print dialog box.

Elements of the Print Dialog Box

Let's go over the options found in the Print dialog box in more detail and learn what you can do with them.

At the top of the box, you'll find your default printer listed. To change this to another printer, click on the **Setup** button and select another printer from the **Printer** drop-down box.

The Print layout list box, as mentioned previously, lists all the available parts of your Schedule+ program that you can print out. Use the scroll bar to view different items in the list.

The Paper format drop-down box lets you choose to print the selected item on paper, a Filofax page (a personal organizer), or on labels.

Use the Schedule range options to control which date you print for the selected item (when applicable). For example, if you're printing your weekly schedule, you can choose the exact week you want to print out.

The options at the bottom of the dialog box let you control how the item prints. For example, if you select the No shading check box, the top of your printout won't be shaded with the default design (which tends to use up a lot of your printer's ink).

Use the three drop-down boxes to the right of the Print layout list to control print quality, font size, and private items on your schedule.

Use the Preview command button to preview how the selected item will look before printing it out. (Learn more about this feature later in this lesson.)

By default, Schedule+ prints each feature with shaded areas (sometimes located at the top of the page, or scattered on your page). To speed up printing, be sure to select the **No shading** check box. This keeps the printer from printing the shaded background used, so you can clearly read any text in the shaded areas.

Use the Print Layout List Box

Each of the items in the Print layout list box lets you print certain portions of your Schedule+ features. To use these items effectively, you need to know what each item prints. The following table explains what kind of printout you'll have after selecting the item for printing.

All text	Prints out all the text items in your daily schedule.
Contact List	Prints the entire list of contacts stored in the Contacts List.
Daily - dynamic	Prints the daily schedule in its most current state of change.
Daily - fixed	Prints the daily schedule.
Monthly	Prints the monthly view of your schedule.

Monthly on Tri-fold graphical	Prints three elements on a single page, including the daily schedule, all 12 months, and the To Do list.
To Do List - mini	Prints the tasks associated with the selected date.
To Do List - normal	Prints the entire To Do list, including all the details associated with each task.
To Do List - text	Only prints the text descriptions of the tasks.
Weekly 5 day	Prints 5 days of the week on a single page.
Weekly 7 day	Prints 7 days of the week on a single page.

There are a few additional details to keep in mind when printing the different layouts:

- All tentative appointments that you schedule will appear in italics on the printout.

- If you schedule lots of appointments throughout the daily schedule you're printing, they may not all fit in the designated space. If this happens, you'll find the overflow of appointments carry over into the Other Appointments box on the printout.

- If you're printing the To Do list or Contacts list, the printout will reflect any sorts you've performed on the columns.

Begin Guided Tour   Print a Schedule

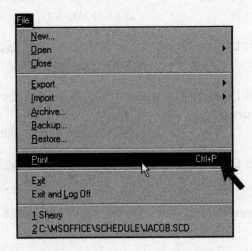

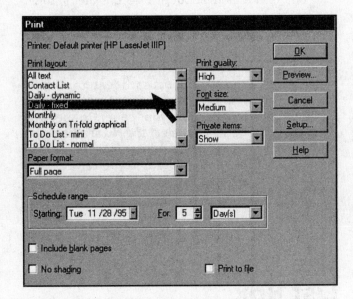

1 Open the Print dialog box by pulling down the **File** menu and selecting **Print**. (You can also access the box by clicking on the **Print** button on the toolbar.)

2 The Print dialog box appears on your screen. Select the layout you want to print from the Print layout list box. (Click on the item to highlight it.) If necessary, select from any of the other printing options. Click **OK**, and the schedule layout you selected will print.

If you choose to, you can print other schedules besides the one you have opened in your program. Select the **Print to File** option, which opens a dialog box for choosing other schedules to print.

HOW TO...

Use Data Together from Different Office Applications

I f you look at any type of business document, you will find that it contains a variety of information. You may find text that explains, describes, or summarizes information; numerical data that provides financial information; charts that give a visual snapshot of the financial data; and so on. As a computer user, therefore, you will most likely work with more than one type of data and use more than one type of application. Perhaps that's the reason you purchased Office.

With Office, you get a collection of the most popular and commonly used applications: Word for word processing, Excel for numerical data and charts, PowerPoint for presentations, and Schedule+ for managing your time and contacts. You can use each of these programs separately, as described in the preceding parts of this book, to create specific types of documents. And you can use these programs together to create a *compound document*: a document that uses data from more than one type of application. Using the applications together is the focus of this part of the book.

What You Will Find in This Section

Use the Microsoft Office Shortcut Bar

To make it easier for you to share data between your applications, Microsoft Office comes with a tool called the *Microsoft Office Shortcut Bar*, which is designed to help you easily switch from one application to another, and even launch applications.

When you turn this feature on, the Shortcut Bar appears at the top of the Windows 95 desktop, and remains in front or on top of any program windows you happen to open. You can quickly change to another Office program or perform a task by clicking on its button. To find out what a button is for, rest the mouse pointer on the button until the ToolTip (a brief description of the button) appears.

The following table explains each of the original Shortcut Bar buttons (you'll learn how to add buttons to the Shortcut Bar later in this section).

The following Guided Tour shows you how to turn the Shortcut Bar on and off and how to use it to create files and perform task . To take more control of the Shortcut Bar, see "Customize the Shortcut Bar," later in this section.

Button	Name	Description
	Start a New Document	Opens a dialog box that provides several sets of templates you can use to create documents in Excel, Word, or PowerPoint. Click on a tab to view a set of related templates, and then click on the template you want to use.
	Open a Document	Displays a dialog box that lets you open a document you already created.
	Send a Message	Starts Microsoft Exchange, and displays a dialog box that lets you send an e-mail message.
	Make an Appointment	Runs Schedule+, allowing you to record the date and time of a new appointment.
	Add a Task	Opens a Schedule+ file and lets you add an item to the list of things you have to do.
	Add a Contact	Runs Schedule+ and allows you to add the name, address, phone number, and other information about a person.
	Getting Results Book	Opens a help book that's included on the CD-ROM.
	Office Compatible	Displays demonstrations of other programs that work with Microsoft Office.
	Answer Wizard	Runs the Microsoft Office help system, which can provide instructions for how to perform most tasks in Office.

Turn the Shortcut Bar Off and On

The Shortcut Bar appears at the top of the Windows desktop whenever you run Windows. If you don't want the Shortcut Bar to appear on startup, take the following steps:

1. Click the **Start** button, point to **Settings**, and click on **Taskbar**. This displays the Taskbar Properties dialog box.

2. Click the **Start Menu Programs** tab, and then click the **Remove** button. The Remove Shortcuts/Folders dialog box appears.

3. Double-click the **StartUp** folder, and then click the **Microsoft Office** Shortcut Bar.

4. Click the **Remove** button and click the **Close** (**X**) button. You return to the Taskbar Properties dialog box.

5. Click **OK** to save your change. The Shortcut Bar will no longer appear on startup. To run the Shortcut Bar, refer to "Turn On Microsoft Office Shortcut Bar" below.

Begin Guided Tour   Turn On Microsoft Office Shortcut Bar

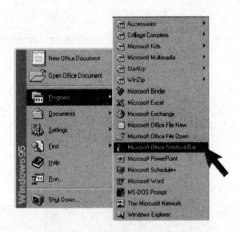

1 Click the **Start** button in the lower left corner of the Windows desktop. The Windows 95 Start menu opens. Move the mouse pointer over **Programs**. The Programs submenu appears, showing you several of the Microsoft Office programs. Click the **Microsoft Office Shortcut Bar**.

2 The Microsoft Office Shortcut Bar appears in the upper right corner of the Windows desktop. The Shortcut Bar is set to remain on top, so it won't become hidden under any application windows you happen to open.

The Shortcut Bar shown in the picture is bigger than the one you'll see. I made the buttons bigger, so they would show up clearly in the figure. To make your buttons bigger, right-click on a blank area of the Shortcut Bar, and click on **Customize**. Click on **Large Buttons**, and click **OK**. You'll learn more about customizing the Shortcut Bar in "Customize the Microsoft Office Shortcut Bar" on page 349.

Begin Guided Tour　Run a Program Using the Shortcut Bar

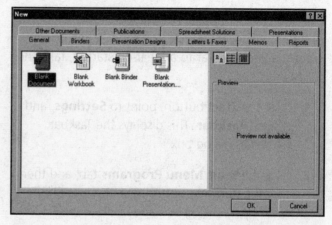

1 The Microsoft Office Shortcut Bar appears in the upper right corner of your screen. Click on the button for the task you want to perform, such as creating a new file or adding a contact to your Schedule+ file.

2 Microsoft Office runs the required application or displays a dialog box that lets you complete the task. For example, if you click the **Start New Document** button, you'll see a set of templates and wizards you can use to create a new document using any of the Office programs. Perform the task as you normally would.

Begin Guided Tour　Turn Off the Shortcut Bar

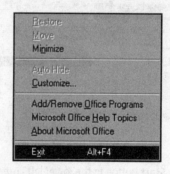

1 If the Shortcut Bar gets in your way, you can turn it off. Click the **Control** button at the left end of the Shortcut Bar to display the Control menu.

2 With the Control menu displayed, click **Exit**. The Shortcut Bar disappears.

Customize the Microsoft Office Shortcut Bar

At first glance, the Microsoft Office Shortcut Bar may not seem very powerful. It simply allows you to create new files, open files you've created, and perform a few simple tasks with Schedule+. However, you can customize the Shortcut Bar to make it a more powerful tool. For example, you can turn on additional buttons for your Windows accessories and for other programs (such as Word and Excel); you can add shortcuts for drives or folders; and you can add icons for your most often used files. In short, you can place just about anything on the Shortcut Bar to make it more convenient.

To customize the Shortcut Bar, simply right-click on a blank area of the Shortcut Bar, and click **Customize**. A dialog box appears, giving you several customization options. You can use the dialog box to turn on additional toolbars (sets of buttons); to add, move, or delete individual buttons; and to change the overall appearance and behavior of the Shortcut Bar. For more detailed instructions on how to customize the Shortcut Bar, take the *Guided Tour*.

As you reconstruct the Shortcut Bar, don't worry about making mistakes. You can undo any change you make and quickly return the Shortcut Bar to its original condition.

Make New Toolbars

The Guided Tour shows you how to turn on toolbars and buttons, but it does not show you how to create your own toolbars. You might want to create a toolbar, for instance, that contains icons for all the programs you use on a daily basis, along with icons for your floppy drive, and maybe for your data folders. To create a toolbar of your own, take the following steps:

1. Right-click on a blank area of the Shortcut Bar and select **Customize**.

2. Click the **Toolbars** tab. A list of existing toolbars appears.

3. Click the **Add Toolbar** button. A dialog box appears, asking if you want to create a toolbar from a folder or create a blank toolbar from scratch.

4. Take one of the following steps:

   Select **Make Toolbar for this Folder**, click on the **Browse** button, and use the dialog box that appears to pick the folder for which you want to create a toolbar. (The resulting toolbar will contain buttons for *all* the files in the specified folder.)

   Select **Create a new, blank Toolbar called** and type a name for the new toolbar. (The resulting toolbar will have no buttons; you must add buttons using the **Buttons** tab.)

5. To add buttons to the new toolbar and remove existing buttons, see "Turn on Additional Toolbars and Buttons" on page 352, starting with step 4.

Begin Guided Tour Change the Look of the Shortcut Bar

1 Initially, the Shortcut Bar appears at the top of the screen. You can click on a blank area of the Shortcut Bar and drag it on top of the Windows desktop or to the left, right, or bottom of the screen to reposition it. The picture here shows the Shortcut Bar dragged to the right side of the screen.

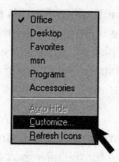

2 To customize the Shortcut Bar in any way, you must first right-click on a blank area of the Shortcut Bar, and then click on **Customize**. (If you moved the Shortcut Bar to the middle of the Windows desktop, right-click on a blank area inside the window to display the shortcut menu.)

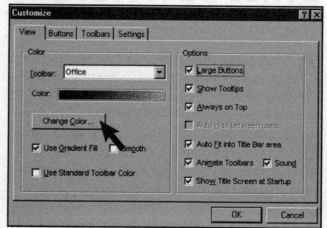

3 You see the Customize dialog box. The first tab, View, lists options that allow you to control the appearance and behavior of the Shortcut Bar. In the Color area, click the **Change Color** button to pick a different color for the Shortcut Bar.

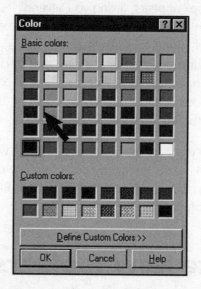

4 A color palette appears, prompting you to select a color. Click the desired color, and click **OK**.

Guided Tour Change the Look of the Shortcut Bar

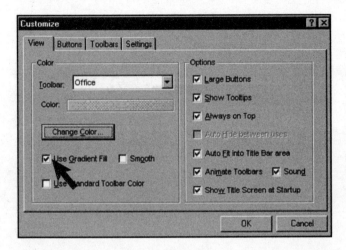

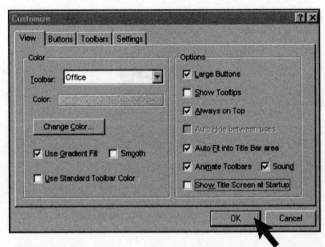

5 When you return to the Customize dialog box, you can use the other Color options to further modify the Shortcut Bar's appearance.

7 Click **OK** to save any changes you've made.

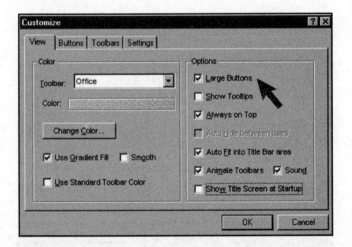

6 In the Options area, click on any option to turn it on or off and change the appearance or behavior of the Shortcut bar. For example, you can click on **Show Title Screen at Startup** to turn this option off and prevent the Microsoft Office title screen from appearing whenever you turn on the Shortcut Bar.

Begin Guided Tour   Turn on Additional Toolbars and Buttons

1 The Shortcut Bar can contain buttons from one or more toolbars. The easiest way to display buttons from another toolbar is to right-click on a blank area of the Shortcut Bar, and click on the toolbar whose buttons you want to add.

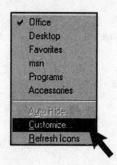

2 Another way to turn on additional toolbars is to right-click on a blank area of the Shortcut Bar, and click **Customize**.

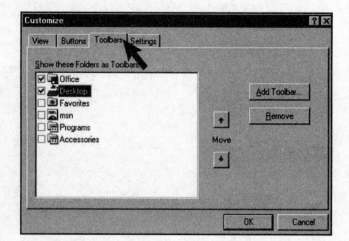

3 In the Customize dialog box, click on the **Toolbars** tab to see a list of toolbars whose buttons you can add. Click on the check box next to a toolbar to add its buttons to the Shortcut Bar. (A check mark indicates that the toolbar is on.)

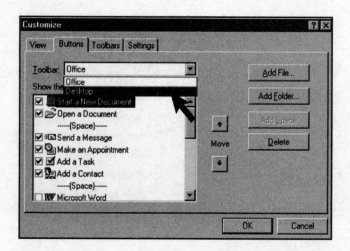

4 When a toolbar is on, you can turn its buttons on or off. Click the **Buttons** tab in the Customize dialog box. Open the **Toolbar** drop-down list, and select the toolbar whose buttons you want to display or hide.

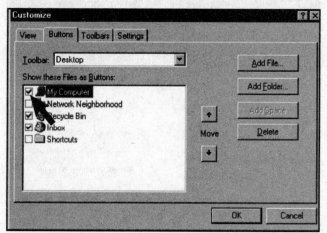

5 When you select a toolbar, the names of its buttons appear. To turn a button on or off, click on its check box. (A check mark indicates that the button will appear in the Shortcut Bar.)

Guided Tour Turn on Additional Toolbars and Buttons

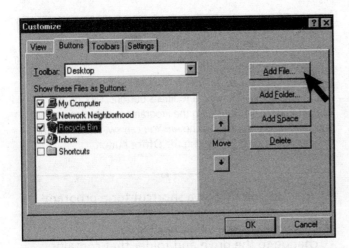

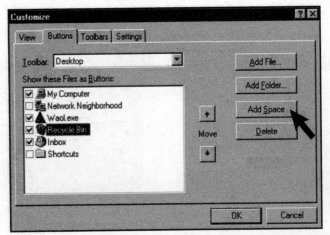

6 You can add a button for a folder or a file (data or program file) to the Shortcut Bar. Click on the name of the button before which you want the new button to appear. Then, click **Add File** or **Add Folder**.

8 To add a space before a button, click on the button before which you want the space inserted, and then click on the **Add Space** button. (This is useful for grouping related buttons.)

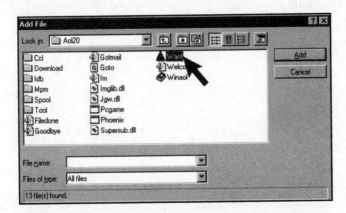

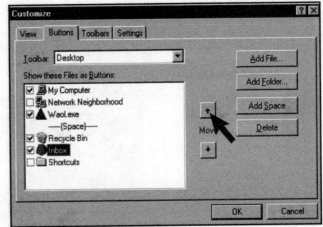

7 A dialog box appears, asking you to pick the file or folder you want to add to the Shortcut Bar. Use the dialog box to select the desired file or folder, and click the **Add** button. The name of the file or folder will appear on the Show These Files as Buttons list.

9 To move a button, click on it in the Show These Files as Buttons list, and then click on the up or down **Move** arrow button to move the item.

(continues)

Guided Tour Turn on Additional Toolbars and Buttons

(continued)

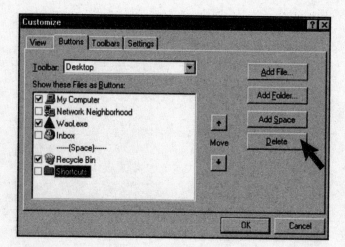

12 A button for activating each toolbar appears in the Shortcut Bar. To view a toolbar's buttons, click on the toolbar button. If you turn on the Programs toolbar, for instance, the Shortcut Bar appears as shown. You can switch back to the original Shortcut Bar by clicking the **Office** button.

You can quickly add a shortcut for a program or data file to the Shortcut Bar. Open My Computer or the Windows Explorer, and change to the drive and folder that contains the file you want to add. Drag the icon for the folder, program file, or data file to the Shortcut Bar, and release the mouse button. You can add shortcuts from the Windows desktop simply by dragging the shortcut to the Shortcut Bar.

10 If you don't use a button in the Shortcut Bar, you can turn it off (as explained in Step 5) or delete it. To delete a button, click on its name, and click the **Delete** button.

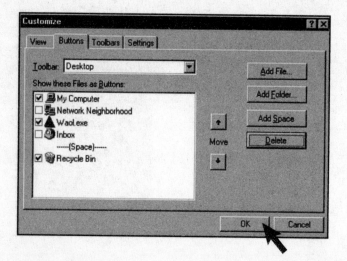

11 Click **OK** to save your changes. The Shortcut Bar appears as you specified.

Share Data Between Applications

As you work with Excel, Word, Schedule+, and your other Windows (and non-Windows) applications, you'll find yourself swapping data between your documents. For example, you might want to copy a graph you created in Excel and paste it into a report you put together in Word.

You can usually share data simply by copying it from the document you created in one application to the document you created in another. But just how is the data between the two documents related? If you change the data in one document, will it automatically be changed in the other one? The answer is, "That depends." It depends how the two applications are set up to share data, and it depends on how you inserted the copied data.

You can share data in any of the following three ways:

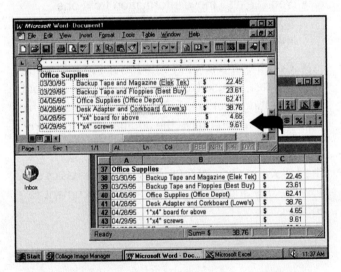

With a link, the shared data updates whenever you edit the file that contains the shared data.

Link: If you're using applications that support OLE (pronounced "Oh-lay," and short for Object Linking and Embedding), you can share data by creating a *link*. With a link, the file into which you pasted the data does not actually contain the linked data; the link is stored in a separate file on the disk. Whenever you edit the linked file, any changes you make to it appear in all

other documents that are linked to the file. For example, say you insert an Excel graph into a Word document as a link. Whenever you change the graph in Excel, those changes will appear in the Word document.

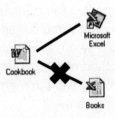

Embedded data breaks the connection with the original file but retains the connection with the program used to create it.

Embed: With OLE, you can also embed data from one file into another file. With embedding, the pasted data becomes a part of the file into which you pasted it. If you edit the file that contains the copied data, your changes will not appear inside the document that contains the pasted data. However, the pasted data retains a connection with the program that you used to create it. If you double-click on the embedded data, Windows automatically runs the associated program, and lets you edit the data.

If an application does not support OLE, you can share data, but any connection between the shared data and its file (or the program used to create it) is broken.

Paste: You can paste data in any number of ways. However, not all applications support OLE. For those applications that do not support OLE, you can still share data between programs by copying and pasting the data. However, the pasted data will have no connection with the application that you used to create it.

Copy and Paste Data Using the Clipboard

Think of copying and pasting as using a photo copier to make a copy. With a photocopy, the original remains intact in the original location, and you have the copy. You can manipulate the copy in any way that you want. You can edit it, delete part of it, highlight it, and so on, all without affecting the original. This method of sharing information works best when you simply want to use the same information in another program.

Here's what you need to remember about copying and pasting:

- Copying and pasting among applications works pretty much the same way as copying and pasting within a document.

- When you copy something, it is placed on the Clipboard, a temporary holding spot. The Clipboard can hold only one piece of information. If you copy something and then copy something else, the last thing that you copied is the only thing on the Clipboard.

- You can copy and paste from one document to another or from one application to another. You can paste to other Office programs and any other type of program that supports copy and paste (for example, a WordPerfect document).

- Usually, when you copy and paste without using a special command, the data is not linked or embedded. If you make a change to the original document, that change is not reflected in the pasted copy.

- The application will try to paste the data into a suitable format in the receiving document. For example, when you paste an Excel worksheet into Word, the information is formatted as a table. In some cases (when you cannot edit the information in the receiving application), the information is pasted as an object; you can double-click on the object to edit it in the program you used to create it.

- You can also move information from one application to another by using the Cut command.

- Copying and pasting data has many advantages. It is fast, simple (you don't have to worry about updating your links), and it results in a small file size (you don't have the additional instructions required by linking or embedding).

The following *Guided Tour* shows you the basics of how to copy and paste data from one document to another.

Begin Guided Tour   Copy and Paste Data Between Documents

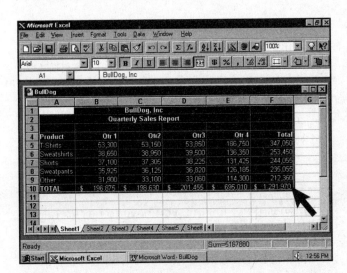

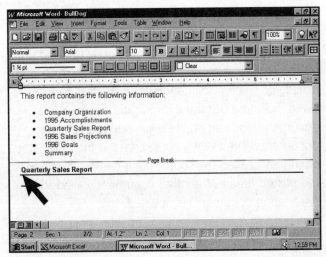

1 Start the application and open the document that contains the data you want to copy. Select the data you want to copy (refer to the other sections of this book to learn the specifics of selecting data in the application you're using.)

2 With the data selected, open the **Edit** menu and choose the **Copy** command. (You can also click on the **Copy** button in the toolbar. In some programs, you can right-click on the selected item and click on **Copy**.)

3 Switch to the application in which you want to paste the data. (You can click on the application's name in the taskbar.)

4 Open the destination document, and move the insertion point to the location where you want to paste the data.

5 Open the **Edit** menu and choose the **Paste** command, or click the **Paste** button in the toolbar. (In some programs, you can simply right-click where you want the data pasted, and then select **Paste**.)

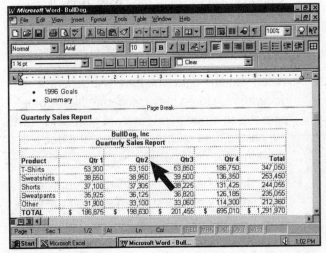

6 The data is pasted in an acceptable format (here as a table). In this example, you could use any of Word's table commands to format and edit the table. The data is not linked to the original worksheet.

Insert Copied Data as a Link

In many cases, you may be creating a document with data from several sources. You could wait until each document is absolutely, completely finished and then copy the appropriate data, but things can—and usually do—seem to change up to the last minute. To avoid including outdated information in your final document, you can create a link between the two documents. Then when copied data in the original document (called the *source* document) is changed, the pasted data in the other document (called the *destination* document) is updated, too.

Here are the key points to remember about linking data:

- You use the Copy command to copy the data you want to link, but you follow a different procedure for pasting the information, as covered in the *Guided Tour*.

- You can link data between Excel, Word, PowerPoint, and any other application that supports OLE, by using the **Paste Special** command on the **Edit** menu. If a program does not support OLE, the Paste Special command will not be available.

- When you link data, you have two separate documents, stored in two separate files. Compare this to embedding (covered next), in which the pasted data becomes a part of the document in which it is pasted.

- Use linking when you need instant updating. Also, linking works best when you use the same data in several documents. You can maintain the one source document without having to worry about updating the documents that use information from the source.

- You can link data in several formats, including RTF (rich text file), as a picture, as an object, or as unformatted text. The format you select

controls how you can edit the data. For example, in picture format, you can edit the link only by double-clicking on it to run the application used to create the linked data. In RTF format, you can edit individual entries in the destination file, but if you close the file and reopen it, any edited entries revert back to the entries used in the original file.

> When you use linking, you have to be careful when moving, renaming, or deleting files. If you take any of these actions, you might break the link between the two files. You can use the **Edit Links** command to edit the link if you move or rename the file. If you delete the file, you will have to recreate it.

Working with Linked Data

Linked data behaves in some fairly unpredictable ways. For example, if you paste data in RTF (rich text format), you can edit entries in the link without affecting the original file. However, if you close the file that contains the linked data, and then reopen it, your edits disappear. The following list will help you understand the way links behave:

- If you paste the link as a picture, you can click on the link to select it. Handles (little black squares) and a border appear around the link. You can drag a handle to change the size or dimensions of the linked object, or you can drag a border to move it. To edit the link, double-click on it; Windows runs the application used to create the link, allowing you to edit it.

- If you pasted the link in RTF format, you can edit individual entries in the linked object. However, editing these entries does not change the original file from which the link was copied. So, when you update the link or reopen the file that contains the link, your changes are replaced by the entries in the original file.

- You can break the link between the linked object and the file from which you copied it. The linked data then becomes a part of the host file, and you cannot edit the data by double-clicking on it or by choosing a link option. To break a link, open the **Edit** menu, select **Links**, click on the link you want to break, and click on the **Break Link** button.

To make permanent changes to the linked data, you must edit the original file from which you copied the link. Although you can edit links by opening the Edit menu, selecting Links, and using the dialog box that appears to modify the link, there's an easier way:

1. Right-click on the link you want to change. A shortcut menu appears, displaying several link options along with other options for changing the object.

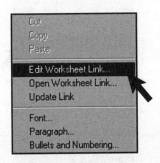

2. Click on the **Edit Worksheet Link** option (the names of the link options vary depending on the application you used to create the object). Windows runs the application used to create the linked object and opens the original file.

3. Edit the data as you normally would, and then save your changes.

4. Switch back to the document that contains the linked data. The changes automatically appear in the linked object.

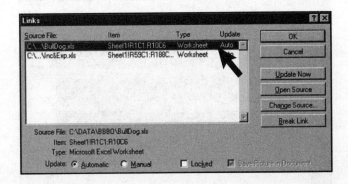

If you open the **Edit** menu and select **Links**, you'll see the dialog box shown here. You can then click on a link to update it, control the way it behaves, break the link, or edit it. Think of this dialog box as control central for all your linked objects. Note the following:

- At the bottom of the dialog box are link update options. **Automatic** tells Windows to automatically update the linked object whenever the original file is changed. If you select **Manual**, you must manually update links by clicking on the Update Now button in this dialog box. If you click on **Locked**, the linked objects will not change when you edit the original file.

- To open a link in its application for editing, click on the link you want to open, and then click on the **Open Source** button. (This opens the original link file so you can edit it as in the previous set of steps.)

- To pick a different file as the link or to specify a different name or location for the linked file (if you moved the link file to a different drive or folder), click on the **Change Source** button. A dialog box appears, allowing you to select the drive, folder, and name of the linked file.

Begin Guided Tour Paste Data as a Link for Automatic Updates

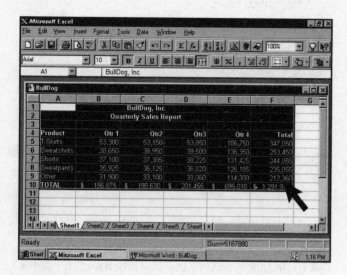

1 Start in the application that contains the data you want to copy. Here you are starting Excel. Then select the data you want to copy.

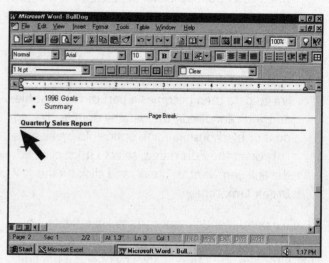

3 Switch to the application and open the document in which you want to paste the data. Move the insertion point to the location where you want the data pasted.

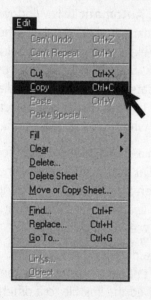

2 With the data selected, open the **Edit** menu and choose the **Copy** command. You can also click the **Copy** button in the toolbar, or right-click the selected data and click **Copy**.

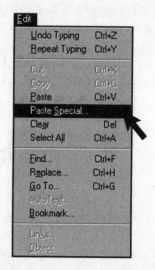

4 Open the **Edit** menu and choose the **Paste Special** command.

Guided Tour Paste Data as a Link for Automatic Updates

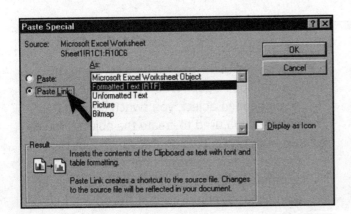

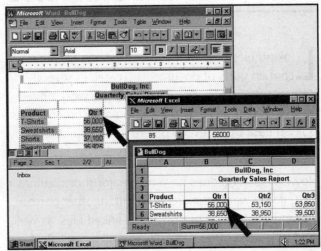

5 You see the Paste Special dialog box. In a Word document, you can paste the data as formatted text, unformatted text, a picture, or a bitmap. Select how you want the data pasted, click the **Paste Link** option button, and click **OK**.

6 The data is pasted and linked to the original. If you edit the original data, the change appears automatically in the linked file. Here the Quarter 1 T-shirt sales are changed from 53,300 to 56,000 in the worksheet.

Embed Copied Data in Another Document

Linking files is great if you create large files that contain parts of documents created in several different programs. It's also great if you work on group projects and you have a single document that pulls in data from several different files maintained by your colleagues or family members.

However, linking does have two major shortcomings. First, if you want to share a file with another person, you must send that person *all* the linked files, as well. And when the other person places all those linked files on her computer, she'll have to update the links to make sure the central document knows where all the contributing files are located. This can be a time-consuming (and frustrating) procedure.

Second, linking allows a file's contents to be edited from more than one location. But say you want the original file to remain unchanged, and you want to modify only the data you pasted into the other document? In such a case, you want to break the link between the two files, allowing them to remain separate.

When you want to share a file with someone else or prevent an original file from being altered, you can embed copied information into a document. What can you do with an embedded object? How is an embedded object different than linking? Read the following list of key concepts to find out:

- When you embed an object, that object is saved with the main document. For example, if you embed part of an Excel worksheet in a Word document, the worksheet data is saved as part of the Word document (not as a separate file). Also, the embedded object is no longer connected to its original document; the embedded object becomes the sole property of the document that contains it.

- You can edit an embedded object using the original application. When you double-click on an embedded object, you switch back to the program you used to create the object. (You can see both documents on the screen, but the toolbar and menu commands change for the appropriate application.) You can then use any commands to edit or format the object. Keep in mind that you must have the original application on your system.

- The major drawbacks to embedding are that you can end up with a pretty big file, and you have to manually update the data contained in this file; the data won't change automatically when you edit the original file.

- You can embed many types of objects from Office applications, from mini-applications (such as Microsoft Draw or WordArt), and from other applications that support embedding. For some specific examples of embedding, see "Insert a WordArt Object into a Document," "Insert a Graph with the Graph Applet," and "Illustrate Documents, Worksheets, and Slides."

- You can embed a document that you have already created, or you can insert a blank embedded document (and then use its application to create it).

Work with an Embedded Object

When you insert cut or copied data as an embedded object, the data doesn't just sit inside the document like an immovable blob. You can click on the object, and then move or resize it; you can even double-click on the object to edit its contents. Whenever you double-click on an embedded object, Windows runs the program associated with the object, allowing you to use the program's tools to modify the object.

When you select an embedded object (usually by clicking on it), tiny black squares (called *handles*) appear around the object. You can then do any of the following to modify the object:

- To move the object, move the mouse pointer to a border (but not a selection handle) and drag the object to the spot you want.

- To resize an object, move the tip of the mouse pointer over a selection handle, and drag the handle to change the object's size or dimensions.

- To delete an object, press **Del**.

- To share the object with another document, drag the object over the Windows desktop. When you release the mouse button, a *scrap* appears on the desktop. You can then drag the scrap into another document.

You can also call up the application you used to create the object and edit the object, as covered in the following *Guided Tour*.

> If you don't have the application that the object was created in, and you try to edit the object, the program you're in will try to convert the object to a format that you can use.

1. Double-click on the linked object. Windows displays the menu bar and toolbar for the application used to create the embedded object. However, you can still see the rest of the document that contains the object.

2. Modify the object as you normally would in the application you used to create it.

3. When you finish making changes, exit the application by clicking inside the main document. The object and document are updated.

Begin Guided Tour   Embed an Existing Object

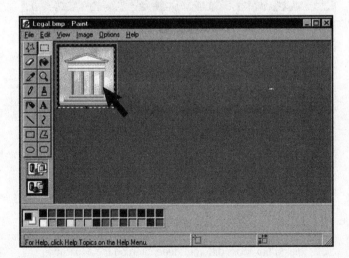

1 Start in the application that contains the data you want to embed. Here you are starting in Windows Paint. Select the data you want to copy.

2 With the data selected, open the **Edit** menu and choose the **Copy** command. You can also click the **Copy** button in the toolbar, or right-click on the selected data and click **Copy**.

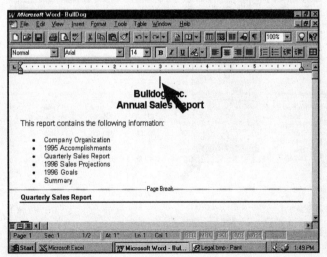

3 Switch to the application and open the document in which you want to embed the copied data. Move the insertion point to the location where you want to paste the copied data.

4 Open the **Edit** menu and select the **Paste Special** command.

(continues)

Guided Tour Embed an Existing Object

(continued)

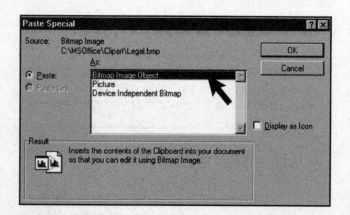

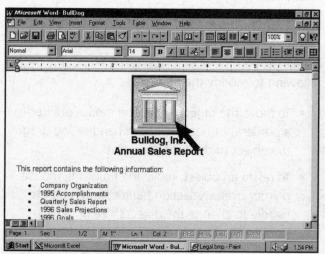

5 You see the Paste Special dialog box. In the **As** list, select the "Object" option. For example, if you're pasting part of a Paint drawing, click on **Bitmap Image Object**. Click **OK**.

6 The data is pasted into the document as an object. Any link between the pasted picture and the original picture file is broken, but the connection between the pasted data and its application remains live. You can double-click on the pasted object to open it in its application and edit it.

Begin Guided Tour Embed a New Object

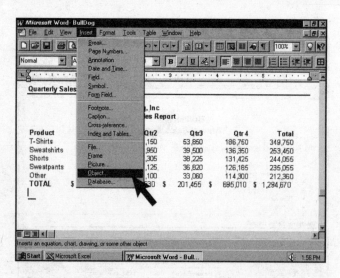

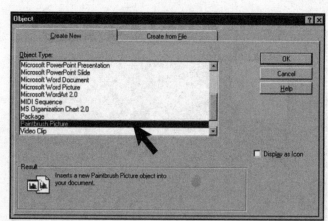

1 Start in the document in which you want to embed the object (here Word). Then open the **Insert** menu and select the **Object** command. (In some programs, you open the **Edit** menu and select **Insert Object**.)

2 You see a list of the types of objects you can insert. (The dialog box looks different depending on the application.) Click on the type of object you want to insert, and then click **OK**.

Guided Tour   Embed a New Object

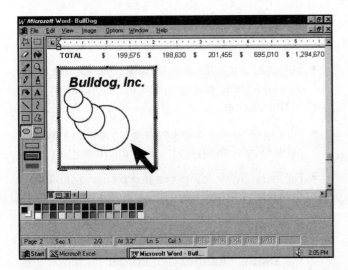

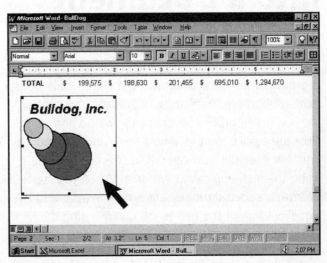

3 The application for the type of object you selected starts. You may not realize that the application started, but if you look at the toolbar and menu commands, you can see that you are in a different application. Create the object using the commands and features of that application.

5 The new object is now embedded in the document. You cannot open the embedded object as a separate file, but you can edit the object by double-clicking on it.

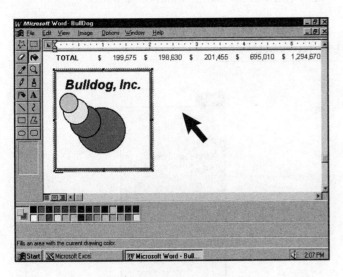

4 When you complete the object, click anywhere inside the document. This closes the application you used to create the embedded object.

Insert a WordArt Object into a Document

Included with Office (and other Microsoft software products) are small programs sometimes called *mini-applications*, *mini-apps*, or *applets*. You can use these special-purpose programs to jazz up and illustrate a document in almost any Windows application. For example, you can create special text effects using the mini-app called WordArt. When you start WordArt, a special toolbar appears. The following list explains some of the things you can do using the WordArt toolbar:

- Select a shape for the text. For example, you can make text slant, create circular text, make the text look like an octagon, and more. To change the shape of text, display the shape drop-down list and then click on the shape you want.

- Select a font, font size, or font style for the text. To make these changes, use the drop-down lists in the toolbar.

- Change the alignment of the text (left, right, or center) by clicking on the alignment button.

- Flip, stretch, or rotate the text by using the **Flip**, **Stretch**, or **Rotation** button in the toolbar.

- Select a different shade, add a shadow, or change the border used to draw the text using the **Shade**, **Shadow**, and **Border** buttons in the toolbar.

You can insert a WordArt object in any of the Office applications; the Guided Tour covers how to insert the object into a Word document (most likely the document you will use as the main document).

Begin Guided Tour Jazz Up a Document with WordArt

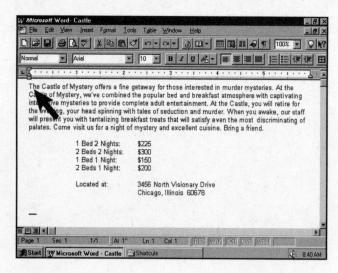

1 Open the document in which you want to insert the WordArt object (here Word), and move the insertion point to the location where you want the object inserted.

2 Open the **Insert** menu and select the **Object** command.

Guided Tour Jazz Up a Document with WordArt

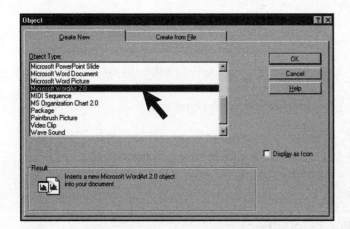

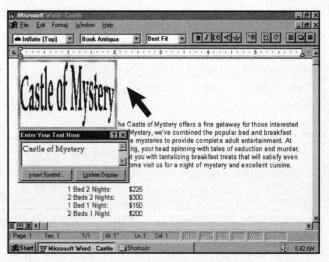

3 You see the Object dialog box. (This dialog box looks a little different in the other Office applications.) In the Object Type list, select **Microsoft WordArt** and click **OK**.

4 You can now use the WordArt applet. You see the toolbar for this applet and a dialog box that prompts you to type your text. Type the text you want to use. Make any formatting changes using the toolbar or any of the menu commands.

5 When you finish creating and formatting the text, click inside the main document to return to it.

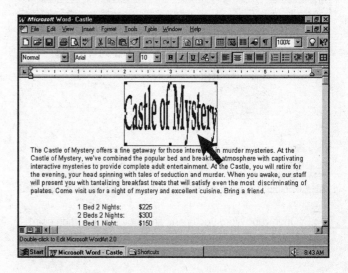

6 Word inserts the WordArt object into the document. To edit the WordArt text, double-click on the object. You can drag the WordArt object to move it or drag a handle to resize it; however, to precisely position the object, you might have to use Word's paragraph formatting features (such as center).

Insert a Graph with the Graph Applet

Another applet included with Office is *Graph*. You can use this program to create simple graphs and insert them in your Word documents or PowerPoint slides, and in other documents you may create.

When you insert a Graph object, a datasheet appears with sample data. This datasheet is similar to an Excel worksheet; it is a grid of rows and columns. You select the cell you want and then replace the existing data. You can add more data or delete sample data you don't need. You can also use the toolbar buttons and menu commands to change the chart type and make other formatting changes.

You can insert a graph in any Office application; take the *Guided Tour* to insert a graph into one of your Word documents.

Begin Guided Tour   Add a Graph to a Word Document

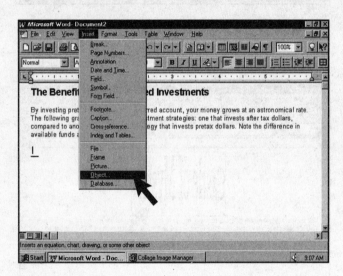

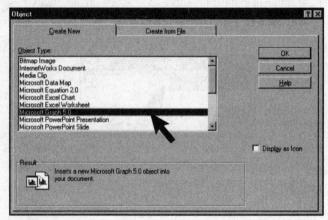

1 Open your Word document, and move the insertion point to the location where you want the graph inserted. Then, open the **Insert** menu and select the **Object** command.

2 You see the Object dialog box, which looks a little different in the various applications. In the Object Type list, select **Microsoft Graph** and click **OK**.

Guided Tour Add a Graph to a Word Document

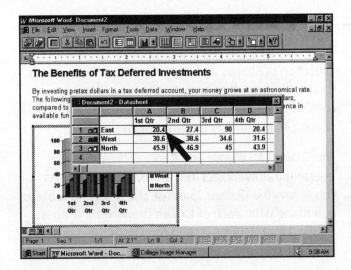

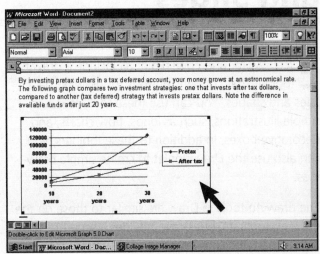

3 Graph starts, and you see the datasheet with sample data. Replace the sample data with the data you want to chart. Make any editing or formatting changes using the menu commands and toolbar buttons in Graph.

5 The new graph is inserted in the document. To move the graph, drag it. To resize the graph, drag one of its handles. To edit the graph, double-click on it.

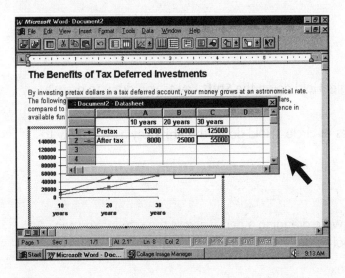

4 When you finish, click inside your Word document to return to it.

Illustrate Documents, Worksheets, and Slides

Excel, Word, and PowerPoint all include a drawing toolbar that contains buttons for drawing basic lines and shapes. You can use these tools to create simple illustrations, such as logos, flow charts, and decorative boxes. In addition to these toolbars, you can also use the *Draw* applet to create simple drawings.

The drawing tools in Draw are similar to those on the drawing toolbars, but Draw provides a separate scratch pad: the Draw window. Also, Draw creates and pastes an object as a single entity rather than as a collection of shapes and lines. If you use the drawing toolbars in the Office applications, your drawing consists of a loose collection of lines and shapes, which can be difficult to move and resize.

The *Guided Tour* leads you through the process of inserting a Draw object into a Word document. As you follow the *Guided Tour*, use the following table to determine what each of Draw's drawing tools does. To use a tool, click on it, and then drag the mouse pointer to draw the line or shape.

Tool	Name	Use This Tool To
	Selection tool	Select objects.
	Line	Draw a line.
	Rectangle	Draw a rectangle. Hold down the **Shift** key as you draw to draw a square.
	Ellipse	Draw an ellipses or circle. (Hold down the **Shift** key as you draw to create a circle.)
	Arc	Draw an arc.
	Freeform	Draw as if you were dragging a pencil across the screen. You can also use this tool to draw shapes such as a triangle.
	Text Box	Create a text box.
	Callout	Create a text box that points to a part of the drawing.
	Format Callout	To format a callout you created, select the callout and click on this button.

Tool	Name	Use This Tool To
	Fill Color	To pick a color to use to fill in an enclosed shape.
	Line Color	Pick a color for the line that defines a shape.
	Line Style	Pick a line thickness and type (for example, a dashed or solid line).
	Bring to Front	Move selected objects to the front, so they cover other objects.
	Send to Back	Move selected objects to the back, so they are covered by other objects.
	Bring in Front of Text	Move the selected object in front of any text boxes and callouts.
	Send Behind Text	Move the selected object behind any text boxes or callouts.
	Group	Group selected objects, so you can move them as a single object.
	Ungroup	Ungroup selected objects, so you can work with them individually.
	Flip Horizontal	Flip the selected objects over a horizontal plane (up or down).
	Flip Vertical	Flip the selected objects over a vertical plane (left to right).
	Rotate Right	Turn a shape as if you were dragging the hands of a clock.
	Reshape	Change the shape of the selected object.
	Snap to Grid	Display a grid that helps you position objects on the screen.
	Align Drawing Objects	Align two objects on the screen.
	Create Picture	Display another Draw screen that lets you create a picture to place on top of this picture.
	Insert Frame	Insert a box on the picture that allows you to add separate objects to the picture.

Begin Guided Tour Insert a Drawing into a Document

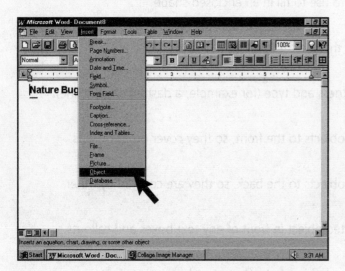

1 Open the document and move the insertion point to the location where you want to insert the drawing. Open the **Insert** menu and select the **Object** command.

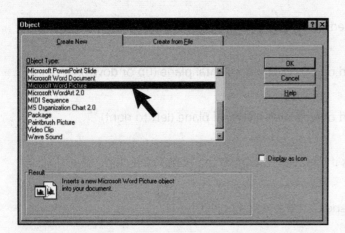

2 You see the Object dialog box (which may look different in Excel and PowerPoint). From the Object Type list, select **Microsoft Word Picture** and click **OK**.

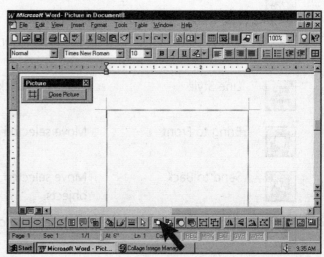

3 You see the Draw applet. A set of drawing tools appears at the bottom of the Word screen. Create the drawing using any of the Draw tools.

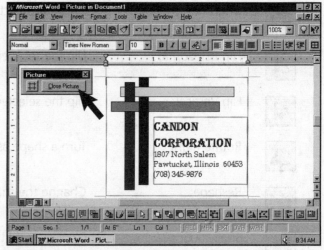

4 When you finish, click the **Close Picture** button.

5 The Draw object is embedded in the document. To move the drawing, drag it. To resize the drawing, drag one of its handles. To change the drawing, double-click on it.

Group Related Documents with Binders

Microsoft Office has a new document management tool called *Microsoft Binder* that lets you "clip" related documents together. For example, if you have a report that consists of a cover letter, one or more Excel worksheets, and a PowerPoint slide show, you can add all these files to a binder in order to work with them as a single document.

Once you've bound several documents together, Microsoft Binder allows you to rearrange the documents, number the pages, and perform other tasks to give your bound documents a consistent look and feel. You can even print all the documents with a single Print command. However, there are some limitations to what you can do in Binder. For example, you can't check the spelling in all the documents with a single command; you must run the spell checker on each document individually.

To understand Microsoft Binder, take a look at this figure. Each document you add to the binder (you'll learn how to add documents later) is shown as an icon in the left pane. The icons appear in the order in which you joined the documents. When you select a document's icon, the contents of the document appear in the right pane, where you can edit the document. The toolbar and menu bar change according to the application you used to create the document.

The *Guided Tour* shows you how to start Microsoft Binder, create a new binder, add documents to a binder, and work on those documents as a group.

> Binders are great for sending more than one document at a time by e-mail. To send a binder, open the **File** menu and select **Send Binder**. This runs Microsoft Exchange, which displays a dialog box asking you to enter the person's name and e-mail address. Refer to your Windows 95 documentation to complete the operation in Microsoft Exchange.

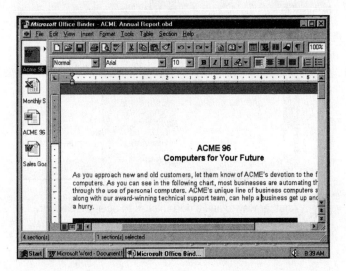

Begin Guided Tour Organize Documents in a Binder

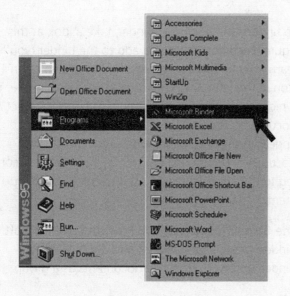

1 To run Microsoft Binder, click the **Start** button, point to **Programs**, and click **Microsoft Binder**.

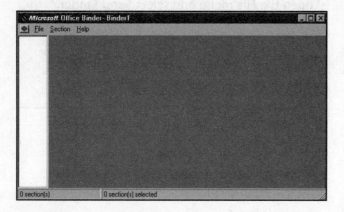

2 The Microsoft Binder window appears, as shown here. Because you haven't yet added files to the binder, it is blank.

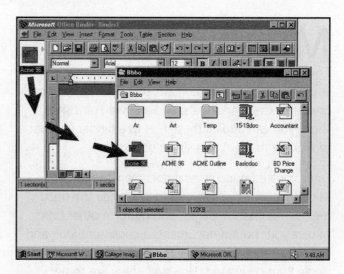

3 The easiest way to add a data file to the binder is to run My Computer or the Windows Explorer, and drag the icon for the file into the left pane of the Binder window.

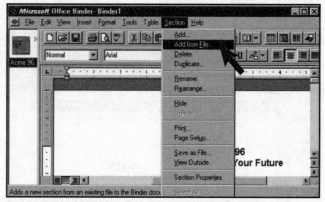

4 Another way to add a document is to open the **Section** menu and select **Add from File**. Use the dialog box that appears to select the file you want to add, and then click the **Add** button.

Guided Tour Organize Documents in a Binder

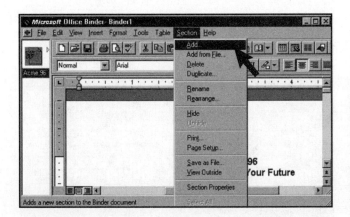

5 To add a new (empty) document, open the **Section** menu and select **Add**. A dialog box appears, asking you to specify the type of document you want to add (Excel chart or worksheet, Word document, or PowerPoint presentation). Select the desired type, and click **OK**.

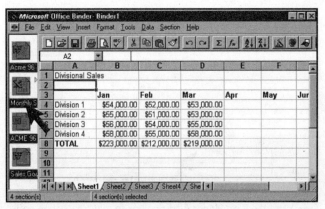

7 To perform a task (such as page numbering) on more than one document, hold down the **Ctrl** key while clicking on the icon for each document you want to act on (this selects the documents). Then, perform the desired task as you normally would.

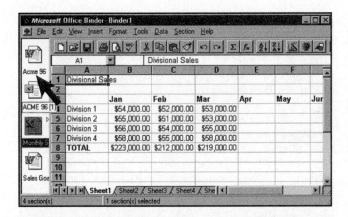

6 You can rearrange the documents in the Binder by dragging a document's icon up or down in the left pane. Release the mouse button.

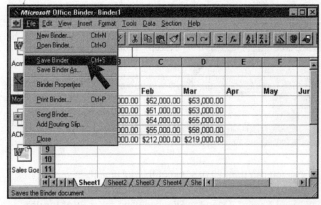

8 To save your binder, open the **File** menu and select **Save Binder**.

(continues)

Guided Tour Organize Documents in a Binder *(continued)*

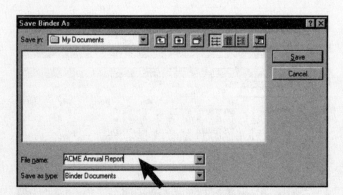

9 Use the Save Binder As dialog box to select a location and enter a name for the new binder file. Once you've named the binder, you can quickly save changes by clicking on the **Save** button or pressing **Ctrl+S**.

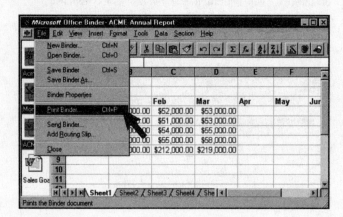

10 You can print all or some of the documents in your binder. To print selected documents, **Ctrl+click** on each document you want to print. Open the **File** menu and select **Print Binder**.

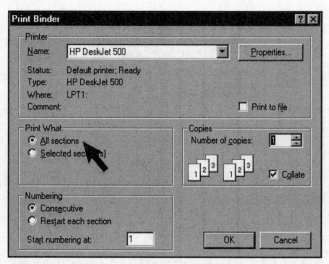

11 Under Print What, click **All sections** to print all the documents in the binder, or click **Selected section(s)** to print only those documents you selected.

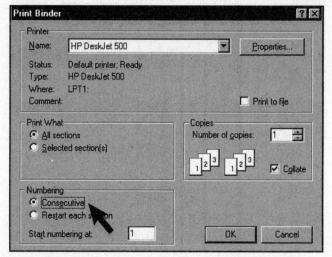

12 Under Numbering, select **Consecutive** to number all the pages in the binder as if they are part of a single document; or select **Restart each section** to number the pages of each document separately.

Guided Tour Organize Documents in a Binder

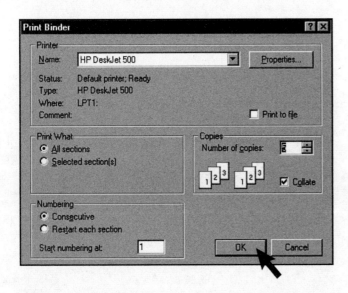

13 Enter any other printing preferences, such as the number of copies you want. To start printing, click **OK**.

PART 2

Do-It-Yourself

Y ou've mastered the basics of using Excel, Word, PowerPoint, and Schedule+. You can create your own workbooks, documents, and presentations, and you may be well on your way to organizing your life with Schedule+. But now that you know your way around the Microsoft Office suite, you'd probably like to explore a little and see how you can put these programs to some practical use.

In this part, you'll learn how to apply the basics you've learned to actual projects. You'll learn how to create a multimedia, interactive résumé in PowerPoint, how to reconcile your checking account with an Excel worksheet, and even how to create a quarterly report that updates itself. In this part, you'll get hands-on experience using the Microsoft Office programs separately and together to make the most of your new investment, and to have some fun in the process.

So, stretch your fingers, and check out the following project sections:

What You Will Find in This Section

DO IT YOURSELF

Combining Excel Data and Charts with Your Word Documents

Now that you are comfortable using the Microsoft Word and Excel products, you are probably using Excel for the worksheets and Word for text creation. That's good, and that's the strength of each product. But what if you need to convey *both* text information and worksheet information? Do you always have to worry about creating and managing two separate documents, one in Word and the other in Excel? Why not combine the advantages of Word and Excel into your single creation? This section describes projects you can perform that mix and match the strengths of each product into a single document or worksheet.

The projects in this section assume that the Microsoft Office Shortcut Bar is on, and that you added buttons for running Excel, Word, and PowerPoint. If this is not the case, see "Customize the Microsoft Office Shortcut Bar," on page [15tbd] for details.

What You Will Find in This Section

Insert an Income Statement into Your Monthly Business Report

Business reports are more effective if they include data, but typing in numbers and trying to align them in columns can be a real pain. It also can be redundant work because you probably already have that data stored in an Excel worksheet, since it's the best tool for handling figures.

Why not combine the best of both worlds? You can insert an Excel worksheet directly into your report in Word. There is no limit to the number of worksheets you can include with your document. For example, you can include an accounting worksheet for each department itemized in a single auditing report. You can create business inventory reports more easily by simply including the inventory worksheet portions directly onto the business report.

To do the task shown here, you'll need to create a document in Word and create a worksheet in Excel.

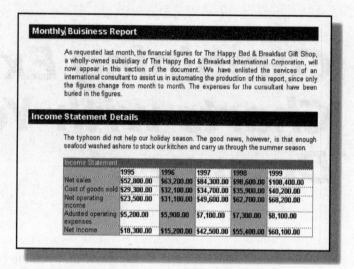

Review the "How to Create a Word Document" section starting on page 77, and "How to Create an Excel Worksheet" section starting on page 137, if you need help doing this.

Begin Do It Yourself Paste Excel Worksheet Data into a Word Document

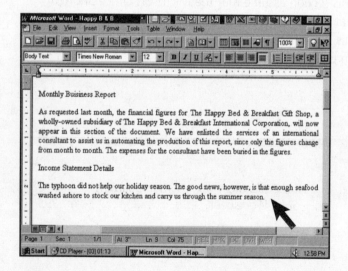

1 Prepare the text for your report in Word. Don't worry about the formatting for now. We will use the report template and automatic formatting capabilities of Word to improve the appearance. Save the report.

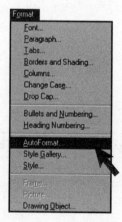

2 Open the **Format** menu, and select the **AutoFormat** command.

Do It Yourself   Paste Excel Worksheet Data into a Word Document

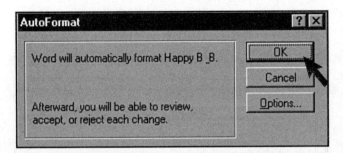

3 The AutoFormat dialog box assures you that if you don't like the changes, you will be able to restore the original format. Click **OK**.

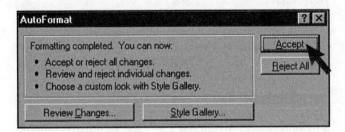

4 The AutoFormat feature improves the appearance of your report and a different AutoFormat dialog box appears so that you can accept or reject the changes. If you like this format, you can click **Accept** and save your report. To find out how much better your report can look, click the **Style Gallery** button.

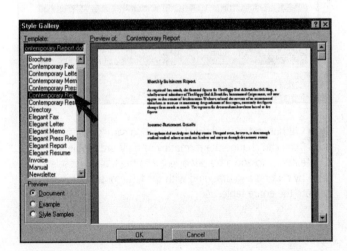

5 Here is the preview of the format chosen by Word. To choose a different format or template, click inside of the Template scroll box on the left. Scroll through the available templates until you find the one you want. Click on the template to select it. For this example, click the **Contemporary** template.

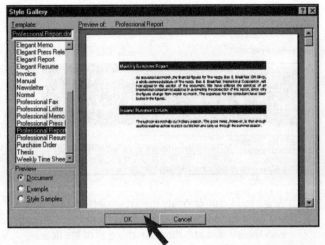

6 The preview shows the template you selected applied to your text. If you don't like the way the template looks, repeat step 5. When you find a template you like, click **OK**.

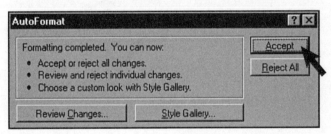

7 You are returned to the AutoFormat dialog box. Click **Accept** to apply the template you selected (Professional Report in the example) to your text. Save your report.

8 Review your report in Word and decide where you want to place the data from an Excel worksheet. Then open Excel by clicking the **Excel** icon on the Microsoft Office Shortcut Bar and locate the file containing the data you want. If it does not yet exist, you can create it now.

(continues)

Do It Yourself Paste Excel Worksheet Data into a Word Document

(continued)

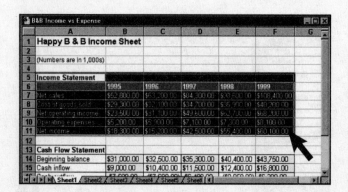

9 When you locate or create the data, select only the data you want to appear in your report by clicking and dragging with the left mouse button to capture all of the data.

10 A selection border and a frame will appear around the object, indicating that you have selected it. To copy the selected data, open the **Edit** menu and click **Copy**.

11 Switch back to Word by clicking the **Word** button in the Microsoft Office Shortcut Bar.

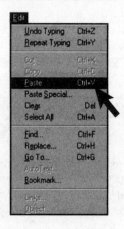

12 Move the insertion point to the location where you want the data inserted. Open the **Edit** menu, and select the **Paste** command.

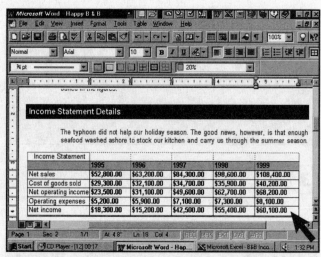

13 The Excel data appears as a table in your report.

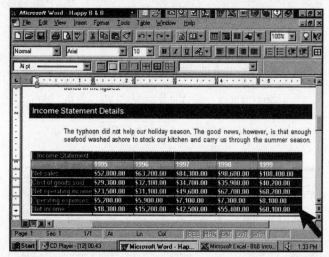

14 Although the worksheet formatting carries over from Excel, you can change the format by using Word's table formatting features. To add a border or color to the table, first select the table by clicking and dragging with the left mouse button to capture the entire table.

Do It Yourself   Paste Excel Worksheet Data into a Word Document

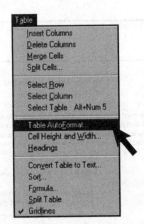

15 With the table selected, open the **Table** menu (or right-click anywhere inside the table) and select the **Table AutoFormat** command.

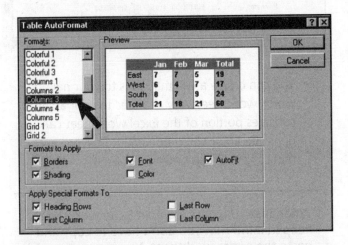

16 The Table AutoFormat dialog box appears and provides you with a large variety of options. For this example, click inside of the Formats scroll box and select **Columns 3**. A preview of your table will appear with the selected formatting options. Click **OK**.

If you are interested in actually linking an Excel worksheet into your report, review the next Do It Yourself called "Create a Quarterly Report That Updates Itself" on page [16tbd].

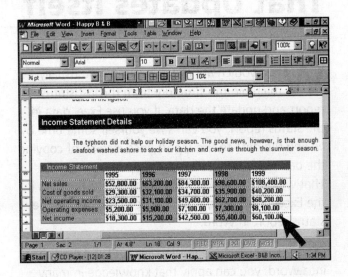

17 The report and formatted data table are now complete. Save your work by using the **File Save** command. You can edit the material in this pasted Excel table just as you would a Word table. It really is a Word table now, and that should be a warning: don't expect to change numbers and have things add up like an Excel worksheet. Each table cell is independent. Try it yourself by clicking on a cell and changing something.

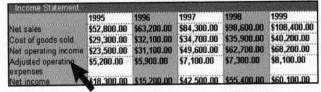

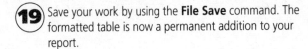

18 Here the text cell entry **Operating expenses** has been selected and changed to **Adjusted operating expenses**. Click anywhere outside of the table to return editing your report.

19 Save your work by using the **File Save** command. The formatted table is now a permanent addition to your report.

Create a Quarterly Report That Updates Itself

When you create a status report, you usually maintain the structure from the last status report and update the data. If you use Excel data in the status report, you can save yourself some time by *linking* the data to the report once instead of copying the data each time you need to update the report. That way, anytime you make a change to the data in the Excel worksheet, that change will appear in the status report in Word.

Once you understand how to link an Excel worksheet into Word, you can apply that knowledge in many ways, especially saving yourself the work of retyping existing information.

- You can automate the monthly creation of a status report that contains a summary chart from a company data worksheet. If anyone makes changes to the data worksheet, your status report will include those latest sales figures automatically.

- If you have a problem with a bank statement, you can draft a letter to the bank that includes the disputed portion of your checkbook worksheet.

- You can create business inventory reports much easier by simply including the inventory worksheet portions directly on the business report.

Buy the Book Bookstore
Quarterly Report

Greetings, loyal investors! Because Buy the Book is an atypical bookstore, we've adopted a somewhat informal format for our quarterly reports. But no matter how the numbers are laid out, you'll be happy to hear that you're still making gobs of money. In fact, we had another record-breaking quarter, compliments of Joe's caffeine klatch (our most recent addition), and the continuing success of our video wing. But enough preliminaries. Here are the raw figures.

	April	May	June
Joe's Caffeine Klatch			
Sales	$8,540.00	$7,654.00	$9,783.00
Purchases	$5,378.00	$4,320.00	$4,536.00
Profit	$3,162.00	$3,334.00	$5,247.00
The Video Wing			
Rentals	$18,763.00	$19,735.00	$17,843.00
Purchases	$1,387.00	$3,862.00	$2,397.00
Profit	$17,376.00	$15,873.00	$15,446.00
Books and Magazines			
Sales	$32,875.00	$29,870.00	$39,021.00
Purchases	$15,830.00	$13,987.00	$18,963.00
Profit	$17,045.00	$15,883.00	$20,058.00

- You can create a will that links to your net worth worksheet. Any changes to your assets or liabilities portion of the Excel worksheet can generate an updated document in Word automatically, the next time you open it.

When inserting data from an Excel worksheet, keep in mind that you don't have to copy and paste the entire worksheet. You can paste only the portion you need. The Do It Yourself steps show an example in which you can omit entire columns from the worksheet by hiding those columns before selecting the data.

Begin Do It Yourself   Paste Worksheet Data So It Updates Itself

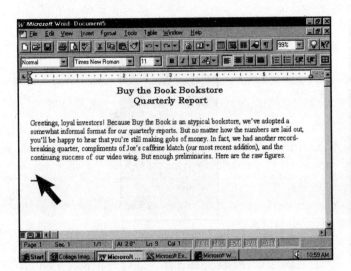

1 Prepare your report in Word and move the insertion point to the location where you want to insert your worksheet data.

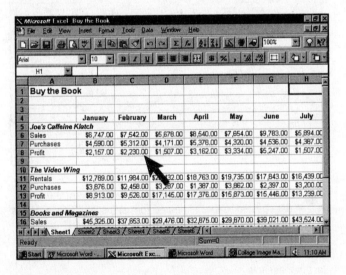

2 Switch to Excel, and open or create the worksheet from which you want to copy the data.

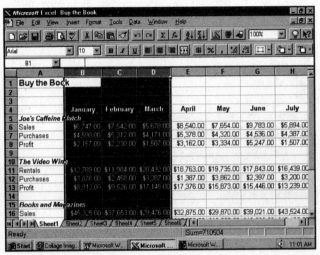

3 In this case, we want to present the income and expenses for only the second quarter. To prevent the first quarter numbers from appearing, you can hide columns B, C, and D. Drag over the column letters at the top of the worksheet.

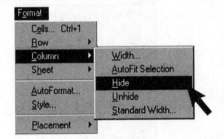

4 To hide the selected columns, open the **Format** menu, point to **Column**, and click on **Hide**.

(continues)

Do It Yourself   Paste Worksheet Data So It Updates Itself

(continued)

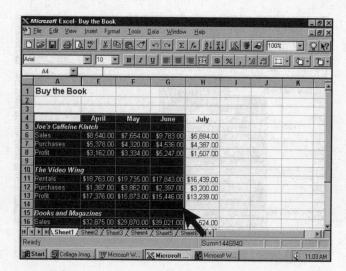

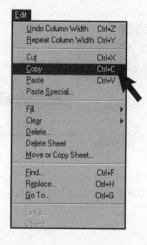

5 Excel hides the selected columns, so you can copy the data in columns A, E, F, and G as a single unit. Drag over the data you want to copy.

6 Open the **Edit** menu and select **Copy**, or click on the **Copy** button in the toolbar.

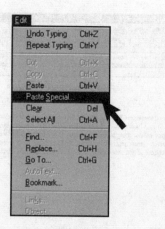

7 Switch back to your Word document. Open the **Edit** menu and select **Paste Special**, so you can insert the copied worksheet data as a link.

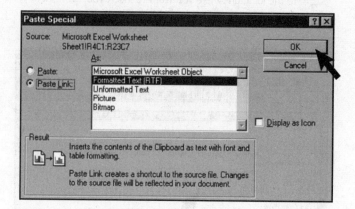

8 The Paste Special dialog box asks how you want the copied data pasted. Click the desired format (usually RTF) in the **As** list, and then click the **Paste Link** option. Click **OK**. RTF (rich text format) inserts the Excel data as formatted text. Microsoft Excel Worksheet Object inserts the data as a picture, making it a little less manageable.

Do It Yourself Paste Worksheet Data So It Updates Itself

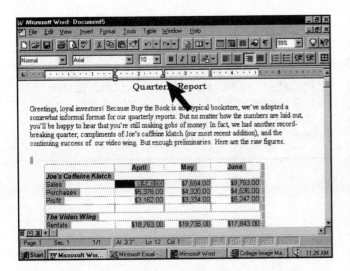

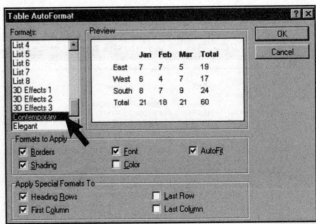

9 The data appears as a table inside your Word document. To change the position of the table, click inside the table, and drag the margin and column width markers, as desired.

11 The Table AutoFormat dialog box appears, allowing you to pick a format for your table. If you select the **Contemporary** format, you'll see the preview table shown here. Click **OK**.

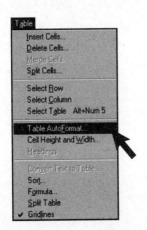

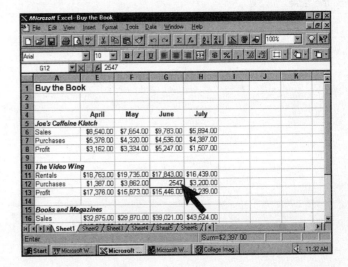

10 To quickly change the look of the table, open the **Table** menu and select **Table AutoFormat**.

12 Let's see how this linked data behaves. Switch back to your Excel worksheet, and change one of the numbers. Here, the Video Wing June purchase amount was changed from 2397 to 2547. Be sure to press **Enter** after typing your change, or the link will not update.

(continues)

Do It Yourself Paste Worksheet Data So It Updates Itself

(continued)

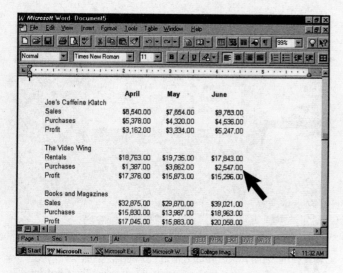

If you hid columns as shown in the Do It Yourself section, and then you unhide the columns, you might run into trouble if you update the link later. When you update the link (using Edit Update Link), Word assumes that you want the hidden columns inserted as well.

13 Switch back to the table in your Word document, and look at the number you changed in your Excel worksheet. As expected, the new entry was automatically inserted into the table.

Copy an Analysis Chart into a Letter to Prospective Investors

Sometimes, numbers alone are overwhelming, and many times, we need to create documents that contain a large amount of raw data. The visual impact of a simple but professional chart can catch the attention of your reader and at the same time make your numbers easier to understand.

Adding Excel charts to Word documents can improve the visual quality of your information. Think about receiving a letter from the lottery commissioner that details your winning the lottery. You have to decide if you want the money monthly, quarterly, or annually. What are the tax implications? Three charts could replace pages of data and make you smile even more.

You can include as many charts in a single letter as you want. You can mix and match the different types of charts—you are limited only by your imagination.

Once you know how to include Charts from Excel into your Word document, your documents can be much more visually stimulating. Here are some ideas to get you started:

- To convince one of your kids (or someone else's kids) to save money, create a graph showing that if the kid sets aside so much money per month, he will have some incredible amount when it's time to leave home.

- You can send a letter requesting a raise to your boss that includes a multiline chart showing the increasing Consumer Price Index and the inflation rate graphed against your meager salary increases.

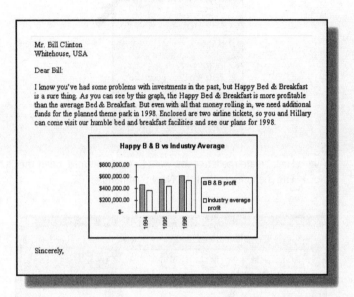

- To convince your spouse to spend less in a particular category, create a pie chart of your monthly budget. When he sees how big a slice of the pie they're devouring, he may think twice when making the next purchase.

- To explain to your IRA representative why you are transferring money out of its fund, you can send a letter with a graph that shows the declining performance of the fund next to the strong performance of the new fund you are considering.

If you need a refresher on charting in Excel, turn back to the "How To Create an Excel Chart" section on page 137.

Begin Do It Yourself Insert an Excel Chart into a Word Letter

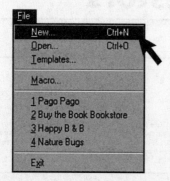

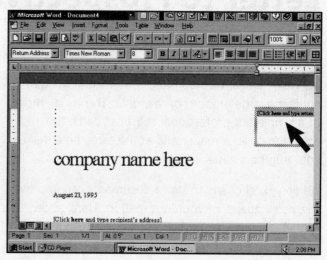

1 First, create the letter you want to send. In Word, open the **File** menu and select the **New** command.

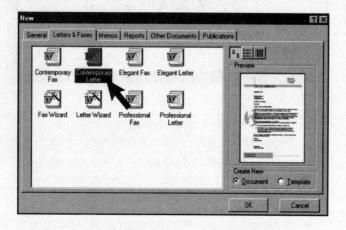

2 The New dialog box appears. Click the **Letters & Faxes** tab, and then click **Contemporary Letter**. Click **OK** to continue.

3 The template for creating a letter is ready for you. Simply click on an item (as instructed in the template), and then type your entry. To change the sample text, drag over it and type your new text.

4 Now, display the Excel chart you want to copy. Open Excel by clicking its icon in the Microsoft Office Shortcut Bar and locate the file containing the chart you want. If it does not yet exist, you can create it now.

Do It Yourself Insert an Excel Chart into a Word Letter

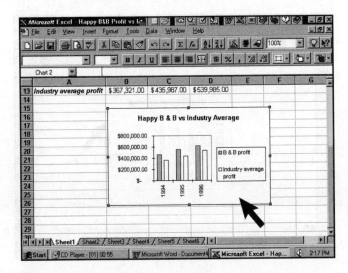

5 When you have located or created the chart, click on it to select it. Selection handles and a frame will appear around the object, indicating that you selected it. If selection handles do not appear around the entire chart, as shown, click outside the chart, and then click on it again.

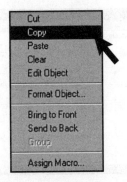

6 Click the right mouse button once anywhere inside the selected chart, and then select **Copy** from the shortcut menu.

7 Switch back to Word by clicking the **Word** button in the Microsoft Office Shortcut Bar or in the taskbar.

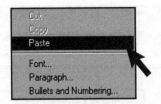

8 In your letter, click where you want the Excel chart inserted. Right-click on the same spot, and then select **Paste** from the shortcut menu.

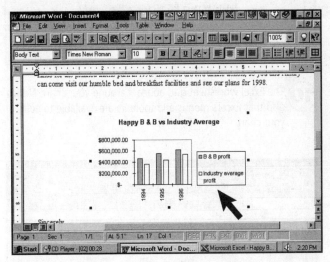

9 You now have a full-featured Excel chart embedded into your Word letter. Existing text moves to accommodate the space taken up by the addition of this new chart. Prove to yourself that it's no ordinary picture by double-clicking on the chart.

(continues)

Do It Yourself Insert an Excel Chart into a Word Letter

(continued)

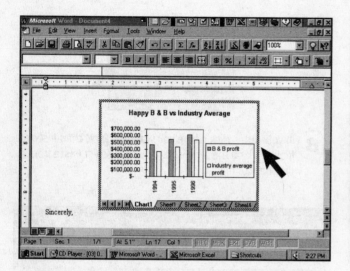

10 The Excel worksheet grid appears around your chart. Notice also that Excel's menus and toolbars are available to edit your chart.

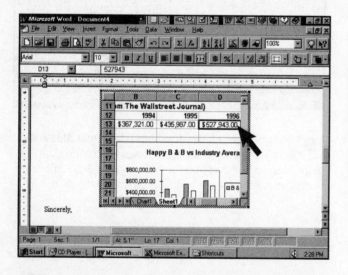

11 After making changes, click on the chart inside your worksheet to select it. Now click anywhere on your original document in Word.

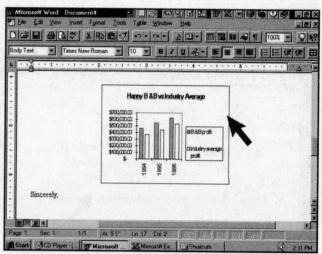

12 The standard Word editing menus reappear. You can now continue with your letter. Remember that this simple pasting of the chart from Excel does not contain a link to the original source document. You can observe this yourself by clicking on the **Excel** button in the Microsoft Office Shortcut Bar.

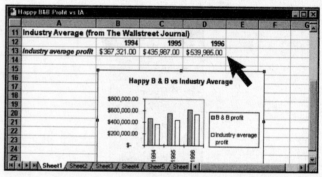

13 Excel will be open with the original chart selected, but your changes after pasting were not reflected back in this source.

Add Explanatory Text to Your Quarterly Sales Worksheet

Worksheets are great for organizing and manipulating rows and columns of numbers, but occasionally, you need to add text to a worksheet to explain the significance of the numbers or to point out an important trend. Although you can type explanatory text directly in your worksheet, the worksheet isn't really set up to handle huge blocks of text. You'll find it difficult to wrap long blocks of text in a cell, edit the contents, format it, and even move around in it.

Because Word is designed to handle text, it makes sense to type your text-intensive material in Word and then copy it into a text box on your Excel worksheet. You can add any number of text boxes to act as an introduction or to sit alongside your data as a running commentary. By combining the text-handling features of Word with the number-crunching expertise of Excel, there's no longer any reason to have a worksheet suffer from a lack of supporting text or documentation.

The Do It Yourself section shows the basics of how to add a Word text box to an Excel worksheet and manipulate the text box. Once you've learned the basics, here are some ideas of other ways you can apply this technique:

- Many charts fail to convey important information that you might want your audience to understand. A well-placed text box can provide a suggested conclusion or a defending argument.

- If your planned business report will contain more data pages than text, it may be less work to create it as a business worksheet in Excel that contains descriptive text from Word.

BullDog, Inc
Quarterly Sales Report

Product	Qtr 1	Qtr2	Qtr3	Qtr 4	Total
T-Shirts	56,000	53,150	53,850	186,750	349,750
Sweatshirts	38,650	38,950	39,500	136,350	253,450
Shorts	37,100	37,305	38,225	131,425	244,055
Sweatpants	35,925	36,125	36,820	126,185	235,055
Other	31,900	33,100	33,060	114,300	212,360
TOTAL	$199,575	$198,630	$201,455	$695,010	$1,294,670

Note the jump in sales in the fourth quarter. Although the increase can be attributed to Christmas sales, we also had a $10,000 special promotion during this time. Let's see what happens if we carry the promotion into the first quarter of the coming fiscal year.

- You can create an expense worksheet that contains icons that open into detailed reports concerning the entry. A worksheet with many icons could even impress the IRS.

- Inventory worksheets can be difficult to understand and maintain, especially if product numbers are arbitrarily designated or ordered. By adding the descriptive text from the corresponding catalog to an adjacent cell, the worksheet can help clarify items conveniently.

You can also add explanatory text to a worksheet by using Excel's Note feature. To add a note to a cell, click on the cell, open the **Insert** menu, and select **Note**. Type the desired text, and then click **OK**. When you rest the mouse pointer on the cell that contains the note, your note pops up in a box that looks sort of like a ToolTip. You can also use the Notes feature to record and attach sound or voice recordings to cells.

Begin Do It Yourself   Paste Word Text into an Excel Worksheet

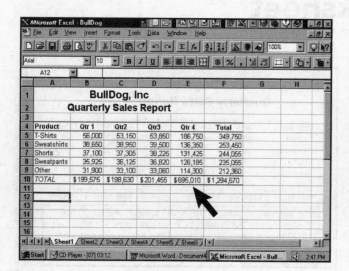

1 Prepare your worksheet in Excel. Decide where it would be appropriate to clarify data by including text from a Word document. In this example, we will add some Word text to clarify the fourth quarter jump in sales.

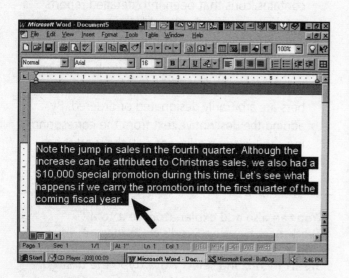

2 Switch to Word, and type the text you want to use or open the Word document containing the text you want. Select the text by dragging over it with the left mouse button. In this example, the entire paragraph was easily selected by clicking three times inside the paragraph.

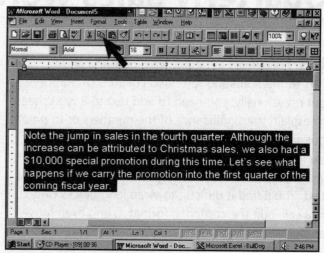

3 The selected text is highlighted. Click the **Copy** button in the toolbar. The text is now copied into the Clipboard.

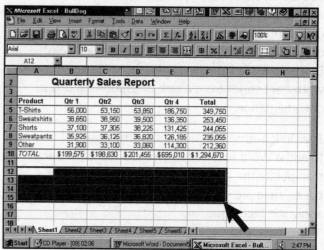

4 Now switch back to Excel (you can click the Excel icon in the Microsoft Office Shortcut Bar), and select the cells to contain your text.

Do It Yourself Paste Word Text into an Excel Worksheet

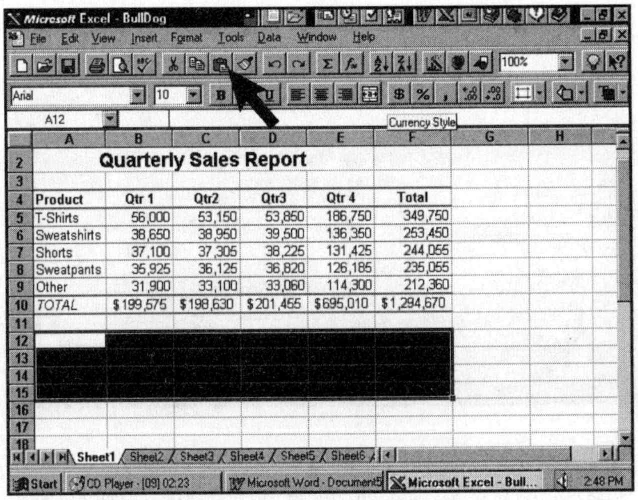

5 Click the **Paste** button in the toolbar.

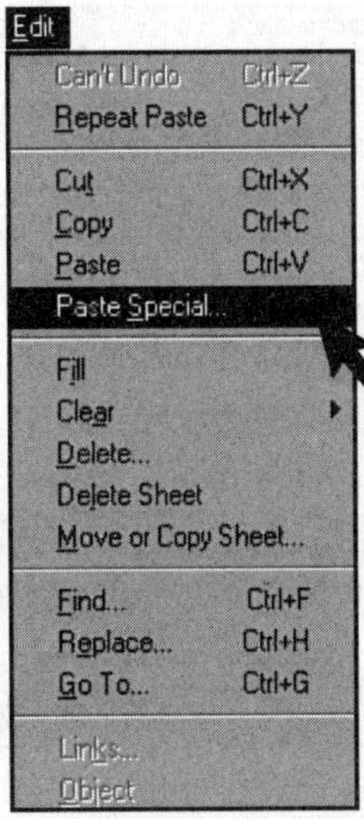

7 Now try opening the **Edit** menu and selecting the **Paste Special** command.

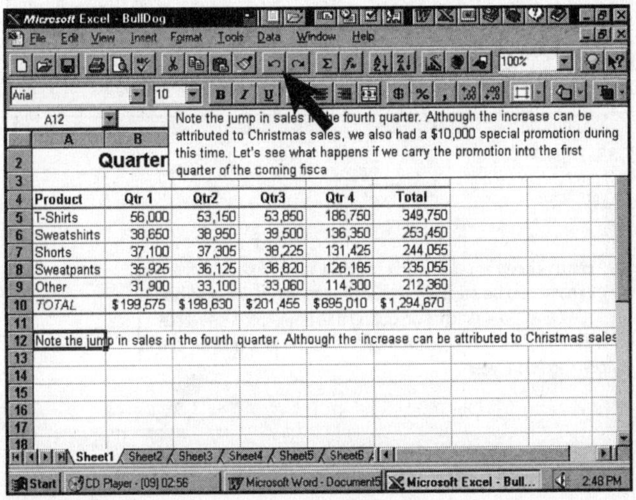

6 Oops! This amount of text was too large for the standard Paste command. The text continues out to the right of the worksheet. Remove this text by clicking the **Undo** button. The text has been removed from the worksheet (but remains on the Clipboard).

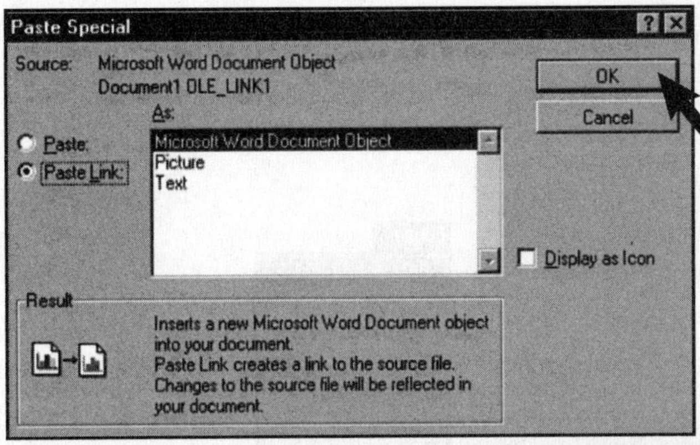

8 The Paste Special dialog box appears. Select the **Microsoft Word Document Object** in the **As** list. Click **OK**.

(continues)

Do It Yourself   Paste Word Text into an Excel Worksheet

(continued)

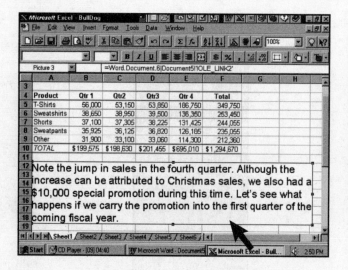

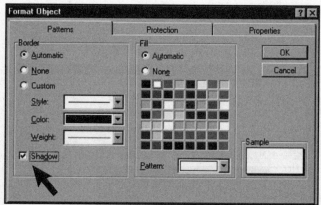

9 This is much better! You now have a text box inside your worksheet that you can drag around to position more precisely. You can also change the height or width of the text box by dragging one of its handles.

10 The text automatically wraps to fit inside the new frame size. To edit or reformat the text, simply double-click on the text box. This opens the file in Word, and you can use Word's tools to change the look of the text.

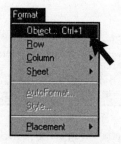

11 You can also change the look of the text box in Excel. Click on the text box to select it, and then open the **Format** menu and select **Object**. (A quicker way to format an object is to right-click on the object and select **Format Object**.)

12 The Format Object dialog box lets you control the border of the text box, shading inside the text box, and other qualities of the text box. Under Border, click **Shadow**. Change any other options, as desired, and click **OK**.

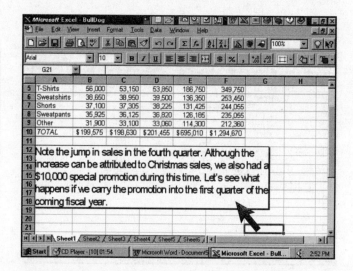

13 A drop shadow appears, giving the text box a more professional look. Save your Excel worksheet.

Another, simpler, way to add text to your worksheets is to add the text inside a text box. Right-click on any toolbar, and select **Drawing** to display the Drawing toolbar. Click on the **Text Box** tool, drag the mouse pointer over the area where you want it to appear, and then type your text.

Insert a Letter into Your Quarterly Report As an Icon

Sometimes, you may want to add an explanation to an Excel worksheet but feel that a text box will take up too much space on the worksheet, and the reader may not need to read the information. In this instance, you can replace the text with an icon. The reader can then read the entire text by double-clicking the document icon or ignore it.

You can add as many icons as you need to clarify your worksheet. Each icon can contain different text from the same Word document or from different Word documents.

Don't forget that these icons link to text from Word and therefore, Word must be available. It may seem obvious to you now because you must have both Excel and Word on your computer to create this project. But if you copy your worksheet to a diskette for someone else to use, they will see your icons representing text, but may not have Word installed on their computer. Without Word installed, a double-click on the icons results in the error that the source application cannot be found.

When you learn the basics of adding icons to your worksheet, you can use the icons to link to graphics,

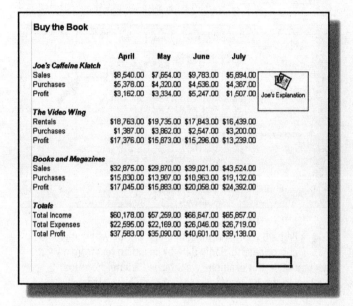

charts, sound recordings, and any other shared data. In addition to using icons for your audience, consider using them for notes to yourself. For example, if you come across a number that doesn't seem right, you might add an icon next to it that displays a question or concern. If you work on group projects, these notes can come in handy for communicating your concerns and questions to your colleagues.

Begin Do It Yourself   Link a Word Document to an Excel Worksheet

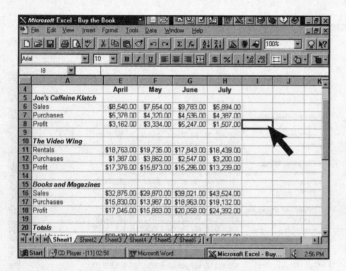

1 Prepare your worksheet in Excel. Decide where it would be appropriate to clarify data by including text from a Word document. In this example, we attached a letter from Joe, explaining the July profit dip at Joe's Caffeine Klatch.

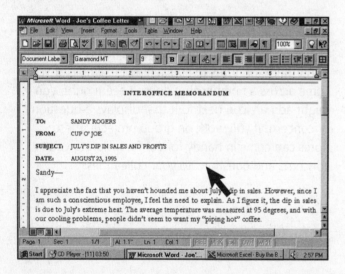

2 Run Word, and open the Word document that contains the text you want to use (or type the text in a new document). You can format the text, if desired.

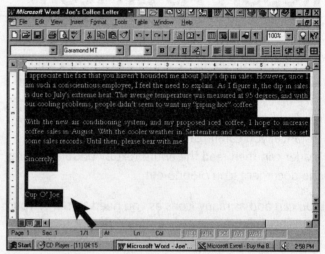

3 Select the text by dragging over it with the left mouse button. In this example, the entire document is selected. (To quickly select the entire document, press **Ctrl+A**.)

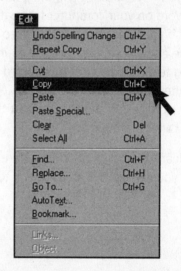

4 The selected text is highlighted. Open the **Edit** menu and select the **Copy** command. The selected text is now copied onto the Clipboard.

Do It Yourself Link a Word Document to an Excel Worksheet

5 Now switch back to Excel by clicking the **Excel** icon in the Microsoft Office Shortcut Bar or in the taskbar.

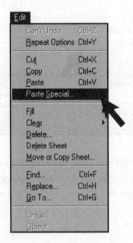

6 Select the cell in which you want the icon to appear; open the **Edit** menu and select the **Paste Special** command. (You can easily move the icon later.)

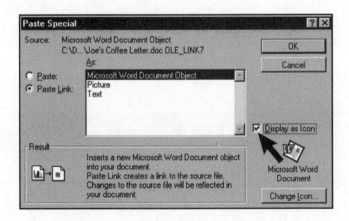

7 The Paste Special dialog box appears. To create a link to the original text source in Word, click the **Paste Link** option. Select the **Microsoft Word Document Object** in the **As** list. Click on **Display as Icon**. The proposed icon appears. You can change this icon to something else by clicking the **Change Icon** button.

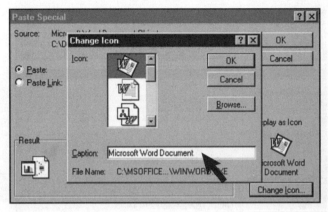

8 In the Change Icon dialog box, you can select one of the available icons from the icon selector by clicking on your choice. You can also change the default icon caption by typing it in the Caption text box.

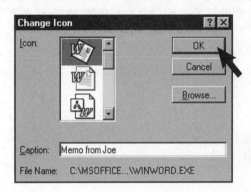

9 When you finish making changes, click **OK** to return to the Paste Special dialog box. Then click **OK** in the Paste Special dialog box.

(continues)

Do It Yourself Link a Word Document to an Excel Worksheet *(continued)*

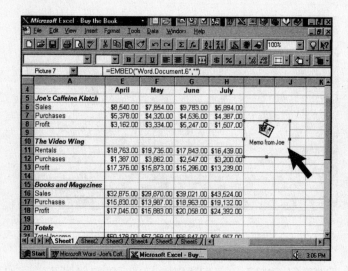

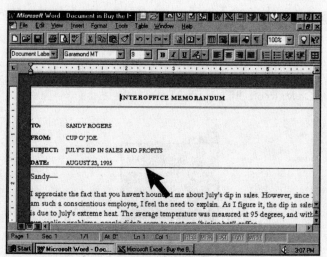

10 You are returned to the worksheet. The Word text is now a part of the Excel worksheet, represented by the icon you created. If the location and size looks good, save your worksheet. To see the actual text, double-click on the icon you created.

11 Microsoft Word is started with the source document containing the selected text. Any changes made to this source text document will always be reflected in your Excel worksheet.

DO IT YOURSELF

Find a Job with Microsoft Office

I n today's competitive job market, searching for a job takes more than just typing a résumé and mailing it to the personnel departments of prospective companies. You usually have to develop a strategy, research several companies, and (most importantly) organize the material you need to effectively market yourself. You have to prepare a résumé; find a list of companies and people to send your résumé to; and pull together all of your records (transcripts, references, evaluations, samples of your work, and so on).

In addition, job seeking has become much more automated. Many employers might ask you to e-mail your résumé or fax it. In many computer-related industries, you can make a big impression by sending a multimedia résumé—a résumé done as a slide show in PowerPoint or as a Word document with icons linking to pictures, sounds, and other documents. And if you're connected to an online service, you can even use your computer to search for potential openings by checking professional bulletin board systems and online want ads.

In this project section, you'll learn how to use Microsoft Office to hone your job search strategies for the '90s. In particular, you'll perform the following projects:

What You will Find in This Section

Create a Résumé in Word

The easiest way to create a cover letter and résumé in Word is to use the Resume Wizard. To use the wizard, you open Word's **File** menu, and click on **New**. Click the **Other Documents** tab, and click **Resume Wizard**. When you click **OK**, Word starts the Wizard, which leads you through the process of creating a résumé (and optional cover letter). To learn more about using Word's templates and wizards, see page 135.

So, if creating a résumé is so easy, why would we include a project about it? Because the résumé that the wizard creates is no award-winning résumé, and because the résumé is difficult to customize.

The project shows a different approach to creating résumés—an approach that uses Word's table feature. The table feature allows you to create résumés that are easily customized. And, once you create your basic paper résumé, the project shows you how to transform it into an interactive multimedia résumé, complete with icons that link to sounds, pictures, worksheet data, and graphs.

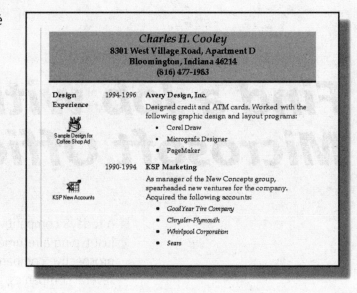

Transforming a Paper Résumé into a Multimedia Résumé

If you are submitting your résumé specifically for a job that requires you to use Microsoft Office, or if you know that the person looking at the résumé uses Microsoft Office, you might be able to impress the person by adding icon links to your résumé. For example, you can add an icon that opens a document showing one of your writing samples. Another icon can link to an Excel worksheet that shows your salary history. You can even include an icon that stores an introductory voice recording or a photo of you.

When inserting icons, take the following two precautions:

- Paste data as an *object* (not as a *link*). If you create a link to the data, you'll have to send the person all the files that act as links, and the person will have to place those files in the same folders you used.

- Do not use data from any program that the person viewing your résumé may not have. For example, if you include a video clip file, and the person does not have a program that can play video clips, the video clip won't run.

The following steps give a general procedure for adding icons to your résumé. For a more interactive and animated résumé, see "Create an Electronic Résumé in PowerPoint" on page 415:

1. Click inside the cell in which you want the icon to appear. If the cell has an entry, move the insertion point to the end of the entry and press **Enter** to create a space for the icon.

2. Run the program used to create the picture, worksheet data, sound file, or other item you want to use in your résumé.

3. Select the desired data, open the **Edit** menu, and select **Copy**.

4. Switch back to your résumé, open the **Edit** menu, and select **Paste Special**.

5. From the **As** list, click the **Object** option (for example, Excel Worksheet Object).

6. Make sure to select the **Paste** (NOT Paste Link) option. By choosing Paste, the data becomes a part of the résumé file, and you don't have to worry about including the original data file on the disk.

7. Click the **Display as Icon** check box, and click the **Change Icon** button.

8. Click the desired icon in the **Icon** list; drag over the text in the **Caption** text box, and type a new caption for the icon. (You might want to type something like "Double-click here to see my transcript," so the person will know what to do.) Click **OK**.

9. You return to the Paste Special dialog box. Click **OK** to insert the data as an icon. The icon appears in your résumé, as shown here.

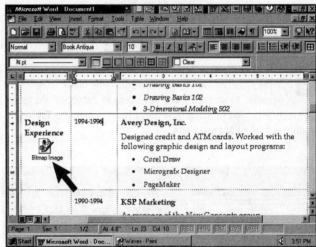

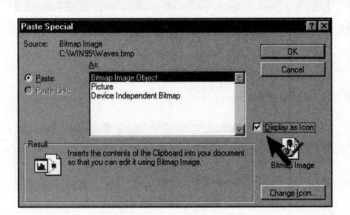

Begin Do It Yourself Create a Résumé

1 Let's start with a blank page in Word. Click the **New** button in the toolbar to create a new, blank document. (To work on the document in Page Layout view, as shown, open the **View** menu and click on **Page Layout**.)

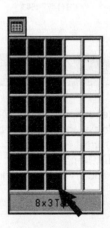

2 The first step in creating the sample résumé is to create a three-column table. Click the **Insert Table** button, and drag over the drop-down grid that appears, until you have a table that's three columns wide and 7 to 8 rows long (you can insert rows later).

(continues)

Do It Yourself Create a Résumé *(continued)*

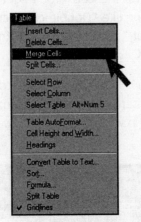

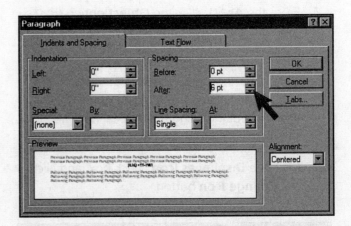

3 When you release the mouse button, the blank table appears. Now, merge the three cells at the top of the table to create a single cell. Drag over the cells; and open the **Table** menu and select **Merge Cells**.

5 Insert some space after the phone number paragraph. Right-click the phone number, and click **Paragraph**. Click the up arrow in the **Spacing After** spin box once to add 6 points after the paragraph. Click **OK**.

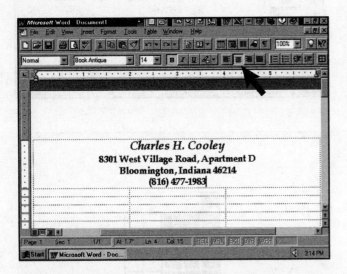

6 To insert a line below your name, address, and phone number, click the **Borders** button to display the Borders toolbar. Then, select a line thickness from the drop-down list (3/4pt in the example), and click the **Bottom Border** button.

4 Click the **Center** button in the Formatting toolbar, and type your name, address, and phone number, pressing **Enter** at the end of each line. Format the text as desired. The text shown here is in Book Antiqua (18-point bold italic for the name, and 14-point bold for the address and phone number).

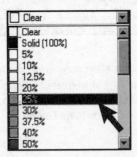

7 You can shade this cell. Open the **Shading** drop-down list in the Borders toolbar, and click the desired shading percent (25% in the example).

Do It Yourself Create a Résumé

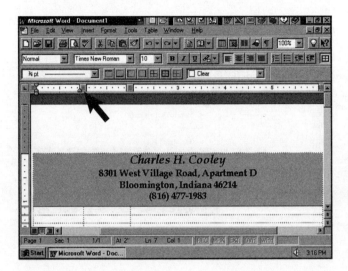

8 Now, set the column widths for the rest of the table. Click inside any cell below the topmost cell. Drag the left column marker to the 1-inch mark on the ruler, and the right column marker to the 2-inch mark. This makes the two left columns 1-inch wide, and the rightmost column 4-inches wide.

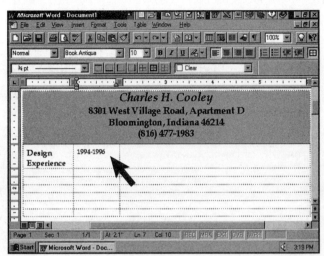

10 Click inside the middle cell and type the appropriate date or date range for the time you held your current job. (You typically list work experience in reverse order, starting with the most recent position.)

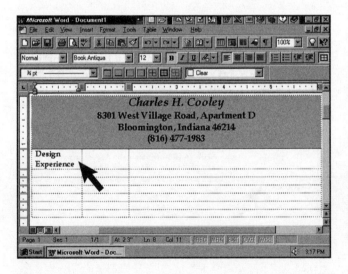

9 Now, you can start typing entries. Click inside the leftmost cell in the second row, and type one of your category names (for example **Design Experience**). Format the text as desired (14-point Book Antiqua bold was used here).

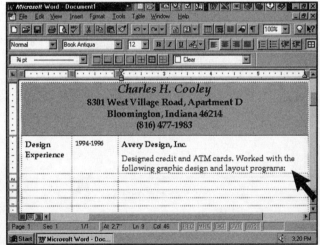

11 In the rightmost cell in row 2, type the name of the company and a brief description of your position. Format the text as desired. The text shown here is in 12-point Book Antiqua MT. The Company name is bold.

(continues)

Do It Yourself Create a Résumé *(continued)*

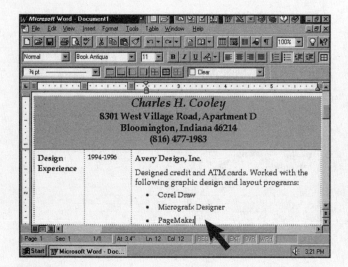

12 Press **Enter**, and type a bulleted list of job responsibilities or key projects. To create the bulleted list, click the **Bullets** button. Before you start typing, change the font to 11-point Book Antiqua italic using the Formatting toolbar.

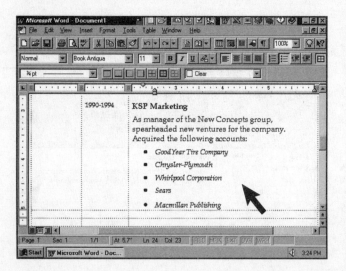

13 If you have another job to list under Work Experience, type the date and job description in the middle and right cells of the next row down. Because you are still in Work Experience, you don't have to retype the category name.

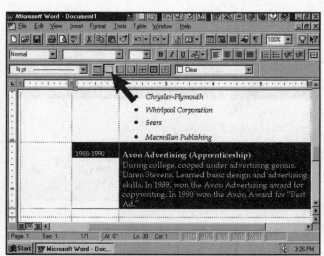

14 When you finish typing your work experience entries, drag over the cells that contain the last date and job description entries. In the Borders toolbar, open the **Line Style** drop-down list, and select **3/4 pt**; then click the **Bottom Border** button to add a line that separates this category from the next one.

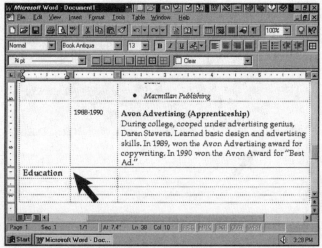

15 Click inside the leftmost cell in the next row down to begin typing your entries for the next category. Type the next category's name (for example, **Education**). Format the text as desired (14-point Book Antiqua bold was used here).

Do It Yourself Create a Résumé

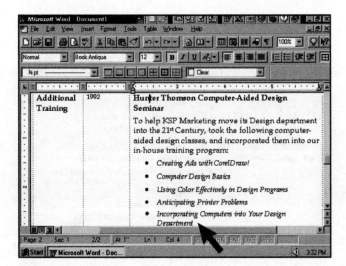

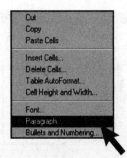

16 Continue typing dates and entries for the various categories, as shown here. You might have categories such as Education, Training, Skills, Awards, Professional Organizations, Special Interests, and Community Service.

18 When you finish, you might notice that some text is awkwardly spaced. It may be too close or too far away from a cell border. To change the spacing, drag over the text that is awkwardly spaced, and then right-click it and select **Paragraph**.

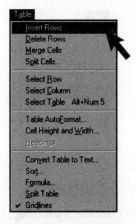

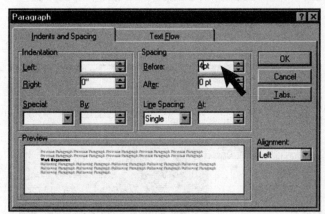

17 If you see that you will need additional rows, it's best to insert rows *before* you type inside the last row, because rows are inserted above the selected row. Click in the selection area to the left of the row above which you want the new row inserted. Then, open the **Table** menu and select **Insert Rows**.

19 The Format Paragraph dialog box allows you to change the layout of your paragraphs. In tables, you can change the space between text and a top or bottom cell border by changing the **Spacing Before** and **After** settings. Usually a 4–6 point change will do the trick.

(continues)

Do It Yourself Create a Résumé *(continued)*

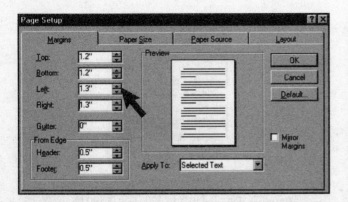

20 If your résumé runs long or short, you can adjust it with the formatting tools. (You typically want a résumé that runs one or two full pages.) Try changing the margins, the point size for various entries, the line spacing, the spacing before and after paragraphs, and so on.

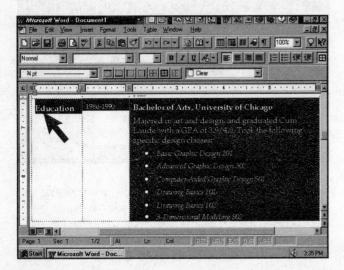

21 Experts suggest that you tailor each résumé you send to make it more appealing to each prospective employer. For example, your education may be more important for one job, whereas your work experience is more important for another. In a table, you can quickly move rows. Drag in the selection area to select the rows you want to move; then, position the mouse pointer over any of the selected text, and drag it up or down.

22 When you release the mouse button, the selected rows move up or down in the table. (Check the bottom borders you added to make sure the lines that divide the categories are still properly positioned.)

23 You can add a clip art image to your résumé to spruce it up. First, click inside the cell where you want the image to appear (usually next to the name and address). Open the **Insert** menu and select **Picture**. (To give yourself more control over the image, insert it into its own cell; you can divide a cell in two by selecting it and then opening the **Table** menu and selecting **Split Cell**.)

Do It Yourself Create a Résumé

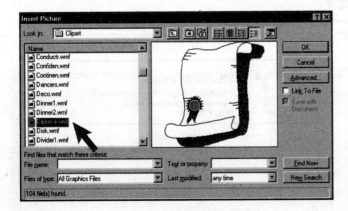

24 Use the dialog box that appears to pick a clip art image you want to use (images are stored in the MSOffice\Clipart folder). Click the desired image and click **OK**.

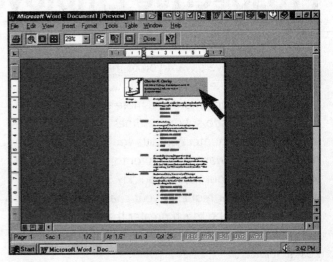

25 Save your work. Before sending the résumé, be sure to spell-check it (as explained on page 97). Click the **Print Preview** button to take a bird's-eye view of the résumé. Tweak the design as needed, till it's perfect.

As you send résumés and cover letters, consider using Microsoft Binder to keep track of them. That way, if you land an interview, you can quickly look back at the cover letter you sent to find out just what you said. It's often useful to review your cover letter and résumé before the interview.

Fax Your Résumé to a Prospective Employer

Most employers want you to mail your résumé and cover letter the old-fashioned way—in an envelope. However, more and more employers are asking applicants to submit résumés via e-mail or fax. In fact, if a headhunter contacts you, chances are the headhunter will want a copy pronto, usually by fax. If you can supply your résumé quickly, and in the form that the employer requests, your chances of landing an interview will be much greater than another person who is working exclusively through the U.S. Postal Service.

This project contains brief instructions on how you can use Word along with Microsoft Fax (which comes with Windows 95) to quickly fax your résumé to an employment service or personnel office. Keep in mind that the receiving fax machine will probably print your résumé in black and white (so don't bother with fancy color formatting or graphics), and that the text may be a little more blurry than you see on-screen. You might want to bump up the point size of your text or use a font that's slightly thinner.

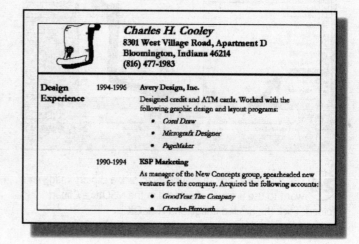

The following steps assume that you chose to install Microsoft Fax when you installed Windows 95. If you did not install Microsoft Fax, it will not appear in the Printer Name drop-down list, as described in Step 3. In that case, you must run the Windows 95 installation program again, to add Microsoft Fax to your system.

Begin Do It Yourself   Fax Your Résumé

1 Change to Word, and open your résumé file. If you have a cover letter you want to send, consider copying its text to a page in front of the first page of the résumé.

Do It Yourself Fax Your Résumé

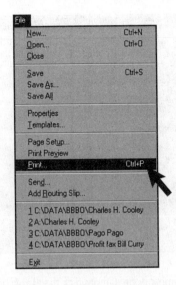

(2) You can fax a file from Word by printing it. Open the **File** menu and select **Print**.

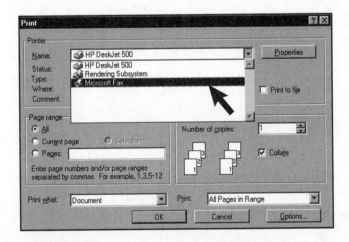

(3) The Print dialog box appears. Open the **Printer Name** drop-down list, and click **Microsoft Fax**. This tells Word to send the document to your fax modem rather than to your printer. Click **OK**.

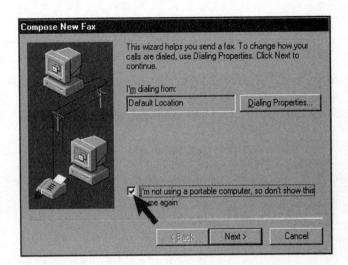

(4) After a moment, the Compose New Fax dialog box appears. If you see this dialog box (and you don't take your computer from one area code to another), click the **I'm not using a portable computer, so don't show this to me again** option, and click **Next**.

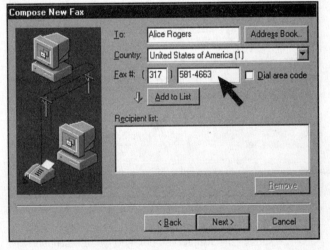

(5) In the next dialog box, type the person's name in the **To** text box and the person's fax number in the **Fax #** text box. Click the **Add to List** button and click **Next**.

(continues)

Do It Yourself Fax Your Résumé *(continued)*

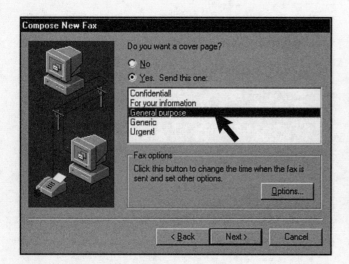

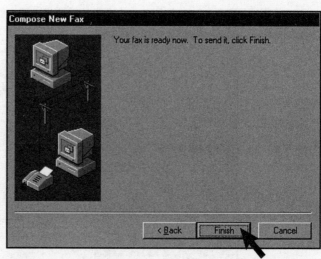

6 The next dialog box asks if you want to add a cover page. Click **Yes**, select the desired cover page, and click **Next**.

8 You're almost done. Simply click the **Finish** button. Microsoft Fax fires up your fax modem, dials the recipient's fax number, and transmits the fax.

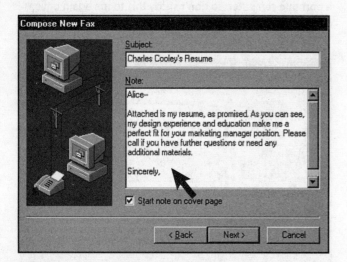

7 This dialog box lets you type a note on the cover page. Click inside the **Subject** text box, and type a description of the fax. Then, click inside the **Note** area, and type a note for the recipient. Click **Next**.

Create an Electronic Résumé in PowerPoint

You've probably seen them on the news—electronic dating services that offer CD-ROM previews of potential mates. You can search for a person by hobbies, interests, education, and annual income, and then pull up a video clip of the person to see what he or she looks like on a good day.

What you rarely see on the news is that this same technology is being used in job searches. You can place your picture, work samples, music clips, video clips, a portion of your résumé, letters of recommendation, and any other material on a disk and then send it off to companies in which you're interested. These electronic résumés are especially effective if you're looking for a job in the computer industry, advertising, marketing, graphics, or writing. An electronic résumé shows not only that you have the basic qualifications for a particular position, but that you can use a computer to effectively present material.

Now that you have PowerPoint, you don't have to wait for your neighborhood résumé service to start producing electronic résumés. You can do it yourself. Simply create a slide show exhibiting your professional skills and abilities.

The following project provides step-by-step instructions that can help you put together a basic PowerPoint résumé. If you need additional help learning how to use PowerPoint's tools to create a slide show, see "How to Create and Edit a PowerPoint Presentation" on page 231 and "Format and Print a PowerPoint Presentation" on page 253.

Begin Do It Yourself Make a Multimedia Résumé

1 To create the electronic résumé, we'll start with one of PowerPoint's sample presentations. Open PowerPoint's **File** menu and select **New**.

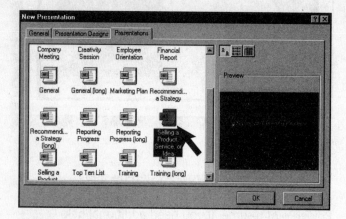

2 The New Presentation dialog box lets you select a design or sample presentation. Click the **Presentations** tab, and then click **Selling a Product or Idea** (you're going to "sell" yourself). Click **OK**.

3 PowerPoint creates an 8-slide slide show. You can keep the slide dark, but I'm going to change it, so it shows up better in this book. To change the background color, right-click the slide, and click **Slide Color Scheme**.

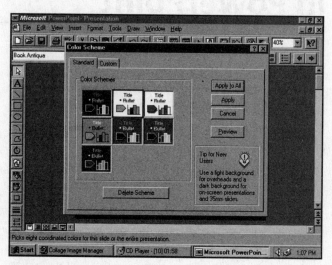

4 Click the desired color scheme, and then click the **Apply to All** button.

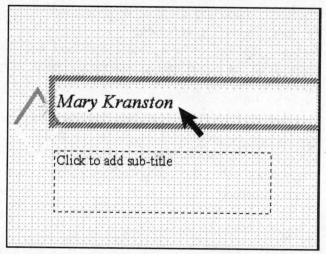

5 Now, we can start working on the content of the slides. On slide 1, drag over **Selling a Product or Idea**, and type your name.

Do It Yourself Make a Multimedia Résumé

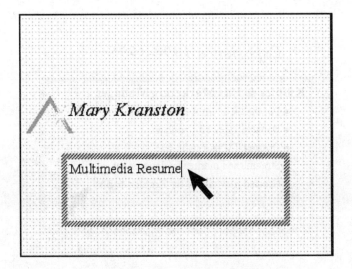

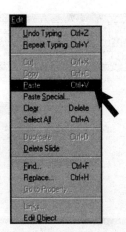

6 Click anywhere inside the **Click to add sub-title** box, and type the job position for which you are applying. Press **Enter** and type **Multimedia Resume**.

8 Return to PowerPoint, and make sure the first slide of your résumé is on-screen. Open the **Edit** menu and select **Paste**.

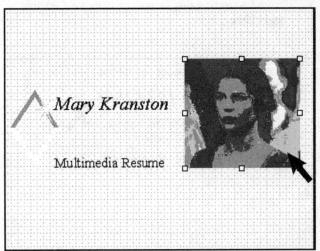

7 If you have a scanned image of yourself, you can put it on the slide. Use Windows Paint, your scanning program, or another graphics program to open the image file. Select the image; then open the **Edit** menu and select **Copy**.

9 PowerPoint places the image on the slide. You can drag the image to move it, and drag any of the handles around the image to change its size.

(continues)

Do It Yourself   Make a Multimedia Résumé

(continued)

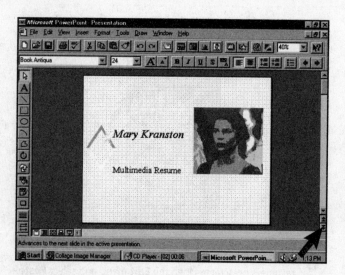

10 Once you've placed the image, there's probably not much room for anything else, so move on to slide 2. Click the **Next Slide** button.

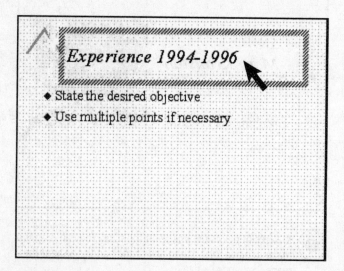

11 Remember, you started with a sales presentation, so you have to change the content. Drag over **Objective** and type **Experience** followed by the years you have held your current position (for example, **Experience 1994-1996**).

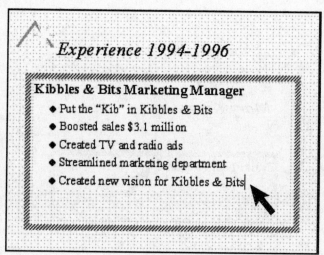

12 Drag over **State the desired objective** and all text that follows it, and then type a list of your job responsibilities and accomplishments at your current position. As you press **Enter** after each item, PowerPoint inserts the bullets for you.

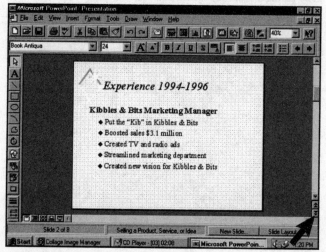

13 When you're done typing a list of accomplishments for your current position, click the **Next Slide** button to create a slide for your previous position.

Do It Yourself Make a Multimedia Résumé

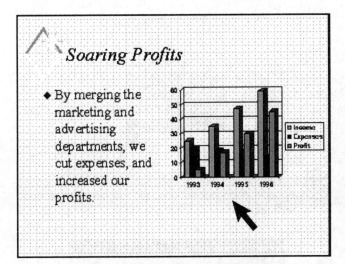

Soaring Profits

◆ By merging the marketing and advertising departments, we cut expenses, and increased our profits.

Kibbles & Bits Sample Ad

14 Continue creating slides to present all the information you would include on a paper résumé, including education, training, awards, and professional organizations. (Don't worry about the order of the slides; you can rearrange slides later.)

16 Once you have the basic text of your résumé typed in, you can start embellishing your résumé with sounds, pictures, video clips, and links to sample work. For example, Windows 95 can play video clips saved as AVI files. If you have a video clip of yourself or your work, create a slide for it; you want to give most of the room on the slide to the video clip.

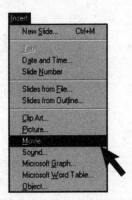

15 If you run out of slides, you can add slides anywhere inside the presentation. Use the **Next Slide** or **Previous Slide** button to display the slide after which you want the new slide inserted. Then, press **Ctrl+M** (or open the **Insert** menu and select **New Slide**).

17 To insert the video clip, open the **Insert** menu, and select **Movie**.

(continues)

Do It Yourself Make a Multimedia Résumé

(continued)

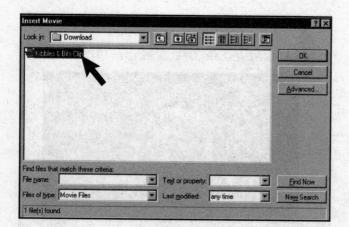

18 In the Insert Movie dialog box, change to the drive and folder that contains the video clip file. Then, click the name of the video clip file you want to insert. Click **OK**.

19 PowerPoint inserts the video clip, but it's too small to see. Drag one of the handles to make the video clip frame larger. You should make it as large as possible on the slide. (Don't worry if it overlaps some text on the slide; we'll hide the clip later.)

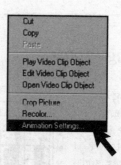

20 Let's make the video play automatically when this slide is displayed. Right-click the video clip, and select **Animation Settings**.

21 The Animation Settings dialog box lets you set several options for the clip. For now, open the **Play Options** drop-down list, and click **Play**, to have PowerPoint play the video clip automatically when this slide appears. Click the **More** button.

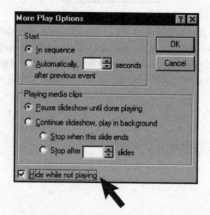

22 To hide the video clip while it isn't playing, click the **Hide while not playing** option. Click the **OK** button. You return to the Animation Settings dialog box. Click **OK** to save your settings.

Do It Yourself Make a Multimedia Résumé

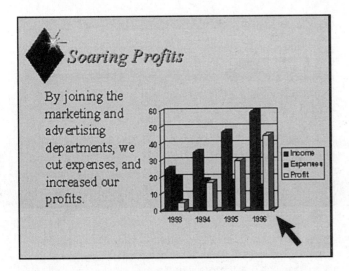

23 You can use the **Insert** menu to add sound clips, pictures, Excel charts, and other items to your slides. For example, here I pasted an Excel chart on a slide to illustrate how Mary Kranston helped boost profits at Kibbles & Bits.

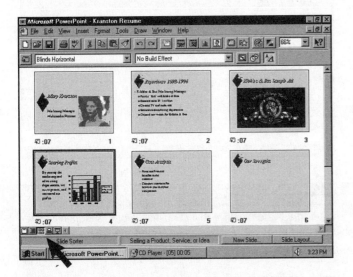

24 Now, let's sort the slides. Click the **Slide Sorter View** button below the slide. In Slide Sorter View, drag the slides around to place them in the desired sequence. As you drag a slide, a line appears to show where the slide will appear.

25 Once the slides are in order, add an animated build, so the slides will advance automatically. First, select all the slides. Open the **Edit** menu and choose **Select All**.

26 Right-click one of the slides, and click **Slide Transition**.

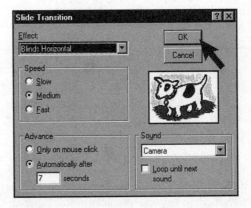

27 Use the dialog box that appears, to control the slide show. Here, I set the build to Blinds Horizontal, at medium speed, using an automatic transition that changes the slides every seven seconds. I also added a camera sound that plays as the next slide comes up. Click **OK**.

(continues)

Do It Yourself   Make a Multimedia Résumé

(continued)

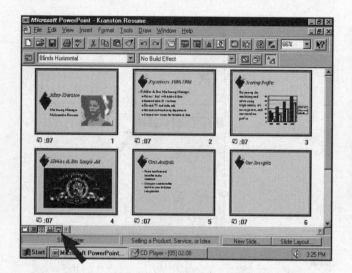

28 To preview your slide show, click the **Slide Show** button below the slide sorter area, and then sit back and watch. Make sure you have enough time to read all the text on each slide. If you don't have enough time, you may have to increase the transition time for that slide.

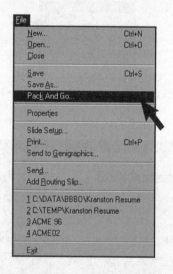

29 Once your résumé is perfect, you can place it on a floppy disk, so you can send it off. PowerPoint can package your résumé with a viewer, so someone who doesn't have PowerPoint can still view it. Make sure you have three or four blank formatted floppy disks on hand. Then, open the **File** menu and select **Pack and Go**.

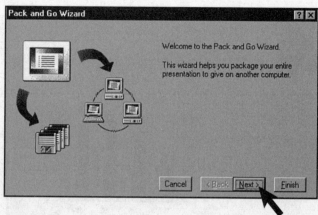

30 The Pack and Go Wizard appears. Follow the on-screen instructions to complete the operation. (It may take more than one disk to store your résumé.)

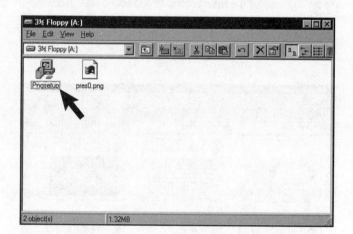

31 Once you store your résumé on floppy disk(s), test it. Insert the first floppy disk into your floppy drive, use My Computer to activate the drive that contains the disk, and then double-click the **Setup** icon. Follow the on-screen instructions to play your résumé.

Although most of your presentation will play on another computer without a glitch, some audio or video clips will not play automatically. In such cases, you might have to insert text under the audio or video clip picture that tells the person to double-click the picture to play the audio or video clip. Likewise, if you're not sure the person will know what to do with your résumé on disk, be sure to include clear instructions (on paper).

Keep Track of Contacts with Schedule+

Any successful job search demands a certain amount of organization and planning. You have to keep track of each company's name, address, and phone number; the position and job responsibilities at that company; the names of any people you've talked with; a phone log of what you've already discussed; and a list of items they sent to you or you sent to them. You can keep track of all this information with Schedule+.

With a complete record such as this, you won't be taken aback when someone from the company calls to set up an interview. You can simply open your Schedule+ file, flip to the page for the company, and scan the pertinent information. You can even type new notes while talking on the phone.

This project shows you how to use Schedule+ to create a separate file for job contacts. The examples also show some of the types of information you should gather, and how to use that information to

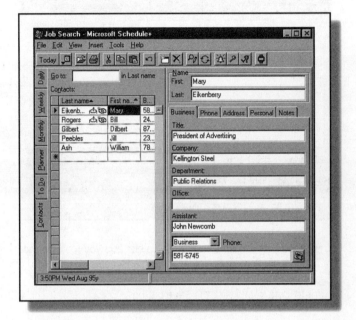

help you land an interview (and hopefully get the job offer).

Begin Do It Yourself   Track Your Contacts

1 Start Schedule+. You can either select it from the **Start Programs** menu, or click the **Microsoft Schedule+** icon in the Microsoft Office Shortcut bar (if you added the icon to the bar), as shown here.

2 Create a new file for your job contacts. Open the **File** menu and select **New**.

(continues)

Do It Yourself Track Your Contacts

(continued)

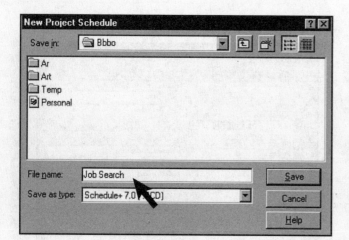

3 The New Project Schedule dialog box asks you to name the new file and pick a folder for it. Type a name (such as Job Search) for the file, change the drive and folder on which you want to store it, and click the **Save** button.

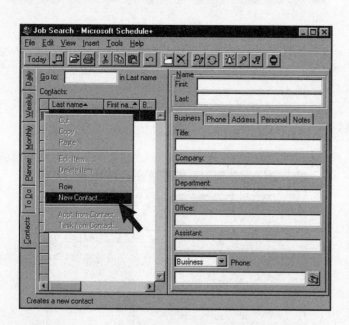

4 Now you can start typing the names of contacts. Click the **Contacts** tab. Right-click one of the buttons in the Contacts list, and then click **New Contact**.

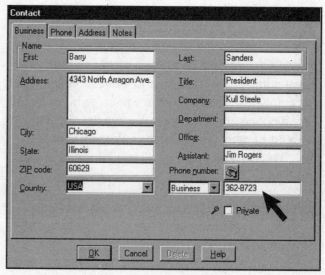

5 The New Contact dialog box appears. Type the required information in each text box. To move to a text box, click inside it, or press the **Tab** key.

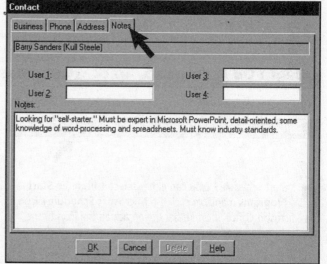

6 Click any additional tabs for which you want to add information, and type entries in the text boxes. The **Notes** tab should hold the most important information. Include any dates you called or submitted material, a list of job responsibilities, company information, or anything else you might find useful.

Do It Yourself   Track Your Contacts

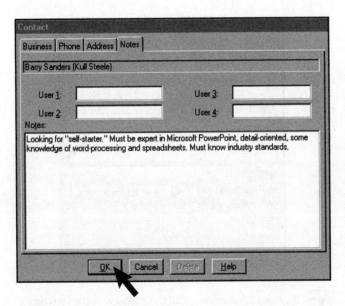

7 Click **OK** when you finish.

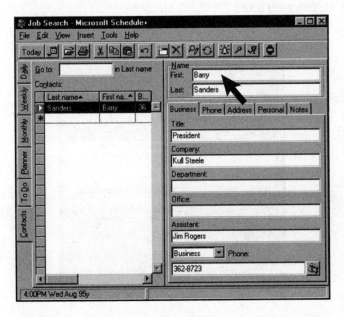

8 You can edit the information for a contact simply by clicking on the contact's name and changing the information on the right side of the scheduler.

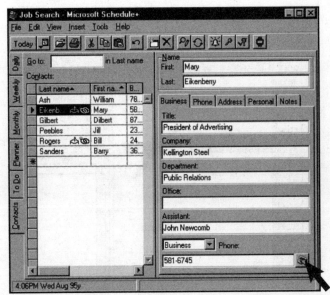

9 To call a contact, you no longer have to shuffle through a stack of papers to find a phone number. Simply click the contact's name, and click the tab that has the phone number. If you have a modem, and your phone is connected to it, click the **Dial Phone** button to have Schedule+ place the call.

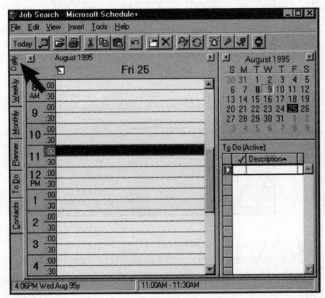

10 You can set appointments for job interviews, and have Schedule+ remind you ahead of time. Click the **Daily** tab, and use the controls on the right to change to the month and day on which you have the interview.

(continues)

Do It Yourself Track Your Contacts

(continued)

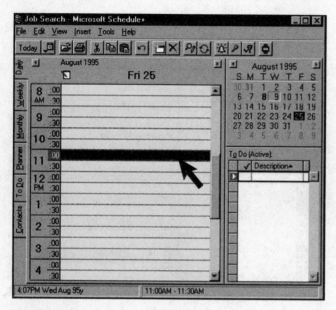

11 Double-click the time of the interview.

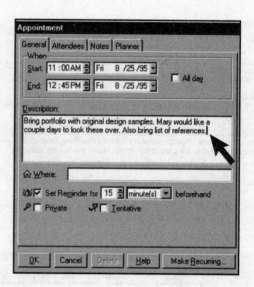

13 Type any information about the interview in the **Description** area. Include the address of and directions to the meeting place, and a list of materials you need to bring to the interview. The first part of the description will appear in your appointment book.

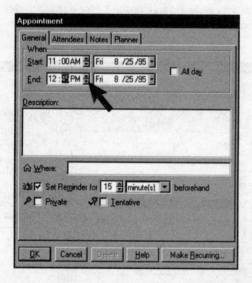

12 The Appointment dialog box shows the starting time of the appointment. To change the expected finishing time for the meeting, click the hour or minute setting in the **End** spin box, and then click the up or down arrow next to the time.

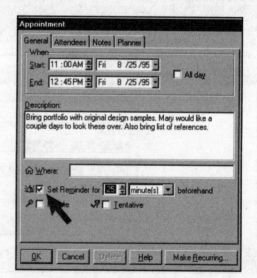

14 To have Schedule+ notify you of the interview ahead of time, make sure there is a check mark in the **Set Reminder** check box. Use the spin box and drop-down list to the right of this option to specify how long in advance you want to be notified. Click **OK**.

Do It Yourself Track Your Contacts

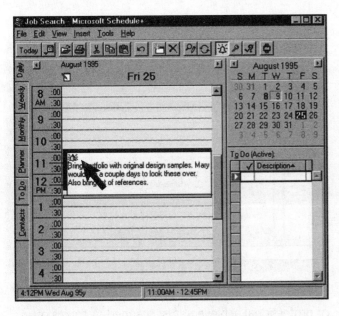

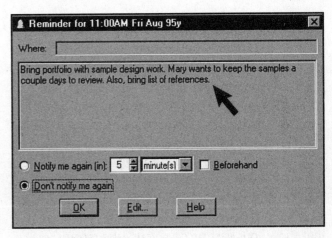

15 The appointment appears on your daily appointment list. The Picture of the bell shows that a reminder has been set.

17 As the interview time approaches, Schedule+ lets you know that you had better start getting ready.

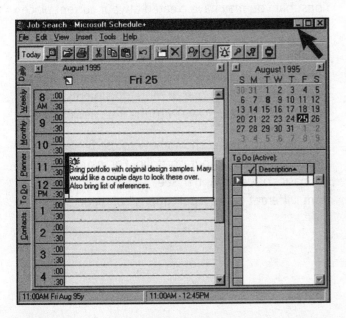

16 In order for Schedule+ to be able to remind you, it must be running. Click the **Minimize** button to shrink the window but keep Schedule+ active.

In order for Schedule+ to notify you of upcoming meetings, the program must be running. Consider placing Schedule+ on Windows' StartUp menu, so it will run automatically when you start Windows. To add Schedule+ to the StartUp menu, right-click a blank area of the taskbar, and then click **Properties**. Click the **Start Menu Programs** tab, and click the **Add** button. Follow the on-screen instructions to add Microsoft Schedule+ to the StartUp menu.

Organize Your Portfolio with Binder

Nothing impresses an interviewer more than details. Interviewers want to know where you went to school, what you studied, your GPA (grade point average), any job skills you've acquired, and specific ways you helped your previous employer improve a product or streamline a process. If you're a graphic artist, the interviewer will want to see your pictures and designs. If you're a writer, you'll have to show some writing samples. Even if you're in a service industry, such as real estate or investments, it helps to have some concrete documents, graphs, and figures that show your past success, your sales records, or even letters of praise from customers and clients. In short, it helps to have a portfolio.

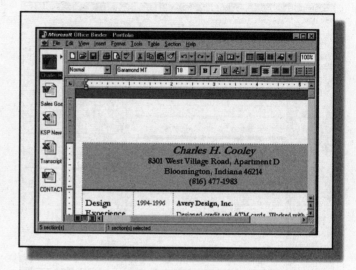

The problem with a portfolio is that it's generally treated like an afterthought; you don't think about putting a portfolio together until someone asks to see it. In addition, a portfolio tends to be a static thing; it contains the same documents regardless of the position you're trying to land.

But portfolios don't have to be so stale and unwieldy. They don't have to be like your grandma's photo album or Uncle Fred's scrapbook. With *Microsoft Binder*, your portfolio can be as flexible and dynamic as any computer document. It can include writing samples, original graphic images or designs, worksheets and charts that illustrate your personal

or professional achievements, scanned-in copies of reviews and evaluations, a list of job references, your salary history, and even sample PowerPoint presentations that you may have created at your current place of employment.

Another advantage of using Binder to maintain your portfolio is that it allows you to quickly rearrange your documents and print one or more documents, so you have fresh copies to leave with the interviewer(s).

The following project shows how to use Binder to create and manage your portfolio. For instructions on the basics of using Binder, see "Use Data Together from Different Office Applications" on page 345.

Begin Do It Yourself   Organize with Binder

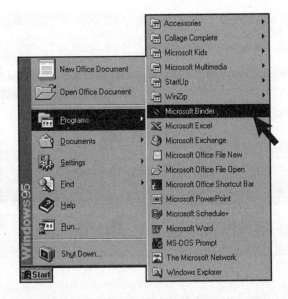

1 To start Binder, click the Windows **Start** button; select **Programs** and **Microsoft Binder**.

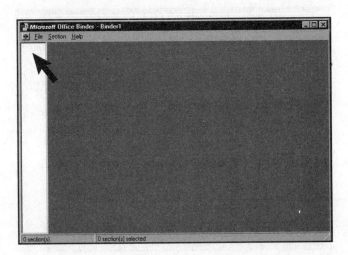

2 Binder starts and displays a blank binder, into which you can start inserting documents.

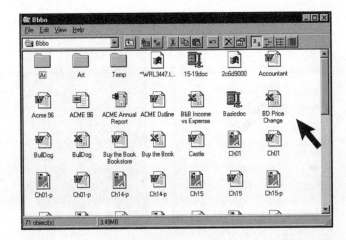

3 You can quickly add documents to the Binder by dragging them from a My Computer or Windows Explorer window into the Binder. Run My Computer or Windows Explorer, and change to the drive and folder that contains the document you want to add.

4 Position the My Computer or Windows Explorer window so that you can see the icon for the document you want to add and the left pane of the Binder window. You can quickly arrange windows by right-clicking on a blank area of the taskbar and then clicking on **Tile Horizontally** or **Tile Vertically**.

(continues)

Do It Yourself   Organize with Binder

(continued)

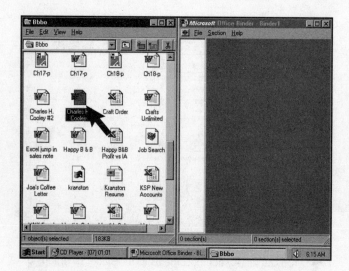

5 Drag the icon for the document you want to add to the Binder into the left pane of the Binder Window.

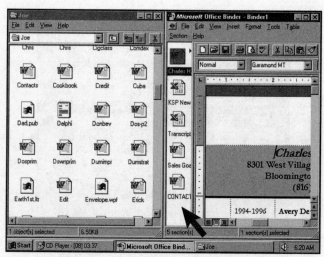

7 Repeat steps 3 to 6 to place additional documents in your portfolio binder. As you add documents, icons are added to the left pane of the Binder window.

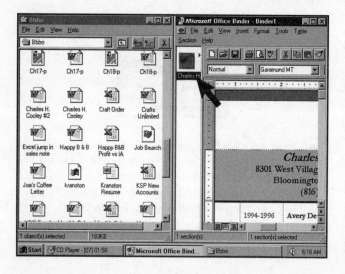

6 The document's icon is added to the left pane of the Binder window, and the first page of the document is displayed in the right pane.

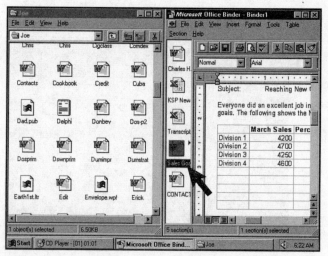

8 You may want to change the order of the documents in the Binder, depending on the job you're trying to land. Click the icon for the document you want to move, and then drag the icon up or down to move it.

Do It Yourself Organize with Binder

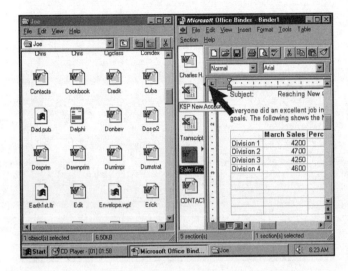

9 As you drag, an arrow appears showing where the document will be moved. When you release the mouse button, the document is moved to the new position.

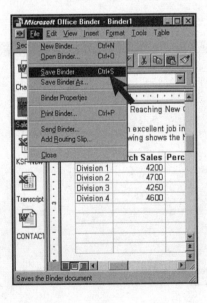

10 To save your electronic portfolio, open the **File** menu and select **Save Binder**.

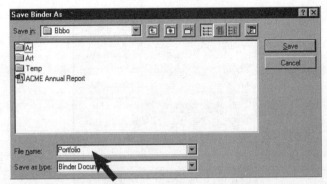

11 The Save Binder As dialog box asks you to name the binder file and specify a folder in which to save it. Select the drive and folder in which you want your portfolio saved. Double-click inside the **File name** text box, and type a name for your portfolio. Click the **Save** button.

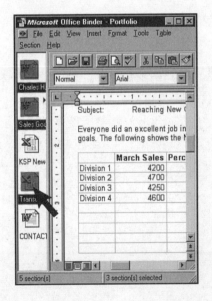

12 Before you head out to your next interview, print out some or all of the documents in your portfolio to take them along. Click the icon for one of the documents you want to print, and then **Ctrl+click** icons for additional documents.

(continues)

Do It Yourself Organize with Binder

(continued)

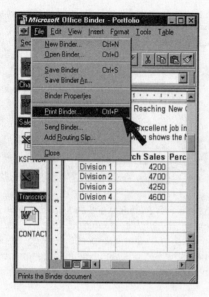

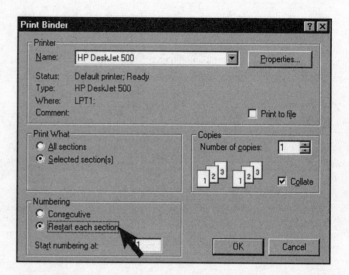

13 Open the **File** menu and click **Print Binder**.

15 Binder will automatically print a page number on each page of your portfolio. Under Numbering, click **Consecutive** to number the pages as if they belong to a single document, or click **Restart each section** to number the pages of each document separately.

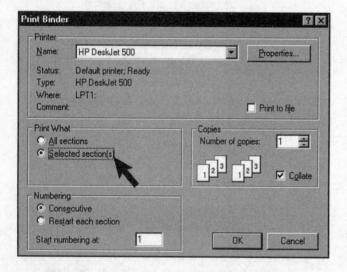

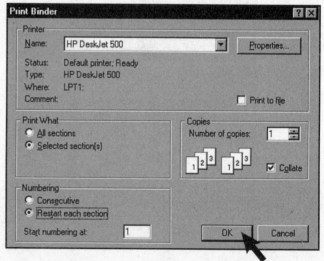

14 The Print Binder dialog box lets you enter print settings. Under **Print What**, click **All sections** to print the entire portfolio, or click **Selected section(s)** to print only the documents you picked in step 12.

16 Click the **OK** button to start printing.

If you have a scanner, consider scanning in any help wanted ads that pique your interest, and save the scans as files. Then, use Microsoft Binder to organize the ads. This is an excellent way to keep in touch with the job market, even when you already have a secure position. If you lose your current position unexpectedly, you have a list of places to start looking.

DO IT YOURSELF

Organize Your Home and Personal Finances

As you get older, your personal life starts to seem more like business than pleasure. You have to balance your checkbook, keep track of your investments, manage your loans, stick to a complicated budget, and keep tabs on your possessions for the insurance company. If you're an ambitious type, you might even try to keep up on all your friends' and relatives' anniversaries and birthdays.

If you have your own family, these daily tasks quickly become overwhelming chores, and your life becomes complicated with stacks of paper, reminder notes, and paper files that are usually not all that important. Keeping the family calendar and bulletin board uncluttered and up to date is a feat in itself.

Fortunately, you can delegate these tasks to your computer… and Microsoft Office. You can use Schedule+ to computerize your address book and keep track of important dates; Excel to balance your checkbook, manage your budget, and calculate loan payments; and Word to save yourself some money on greeting cards. The following projects in this section show you just what to do:

Reconcile Your Checkbook Balance

If you already have a personal finance program, such as Quicken, that you use to record checking account transactions and keep track of your budget, you don't really need another tool to perform the same tasks. Personal finance programs are specialized spreadsheets that come complete with advanced tools for managing your money.

However, if you don't have one of these specialized programs, you can use Excel to manage your checking account. The following project shows you how to transfer the information from your checkbook to an Excel worksheet. After setting up the worksheet, you can simply type your transactions in the appropriate cells; the formulas in the Balance column automatically recalculate your checking account balance.

In addition, the worksheet you are about to create helps you reconcile your checking account balance with your monthly bank statement. You mark the cleared transactions in the checkbook register and

enter the ending balance from the bank statement; the worksheet adds any uncleared transactions to the bank statement balance, to determine whether your registry matches the bank statement. But, enough for the preliminaries—let's begin.

Number	Date	Description of Transaction	Payment/Debit	Cleared	Deposit/Credit	Balance
						$30.00
1001	5/3	PC Computing Subscription	$34.97	Y		($4.97)
	4/30	Monthly Service Charge	$2.00	Y		($6.97)
	5/4	Transfer from Savings		Y	$100.00	$93.03
1002	5/9	Void		Y		$93.03
1003	5/15	A New Song	$15.00	Y		$78.03
1004	5/16	IQuest	$15.00	Y		$63.03
1005	5/16	Deputy Sheriff	$25.00	Y		$38.03
	5/19	Transfer from Savings		Y	$100.00	$138.03
	6/9	Deposit Royalty Check		Y	$1,000.00	$1,138.03
1006	6/12	Visa Payment	$487.55	Y		$650.48
	4/30	Monthly Service Charge	$2.00	Y		$648.48
	6/12	Transfer from Savings		Y	$2,384.79	$3,033.27
	6/13	Deposit June Contract Pmt		Y	$1,500.00	$4,533.27
	6/15	Transfer from Savings		Y	$400.00	$4,933.27
1007	6/15	IRS Q2 Pmt	$4,030.00	Y		$903.27
1008	6/15	State Q2 Tax Pmt	$780.00	Y		$123.27
1009	6/15	IQuest	$15.00	Y		$108.27
1010	6/16	Direct Delivery	$7.00	Y		$101.27
1011	6/17	Galyans	$38.82	Y		$62.45
1012	6/27	Direct Delivery	$23.00	Y		$39.45
1013	7/11	Direct Delivery	$11.00	Y		$28.45
	6/5	Check Order	$15.65	Y		$12.80
	7/11	Deposit July Contract Pmt		Y	$500.00	$512.80
1014	7/19	IQuest	$15.00	Y		$497.80

Begin Do It Yourself Make a Checkbook Register

1 Start Excel, and create a worksheet for your checkbook. Right-click on the **Sheet1** tab, and click on **Rename** to name it.

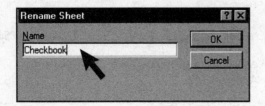

2 The Rename Sheet dialog box lets you type a tab name. Type **Checkbook** and press **Enter**.

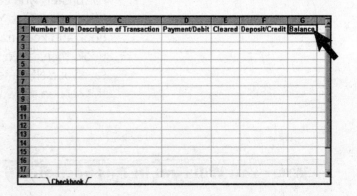

3 The tab name changed to **Checkbook**. Now, in row 1, type the column headings as they appear here. (Don't worry if the headings don't fit in the cells; you can fix that later.)

Do It Yourself   Make a Checkbook Register

4 Lock the headings in place, so they won't scroll off the top of the screen when you scroll down. Click inside cell **A2** (just below **Number**), and then open the **Window** menu and click **Freeze Panes**.

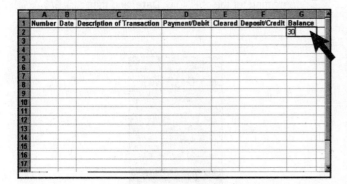

5 In the cell just below **Balance**, type the starting balance of your account. (This will be the only entry in row 2.)

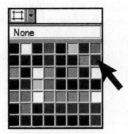

6 Drag over cells A2 through F2 to block them out. Then, open the **Color** drop-down list, and select a dark color to indicate that you don't want to type anything in these cells.

7 You can now enter the formulas in the **Balance** column that calculate your running checkbook balance. Click inside cell G3, type **=IF(C3="","",G2-D3+F3)**, and press **Enter**. This formula tells Excel that if cell C3 (in the Description of Transaction column) is empty, then keep cell G3 blank; otherwise, subtract any amount in the Payment/Debit cell and add any amount in the Deposit/Credit cell to the previous balance.

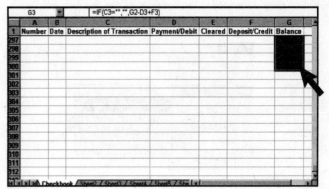

8 To save time, copy the formula from G3 down into the next 298 cells in column G. Drag the fill box in the lower right corner of cell G3 down till you select all cells in column G up to G300. (This gives you room for recording about 300 transactions.)

9 If you click cell G300, and look at the formula in the formula bar, you can see that Excel automatically updated the cell references in this formula so they pertain to the entries in row 300.

(continues)

Do It Yourself Make a Checkbook Register *(continued)*

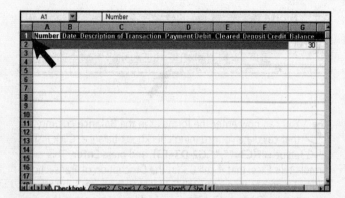

10 You can start formatting the worksheet. Click the 1 to the left of row 1 to select the entire row. Then, click B (Bold button) in the Formatting toolbar to make the headings bold.

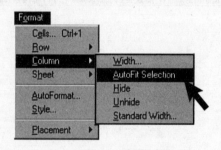

11 While row 1 is selected, widen the columns so the headings will fit in the cells. Open the **Format** menu; select **Column** and **AutoFit Selection**.

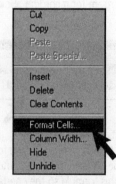

12 Right-click **B** at the top of the second column, and select **Format Cells**.

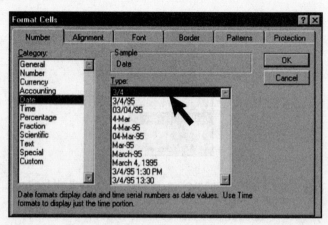

13 The Format Cells dialog box lets you change the number formatting for the cells. Click **Date**, and then click **3/4** under **Type**. This keeps the date entry short and sweet. Click **OK**.

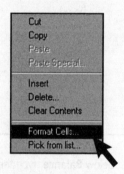

14 Now, change the style for columns D, F, and G to display dollar amounts. Click the D at the top of the fourth column, and **Ctrl+click** F and G at the top of their columns. Then, right-click any of the selected cells, and click **Format Cells**.

Do It Yourself   Make a Checkbook Register

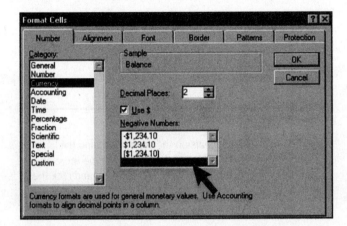

15 In the Format Cells dialog box, under Category, click **Currency**. Make sure there is a check mark in the **Use $** check box. In the **Negative Numbers** list, click the fourth option to display negative numbers as red text in parentheses. Click **OK**.

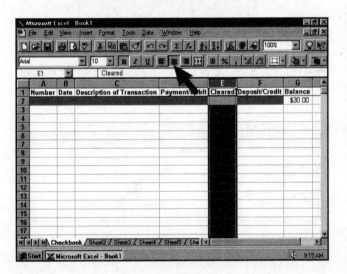

16 In column E, you'll type **Y** if a transaction has cleared. It'll look better if the Y is centered. Click the E at the top of the fifth column, and click the **Center** button in the Formatting toolbar.

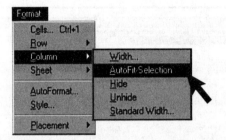

17 Ready? Start typing the transactions from your checkbook into the appropriate cells in the worksheet. If one of your entries is too wide for a column, it may appear chopped off or (in the case of a number) appear as **######**. If this happens, click the letter at the top of the column. Open the **Format** menu; select **Column** and **AutoFit Selection**.

18 When you enter an amount in the Debit or Deposit column, your worksheet automatically calculates the new balance and inserts it in the Balance column.

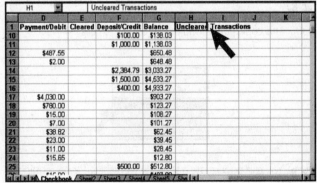

19 When you receive your next bank statement, you can modify your worksheet to help you reconcile your balance with the ending balance on the bank statement. First, type a new heading in cell H1 called **Uncleared Transactions**.

(continues)

Do It Yourself Make a Checkbook Register *(continued)*

	D	E	F	G	H	I	J	K
1	Payment/Debit	Cleared	Deposit/Credit	Balance	Uncleared Transactions			
2				$30.00				
3	$34.97			($4.97)	-34.97			
4	$2.00			($6.97)				
5			$100.00	$93.03				
6				$93.03				
7	$15.00			$78.03				
8	$15.00			$63.03				
9	$25.00			$38.03				
10			$100.00	$138.03				
11			$1,000.00	$1,138.03				
12	$487.55			$650.48				
13	$2.00			$648.48				
14			$2,384.79	$3,033.27				
15			$1,500.00	$4,533.27				
16			$400.00	$4,933.27				
17	$4,030.00			$903.27				

Checkbook / Sheet2 / Sheet3 / Sheet4 / Sheet5 / She

20 Click inside cell **H3**; type the formula **=IF(E3="y","",F3-D3)** and press **Enter**. This tells Excel that if the cell in E3 has a **Y** in it (indicating the transaction has cleared), then insert nothing in cell H3. If cell E3 does not have a Y in it, Excel inserts any deposit from cell F3 minus any debit from cell D3, showing the amount of the uncleared transaction. (If desired, format column H3 to display numbers as currency amounts.)

H3 =IF(E3="Y","",F3-D3)

	D	E	F	G	H	I	J	K
1	Payment/Debit	Cleared	Deposit/Credit	Balance	Uncleared Transactions			
294								
295								
296								
297								
298								
299								
300								
301								
302								
303								
304								
305								
306								
307								
308								
309								

Checkbook / Sheet2 / Sheet3 / Sheet4 / Sheet5 / She

21 Click cell **H3**, and drag the fill box in the lower right corner of the cell down until you select all cells in column H up to H300. This copies the formula from cell H3 to cells H4–H300.

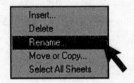

Insert...
Delete
Rename...
Move or Copy...
Select All Sheets

22 You can now create a separate worksheet for performing the reconciliation. Right click the **Sheet2** tab and click **Rename**. Type **Reconcile** and press **Enter**.

A7 Difference (Should be Zero)

	A	B	C	D	E	F	G	H	I
1	Reconcile Checkbook with Bank Statement								
2									
3	Bank Statement Ending Balance								
4	Uncleared Transactions (from Checkbook)								
5	Final Balance (Ending+Uncleared)								
6	Recorded Bankbook Balance								
7	Difference (Should be Zero)								
8									
9									

23 The new name appears on the second tab, and the Reconcile sheet is activated. In column A, type the row headings as shown here. Then, drag over the cells, and click the **Bold** button in the Formatting toolbar.

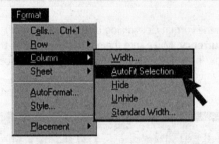

Format
  Cells... Ctrl+1
  Row   ▶
  Column   ▶   Width...
  Sheet   ▶   AutoFit Selection
                     Hide
  AutoFormat...   Unhide
  Style...   Standard Width...
  Placement   ▶

24 Click **A** at the top of column 1, and then open the **Format** menu. Select **Column** and **AutoFit Selection**.

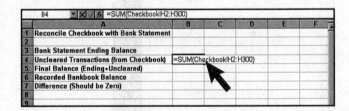

B4 =SUM(Checkbook!H2:H300)

	A	B	C	D	E	F
1	Reconcile Checkbook with Bank Statement					
2						
3	Bank Statement Ending Balance					
4	Uncleared Transactions (from Checkbook)	=SUM(Checkbook!H2:H300)				
5	Final Balance (Ending+Uncleared)					
6	Recorded Bankbook Balance					
7	Difference (Should be Zero)					
8						
9						

25 Click inside cell **B4**; type **=SUM(Checkbook!H3:H300)** and press **Enter**. This function inserts the total from the Uncleared Transactions column on the Checkbook page. (Excel uses the exclamation point in formulas and functions to reference different worksheets in the same workbook.)

Do It Yourself   Make a Checkbook Register

B5	▼	✕	✓	ƒ	=B3+B4	
	A		B	C	D	E	F
1 Reconcile Checkbook with Bank Statement					
2					
3 Bank Statement Ending Balance					
4 Uncleared Transactions (from Checkbook)		711.8			
5 Final Balance (Ending+Uncleared)		=B3+B4			
6 Recorded Bankbook Balance					
7 Difference (Should be Zero)					
8					
9					

26 Click inside cell **B5**; type **=B3+B4** and press **Enter**. This formula adds any uncleared transactions to your bank statement balance to bring the balance up to date with your records.

B7	▼	✕	✓	ƒ	=B5-B6	
	A		B	C	D	E	F
1 Reconcile Checkbook with Bank Statement					
2					
3 Bank Statement Ending Balance					
4 Uncleared Transactions (from Checkbook)		711.8			
5 Final Balance (Ending+Uncleared)		711.8			
6 Recorded Bankbook Balance					
7 Difference (Should be Zero)		=B5-B6			
8					
9					

27 Finally, click inside cell **B7**; type **=B5-B6** and press **Enter**. This formula subtracts your checkbook balance from the bank statement's ending balance (plus any uncleared transactions). If there are no discrepancies between your records and the bank's, this number should be zero.

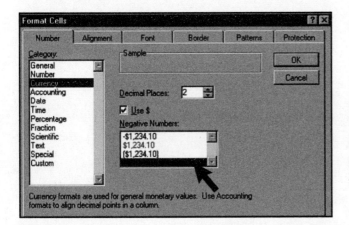

28 Now, right-click **B** at the top of the second column, and select **Format Cells**. Under Category, click **Currency**. Make sure there is a check mark in the **Use $** check box. In the **Negative Numbers** list, click the fourth option to display negative numbers as red text in parentheses. Click **OK**.

E18	▼		Y				
	D	E	F	G	H	I	J	K
1 Payment/Debit	Cleared	Deposit/Credit	Balance	Uncleared Transactions			
2			$30.00			
3 $34.97	Y		($4.97)			
4 $2.00	Y		($6.97)			
5	Y	$100.00	$93.03			
6	Y		$93.03			
7 $15.00	Y		$78.03			
8 $15.00	Y		$63.03			
9 $25.00	Y		$38.03			
10	Y	$100.00	$138.03			
11	Y	$1,000.00	$1,138.03			
12 $487.55	Y		$650.48			
13 $2.00	Y		$648.48			
14	Y	$2,384.79	$3,033.27			
15	Y	$1,500.00	$4,533.27			
16	Y	$400.00	$4,933.27			
17 $4,030.00	Y		$903.27			

29 Okay, now you're ready to reconcile. Click the **Checkbook** tab. In the **Cleared** column, type **Y** next to each transaction listed on the statement you received from the bank. You should also check to make sure the amount of each transaction on the bank statement matches the transaction amount as you recorded it.

D35	▼		2				
	A	B	C	D	E	F	G
1 Number	Date	Description of Transaction	Payment/Debit	Cleared	Deposit/Credit	Balance	
34 1020	8/7	Direct Delivery	$45.00			$743.80	
35	7/31	Monthly Service Charge	$2.00	Y		$741.80	
36							
37							
38							
39							
40							
41							

30 If your bank statement lists any transactions that you have not recorded (such as monthly service charges), enter those transactions and mark them as cleared.

B3	▼	✕	✓	ƒ	786.8	
	A		B	C	D	E	F
1 Reconcile Checkbook with Bank Statement					
2					
3 Bank Statement Ending Balance		786.8			
4 Uncleared Transactions (from Checkbook)		($45.00)			
5 Final Balance (Ending+Uncleared)		$741.80			
6 Recorded Bankbook Balance					
7 Difference (Should be Zero)		$741.80			
8					
9					

31 When you finish checking off cleared transactions, click the **Reconcile** tab. Click inside cell **B3** (to the right of **Bank Statement Ending Balance**); type the ending balance from your bank statement and press **Enter**.

(continues)

Do It Yourself   Make a Checkbook Register   *(continued)*

B6	▾ ✕ ✓ ƒ	741.80				
	A	**B**	**C**	**D**	**E**	**F**
1	Reconcile Checkbook with Bank Statement					
2						
3	Bank Statement Ending Balance	$ 786.80				
4	Uncleared Transactions (from Checkbook)	($45.00)				
5	Final Balance (Ending+Uncleared)	$741.80				
6	Recorded Bankbook Balance	741.80				
7	Difference (Should be Zero)	$741.80				
8						
9						

32 Copy the current checkbook balance (the last number in the Balance column of your Checkbook page) into cell B6 (you can type the amount, or use the Copy and Paste commands). (This is your current checkbook balance according to your records.)

B7	▾	=B5-B6				
	A	**B**	**C**	**D**	**E**	**F**
1	Reconcile Checkbook with Bank Statement					
2						
3	Bank Statement Ending Balance	$ 786.80				
4	Uncleared Transactions (from Checkbook)	($45.00)				
5	Final Balance (Ending+Uncleared)	$741.80				
6	Recorded Bankbook Balance	$741.80				
7	Difference (Should be Zero)	$0.00				
8						
9						

33 The formulas on the Reconcile sheet compare the bank statement balance with your checkbook balance, and determine if there is a discrepancy. If the difference is not zero, you should go back and check the bank statement against your records.

Because you'll make frequent use of your checkbook, consider making a shortcut for it on the Windows desktop. Use My Computer or Windows Explorer to change to the drive and folder where you store the checkbook file. Then use the right mouse button to drag the checkbook file icon onto the Windows desktop. After releasing the mouse button, click **Create Shortcut(s) Here**.

Create an Address Book

If you're anything like me, you have a hand-scribbled phone list stuck to a corkboard in your kitchen, and you have a drawer full of envelopes, so you can keep track of addresses of friends and relatives. Well, it's about time that we both organize our lives and place our phone numbers and addresses in an easily accessible book, a computerized address book.

With Schedule+, creating such an address book is a snap. You simply fire up the program and then start typing the names, addresses, and phone numbers of all your friends and family members. You can even mark special dates, such as birthdays and anniversaries. In addition, you'll be able to quickly look up any name in your address book, and (if you have a modem with a phone connected to it) you can have Schedule+ dial phone numbers for you.

This project shows you how to transfer the information from your current paper address book (or stack of notes) into Schedule+ and use that information to save valuable time.

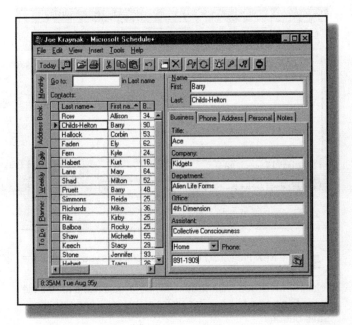

Begin Do It Yourself Make an Electronic Address Book

1 Start Schedule+. You can either select it from the **Start Programs** menus, or click the **Microsoft Schedule+** icon in the Microsoft Office Shortcut bar (if you added it to the bar), as shown here.

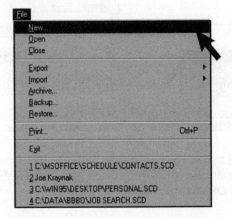

2 Create a new file for your friends and relatives, or use the existing file. To create a new file, open the **File** menu and select **New**.

(continues)

Do It Yourself Make an Electronic Address Book *(continued)*

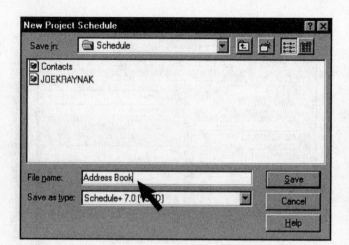

3 The New Project Schedule dialog box asks you to name the new file and pick a folder for it. Change the drive and folder in which you want to store the file, type a name for the file in the **File name** text box (for example, Personal), and click the **Save** button.

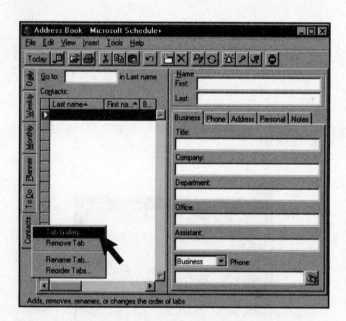

4 Scheduler+ displays the new file, but it's set up more for business use than for home use. Let's change that. Right-click the **Contacts** tab, and click **Tab Gallery**.

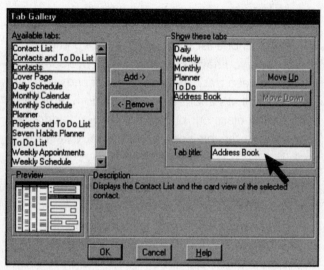

5 The Tab Gallery dialog box gives you control over the pages that appear in your schedule. To rename the Contacts page, click on **Contacts** in the Show these tabs list, double-click inside the **Tab title** text box, and type **Address Book**. Click on **Contacts** in the Show these tabs list, and the new name appears.

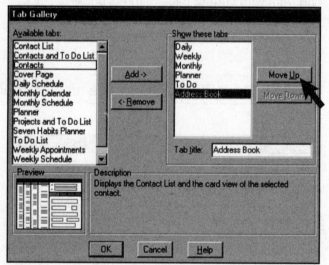

6 For convenience, move the Contacts tab to the front of your address book. Make sure **Address Book** is selected in the Show these tabs list; then click the **Move Up** button five times to move Address Book to the top.

Do It Yourself Make an Electronic Address Book

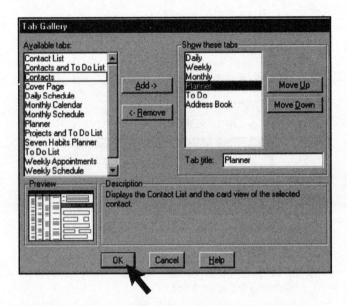

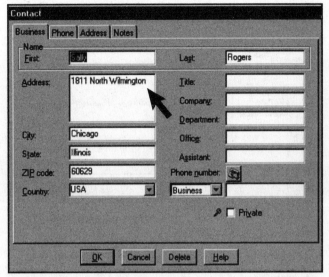

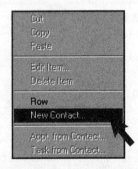

7 Now, remove any tabs you don't plan on using. Simply double-click the tab's name in the **Show these tabs** list. Click **OK** when you're done.

8 Now you can start typing the names, addresses, and phone numbers of your friends and relatives. Click the **Address Book** tab. Right-click one of the buttons in the **Contacts** list, and then click **New Contact**.

9 The Contact dialog box appears. Type the required information in the appropriate text boxes (it's okay to leave some text boxes blank). To move to a text box, click inside it, or press the **Tab** key.

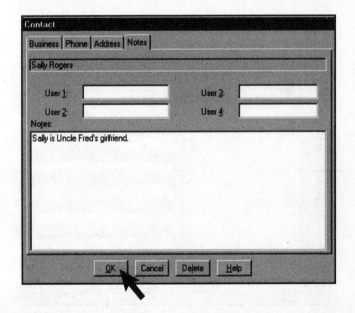

10 Click any additional tabs for which you want to add information, and type entries in the text boxes. Click **OK** when you're done.

(continues)

Do It Yourself Make an Electronic Address Book

(continued)

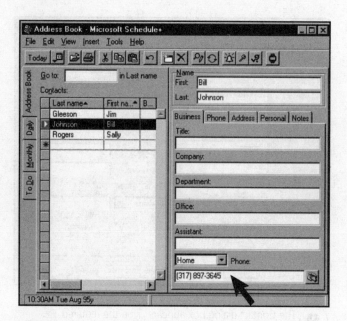

11 You can edit the information for a person simply by clicking on the person's name, and changing the information on the right side of the scheduler.

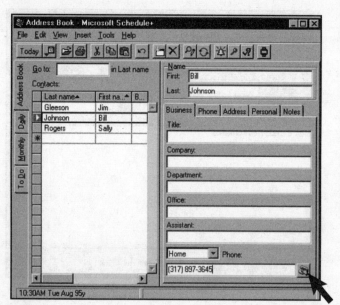

12 To call a person (or your favorite pizza joint), you no longer have to shuffle through a stack of papers to find a phone number. Simply click the person's name, and click the tab that has the phone number. If you have a modem, and your phone is connected to it, click the **Dial Phone** button to have Schedule+ place the call.

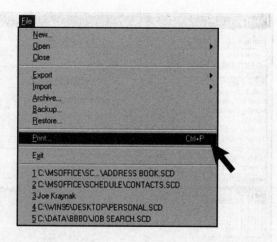

13 When Christmas rolls around, you can print mailing labels for all the people in your address book. Simply open the **File** menu and select **Print**.

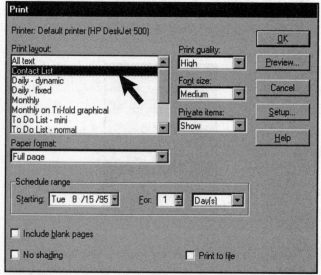

14 In the **Print layout** list, make sure to select **Contact List**.

Do It Yourself Make an Electronic Address Book

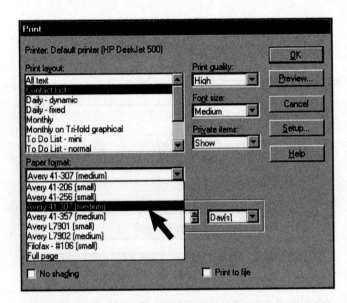

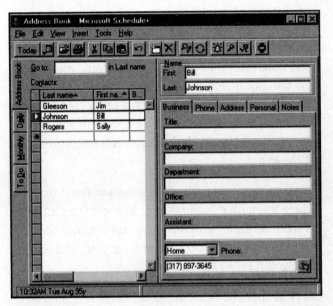

 15 Open the **Paper format** drop-down list, and click the type of labels you plan on printing on. Make sure you load the labels in your printer; then click **OK**.

16 When you're done with Schedule+, don't worry about saving your file; Schedule+ saves the information automatically as you enter it. Simply click the **Close** button in the upper right corner of the Window.

Calculate Interest on Personal Loans

If you've ever taken out a loan to buy a car or to go to college, taken out a mortgage, or made any other purchases that you just can't afford, you know how mind boggling the process is. You usually place complete trust in a stranger with a fancy calculator to tell you how much you can afford, how much your payments will be, and how long it will take you to pay off the loan.

If you want to play with the numbers yourself (to reduce the term or payment, or to see if you can pay off the loan early), you have to jump through hoops to get the person to do the math for you. And even then, you have to trust their answers.

But now that you have Microsoft Excel, and a nifty template that's included with it, you can play the numbers game in the comfort and privacy of your own home. With the Loan Manager template, you can immediately see how your payments are affected if you borrow more or less money. You can see how much you'll save by taking out a 15-year mortgage rather than a 30-year mortgage, and how much your

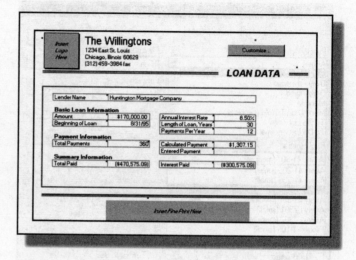

monthly payment will increase. You can even determine how fast you'll pay off a loan if you pay extra toward the principal each month.

The following project shows you how to use the Loan Manager template, and how to customize it for a specific loan.

Begin Do It Yourself Manage Your Personal Loans

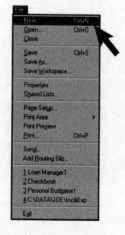

1 To use the Loan Manager template, run Excel, and then open the **File** menu and select **New**.

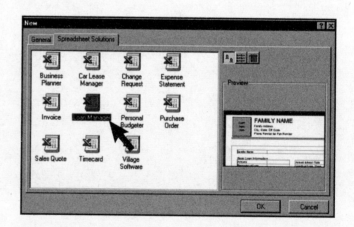

2 Click the **Spreadsheet Solutions** tab, click **Loan Manager**, and click **OK**.

Do It Yourself   Manage Your Personal Loans

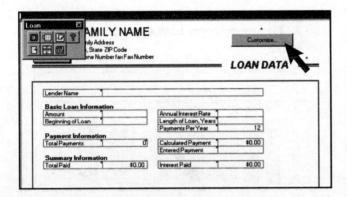

3 The Loan Manager template appears. Before you start entering data, customize Loan Manager for this particular loan. Click the **Customize** button.

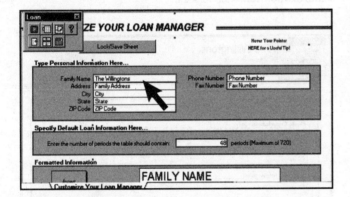

4 You can now enter your name and address. Click inside the **Family Name** cell, type your name, and press **Enter**. Continue clicking on cells and typing entries for your address, city, state, ZIP code, and phone number.

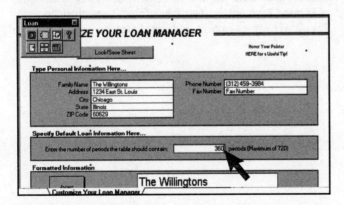

5 Click inside the periods cell, and type the number of pay periods for which you are borrowing the money. (To determine the number of pay periods, multiply the number of years by 12; for example, a 30-year mortgage would have 360 pay periods.) Press **Enter**.

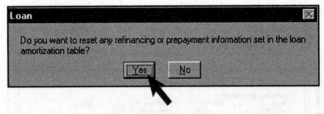

6 If you change the number of pay periods, the dialog box shown above appears. Click **Yes**, so the template can automatically customize itself for the specified number of periods.

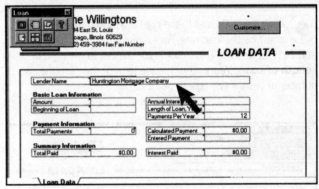

7 Now, enter specific information about the loan. Click the **Loan Data** tab. The green shaded boxes you see will contain calculated amounts, so don't type any data in them. Click inside the cell to the right of **Lender Name**, and type the name of the bank or mortgage company from which you are borrowing the money.

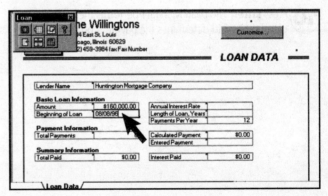

8 Click inside the cell to the right of **Amount**, and type the dollar amount you are borrowing. Then, click inside the cell to the right of **Beginning of Loan**, and type the date on which you intend to borrow the money.

(continues)

Do It Yourself Manage Your Personal Loans

(continued)

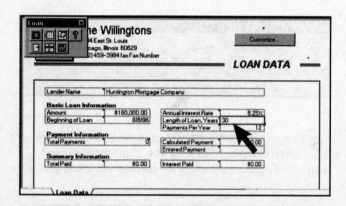

9 Click inside the cell to the right of **Annual Interest Rate**, and type the loan rate. For example, if you're borrowing at 8.25%, type 8.25. Then, click inside the cell to the right of **Length of Loan, Years**, and type the term of the loan (the number of years it will take to pay it off).

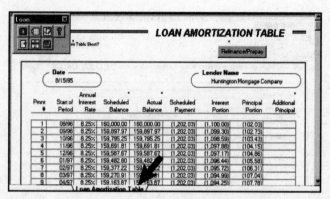

11 Loan Manager also creates an amortization table that breaks down each payment into the amount of the payment that applies to interest and principal. Click the **Loan Amortization Table** tab to see it.

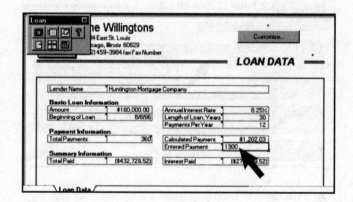

10 Press **Enter**. The Loan Manager performs the necessary calculations and determines the payment on the loan.

12 Now, let's have some fun. Play with the payment amounts to see how much you can save by making larger payments. Click the **Loan Data** tab, and then click inside the cell to the right of **Entered Payment**. Type an amount that's larger than the Calculated Payment amount, and press **Enter**.

Do It Yourself Manage Your Personal Loans

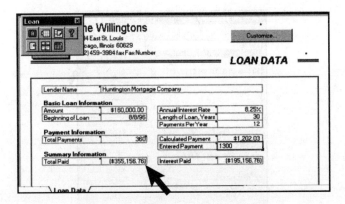

13 As you can see, on a 30-year $160,000 loan at 8.25%, if you pay an additional $98 per payment, you'll save over $77,000 over the life of the loan. If you pay an additional $198 per month, you'll save over $117,000!

15 If you get serious about playing with the loan amounts, percentages, and terms, consider using Scenario Manager to keep track of the various possibilities. First, click the **Loan Data** tab. Next, open the **Tools** menu and click **Scenarios**.

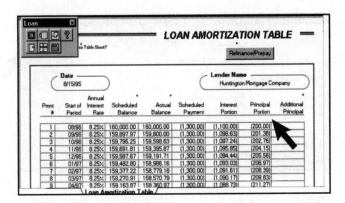

14 To see how this works, click the **Amortization Table** tab. As you can see, you are now paying much more toward principal each month, reducing the amount of the actual loan, hence reducing the amount of interest you pay.

16 To create a new scenario, click the **Add** button.

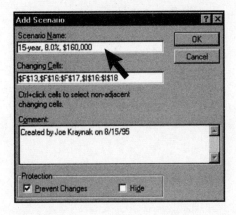

17 The Add Scenario dialog box appears. Type a descriptive name for the scenario; for example, type 15-year, 8.0%, $160,000. Click **OK**.

(continues)

Do It Yourself Manage Your Personal Loans

(continued)

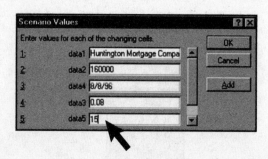

18 The Scenario Values dialog box appears, allowing you to enter different values for term, percentage rate, and loan amount. Double-click inside a cell (or tab to it) and type the desired value. (You can change the values in more than one text box.) Click **OK** when you're done.

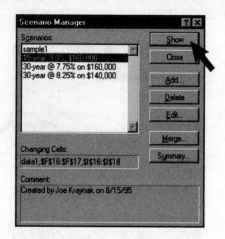

19 You can add more scenarios, as desired. When you want to see a scenario in action, simply click its name, and click the **Show** button. (You may have to drag the Scenario Manager title bar to move the dialog box out of the way, so you can see the results.)

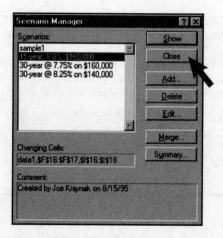

20 When you're done playing with numbers, click the Scenario Manager's **Close** button.

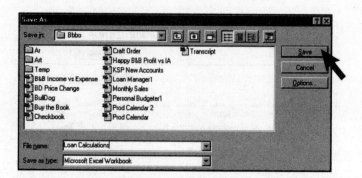

21 Be sure to save your loan spreadsheet when you're done. Open the **File** menu and select **Save**. Then complete the dialog box that appears, to name the file and select a folder in which to store it.

Create a Workable Budget

If you don't keep track of how much money you spend, you'll never have enough, no matter how much money you earn. If you have expensive taste in clothes, you can't live without the latest CD, or if you just enjoy eating out at fine restaurants, you can piddle away more money per month than is coming in.

To track the incoming and outgoing money, you should keep a budget. At first, you might set some goals for various categories, such as food, clothing, entertainment, rent, and utilities. As you work with the budget, you can readily see which categories you guessed wrong on. You can then adjust the numbers (for instance, set aside more for entertainment and less for groceries). And, if you can live within the budgeted amounts in each category, you will quickly see your savings mount. You might even save enough money to start investing it in stocks or bonds.

But how do you start a budget? How do you categorize your expenses? Excel comes with a Personal

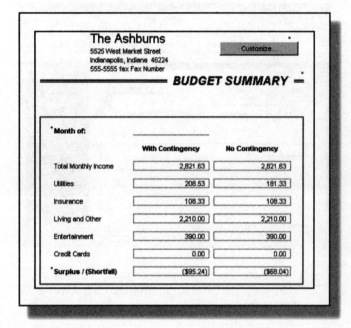

Budgeter template to help you start. This project shows you how to open the Personal Budgeter workbook and use it to create your own custom budget.

Begin Do It Yourself   Create a Budget

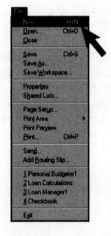

1 To open the Personal Budgeter, run Excel, open the **File** menu, and select **New**.

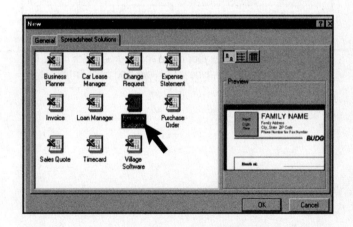

2 In the New dialog box, click the **Spreadsheet Solutions** tab, and then click **Personal Budgeter**. Click **OK**.

(continues)

Do It Yourself Create a Budget

(continued)

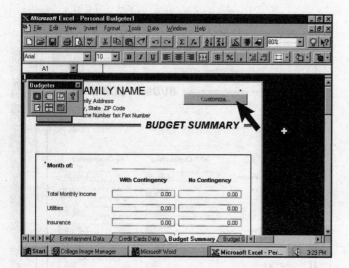

3 The Personal Budgeter appears, displaying the summary worksheet. Let's customize the workbook first. Click the **Customize** button.

4 You can now enter your name and address. Click inside the **Family Name** cell, type your name, and press **Enter**.

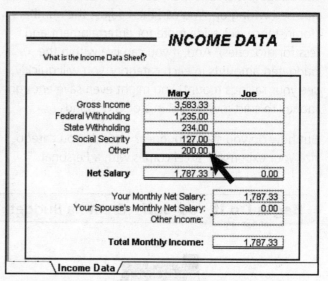

5 Continue clicking on cells and typing entries for your address, city, state, ZIP code, and phone number.

6 When you're done entering personal information, grab your last few paychecks, and click the **Income Data** tab. Enter your gross monthly pay and any tax deductions in the specified cells. (If you have additional deductions, such as 401K contributions or health insurance payments, add them and enter the total in the cell to the right of **Other**.)

Do It Yourself Create a Budget

```
═══════════ INCOME DATA ═══
What is the Income Data Sheet?

                            Mary          Joe
        Gross Income       3,583.33     3,298.25
  Federal Withholding      1,235.00     1,145.00
    State Withholding        234.00       215.00
      Social Security        127.00       117.00
                Other        200.00
          
          Net Salary       1,787.33     1,821.25

        Your Monthly Net Salary:       1,787.33
Your Spouse's Monthly Net Salary:      1,821.25
                  Other Income:

            Total Monthly Income:      3,608.58

\ Income Data /
```

7 If you're married, enter information from your spouse's paycheck into the specified cells. Make sure the net income amount matches the net income shown on your paycheck stub. The Personal Budgeter automatically adds the two net incomes to determine the total net income.

```
═══════════ UTILITIES DATA ═══
What is the Utilities Data Sheet?

              Amount ($)      MM/DD/YY      Ave Bill
Electricity     56.00         05/07/95       45.33
                43.00         06/07/95
                54.00         07/07/95
                32.00         08/07/95
                45.00         09/07/95
                42.00         10/07/95
                                             Ave Bill
Cable           15.00         05/15/95        15.67
                17.00         06/15/95
                14.00         07/15/95
                16.00         08/15/95
                17.00         09/15/95
                15.00         10/15/95
\ Utilities Data /
```

8 Now, get your utility bills for the last six months, and click the **Utilities Data** tab. Type the monthly amount you spent on each utility that's listed. You can use the **Other** area to list additional utility expenses, such as water and sewer. (You can also change the names of some of the listed utilities that you don't have, such as Cable.)

```
Other        *Amount ($)      MM/DD/YY       Ave Bill
                                               0.00


Total Anticipated Utilities                  175.00

Contingency Percentage (%)                    15%
(15% recommended)

Total Monthly Utility Expenses               175.00

                Insert Fine Print Here
\ Utilities Data /
```

9 Be sure to enter a percentage in the **Contingency Percentage** cell to account for any unseen increases in utility bills. (This provides you with a worst-case scenario of how much you'll have to pay in utility bills.)

```
═══════════════════ INSURANCE DATA ═══
What is the Insurance Data Sheet?

                                                              Monthly    # of
Policy Type / Name  Policy Number  Agent    Policy Period     Amount   installments
Car
Volkswagon          564987-01      McCollugh  1-1-96 to 1-6-96  125.45      6
Olds                564987-02      McCollugh  1-1-96 to 1-6-96  119.85      6

Medical


Homeowner's
Residence           564987-03      McCollugh  1-1-96 to 1-6-96   98.75      6
\ Insurance Data /
```

10 Fetch your most recent insurance statements, and click the **Insurance Data** tab. Enter all information for your auto, home, health, and life insurance. (If you already accounted for a health or life insurance payment as an automatic deduction on your paycheck, do not include it here.)

(continues)

Do It Yourself Create a Budget *(continued)*

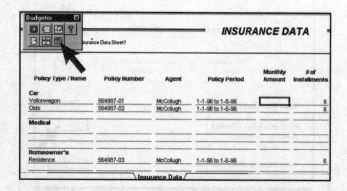

11 Because most insurance companies bill you twice per year, you might have to figure the monthly amount yourself. Click the **Calculator** button in the floating toolbar.

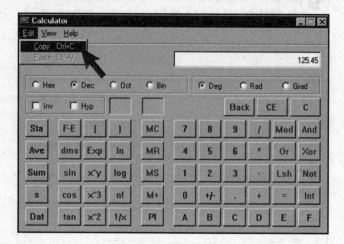

12 Key in the amount of the 6-month payment, click the **/** (division) button, type in **6** (to divide the 6-month payment by 6 months), and then click the **=** button. Open the **Edit** menu and select **Copy**.

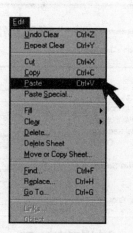

13 Click inside the cell into which you want to add the monthly payment information; open the **Edit** menu and select **Paste**. This inserts the copied amount from the Calculator into the selected cell.

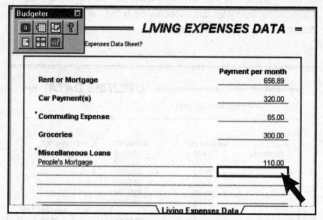

14 When you finish entering insurance payment information, click the **Living Expenses Data** tab, and enter your living expenses in the appropriate blanks.

Do It Yourself Create a Budget

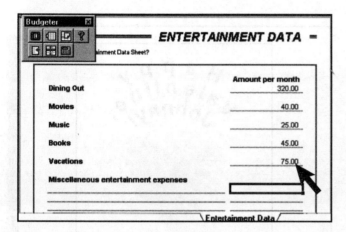

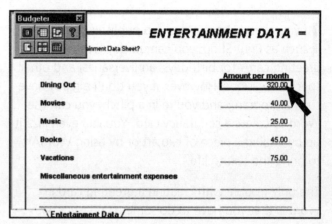

15 Continue clicking on tabs and entering information for entertainment expenses, credit card charges, and any other miscellaneous expenses you might have.

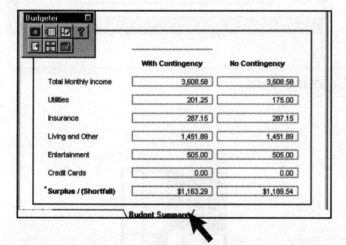

16 When you finish, you can see how much money you have free each month (or how much you're going in the hole each month). Click the Budget Summary tab, to see how you're doing so far.

17 You can now start to play with numbers, to determine just where you should cut back on expenses to save money. You might want to start with paring down entertainment expenses and possibly consumables, such as groceries. Once you bring your expenses in line, think about trimming your credit card debt.

18 A budget takes a long time to assemble. Be sure to save your work. Press **Ctrl+S**, and then use the Save As dialog box to type a name for the budget file and select a folder in which to store it.

Create Greeting Cards

If you already have a desktop publishing program such as Print Shop, you can quickly create custom greeting cards for birthdays, anniversaries, and other special occasions. However, if you don't already have such a program, and you're in a pinch, you can use Word to create a semifancy card. You can even jazz it up by adding a piece of clip art or by using WordArt to bring the text to life.

The only trouble with creating a greeting card in Word is that you have to do some gymnastics with the page layout to make the paper fold correctly into a card. The following project teaches you how to do this, and how to add clip art, WordArt objects, and other items to embellish your creation.

Begin Do It Yourself Create Your Own Greeting Card

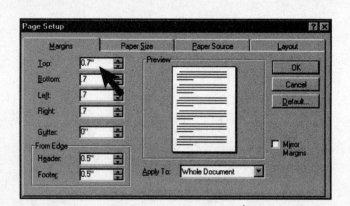

1 Run Word, and create a new document. Change the margins to give yourself some real estate to work on. Open the **File** menu and select **Page Setup**. In the Page Setup dialog box, click the **Margins** tab, and then enter a margin setting of **.7** for the left, right, top, and bottom margins. Click **OK**.

3 x 3 Table

2 Use the Tables feature to create the general card layout. Click the **Insert Table** button, and then drag the mouse pointer down and to the right to select a table that's three-by-three. (To work in Page Layout view, as shown here, open the **View** menu and select **Page Layout**.)

Do It Yourself Create Your Own Greeting Card

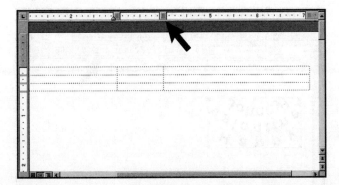

3 Word plops the table on the page. Now, drag the column markers in the ruler to set markers at the following marks: 3", 4", and 7". This gives you two columns that are 3 inches wide and a column in the middle (where you'll fold the card) that's 1 inch wide.

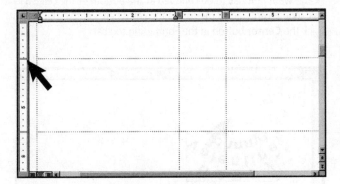

4 Drag the row markers to set the row heights for the table. You want row markers at the following positions: 4", 5.5", and 9.5". This gives you two cells that are 4 inches high with a 1 1/2-inch space between them.

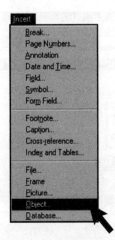

5 Now, insert your greeting on the front of the card. Click inside the upper left cell. Then, open the **Insert** menu and select **Object**.

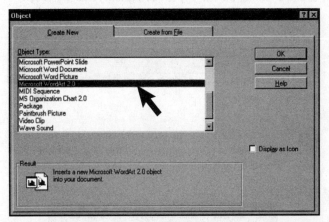

6 In the Insert Object dialog box, scroll down the Object Type list, and click **Microsoft WordArt 2.0**. Click **OK**.

(continues)

Do It Yourself Create Your Own Greeting Card

(continued)

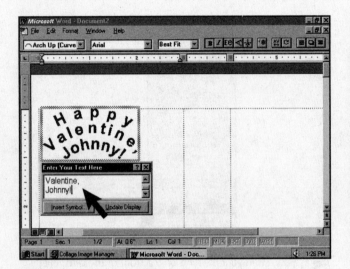

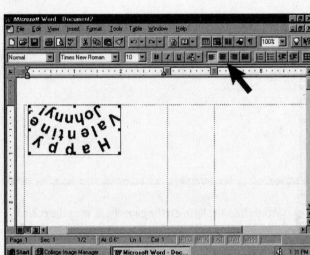

7 In the text box that appears, type the text you want to appear on the front of the card. Use the WordArt toolbar to pick a font for the text and to add any fancy text effects or embellishments. The text shown here curves up.

11 The text is flipped alright, but it's still not positioned as we want it. It has to be centered at the bottom of the cell (so it will appear centered at the top of the cell when you fold the card). Click the **Center** button in the Formatting toolbar.

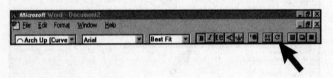

8 You now have to flip the text upside down, so it will be positioned correctly when you fold the card. Click the **Special Effects** button, as shown here.

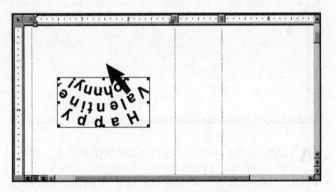

12 Click to the right of the new WordArt object, and press **Enter** eight times. This inserts eight centered paragraphs below the object, so you can move it down. Then, drag the WordArt object down to the bottom paragraph in the cell.

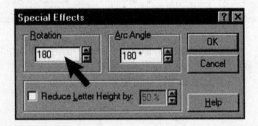

9 In the Rotation text box, type **180** to flip the text completely upside down. Click **OK**. (You have to flip everything upside down in this cell, so that when you fold the paper, this panel will appear rightside up.)

10 Click anywhere outside the box that contains the text you entered. This exits WordArt. (You can run WordArt at any time by double-clicking on this text.)

Do It Yourself   Create Your Own Greeting Card

13 You can also insert a centered piece of clip art in this cell. Click inside the cell, one or two paragraphs above the WordArt object. Then, open the **Insert** menu and click **Picture**.

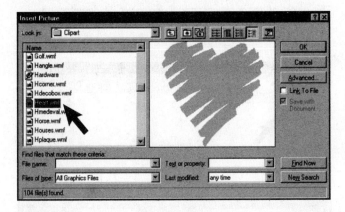

14 Use the dialog box that appears, to select a clip art image. (Clip art images are stored in the MSOffice/Clipart folder.) Click **OK** when you find the image you want to insert.

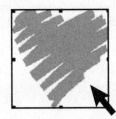

15 The image is inserted, but it's not upside-down. Double-click the image to edit it.

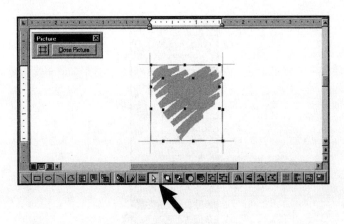

16 Some drawings consist of more than one part, so you have to select all the parts before rotating. Click the **Select Drawing Objects** button in the Drawing toolbar, and then drag a box around the entire drawing (including the frame).

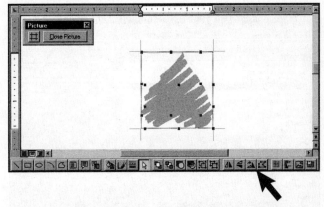

17 All the parts that make up the drawing appear. Click the **Rotate Right** button twice to flip the image upside-down. Click the **Close Picture** button to return to the Word document. (You can drag the drawing up or down to position it in relation to the WordArt object.)

(continues)

Do It Yourself Create Your Own Greeting Card *(continued)*

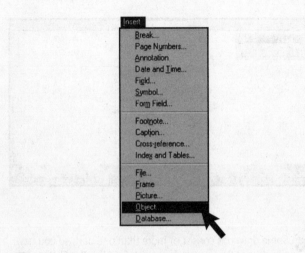

18 Now for the back of the card (this is optional). Click inside the upper right cell in the table. Then, open the **Insert** menu and select **Object**.

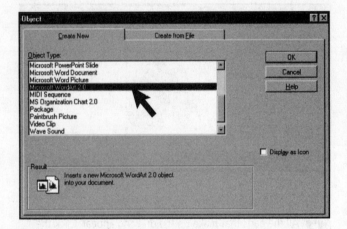

19 In the Insert Object dialog box, scroll down the Object Type list, and click **Microsoft WordArt 2.0**. Click **OK**.

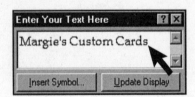

20 In the text box that appears, type something like **Margie's Custom Cards** or some other corny text to show that you made the card. You can use the WordArt toolbar to style the text, and flip it upside-down, as you did in steps 9 and 10.

21 When you're done, click outside the text box, and then click the **Center** button in the Formatting toolbar, to center the WordArt object.

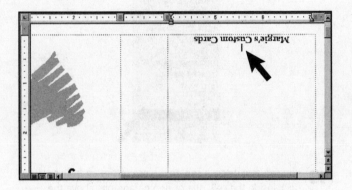

22 Click to the right of the WordArt object, to place the insertion point just to the right of it. Then, press **Enter**. This gives you room for entering a decorative divider above the WordArt object.

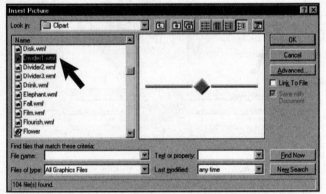

23 Open the **Insert** menu, and select **Picture**. Use the dialog box, as shown here, to select one of the Divider clip art images that comes with Office (in the MSOffice/Clipart folder). Click the **OK** button.

Do It Yourself Create Your Own Greeting Card

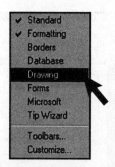

24 Now for the easy stuff, some plain, rightside-up text. Click inside the lower right cell in the table, to enter the text for the inside of the card. We'll create a text box using the Drawing toolbar. Right-click on one of the toolbars, and click **Drawing**.

27 A text box appears complete with its own insertion point. Type the text you want to appear on the inside of the card. You can style the text, as you would style any Word text. The text shown here is Book Antiqua set in various point sizes.

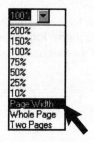

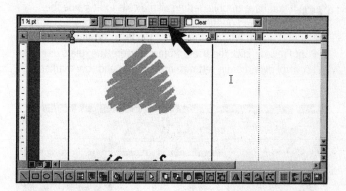

25 To draw the text box effectively, you need to see the entire cell. Open the **Zoom Control** drop-down list in the Standard toolbar, and click **Page Width**. Use the scroll bars to bring the entire cell into view.

28 You can quickly place a border around any cell. Simply click a blank area inside the cell (don't click a picture or WordArt object). Then, click the **Border** button in the Formatting toolbar, and use the Border toolbar to select the thickness and position of the border.

(continues)

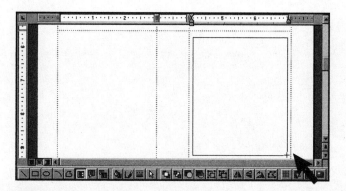

26 Click the **Text Box** button (in the Drawing toolbar), and use the mouse pointer to drag a text box inside the lower right cell.

Do It Yourself Create Your Own Greeting Card

(continued)

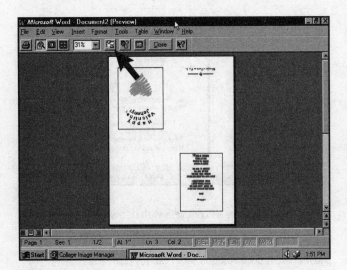

29 If you have trouble getting all the cells to fit inside the margins and on the same page, you can quickly adjust the cell boundaries in Print Preview. Click the **Print Preview** button. In Print Preview, click the **View Rulers** button. The rulers give you full control over margin settings, and column and row markers.

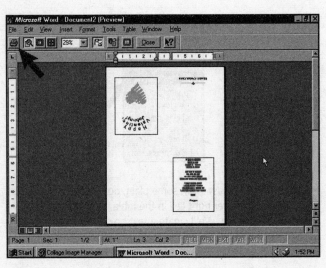

31 When you finish fine-tuning the layout for your card, you can quickly print it from Page Preview. Simply click the **Print** button in the toolbar.

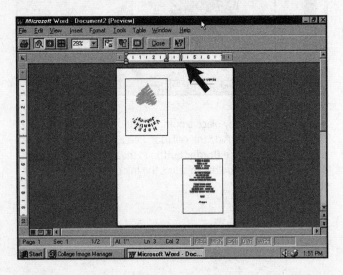

30 Drag the column markers in the top ruler to change the column widths. Drag the row markers (the double lines) in the left ruler to change the row heights. You can also drag margin markers to change the page margins.

Keep Track of Birthdays and Anniversaries

If you have a large family or lots of friends, you might have a little trouble keeping track of birthdays, anniversaries, and other important dates. If you currently keep a calendar of dates, you have to face the monotony of copying those dates to each new calendar you get. Then, you have to remember to look at the calendar. If you keep track of important dates in your address book, you have an even more unreliable tool to remind you.

To save yourself some time, and avoid the embarrassment of missing dates, consider using Schedule+ to track dates for you. With the **Insert Event** command, you enter the date once, and Schedule+ copies the date for every subsequent year. Schedule+ can even notify you days in advance of the upcoming date, so you can get a card in the mail before it's too late.

The following project assumes you know the basics of Schedule+. You can create a new Schedule+ file for keeping track of dates, or you can use an existing address book (if you created one in an earlier project).

Setting Schedule+ to Run Automatically on Start Up

No program can do its job if it isn't running, and Schedule+ is no different. If you use Schedule+ to keep track of important dates or appointments, you must keep it running, so it can notify you. The following steps explain how to add Schedule+ to the Windows StartUp group, so Schedule+ will run automatically whenever you turn on your computer.

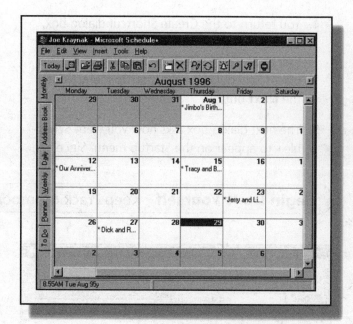

1. Click the Windows **Start** button; then, select **Settings** and click on **Taskbar**.

2. In the Taskbar Properties dialog box that appears, click the **Start Menu Programs** tab, and click the **Add** button.

3. In the Create Shortcut dialog box, click the **Browse** button, and use the dialog box that appears, to select the **Microsoft Schedule+** program icon (it's in the MSOffice folder). Click the **Open** button.

4. You return to the Create Shortcut dialog box. Click the **Next** button, and use the dialog box that appears, to select the **StartUp** icon. (This places Schedule+ on the StartUp menu.) Click the **Next** button.

5. The next dialog box asks how you want Schedule+ to appear on the Startup menu. Since

Microsoft Schedule+ seems logical, click the **Finish** button. Windows adds Schedule+ to the StartUp menu. Whenever you run Windows, Schedule+ will run automatically.

> If you don't use your computer much, at least turn it on every couple of days to see if any important dates are on the horizon. Remember, Schedule+ can't remind you unless your computer is on and Schedule+ is running.

Begin Do It Yourself   Keep Track of Important Dates

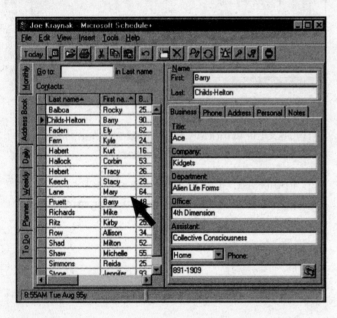

1 Run Schedule+, and open the file you want to use to keep track of dates (or use the file that appears when you run Schedule+).

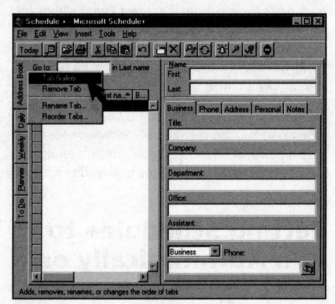

2 If you already have a Monthly tab, click it and skip to step 4. Otherwise, right-click one of the tabs, and click **Tab Gallery**, so you can add a Monthly tab to your schedule, and move onto step 3.

Do It Yourself Keep Track of Important Dates

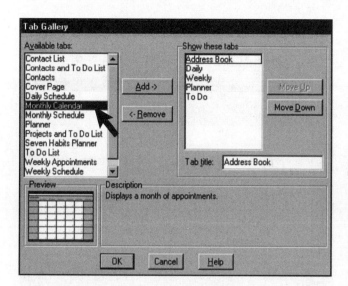

3 In the Tab Gallery dialog box, click **Monthly Calendar** in the **Available tabs** list; then click the **Add** button. Click **OK** to insert the tab and return to your schedule.

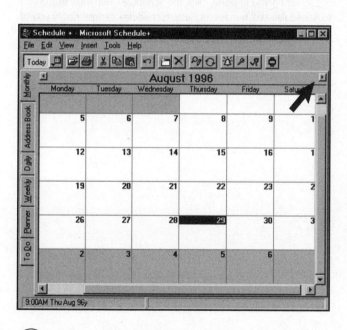

4 Click the back or forward button above the monthly calendar to display the month in which the date falls. As you click the arrow buttons, Schedule+ displays the previous or next month.

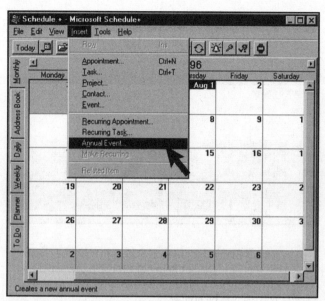

5 Click the date you want to mark as special, and then open the **Insert** menu and click on **Annual Event**.

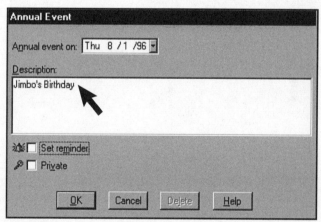

6 The Annual Event dialog box lets you type a description of the date. Type a brief description, such as Jimbo's Birthday.

(continues)

Do It Yourself Keep Track of Important Dates   *(continued)*

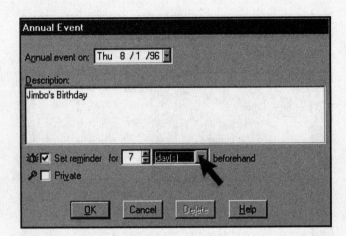

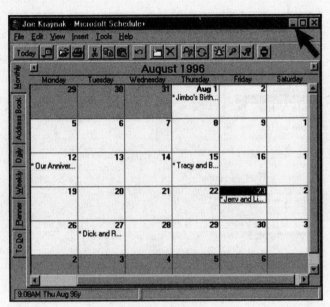

7 Click **Set Reminder**, to place a check mark in the check box. Then, use the **Set Reminder for** spin box and drop-down list to specify the number of days (or weeks or months) in advance you want to be notified.

8 Click **OK** to set the date.

9 Continue entering important dates, until you're finished. When you're done, click the Schedule+ Minimize button, so Schedule+ will remain running. (Schedule+ cannot notify you of upcoming dates if it is not running.)

Create a Family Tree

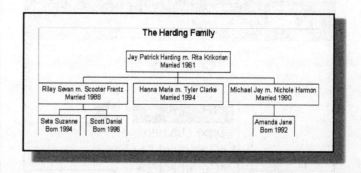

ave you ever gone to a family reunion and wondered how exactly you are related to great Aunt Polly? Is it getting more difficult to keep track of your growing family? Then you need to create a family tree.

Family trees give you and your family a detailed permanent record of your family history. A family tree is a great conversation piece at a family reunion or a fabulous gift to all of your family members.

You don't have to run out to the nearest computer store and purchase a special program. You can use Microsoft Word to create your family tree. The organization chart mini-application in Word is meant to create a visual tree structure of the employees in an organization. If you think about it, that's what a family tree is, too. Therefore, why not use Word's organization chart to create a family tree?

Begin Do It Yourself   Create Your Family Tree

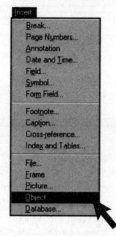

1 In Word, open the **Insert** menu and click **Object**.

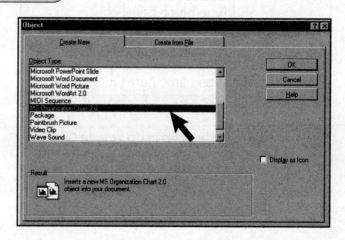

2 In the Object dialog box, select **Microsoft Organization Chart 1.0** from the object list and click **OK**.

(continues)

Do It Yourself Create Your Family Tree (continued)

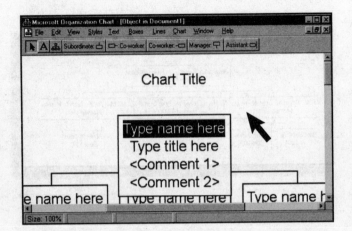

3 You will see the Microsoft Organization Chart window. I have maximized the window so we can see more of it by clicking on the **Maximize** button.

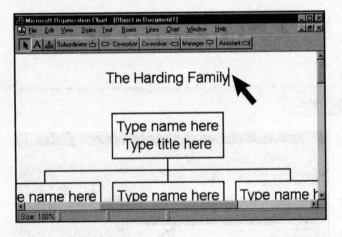

4 Add a title to your family tree by clicking in the **Chart Title** area and typing in your own title. You can delete the words "Chart Title" by highlighting them and pressing the **Delete** key.

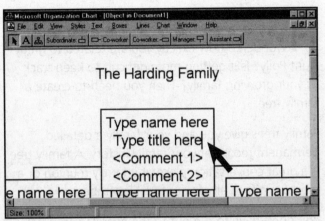

5 Double-click the first level box. Several lines appear where you can input the family member's name and other important information like their birth, wedding, or death dates. Type in the appropriate text and click outside of the box. Continue double-clicking in boxes and adding family members.

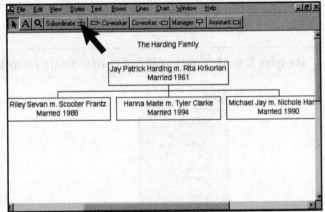

6 When you run out of boxes and you want to add more, click the appropriate button on the icon bar at the top of the window. The picture on the button should give you a clue as to how the box will be inserted into the tree. After clicking on the icon, click the box where you want the new box inserted next to or below. In the example, I clicked on the Riley Sevan m. Scooter Frantz box to add their children.

Do It Yourself Create Your Family Tree

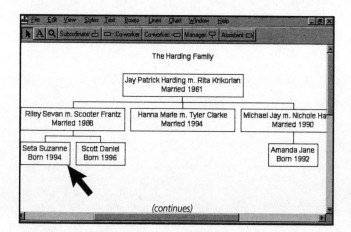

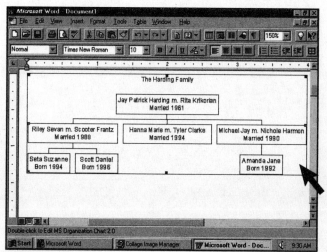

7 Double-click the new box and add the family member's name and information. Continue adding family members by repeating steps 6 and 7 as many times as necessary.

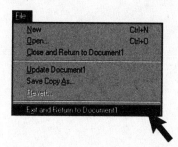

8 To add the family tree into the Word document, open the **File** menu and click the **Exit and Return to Document** command. You may see a dialog box asking you to update the document. Click **Yes**.

9 The family tree is an object in Word. So, if you are not happy by its size, click the tree and drag the black selection handles to the desired size.

10 Save and Print your family tree as you would any Word document.

DO IT YOURSELF

On the Job with Microsoft Office

I n this day and age of information and communication, it's easy to overload people with the tons of information on a daily basis. You want people to notice your important documents; therefore, you need to create impressive and attention-grabbing documents. Microsoft Office products are the key to creating dynamic documents and presentations.

You can use the Microsoft Office programs to their full potential in an office or business environment. Whether you are an assistant or manager in a large corporation, own a small business, or work out of your home office, the Office products can make you look as professional as if you worked for a Fortune 500 company.

This section has projects to help you effectively present yourself and your business in a positive and professional light with impressive and eye-catching documents.

What You Will Find in This Section

Compose a Newsletter

Newsletters are one of the most common ways to communicate information, news, and upcoming events. In this day and age of communication, you have to struggle to catch the attention of most people. They are inundated daily with piles upon piles of information. Newsletters are a great way to grab attention and communicate your message for business, school, and even home.

Newsletter text usually appears in columns, resembling a newspaper. Like a newspaper, headings are usually in a larger and bolder font to identify subject matter. You can place graphics or art in the body of your newsletter to draw attention to an element or headline.

You are not limited to the fonts, font sizes, margins, graphics, or layout described in the steps. These are merely suggestions to creating the newsletter shown here. You can change and modify any of the settings as you need for your newsletter.

Add a Graphic to Your Newsletter

You can really jazz up your newsletter by adding *graphics*, or pictures, to your newsletter to make it appear more professional. You can insert clip art included with Microsoft Office (these steps explain how) or insert your own graphics by using the **Insert Picture** command and then selecting the file. Here are the steps on how to insert a graphic from the Microsoft ClipArt Gallery:

1. To insert a graphic or clip art into your newsletter, open the **Insert** menu and select **Object**.

2. In the **Object** dialog box, select the **Microsoft**

ClipArt Gallery from the Object Type list and click **OK**.

3. In the Microsoft ClipArt Gallery 2.0 window, you see a list of categories on the left and the pictures or clip art in the selected category on the right.

4. Click on the category you want to look in, and then click on the clip art picture you want to insert into the newsletter (a blue box surrounds the clip art you have clicked on).

5. When you select the clip art you want to insert, click the **Insert** button.

6. If the graphic is not the size you want in the document, click the graphic (selection handles appear around the graphic). Drag one or all of the selection handles until the graphic is the size you want.

Begin Do It Yourself Put Together a Newsletter

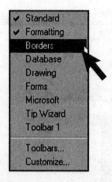

1 In Word, start with a blank document by clicking the **New** button. Display the Borders toolbar by clicking the **Borders** button (the last button) on the Formatting toolbar.

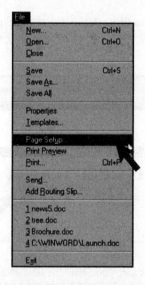

2 Set the page margins by opening the **File** menu and selecting the **Page Setup** command.

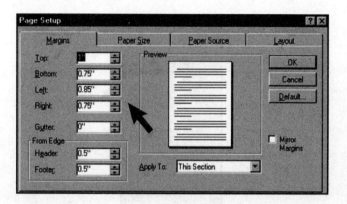

3 In the Page Setup Dialog box, click the **Margins** tab. Change the margin setting to Top: **1"**, Bottom: **.75"**, Left: **.85"**, and Right: **.75"**. Click **OK**.

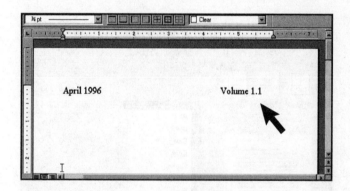

4 Set the Font to **Times New Roman** and the font size to **18** using the buttons on the Formatting toolbar. Then, type the date and volume number of the newsletter. Press **Enter** to move to the next line.

(continues)

Do It Yourself Put Together a Newsletter

(continued)

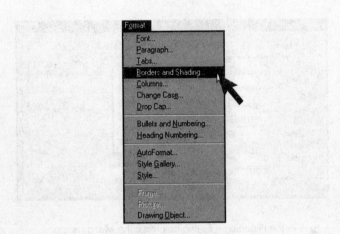

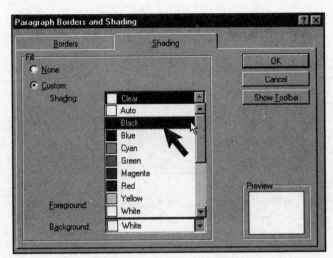

5 Select or highlight the line you just typed; open the **Format** menu and select **Borders and Shading**.

7 Click the **Shading** tab and click the **Background** drop-down list. From the list, click **Black**. Click **OK**.

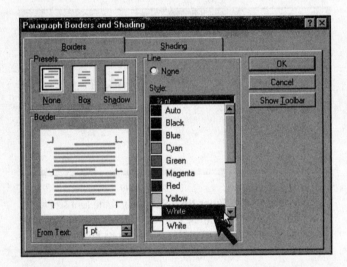

6 In the Paragraph Borders & Shading dialog box, click the **Border** tab; click the **Color** drop-down list and click **White.**

8 Move to the blank line after the date and volume and change the Font Size to **48**; type the title to your newsletter (in this case, **Legends Ledger**). Click the **Center** button on the toolbar to center the title and press **Enter** to move to the next line.

Do It Yourself Put Together a Newsletter

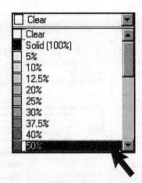

9 Select the title you just typed in and click the **Shading** drop-down list on the Borders toolbar. Click **50%**.

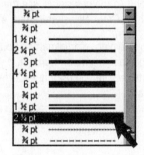

10 Click the **Line Style** drop-down list on the Borders toolbar and click **2 1/4pt double underline** style. Then click the **Bottom Border** button.

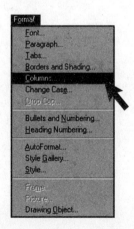

11 Move to the blank line under the title and click the **Font Size** button; set the font size to **10**. Then click the **Align Left** button on the toolbar. Now put your newsletter into three columns. Select or highlight the empty line you inserted under the title and open the **Format** menu and select **Columns**.

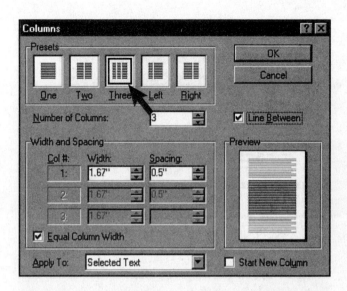

12 In the Columns dialog box, click **Three** under **Presets** and click the **Line Between** check box to turn it on. Click **OK**.

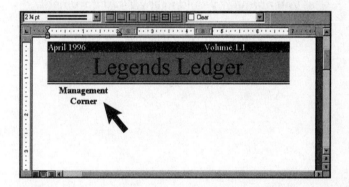

13 The insertion point now rests in the first column of your three-column newsletter. To enter a heading, click the **Font Size** button on the toolbar and select **18**. Click the **Bold** button and then click the **Center** button. Now you're ready to type your heading.

(continues)

Do It Yourself Put Together a Newsletter

(continued)

14 To enter the body text, click the **Font Size** button and select **10**; then click the **Align Left** button. Type your body text.

You can add bullets and numbered lists and change indents, fonts, font sizes, styles, and more. Basically, add or change any formatting as you normally would in any Word document.

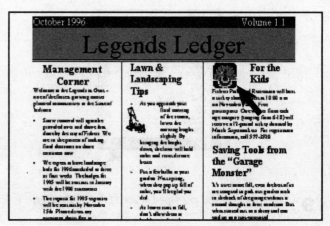

15 To add a graphic to the newsletter, see the steps in the "Add a Graphic to Your Newsletter" task 472.

16 When you finish typing and formatting your text in the newsletter, you should save and print it. If you want to preview the newsletter before you print it, click the **Print Preview** button on the toolbar.

Create an Invoice

Have you ever delivered a product or service to a company and they wanted an invoice before they will pay you? Scratching out a quick invoice on a piece of paper doesn't present a professional image of your company or business. Don't worry. You don't have to go out and purchase an expensive-looking invoice.

The people at Microsoft were kind enough to provide an invoice *template* in Excel. All you have to do is fill in the blanks. The steps in this task will walk you through creating a custom invoice for your own personal needs.

If you are not happy with the invoice template, you can create your own invoice from scratch and save it as a template. Use the **File Save** command, click the **Save as type** drop-down list and then **Template**. Then click **Save**.

If you are basically happy with the invoice template but want a few additions such as new text, a different term agreement, and so on, don't hesitate to add and delete elements from the existing template. Once you have made the changes, select the **File Save** command, click the **Save as type** drop-down list and then **Template**. If you want to give a new name to your template, type the name in the **File name** text box and click **Save**. If you want to write over the existing template, simply click **Save**.

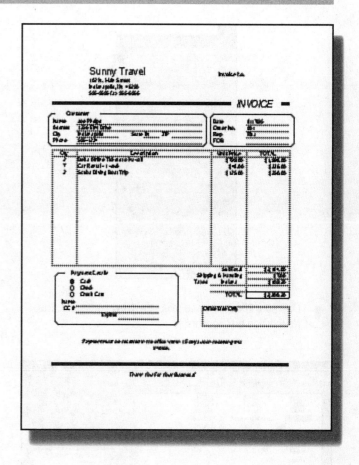

Begin Do It Yourself   Create an Invoice Form

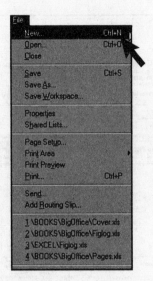

1 Open the **File** menu and select the **New** command. The New dialog box appears.

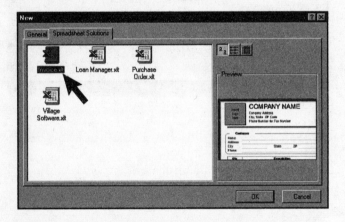

2 Click the **Spreadsheet Solutions** tab and then click the **Invoice** icon. Click **OK**.

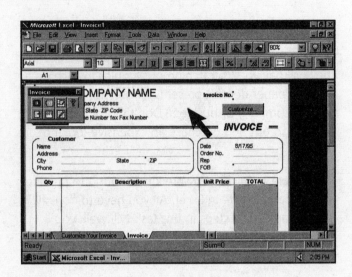

3 The Invoice template appears on-screen. You will also notice a new floating toolbar called **Invoice**. Begin filling in the information on the template by clicking in the cell you want to change or add to; then type. However, I suggest you customize the template to your needs, for example, to fill in your company name in the appropriate area. Follow the steps in the following section, "Customize the Invoice Template." If you don't want to customize, skip to the steps titled "Fill in the Invoice."

To move the floating toolbar out of the way so you can see more of the screen in the steps, move it (as I have in the figures) underneath the Formatting toolbar by clicking on the title bar and dragging.

Begin Do It Yourself   Customize the Invoice Template

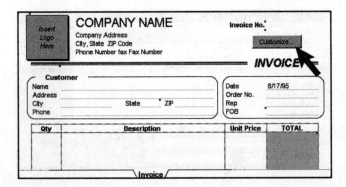

1 Before you begin typing information on the template, you need to make some custom changes, such as adding your company name. Click the **Customize** button in the top right corner of the Invoice template.

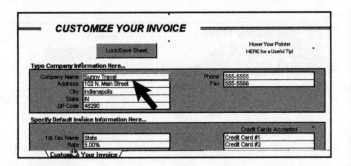

2 You'll see a screen that says **Customize Your Invoice**. In the **Type Company Information Here...** area, type your company name and address in the text boxes.

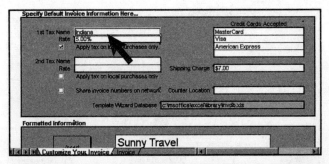

3 In the **Specify Default Invoice Information Here...** area, enter pertinent information such as your state's tax rate, what credit cards you accept, and shipping charges. Select the check boxes that apply to your situation.

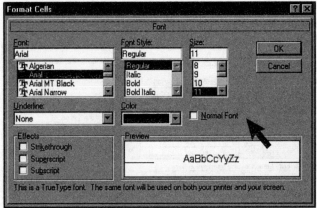

4 In the **Formatted Information** area, you will notice the company name shows the information you entered in step 2. If you want to change the font or font size, click the **Change Plate Font button**. The Format Cells dialog box appears. Make any changes in the dialog box you want and click **OK**.

(continues)

Do It Yourself Customize the Invoice Template *(continued)*

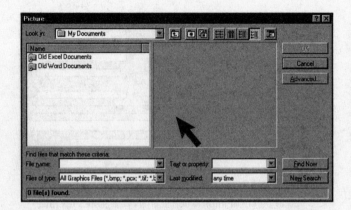

5 If you would like to add your company logo or a graphic to the invoice, click the **Select Logo** button. In the Picture dialog box, select the file that contains your logo or the graphic you want to use and click **OK**.

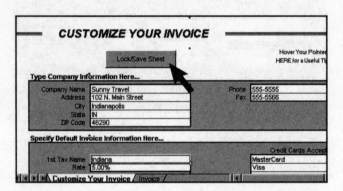

6 When you finish making the selections for customizing the invoice template, click the **Lock/Save Sheet** button.

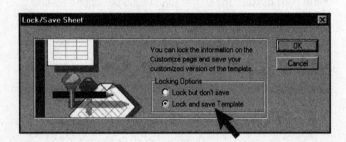

7 In the Lock/Save Sheet dialog box, click the **Lock and save Template** option button and click **OK**.

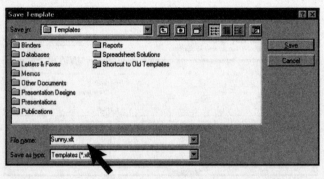

8 In the Save template dialog box, type a name for your customized template in the **File name** text box and click **Save**. This doesn't overwrite the original invoice template. It creates another version of the template for you to use in the future.

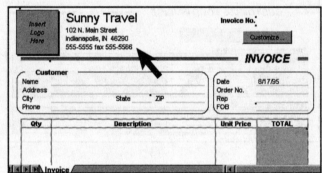

9 You'll notice that the information you entered when you customized the form, such as your company name and address, appears on the invoice.

Begin Do It Yourself   Use the Customized Template to Create Your Invoice

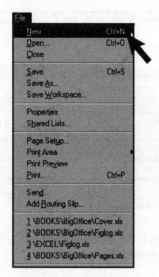

1 Open the **File** menu and click the **New** command.

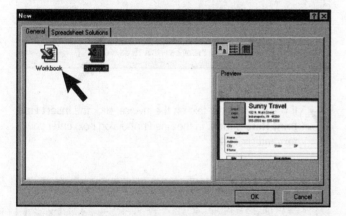

2 Click the template you saved in the previous set of steps; then click **OK**.

3 Fill in the information as outlined in the next set of steps called Fill In the Invoice.

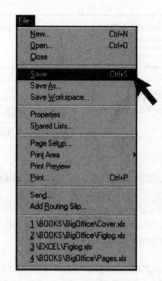

4 Save the invoice as an Excel workbook with the **File Save** command as you normally would save a workbook.

Begin Do It Yourself Fill In the Invoice

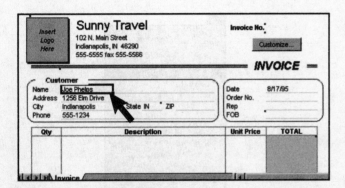

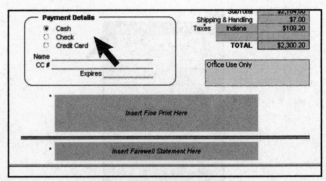

1 In the **Customer** area of the invoice, click the line you want to fill in and begin typing. Continue until you fill in all of the customer information.

2 To the right of the **Customer** area, Excel adds the current date (if you want to change it, click on the field and type the new date). To fill in the remaining fields, click in the field and begin typing.

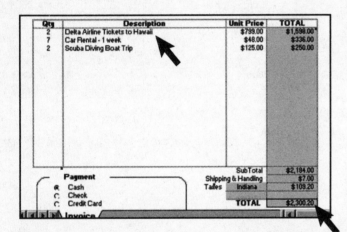

5 Fill in the **Payment Details** information areas as needed.

6 (Optional) In the **Office Use Only** area, fill in any information necessary.

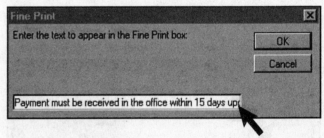

7 If you want special text on the invoice, click the **Insert Fine Print Here** button. In the Fine Print dialog box; enter your text and click **OK**.

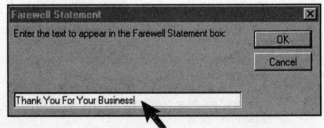

3 To fill in the body of the invoice, click in the **Qty** field and enter your quantity per item. Enter a description of the item in the **Description** field and the individual price per unit in the **Unit** Price field. Excel automatically calculates the amount and places it in the **Total** field.

4 Continue entering your invoice information. Excel displays the grand total automatically at the bottom of the invoice after adding in the shipping charges and taxes.

8 To add a closing statement to your invoice, click the **Insert Farewell Statement Here** button. In the Farewell Statement dialog box, enter your statement and click **OK**.

9 To see a preview of your invoice as you create it, click the **Print Preview** button on the toolbar. When you finish your invoice; remember to save and print it.

Any time you see a little red dot next to a cell, the cell includes a *CellTip* with helpful information on filling in the information. To see the CellTip, point at the red dot.

Put Together a Custom Purchase Order

If you do a lot of purchasing for your business (and even if you don't), a purchase order is a necessity for staying organized. Using a purchase order form is a clear and concise way to purchase items from a vendor. You give the vendor visual proof of what you are ordering so there are not any mistakes or misunderstandings, which may result from verbal orders.

Using a purchase order every time you purchase an item also allows you to assign a number to each purchase order. This provides an efficient way of tracking orders.

Microsoft Excel comes with a template for creating a professional looking purchase order. You are not limited to the existing template; you can customize it to meet your business needs.

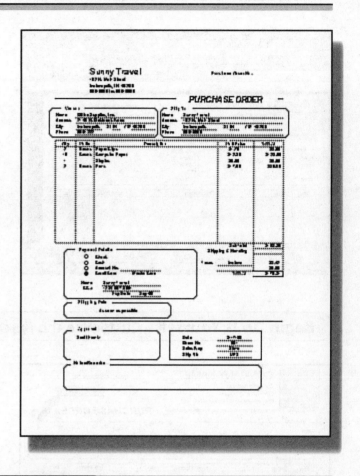

Begin Do It Yourself Create a Purchase Order Form

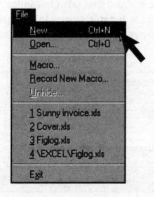

1 In Microsoft Excel, select the **File** menu and the **New** command.

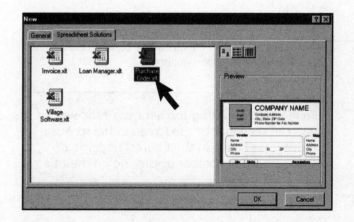

2 Click the **Spreadsheet Solutions** tab, click the **Purchase Order** icon, then click on **OK**.

(continues)

Do It Yourself   Create a Purchase Order Form

(continued)

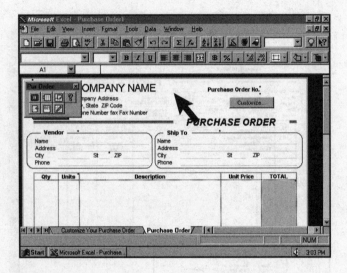

3 The Purchase Order template appears on-screen. You will also notice a new floating toolbar called **Pur Order**. You can begin filling in the information on the template by clicking in the cell you want to change or add; then begin typing. However, I suggest you customize the template to your needs, for example, to fill in your company name in the appropriate area. Follow the steps in the following section, "Customize the Purchase Order Template." If you don't want to customize, skip to the steps titled "Fill In the Purchase Order."

Any time you see a little red dot next to a cell, the cell includes a *CellTip* with helpful information on filling in the information. To see the CellTip, point at the red dot.

Begin Do It Yourself   Customize the Purchase Order Template

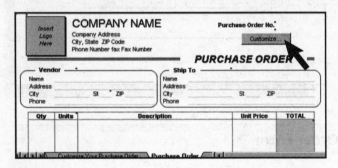

1 Before you begin filling in the information on the template, you need to make some custom changes such as adding your company name. Click the **Customize** button in the top right corner of the purchase order template.

To move the floating toolbar out of the way so you can see more of the screen in the steps, move it (as I have in the figures) underneath the Formatting toolbar by clicking on the title bar and dragging.

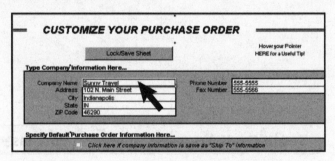

2 You'll see a screen that says **Customize Your Purchase Order**. In the **Type Company Information Here...** area, type your company name and address in the text boxes.

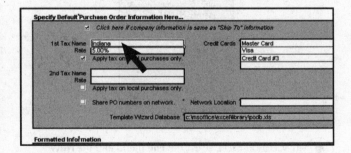

3 In the **Specify Default Purchase Order Information Here...** area, enter the pertinent information such as your state's tax rate and your credit card number(s). Select the check boxes that apply to your situation.

Do It Yourself   Customize the Purchase Order Template

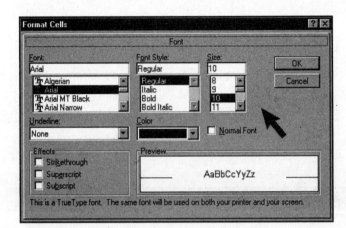

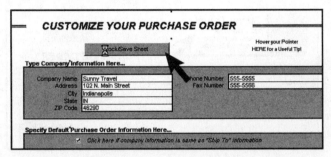

4 In the Formatted Information area, you will notice the company name has been updated with the information you entered in step 2. If you want to change the font or font size, click the **Change Plate Font** button. The Format Cells dialog box appears. Make any changes in the dialog box you want and click **OK**.

6 When you finish making the selections for customizing the purchase order template, click the **Lock/Save Sheet** button.

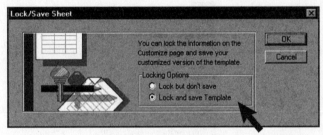

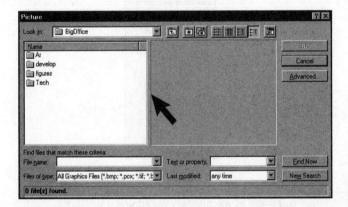

7 In the Lock/Save Sheet dialog box, click the **Lock and save Template** option button and click **OK**.

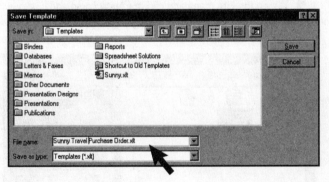

5 If you would like to add your company logo or a graphic to the purchase order, click the **Select Logo** button. In the Picture dialog box, select the file that contains your logo or the graphic you want to use and click **OK**.

8 In the Save template dialog box, type a name for your customized template in the **File name** text box and then click **Save**.

(continued)

Do It Yourself Customize the Purchase Order Template *(continued)*

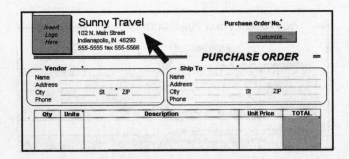

9 You see the information on the purchase order that you entered when you customized the form (such as your company name and address).

Begin Do It Yourself Use the Customized Template to Create Your Purchase Order

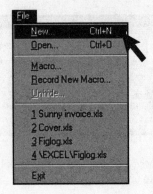

1 Open the **File** menu and click the **New** command.

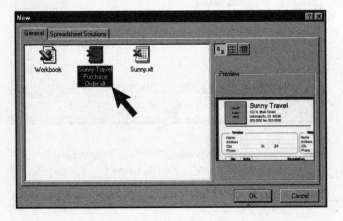

4 Save the invoice as an Excel workbook with the **File Save** command as you normally would save a workbook.

2 Click the template you saved in the previous set of steps; then click **OK**.

3 Fill in the information as outlined in the next set of steps.

Begin Do It Yourself   Fill in the Purchase Order

1 In the **Vendor** area of the invoice, click the line you want to fill in and begin typing. Continue until you fill in all of the vendor information.

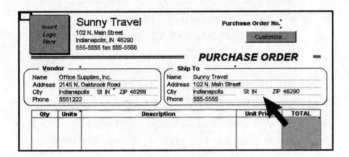

2 In the **Ship To** area, click the line you want to fill in and begin typing. Continue until you type in all of the Ship To information.

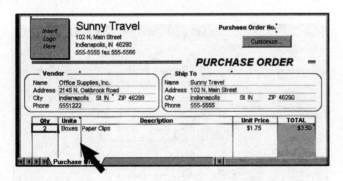

3 To fill in the body of the purchase order, click in the **Qty** field and enter your quantity per item. In the **Units** field, enter the unit size as it applies to the unit price, such as a case, box, dozen, and so on. Enter a description of the item in the **Description** field, and the individual price per unit in the **Unit Price** field. Excel automatically calculates the amount and places it in the **Total** field.

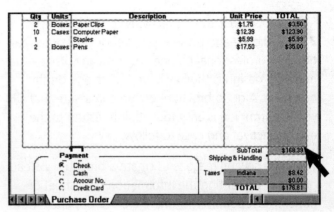

4 Continue entering your purchase order information. Excel will display the grand total automatically at the bottom of the invoice after adding in the shipping & handling charges and taxes.

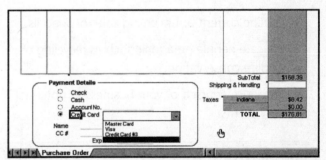

5 In the **Payment Details** information area, click the method of payment. If you select **Credit Card**, a drop-down list appears with the credit cards you entered when you customized the purchase order. Click a credit card and Excel adds the information about that card in the appropriate fields. Fill in all of the remaining fields as needed. Simply click in the field and begin typing.

6 To see a preview of your purchase order as you create it, click the **Print Preview** button on the toolbar. When you finish your purchase order, remember to save and print it.

Create a Brochure

A brochure is the perfect way to reach a target audience and present yourself or your organization in a professional manner. As with any other visual material, design is the key to your message on the brochure. A good brochure design can assure that your information is easy to read, interesting to the eye, attractive, and easy to follow.

There are several reasons to create a brochure instead of simply presenting the information on a sheet of paper. Most people will ignore a piece of paper with text. A brochure usually includes graphics, adds an element of professionalism, and tells the reader that it wants his attention. However, creating a brochure is very easy using Microsoft Word. You can create a brochure to:

- Outline current or upcoming sales or specials.

- Educate people on a topic such as recycling or wildlife conservation.

- Introduce yourself or your business to potential new clients.

- Use as an invitation or an announcement to a special gathering or event.

- Hand out to your clients. For example, if you are in the restaurant business, you can create a brochure that has a miniaturized copy of your menu.

There are usually two kinds of brochures: two-fold and three-fold (or tri-fold). The following Do It Yourself steps will walk you through creating a two-fold brochure. If you want to create a three-fold brochure, simply select three columns instead of two in step 3.

Begin Do It Yourself Make a Brochure

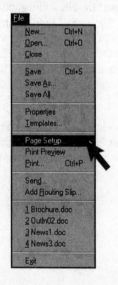

1 Start with a blank screen (click the **New** button on the toolbar) in Microsoft Word. Select the **File** menu and the **Page Setup** command.

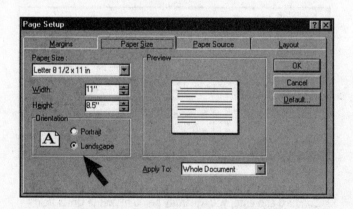

2 In the Page Setup dialog box, click the **Paper Size** tab. Click the **Landscape** option button; click **OK**.

Do It Yourself Make a Brochure

3 Click the **Columns** button on the toolbar. A drop-down list of columns appears. Drag the mouse over two columns.

> To see the columns you created in step 3, you must be in Page Layout view. Click the **Page Layout** button on the bottom of the document window. If you need a refresher course on moving around in columns, see "Set Up Columns" on page 132.

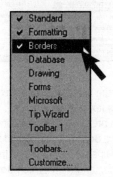

4 Display the Borders toolbar by clicking the **Borders** button (the last button) on the Formatting toolbar.

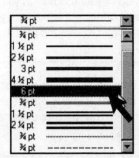

5 Press **Enter** several times to move to the bottom of the first column. Once there, click the **Line Style** drop-down list on the Borders toolbar and select the **6 pt** line. Then click the **Top Border** button on the toolbar.

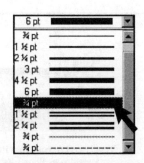

6 Click the **Line Style** drop-down list and select **3/4 pt** double underline from the list; then click the **Bottom Border** button.

7 Underneath the lines you just drew, type your company information. For the example, I clicked the **Center** button and then the **Bold** button, set the font at **Times New Roman**, and set the font size to **18** before typing in the information.

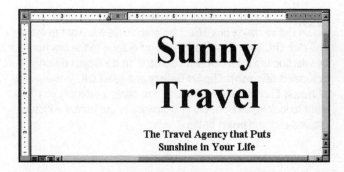

8 Move to the second column on the first page and set the font size, click the **Center** button, click the **Bold** button, and then type in the title of the brochure. In this example, I set the font size to **72**, clicked the **Center** button, and clicked the **Bold** button for Sunny Travel. I reduced the font size to **20** for the remaining text.

(continues)

Do It Yourself Make a Brochure

(continued)

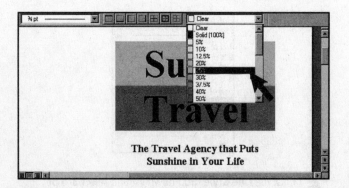

9 Add shading to the text to add pizzazz. In this example, I selected the word **Sunny**, clicked on the **Shading** drop-down list from the Borders toolbar, and selected **25%**. For the word Travel, I selected **50%** shading from the same drop-down list.

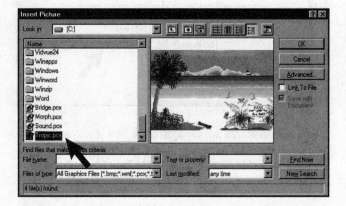

10 To add graphics, select the **Insert Picture** command. In the Picture dialog box, select the graphic file you want to insert and click **OK**. You can also add a clip art graphic to the brochure by selecting the **Insert Object** command. In the Object dialog box, select **Microsoft ClipArt Gallery** and select **OK**. In the Microsoft ClipArt Gallery 2.0 dialog box, select a category you want to look in, click the clip art you want to use from the **Picture** list, and click the **Insert** button.

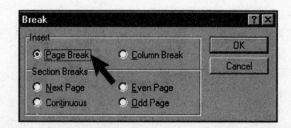

11 Move to the second page of the document by either pressing **Enter** until you are on the second page or selecting the **Insert Break** command. In the Break dialog box, click the **Page Break** option button; click **OK**.

12 Beginning in the first column on the second page, enter the remaining text for the brochure. In this example, I have inserted headings to break up the information. I changed the font size to **22**, clicked the **Bold** button, clicked the **Align Right** button, selected the line style of **4 1/2 pt** from the **Line Style** list on the Borders toolbar, and then clicked **Bottom Border** button.

13 For the body text in this example, I used the **Align Left** button with the font size of **14**.

14 To see a preview of your brochure as you create it, click the **Print Preview** button on the toolbar. If you are done with your brochure, don't forget to save and print it.

> You will see that I used bullets in some of the text. To add bullets, simply click the **Bullets** button on the Formatting toolbar and begin typing.

Write a Memo

Memos are an essential part of any interoffice communication. Most memos include an information area where the date, author of the memo, receiver(s), and subject are identified. The remainder is usually devoted to the body text of the memo.

Often, piles upon piles of memos cover the tops of business people's desks. If your information is important and you need it to stand out from the other memos littering a co-worker's desk, then you need an attention-grabbing memo.

Use Microsoft Word to create your impressive memo. There are several ways you can do this:

- You can go the easy route and use Word's three types of memo template. You can choose from Contemporary, Elegant, or Professional.

- You can use Word's Memo Wizard. This wizard will walk you through the steps to create a memo.

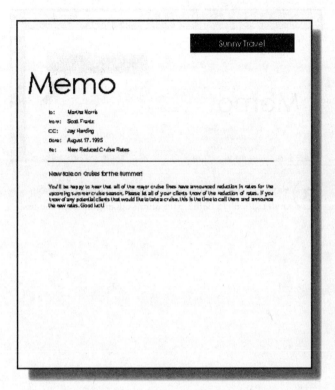

- You can start with a blank document and design your own memo. Once you finish, you can save it as a template to use over and over again.

Begin Do It Yourself　Create a Memo Using a Template

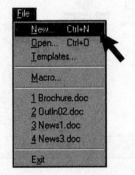

1 Open the **File** menu and click **New**.

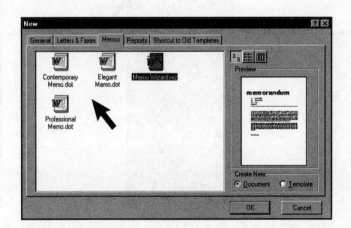

2 In the New dialog box, click the **Memos** tab. Click the type of template you want to create. You can choose from **Contemporary**, **Elegant**, or **Professional**. To see an example of the template, look in the **Preview** area. Once you select the template, click **OK**. In this example, I selected the Professional template.

(continues)

Do It Yourself Create a Memo Using a Template (continued)

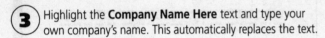

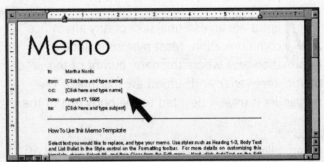

3 Highlight the **Company Name Here** text and type your own company's name. This automatically replaces the text.

4 You'll notice the "click-here-and-type" feature at work on the memo. To fill in any of the information area, simply click anywhere in the bracketed area and begin typing your text. You'll notice Word filled in the date for you. Enter, edit, or format text as you normally would for the remainder of the memo.

5 When you are adding or changing text in the memo, you can select from one of the many preformatted styles. Click the **Style** drop-down list from the Formatting toolbar and select the style you want to use from the list.

6 To see a preview of your memo as you create it, click the **Print Preview** button on the toolbar. When you finish your memo, remember to save and print it.

Begin Do It Yourself Create a Memo Using the Memo Wizard

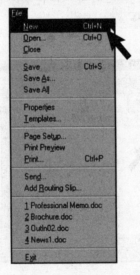

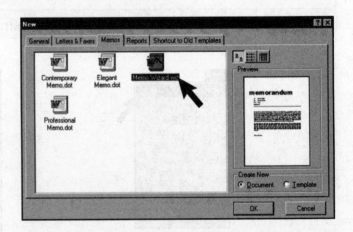

2 In the New dialog box, click the **Memos** tab. Click the **Memo Wizard** icon and click **OK**.

1 Open the **File** menu and click **New**.

Do It Yourself Create a Memo Using the Memo Wizard

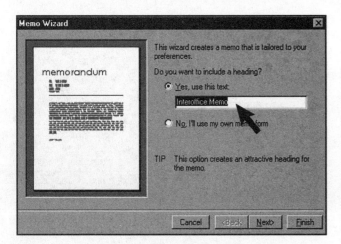

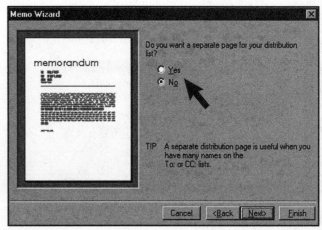

3 The Memo Wizard window appears and asks if you want Word to add a heading or if you want to use your own. Click in the appropriate check box. If you want Word to add the heading, enter the heading you want to include in the text box. Click **Next**.

> Click the **Back** button to go to the previous window(s) in the Memo Wizard.

5 Click the **Yes** or **No** option button, depending on if you want a separate page for your distribution list. Click **Next**.

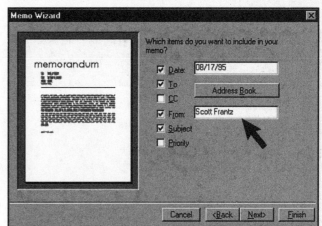

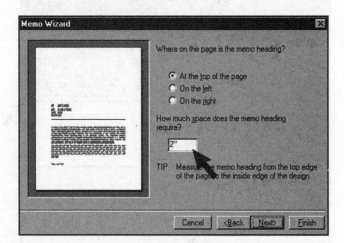

4 If you opted to have your own heading, you will see this window. Click the option button to tell Word where you want the memo heading placed. Also enter the number of inches the heading should take up on the page. Click **Next**.

6 Click in the check boxes next to the items you want to include in your memo. A check mark indicates that an option is turned on. If you want to use a different date than today's, change the date in the text box. If you want to use names from an address book, click the **Address Book** button and select the names for your distribution list. If you want to change who the memo is from, change the name in the **From** text box.

(continues)

Do It Yourself Create a Memo Using the Memo Wizard (continued)

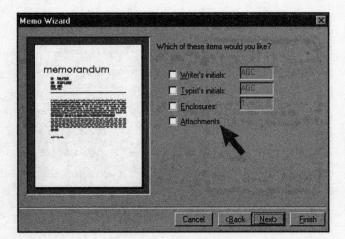

7 Click in the check box next to the items you want to include. If there is a text box next to the item, type in the appropriate information. Click **Next**.

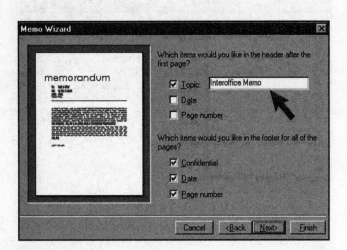

8 At the top of the window, select the check boxes you want included in the header of the second page of the memo. At the bottom of the window, select the check boxes you want to include in the footer of the memo. Click **Next**.

9 Click the option button next to the type of memo you want (**Professional**, **Contemporary**, or **Elegant**). Click **Next**.

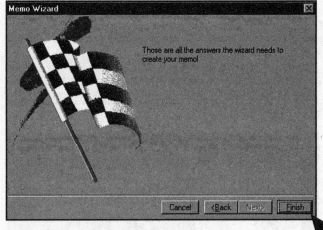

10 In the last window, click **Finish**.

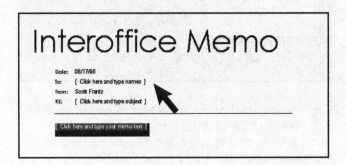

11 You'll notice the "click-here-and-type" feature at work on the memo. To fill in any of the information area, simply click anywhere in the bracketed area and begin typing your text. Enter, edit, or format text as you normally would for the remainder of the memo.

Prepare a Comprehensive Report

Have you ever had to prepare a plan, proposal, or a report? It can be a time-consuming and frustrating experience. You probably have all of the information you need for the report but don't have a clue how to put it all together to make it look professional—and impressive.

You don't have to be frustrated anymore. Microsoft Word has three templates that you can use to create your report: Contemporary, Elegant, or Professional.

These report templates include a cover page and formatting for the body of the report. The report templates include formatting, as well as styles for headings, body text, block quotation, bulleted lists, numbered lists, and tables. Word has done all of the work for you! You simply enter your report information, customize by adding tables, charts, graphics, and so on, and you're on your way.

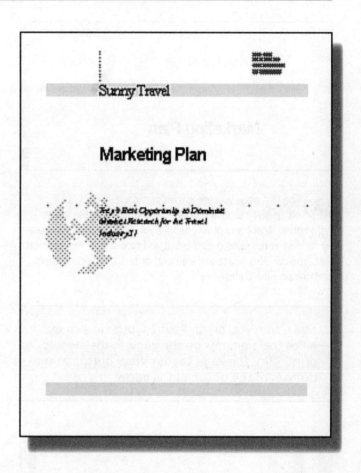

Begin Do It Yourself   Create a Report

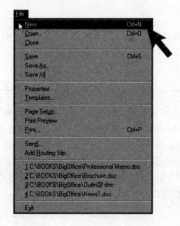

1 In Microsoft Word, select the **File** menu and then **New**.

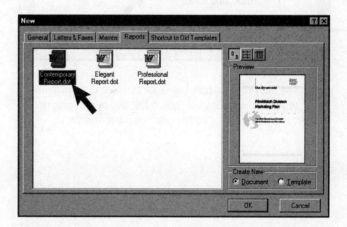

2 In the New dialog box, click the **Reports** tab; click the template you want to use: **Contemporary**, **Elegant**, or **Professional**. To see what each template looks like, look in the **Preview** area. When you select a report, click **OK**. In this example, I selected the Contemporary template.

(continues)

Do It Yourself   Create a Report *(continued)*

3 The first page you see is the cover page. Enter your company's name and address in the frame in the upper right corner. Make any other changes you want to the cover page by clicking or dragging over the text and typing your replacement text. You can also delete any elements or text by selecting them and pressing the **Delete** key.

Make sure you are in Page Layout view to see all of the elements on the page as they would print. Click the **Page Layout View** button at the bottom of the document window.

4 The body of the report begins on the second page of the template. Make any changes to the text by dragging over the text and deleting it or adding additional information.

5 When you are adding or changing existing text, you can select from one of the many preformatted styles. Click the **Style** drop-down list from the Formatting toolbar, and select the style you want to use from the list.

6 To delete a graphical element or object, click the object to select it; press the **Delete** key.

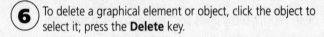
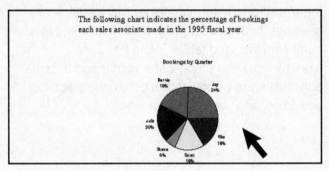

7 If you have information you need to include in the report from another program, you can *embed* or *link* it in your report. For more detailed information on how to share information between programs, see "Use Data Together from Different Office Applications" on page 345. In this example, I placed a chart created in Excel in the text portion of the report.

8 To see a preview of your report as you create it, click the **Print Preview** button on the toolbar. If you are done with your report, don't forget to save and print it.

The report templates also come with styles for a table of contents and an index. To add these elements, select the **Insert** menu and then **Index and Tables**. Click the tab of the element you want to insert. Make any of the changes you want in the dialog box.

PART 3

101 Quick Fixes

This is the section of the book that no one really wants to read. If you have turned here, it means you are having a problem. But don't despair, here are 101 of the most common problems along with their solutions. You won't have to fumble through the whole book saying, "I know I've seen the solution in here somewhere." The problems and solutions are here for easy reference.

To use this section look for your problem in the Quick-Finder table. It is broken down into sections, for example, Word Problems, Excel Problems, File Saving problems, and so on. If you can't find your particular problem, try looking in the Integration Problems, which covers problems that affect all of the Office programs. Once you find your problem in the table, turn to the Quick Fix to find the solution.

Quick-Finder Table

Installation Problems

Problem	Quick Fix	Page
All files not removed after uninstall	7	509
Can't make backup of installation disks	6	509
Could not finish installation	1	506
Error when copying installation disks	6	509
Installation did not complete successfully error message	1	506
Not enough disk space error message	2	506
Not enough disk space when Setup said there was	3	507
Required disk space less than available disk space	2	506
Setup calculated required disk space incorrectly	3	507
Setup could not open FINDFAST.CPL: error message	5	509
Setup keeps asking for disk 2	4	507
Setup won't get past second disk	4	507
Subfolders remain after uninstall	7	509

Word Problems

Problem	Quick Fix	Page
Accidentally added incorrect word to custom dictionary	20	516
Accidentally deleted a whole paragraph	15	514
Accidentally deleted text	15	514
Accidentally got drag-and-drop cursor	29	519
AutoCorrect changes text that shouldn't be changed	32	520
Bullet is added when I press **Enter**	16	514
Can enter only one line in table row	18	515
Can only see one column on the screen	11	510
Can see only half the document at once	25	518
Can't add page numbers	30	520
Can't delete blank line after paragraph	23	517
Can't delete bullet	17	515
Can't delete page number on page one	31	520
Can't find wizard in New dialog box	33	521

(continues)

Word Problems *Continued*

Excel Problems

(continues)

Excel Problems *Continued*

Problem	Quick Fix	Page
Need to recalculate worksheet	42	525
Number format is not correct	36	523
Report Manager option not available	48	528
Report Manager was not installed	48	528
Text of calculation appears instead of answer	39	524
There is a flashing bar in one of the cells	43	526
Titles are sorted with data	44	526
Total didn't change after changing numbers	42	525

PowerPoint Problems

Problem	Quick Fix	Page
Accidentally deleted slide from presentation	51	529
Can't change some of the objects on the slide	60	533
Can't change template	50	529
Can't display hidden slides in presentation	55	530
Can't find ClipArt in the ClipArt Gallery	57	531
Can't find hidden slide	55	530
Can't remove bullets	53	530
Can't select bullets	53	530
Can't select certain objects	60	533
Can't select objects on slide master	60	533
ClipArt fills entire screen	59	532
Couldn't find ClipArt after choosing it in the Gallery	58	532
Erased the wrong slide	51	529
Line is too long for slide	52	529
Need to change size of picture	59	532
Need to change transition speed	54	530
Need to refresh ClipArt Gallery	58	532
New ClipArt wasn't added to the ClipArt Gallery	57	531
Selected wrong template in wizard	50	529
Size of ClipArt is wrong	59	532
Text does not wrap	52	529
Text goes off the edge of the slide	52	529
Tip of the Day appears at startup	56	530
Transitions are too fast in presentation	54	530

Schedule+ Problems

Problem	Quick Fix	Page
Can't find the Yearly calendar	62	534
Can't share schedule with coworker	63	535
Do I want to work alone	61	533
Group-enabled mode problem	61	533
Need to add view tab	62	534
Need to change permissions	63	535
Need to turn off dual time zones	64	536
Two times listed on schedule	64	536
Two time zones on schedule	64	536

Miscellaneous Problems

Problem	Quick Fix	Page
Buttons are missing from the toolbar	67	537
Can't find What's New opening screen	65	536
Commands are missing in menus	68	537
Incorrect buttons on toolbar	67	537
Incorrect items in menus	68	537
Need to change toolbar back to default	67	537
Opening screen no longer opens at startup	65	536
The toolbar is in a box in the middle of the screen	66	536
The toolbar is no longer displayed	66	536
The toolbar turned into toolbox	66	536
Want to change menus to default	68	537

Integration Problems

Problem	Quick Fix	Page
Broken link between Excel and Word	71	539
Cannot open Word outline in PowerPoint	69	537
Can't change the name of the buttons on the Shortcut bar	77	540
Can't edit Excel worksheet in Word	76	540
Can't edit linked object	75	540
Can't link Excel file to Word	70	538
Can't rename buttons on the Shortcut bar	77	540
Double-clicking object did not open source application	75	540
Error message when opening Word outline from PowerPoint	69	537
Excel data not lined up in PowerPoint	72	539

(continues)

Integration Problems *Continued*

Problem	Quick Fix	Page
Excel data too large for PowerPoint slide	73	539
Excel won't open when double-clicking linked object in Word	76	540
Excel worksheet did not copy correctly to PowerPoint	72	539
Excel worksheet does not update in Word	70	538
Excel worksheet linked to Word is not updated	71	539
Excel worksheet won't fit on PowerPoint slide	73	539
File in use error message when opening Word outline from PowerPoint	69	537
Find did not locate my document	74	540
Find didn't find a document I know is there	74	540
Linked worksheet does not update in Word	71	539

Printing Problems

Problem	Quick Fix	Page
Blank page prints after document	79	541
Can't print because the print option is grayed out	78	541
Can't print lines around Word table	81	542
Correct date does not print from date field	89	545
Date field is not updated when printing	89	545
Edges of text are cut off when printing	86	544
Excel numbers all pages 1 from Report Manager	88	545
Excel report pages are all numbered 1	88	545
Fonts do not print correctly	82	542
Graphics look terrible when printed	83	543
Gridlines are displayed in Word but not printed	81	542
Laser printer does not have enough memory to print entire slide	84	543
Laser printer only prints half of PowerPoint slide	84	543
Last page is on top after printing	80	541
Lines are jagged when printing graphics	83	543
Need to change print order	80	541
Need to print an Excel chart embedded in a worksheet	87	545
Need to tell printer driver I am using legal paper	85	544
No printer is installed	78	541
Only half of PowerPoint slide will print	84	543
Pages print in reverse order	80	541
Print option is unavailable	78	541
Printer font is different than screen font	82	542
Printer resolution is too low	83	543

File Creating and Saving Problems

System Problems

Installation Problems

1: Halfway through installation, it stopped and said *Installation did not complete successfully*. What do I do now?

Any other application that is running can interfere with the installation. Make sure you close all other applications (especially virus checking software) and run the installation program again.

2: I got part way through installation and Office told me that I didn't have enough disk space.

Office can take up a lot of disk space. The typical installation needs 50 MB of disk space. The compact installation needs 25 MB. There are a few different options you can take at this point. You can click the **Exit Setup** button and try to free up some disk space. Copy files to floppy that you no longer need, and delete the files from your hard drive. Run Setup again. If you were unable to free up enough space, you can install only some of the Office components. Follow these steps to change the setup options:

1. From the Setup dialog box, click the Change Option button.

2. Click the **Compact** button to install only the bare minimum to run Office. Skip the remaining steps and continue with setup. If you would rather choose which options to install, click the **Custom** button. The Microsoft Office for Windows 95 - Custom dialog box appears.

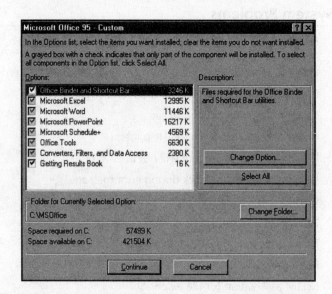

3. Uncheck the options you don't need right now by clicking on the option's check box. Remember, you can always add or remove options after you have installed Office. You can also highlight an option and click on the **Change Option** button to uncheck individual components of an option.

4. Continue to uncheck options until the required disk space is less than the available disk space (you can see the totals at the bottom of the dialog box). Click the **Continue** button to finish the installation.

3: Setup told me I had enough disk space, but when it was almost finished, it told me it couldn't finish because there wasn't enough disk space.

You are probably using a disk compression program such as DriveSpace. When you use a disk compression program, the amount of hard drive space that Setup thinks you have is only an estimate of how much free disk space you actually have. Since DriveSpace doesn't know what kind of files you will be adding or how much they will be able to be compressed, the free space reported is only an educated guess. Even though Setup thought you had enough space, you really didn't. Follow the steps in Quick Fix #2 to free up disk space or deselect some of the Office components.

4: During installation, Setup asked me to insert disk 2. I inserted disk 2 and it asked me again to insert disk 2.

This problem can be caused by two different things. Either you have bad disks or there is a problem with your floppy drive. We'll address the bad disk theory first. Exit the setup program by clicking the **Exit Setup** button and do the following:

> The following commands assume that your drive A is the drive you are installing from. If you are using drive B:, substitute **B** for **A** in the commands.

1. From the **Start** menu in Windows, point to **Programs**, and click **MS-DOS Prompt**.

2. All of the disks except for disk 1 are in the DMF format. This format allows Microsoft to store more information on a floppy disk, but it keeps you from using standard copy commands on the disk. Therefore, you will have to use the EX-TRACT program to test the other disks. Create a temporary folder on your hard drive to test the disks. You can call it OFFTEMP. Type the following to create the folder:

    MD C:\OFFTEMP

3. Copy all files from the Setup disk to the temporary folder by typing:

   Copy A:*.* C:\OFFTEMP

4. You now need to extract the Cabinet files from disk 2 to your temporary folder. Insert disk 2 in your A drive and type the following:

   A:FOR %1 IN (*.*) DO C:\OFFTEMP\EXTRACT /C A:\%1 C:\OFFTEMP\%1

If you cannot extract these files successfully, disk 2 is bad. Contact Microsoft for replacement disks.

> If disk 2 checked out okay and you would like to check the rest of your disks, you can check them using the same command as in step 4. Insert each disk in your A drive and repeat step 4.
>
> If you don't have any problems extracting all of the disks, your disks are okay. You can delete the files from the OFFTEMP folder to free up disk space.

If all of the disks checked out, there could be a problem with how your floppy drive is communicating with your computer. To alleviate the problem, do the following:

1. From the **Start** menu, point to **Programs,** point to **Accessories**, and click on **Notepad**. Use the **Open** command on the **File** menu to open **C:\CONFIG.SYS**. Scroll down to a blank line and add the following command:

   If your 1.44 MB floppy drive is drive A:

   DRIVPARM=/d:0 /f:7

   If your 1.44 MB floppy drive is drive B:

   DRIVPARM=/d:1 /f:7

2. Now, check your CONFIG.SYS file to make sure you do not have the following line:

   DEVICE=DRIVER.SYS

   If you do have this line in CONFIG.SYS, type **REM** in front of the line to disable it.

3. Restart your computer and run Setup again.

If setup still does not work properly, remove the statement you added in step 1 from the CONFIG.SYS file. If you typed **REM** in front of any lines in step 2, delete the **REM** that you added. Contact your computer manufacturer and tell it that change-line support is not functioning properly.

5: Part way through installation I got the error message: *Setup could not open FINDFAST.CPL: it is in use by another application.*

You probably ran Setup from **Add/Remove Programs** in the Control Panel, or you had Control Panel open for another reason. Whatever the reason, having the Control Panel open is your problem. Click **Control Panel** on the taskbar to switch to Control Panel. Close Control Panel and switch back to Setup. Click the **Retry** button in the message box and Setup will continue.

6: I want to make backup copies of the installation disks but I keep getting an error.

Microsoft invented a way to store 1.7 megabytes of data on a 1.44 megabyte floppy drive. This saves it money because it doesn't have to distribute as many disks. Unfortunately, it also means that you cannot make backup copies of the disks. If it's any consolation, Microsoft will replace defective disks at no charge.

7: After I uninstalled one of the Office applications, the subfolders were still on my hard disk.

Office leaves the subfolders and any setup files on the hard disk. Most of these subfolders will be empty, so they really don't take much space. If you leave these subfolders on the hard disk, Office will use any custom settings that you changed in your application if you reinstall it. If you're sure that you won't be installing the program again, or if you don't care about any changes you've made to the setup, you can delete these subfolders.

Word Problems

8: I moved the selection bar to a different paragraph, but when I started typing, it showed up where I was before.

Simply moving the selection bar to a different place does not move the insertion bar (the flashing bold vertical line). You must move the selection bar to where you want it and then click the left mouse button to move the insertion bar. Now when you type, the text will go where you want it to.

9: When I try to add text in the middle of a document, it types over the text that is already there.

You have accidentally hit the insert key on your keyboard. This puts you in Overtype mode, which allows you to type over text you have written. It will be indicated by OVR in the status bar. If you find that Word always starts in Overtype mode (and you don't want it to), follow these steps to change the default:

1. Select **Options** from the **Tools** menu.

2. Click the **Edit** tab in the Options dialog box and uncheck the check box next to **Overtype Mode**.

3. Click **OK** to close the dialog box.

10: All the toolbars and menus are gone. The only thing on my screen is the document. How can I get them back?

You are in full screen mode. In this mode, all that is visible is your document, which can be handy if you just want to type or read what you have written. You can still use the menus if you remember the shortcut keys to bring them up. When you are ready to return to the regular screen, click the button that is located at the bottom right corner of the screen. By the way, if you ever want to try full screen mode again, select **Full Screen** from the **View** menu.

11: I've set up Word to have two columns, but there is only one column on the page.

You are in Normal view. Normal view is the view you will use most of the time. You can see more of what you are typing and Word runs faster in Normal view. Unfortunately, you cannot see graphics characters, headers and footers, or columns in Normal view. Your columns will print correctly even though they do not appear on-screen. To view your columns, choose **Page Layout** from the **View** menu, or click the **Page Layout** button in the lower left corner next to the horizontal scroll bar.

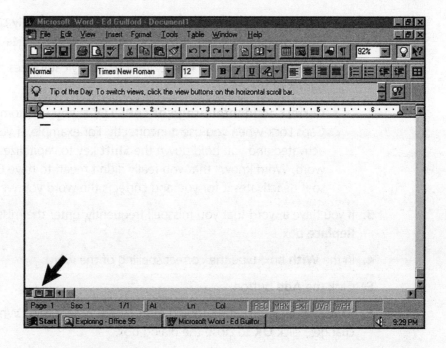

12: When I type things, Word keeps changing them. What's going on?

Word is actually helping you out. This is the AutoCorrect feature. It automatically corrects common typing errors as you enter them. Follow these steps to edit which mistakes Word automatically corrects:

1. Select **AutoCorrect** from the **Tools** menu. The AutoCorrect dialog box appears.

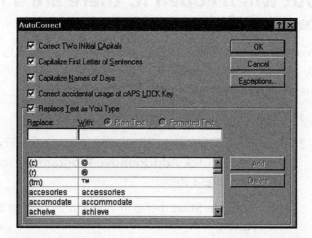

2. In the AutoCorrect dialog box, you can check the check boxes next to the following options to turn them on:

- **Correct TWo INitial CApitals** Automatically changes the second letter to lowercase if you accidentally capitalize the first two letters of a word.

- **Capitalize First Letter of Sentences**   Automatically capitalizes the first letter of the first word when you begin a new sentence.

- **Capitalize Names of Days**   Automatically capitalizes the first letter of the names of the days.

- **Correct accidental usage of cAPS LOCK key**   Automatically deactivates Caps Lock when you use it incorrectly. For example, if you have **Caps Lock** activated and you hold down the **Shift** key to capitalize the first letter of a word, Word knows that you really didn't mean to have Caps Lock activated, so it deactivates it for you and corrects the word you were typing.

3. If you have a word that you misspell frequently, enter the misspelled word in the **Replace** box.

4. In the **With** box, type the correct spelling of the word.

5. Click the **Add** button.

6. Repeat steps 3 through 5 to add more words if necessary. When you finish making changes, click **OK** to close the dialog box.

If you don't like the AutoCorrect feature at all, you can turn it off by clearing the **Replace Text as You Type** check box in the AutoCorrect dialog box.

13: I want to open a document I created in MS Works, but when I open it, there are a lot of funny characters on the screen.

Word did not convert your Works file correctly. The MS Works converter is not installed by default. You can install this converter along with a bunch of others by following these steps:

1. Close all open applications, including Word.

2. From the Office Shortcut Bar, click the puzzle piece in the top left corner of the Shortcut Bar. Click **Add/Remove Programs**. If you are not running the Shortcut bar, follow these steps:

   a. From the **Start** menu in Windows, point to **Settings** and click **Control Panel**.

   b. Double-click the **Add/Remove Programs** icon and click the **Install/Uninstall** tab.

   c. Click **Microsoft Office** from the list of programs and click the **Add/Remove** button.

3. Windows will prompt you to insert your Office disk 1 or Office CD (depending on how you installed it). Insert it into the appropriate drive and click **OK**.

4. When the Microsoft Office for Windows 95 dialog box opens, click the **Add/ Remove** button.

5. In the Options box, click **Converters**, **Filters**, and **Data Access**, and click the **Change Option** button.

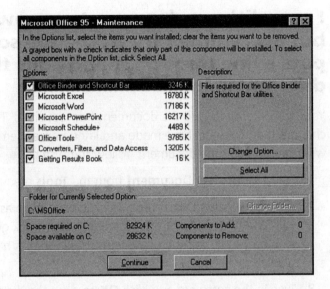

6. In the **Options** box, click **Converters**, and click the **Change Option** button again.

7. In the **Options** box, check the check box next to **Works for Windows 3.0** or **Works for Windows 4.0** (if you're unsure which version of Works you were using, check them both). You can also check other converters if you think you might need them.

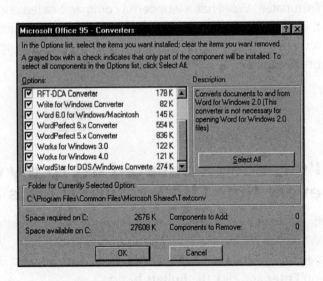

8. Click **OK**. Click **OK** again, and click **Continue**.

9. A message box will pop up telling you when Office setup is complete. Click **OK** to close the message box.

The next time you try to open your Works document, it will be converted correctly.

14: I am editing a document my coworker gave me, but every time I try to change something, Word puts a line through it and adds the new text in a different color.

Your coworker protected the document from revisions. This allows them to see the changes that reviewers have made and later merge them into the document. If you want to unprotect the document, follow these steps:

1. Select **Unprotect Document** from the **Tools** menu.

2. If the **Unprotect Document** dialog box pops up asking you for a password, you will have to get it from your coworker. Good luck getting it, though. If they wanted you to edit the document, they wouldn't have protected it in the first place.

3. Type in the password and click **OK** to close the dialog box. The document will now be unprotected.

15: I accidentally deleted a whole paragraph. Is there any way to get it back?

Fortunately, Word has a wonderful command called undo. You can select **Undo** from the **Tools** menu, or click the **Undo** button on the toolbar. If you did something else after you deleted the paragraph, you can keep selecting undo until it brings the paragraph back.

16: I've added a bulleted list to my document. Now every time I hit a return it adds a new bullet.

If you want a blank line between bullets you can hold the **Shift** key and press **Enter**. When you release the Shift key and press **Enter** again, Word will start a new line beginning with a bullet. When you finish with your list, move to the next line by pressing **Enter** and click the **Bullets** button.

17: I want to get rid of the bullet, but Word won't let me delete it.

To remove a bullet, move the insertion bar next to the bullet and click the **Bullets** button. Or choose **Bullets and Numbering** from the **Format** menu, and click the **Remove** button. If you want to remove bullets from more than one item, highlight the items where you no longer want bullets, and click the **Bullets** button. You can use the same procedure for a numbered list except click the **Numbering** button instead of the **Bullets** button.

18: I'm entering text in a table, but it won't all fit. Can't the table automatically adjust to fit my text?

You need to change the row height of your table to Auto. This will allow the height of the row to grow large enough to fit the contents. Follow these steps to change the row height:

1. Highlight the row(s) of your table that you want to change. If you want to select the entire table, click in the table and, with Num Lock off, press **ALT+5** on the numeric keypad.

2. Select **Cell Height and Width** from the **Table** menu.

3. Click the **Row** tab, and select **Auto** from the drop-down list in the **Height of Row** box.

4. Click **OK** to close the dialog box.

19: I changed the paragraph alignment to justified. Now there are big gaps between the words.

When you use justified alignment, Word makes the left and right edges of your paragraph even with the left and right margins. The only way Word can do this is by adding space between words to spread them out. To avoid large gaps, you must use hyphenation. The easiest way to hyphenate is to let Word do it for you automatically. Follow these steps to turn on automatic hyphenation:

1. Select **Hyphenation** from the **Tools** menu.

2. In the Hyphenation dialog box, check the **Automatically Hyphenate Document** check box.

3. Click **OK** to close the dialog box. Word will go through your document and hyphenate words at the appropriate places.

If you would like more control over your hyphenation, you can have Word ask you what words you want to hyphenate. To do this, click the **Manual** button in the Hyphenate dialog box. Word will go through your document one line at a time and suggest words to hyphenate. When the suggested word appears, there will be a hyphen in all the places it is possible to hyphenate the word. Click on one of the hyphens in the word to select the desired hyphenation point. Click **Yes** to hyphenate the word, **No** to not hyphenate the word, or **Cancel** to quit manual hyphenation.

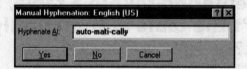

20: While using the spelling checker I accidentally added a word to the custom dictionary that was spelled incorrectly. How can I change it?

You need to edit your custom dictionary to delete the incorrectly spelled word. The dictionary can be edited as a Word document. Follow these steps to open your custom dictionary:

1. Choose **Options** from the **Tools** menu.

2. Click the **Spelling** tab in the Options dialog box and click the **Custom Dictionaries** button (see the previous Quick Fix for a picture of the Custom Dictionaries dialog box).

3. In the Custom Dictionaries dialog box, click the check box next to the name of your custom dictionary (it is usually called CUSTOM.DIC) to check it. Click the **Edit** button.

4. A message box will open telling you that Word will disable automatic spell checking when you edit the dictionary. Click **OK** to continue.

5. Your custom dictionary will open in Word. You will see a single column of words. Scroll through the dictionary until you find the word that you incorrectly added to the list. Highlight the word and press the delete key to erase it. If there are other words that you do not want in the dictionary, go ahead and delete them too.

6. When you are finished editing the dictionary, choose **Close** from the **File** menu. Word will ask you if you want to save the changes. Click **OK** to save the dictionary. Word will tell you that the document contains formatting that cannot be saved in text format. Click the **Yes** button. Word will then tell you that your dictionary is a Text Only document. Click the **Text Only** button to save the dictionary in Text Only format.

7. Since automatic spell checking was disabled in step 4, you will need to manually turn it back on. Choose **Options** from the **Tools** menu. Click the **Spelling** tab and check the check box next to **Automatic Spell Checking**. Click **OK** to close the Options dialog box.

21: I've looked up several meanings in the Thesaurus, and I can't remember what the original word was.

Click the drop-down box in the **Looked Up** section of the Thesaurus dialog box. The word you started with is always at the top of the list.

22: The last two lines of my paragraph are on the second page. How can I keep them all on the first page?

If you have just a line or two on the last page of the document, there is an easy way to move those lines to the previous page. Select **Print Preview** from the **File** menu and click the **Shrink to Fit** button in the toolbar. This will compress the lines on the previous page to allow all the lines to fit. Use the **Magnifier** tool to make sure you are happy with the appearance of the shrunken lines. If you're not, select **Undo** from the **Edit** menu to return your document to regular size.

23: There is a blank line at the end of all my paragraphs, but Word won't let me delete them.

Word allows you to automatically add spacing before or after a paragraph. With this option you can separate your paragraphs without having to manually add a line each time you start a new paragraph. To set the spacing, follow these steps:

1. Highlight the paragraph(s) you want to set the spacing for.

2. Click the **Paragraph** option in the **Format** menu.

3. In the Paragraph dialog box, click the **Indents and Spacing** tab. In the Spacing section, you can either add space before or after the paragraph using the **Before** or **After** options. The spacing is given in point size. If you're using a 12-point font, 6 points would be half a line; 12 points would be a whole line. To eliminate the spacing, set these values to zero.

4. When you finish, click **OK** to close the dialog box.

If you find this problem occurring in all your paragraphs, you may want to change the Style. Click in the paragraph that you need to change the Style and choose **Style** from the **Format** menu. Click the **Modify** button in the Style dialog box. In the Modify Style dialog box, click the **Format** button and click **Paragraph**. Adjust the spacing as described in step 3 above and click **OK**. Click **OK** again and click **Apply**. This will change the Style for all paragraphs that are based on the Style.

24: I see dots between all my words and paragraph marks at the end my paragraphs. How can I get rid of them?

You have inadvertently clicked the **Show/Hide** button on the toolbar. With this button activated, you see paragraph marks at the end of each paragraph and dots to indicate spaces, but these characters will not print with your document. If you don't want to look at them, simply click the **Show/Hide** button again.

25: I have changed to a larger font and can only see half the width of a page at a time. How can I see more of the page?

You can see more of the document by adjusting the Zoom Control on the toolbar. If you want to see the entire width of the page, click the arrow to the right of the Zoom Control box and click **Page Width**. Or you can experiment with different percentages to get the size you like the most. Even though your type looks smaller on-screen, it will print full size.

26: After I move a table, I can't see enough of my document.

Sometimes, when you move a table, it shifts the view point of the document past the left or right margins. This shows a column of blank space to the left or right of your text. To display the document correctly, click to the right of the horizontal scroll box; then move the scroll box all the way to the left.

27: When I tried to move one item in a numbered list, the text moved but the number didn't. How can I get them to move together?

To move the number along with the text, you have to include the paragraph mark with the selection. To be sure that you have selected the paragraph mark, click the **Show/Hide** button on the toolbar to make the paragraph marks visible. Select the paragraph mark along with your text, and the number or bullet will move with the text.

28: I changed the font at the beginning of the document, but it keeps changing back to the original font.

Word will revert back to the default font for the template you used to create your document. One way to change the font throughout your document is to wait until you have typed the whole document and then select the entire document by pressing **Ctrl+A**. Now, change the font. If you always want to use this font for the template your document is based on, follow these steps to change the default font:

1. Choose **Font** from the **Format** menu.

2. Choose the desired font from the dialog box and click the **Default** button. A message box opens asking if you are sure you want to change the default font. Remember, this will change the default font in all documents you have created using this template. If you are sure you want to change the default font, click **Yes**.

29: I selected a block of text and my cursor changed to an arrow with a box around the tail. What's happening?

This is the *drag-and-drop* pointer. Drag-and-drop allows you to save time by not having to click the Cut and Paste buttons to move a block of text. To use drag-and-drop, follow these steps:

1. Select the block of text you want to move.

2. Click the text again and hold down the mouse button to bring up the drag-and-drop pointer.

3. Move the cursor to the point in the document where you want the beginning of the selected text to be moved to. Release the mouse button, and the block of text moves to the new location.

If you accidentally got the drag-and-drop cursor, immediately move the cursor into the selected text and click the mouse again. This will cancel your selection. If you don't use drag-and-drop, and this feature annoys you, you can turn it off. Choose **Options** from the **Tools** menu and click the **Edit** tab. Uncheck the Drag-and-Drop Text Editing check box and click **OK**.

30: I want to add page numbers, but Page Numbers is gray in the Insert menu.

You are in Outline view. You cannot add page numbers in outline view, so choose Normal or Page Layout view by clicking on their button in the lower left corner of the window.

31: When I print a Word document, it numbers page 1. How can I get it to only number page 2 and greater?

By default, when you add page numbers to a document, Word numbers all of the pages. In some documents, however, you may not want to number the first page. Fortunately, there is an easy way to suppress the page number on the first page. Follow these steps:

1. Choose **Page Numbers** from the **Insert** menu.

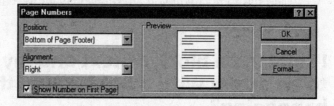

2. In the Page Numbers dialog box uncheck the **Show Number on First Page** check box.

3. Click **OK** to close the dialog box.

32: When I type in (c), Word changes it to ©.

AutoCorrect is changing the text for you. With this feature, you can easily insert the © symbol. Unfortunately, it is very difficult to insert **(c)**. If you need to use **(c)** in your document, follow these steps to tell AutoCorrect that you don't want to change it to ©:

1. From the **Tools** menu, choose **AutoCorrect**.

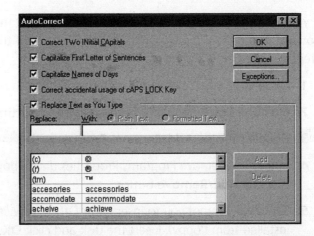

2. At the bottom of the AutoCorrect dialog box, select the (c) entry.

3. You now have two choices, you can completely delete the © shortcut, or you can define a different key sequence to type to make the © symbol appear.

- To delete the © shortcut, click the **Delete** button.

- To define a new sequence, type the new sequence (for example, **((c))** in the **Replace** box and click the **Add** button. Now highlight the original **(c)** and click the **Delete** button.

4. Click **OK** to close the dialog box.

33: I want to use a wizard, but when I try to open a new document, the wizard I want is not available.

It's not obvious where Word keeps the wizards when you are opening a new document. They do not all appear when you choose **New** from the **File** menu. Try clicking through all the tabs in the New dialog box. Each tab has a different set of templates and wizards.

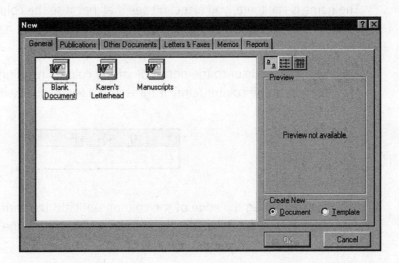

If you still can't find the wizard you are looking for, it may not have been installed when you installed Office. In a typical installation, not all of the wizards install. Follow these steps to install more wizards:

1. Close all of your open applications.

2. From the **Start** menu in Windows, point to **Settings** and click **Control Panel**.

3. Double-click the **Add/Remove Programs** icon.

4. In the Add/Remove Programs Properties dialog box, click **Microsoft Office** and click the **Add/Remove** button.

5. Setup will prompt you to insert your Office for Windows 95 CD (or disk 1 if you installed from floppy). Insert the disk and click **OK**.

6. In the Setup dialog box, click the **Add/Remove** button.

7. Click **Microsoft** Word in the **Options** box and click the **Change Option** button.

8. Click **Wizards**, **Templates**, and **Letters** in the **Options** box and click the **Change Option** button again.

9. Scroll through the Options list and click the wizards you want to install. Click **OK**.

10. Click **OK** to close the dialog box, and click the **Continue** button.

11. A message box will open telling you that Microsoft Office Setup was completed successfully. Click OK to close the message box.

Excel Problems

34: If I type a long name in Excel, the end of it cuts off when I type something in the next column.

The name is still there; you just can't see it all because the column is not wide enough to show the full name. The easiest way to change the column width is with your mouse. Follow these steps:

1. Move your cursor to the right side of the column heading (the gray-lettered area at the top of the column) until it turns into a vertical bar with arrows on each side.

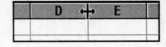

2. Click-and-drag the edge of the column until it is the width you want. If you double-click the right side, the column width will change to fit the largest value you have in that column.

35: I set up a calculation to add the numbers in a column, but Excel displays ########.

The result of your calculation is too wide to fit in the cell. Change the column width using the technique in Quick Fix #34 until it is wide enough to display the result.

36: If I type in *100000000* Excel displays *1E+08*. How can I get it back to *100000000*?

You need to format the cells to display the number in the way you prefer. Follow these steps to change the number format:

1. Highlight the range of cells you want to format.

2. From the **Format** menu, choose **Cells** and click the **Number** tab.

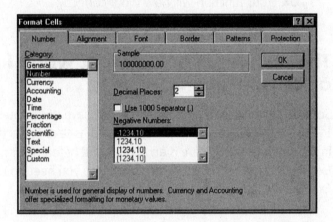

3. In the Format Cells dialog box, choose **Number** in the **Category** box. There is a sample at the top of the dialog box that shows you how your numbers will look with the selected format.

4. If you like, you can also use the 1000 separator to make your number look like 100,000,000. Just select the check box next to **Use 1000 Separator (,)**. You can also change the number of decimal places that are in the **Decimal Places** box.

5. Once you have the number looking like you want it, click **OK** to close the dialog box.

After you finish, if the number looks like ########, your column width is too small. Use the technique in Quick Fix #35 to change the column width.

37: I entered a function in a cell, but Excel displays #NAME?.

There are two things that could be causing this problem. First, make sure that you have spelled the function correctly. If it isn't misspelled, you may have used a range name that doesn't exist. To check, click the arrow toward the left edge of the formula bar to drop down a list of valid range names. If there are no names on the list, or the one you specified isn't there, you need to define the range you wanted to calculate. Follow these steps to define a range:

1. Highlight the range of cells you want to name.

2. Point to **Name** on the **Insert** menu and click **Define**.

3. In the Define Name dialog box, type in a name for your range in the **Names in Workbook** box (make sure it's the same name that's in your function) and click **OK**. Your function will now work correctly.

38: The answer is not correct when I calculate a range of cells.

Some of the entries in the range may not have been entered correctly. Check each cell to ensure that the numbers are not stored as text. To do this, click the cell and look it up in the formula bar. If there is an apostrophe before your number, it is formatted as text. Excel won't use text in your calculations, so you need to remove the apostrophe to let Excel know you have a number in the cell.

39: I entered a calculation in a cell, but it displays the text of the calculation instead of the answer.

You have forgotten to put an equal sign before your formula. Excel needs this to let it know there is a formula in the cell. Edit the cell, insert the equal sign, and your calculation will work correctly.

40: When I entered a date in a cell, Excel changed it to a number.

Most of the time, when you enter a date in a cell, Excel is smart enough to know that it is a date. However, if you already have the cell formatted in something other than date format, Excel will change it to the format you have specified. Follow these steps to fix the problem:

1. Highlight the range of cells that contain the dates.

2. Select **Cells** from the **Format** menu and click the **Number** tab.

3. In the Format Cells dialog box, select **Date** from the **Category** box and select the desired date format from the **Type** box.

4. Click **OK** to close the dialog box.

41: I am trying to enter 01214 (a ZIP Code) into my worksheet, but the first zero doesn't display.

By default, Excel drops all leading zeros in your numbers. To display the leading zeros, you need to use the ZIP Code format for the range of cells that contains your ZIP Codes. Follow these steps to change the format:

1. Highlight the range of cells that contain the ZIP Codes.

2. Choose the **Cells** option from the **Format** menu and click the **Number** tab.

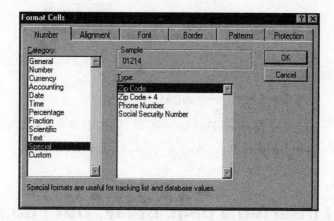

3. In the Format Cells dialog box, select **Special** in the **Category** box.

4. In the **Type** box, select **Zip Code** or **Zip Code + 4** (depending on which one you are using).

5. Click **OK** to close the dialog box.

42: I changed some numbers in a column, but the total didn't change.

You probably have automatic calculation turned off; this is a useful way of speeding up your work if you have a very large worksheet because Excel can take awhile to recalculate. To see the correct total press **F9**. Excel will recalculate the worksheet. If you want Excel to calculate automatically, follow these steps:

1. Choose **Options** from the **Tools** menu and click the **Calculation** tab.

2. Choose **Automatic** from the Calculation section of the Options dialog box.

3. Click **OK** to close the dialog box.

43: There is a flashing bar in one of the cells. What does it mean?

If you double-click a cell you can edit its contents right in the cell. This is a convenient way to edit because you don't have to keep moving to the formula bar when you are editing cells. The flashing bar simply indicates you are in Edit mode and shows you where the insertion point is.

44: I want to sort my data, but Excel sorts the column headings too.

There are two ways to fix this problem. The easiest way is to select the range of cells you want to sort (don't include the headings) and click the **Sort Ascending** or **Sort Descending** button.

Another way is to do the following:

1. Select **Sort** from the **Data** menu.

2. In the **My List Has** section of the Sort dialog box, click **Header Row**.

3. Click **OK** to close the dialog box and sort the data.

45: I inserted a page break, but I don't want it there anymore. How can I remove it?

This can be a little tricky because the **Remove Page Break** option doesn't even appear in the **Insert** menu until you select the correct cell. To select a horizontal page break, select a cell directly below the page break. To select a vertical page break, select a cell directly to the right of the page break. To remove the page break, choose **Remove Page Break** from the **Insert** menu.

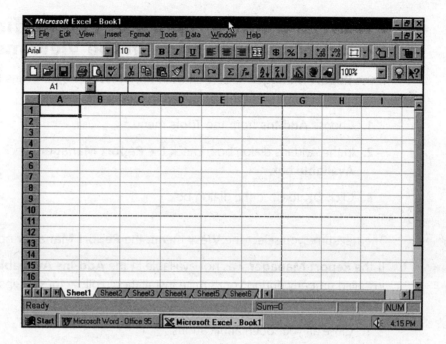

46: I entered a formula, and Excel displays the message: *Error in formula*.

Excel will try to help you by moving the cursor to the part of the formula that has the error. If you're not sure what the problem is, click the **Help** button in the error message dialog box. Excel will give you a list of common mistakes to look for, like having the wrong number of arguments in a function, invalid characters, missing operand (such as =2+3+), or an external reference without a workbook name (such as =!B2). These types of mistakes can be frustrating to find because they usually involve a simple typing error or a missing sign. If you get tired of looking at the formula, remove the equals sign at the beginning of the formula and press **Enter**. This will allow you to continue working and come back to the formula later. When you are ready to tackle the formula again, make sure you reenter the equals sign.

47: When I enter a formula, Excel displays the error message: *Parentheses do not match*.

Remember, when you use parentheses in a formula, they must equal out. That is, for every open parenthesis there must be a closed parenthesis. Carefully check your formula to be sure you have used the parentheses correctly. To have Excel help you find the missing parenthesis, click at the left edge of the formula in the formula bar. Move the insertion point through the formula with the right arrow key. As you move through the formula, matching parentheses will bold. This may tip you off to where you need to add the missing parenthesis.

48: I want to create a report, but I can't find the Report Manager option in the View menu.

If the **Report Manager** option is not in the **View** menu, it means the Report Manager is not loaded with the Add-Ins. To load it, follow these steps:

1. Choose **Add-Ins** from the **Tools** menu.

2. In the Add-Ins dialog box, check the **Report Manager** check box in the **Add-Ins Available** box.

3. Click **OK** to close the dialog box.

The next time you select the **View** menu, the **Report Manager** option will be available.

If the **Report Manager** was not available in the **Add-Ins Available** box, it was not installed properly during your Office installation. Follow these steps to install the Report Manager:

1. Close all your open applications.

2. From the **Start** menu in Windows, point to **Settings** and click **Control Panel**.

3. Double-click the **Add/Remove Programs** icon.

4. In the Add/Remove Programs Properties dialog box, click **Microsoft Office** and click the **Add/Remove** button.

5. Setup will prompt you to insert your Office for Windows 95 CD (or disk 1 if you installed from floppy). Insert the disk and click **OK**.

6. In the Setup dialog box, click the **Add/Remove** button.

7. Click **Microsoft Excel** in the **Options** box and click the **Change Option** button.

8. Click **Add-ins** in the **Options** box and click the **Change Option** button again.

9. Check the **Report Manager** check box and click **OK**.

10. Click **OK** to close the dialog box, and click the **Continue** button.

11. A message box opens telling you that Microsoft Office Setup was completed successfully. Click **OK** to close the message box.

49: I tried to center text across several columns, but the Center Across Selection command did not work.

The **Center Across Selection** command will not work properly if the cells you are centering across (except for the cell with the data in it) are not empty. To be sure there is no data in the cells, select the seemingly empty cells and press the **Delete** key. The easiest way to center across the selection is to highlight the range of cells you want to center across (including the cell with the data in it) and click the **Center Across Columns** button in the toolbar.

PowerPoint Problems

50: I accidentally selected the wrong template in the wizard I used to create my presentation. How can I change it?

It's easy to change the design template in a presentation. Just follow these steps:

1. Choose **Apply Design Template** from the **Format** menu.

2. In the Apply Design Template dialog box, choose the desired template from the list in the **Name** box. If you're not sure which one you want, click a template and you will see a preview of what it will look like.

3. Once you have chosen the correct template, click the **Apply** button.

51: I accidentally deleted a slide from my presentation. How can I get it back?

Choose **Undo** from the **Edit** menu to bring back the slide. If you've done a few things since you deleted the slide, keep selecting **Undo** until the slide comes back. Unfortunately, you will lose anything you have done after you deleted the slide.

52: When I add a long line of text to my slide, it goes off the edge of the slide.

You have entered your text as a label instead of in a text box. You did this by selecting the **Text Tool** from the drawing toolbar and clicking and releasing the mouse button somewhere on your slide. When you entered the text as a label, the text box expanded to fit whatever you were typing and did not wrap to the next line. If you would rather have the text wrap automatically, you need to create a text box. To do this, click the **Text Tool** button and click the mouse button at the upper left corner of where you want the box to start. While holding the mouse button down, drag the box to the desired size. Now, the text you type will wrap when it gets to the edge of your text box.

53: I want to remove the bullets from my slide, but PowerPoint won't let me.

To remove the bullets, select the lines beside the bullets you want to remove and click the **Bullet On/Off** button in the toolbar.

54: I added transitions in my slide presentation, but they are too fast to see.

The transition speed is set to fast by default. You can change the speed to slow or medium if fast is not effective. Follow these steps to change the transition speed:

1. Switch to Slide Sorter View by clicking the **Slide Sorter View** button in the lower left corner of the window.

2. Select all the slides that have too fast of a transition and click the **Slide Transition** button.

3. In the Slide Transition dialog box select **Slow** or **Medium** in the **Speed** section.

4. Click **OK** to close the dialog box.

55: I have some hidden slides in my presentation. How can I show them?

Hidden slides can be very useful tools for presentations when you may need to show a little more data than you expected. When your presentation gets to the slide just before the hidden slide, click the right mouse button to bring up the menu. Point to **Go To** and click **Hidden Slide**. If you'd rather use the keyboard just press the **H** key.

56: PowerPoint shows a tip every time I start it. How can I tell PowerPoint to stop showing me tips?

The easiest way is to uncheck the **Show Tips at Startup** check box when the tip comes up. If the Tip of the Day screen is gone, choose **Tip of the Day** from the **Help** menu. This will bring up the next tip and allow you to uncheck the check box.

57: I installed some new ClipArt on my computer, but I can't find it in the ClipArt Gallery.

Whenever you install new ClipArt, you have to add it to the ClipArt Gallery. Follow these steps to add your new pictures:

1. Choose ClipArt from the **Insert** menu and click the **Organize** button.

2. Click the **Add Pictures** button in the Organize ClipArt dialog box.

3. If PowerPoint recognized the ClipArt package that you installed, it will tell you that it found it. In the Add New Pictures dialog box, click the **Add All** button to add the new ClipArt package to the ClipArt gallery. When PowerPoint is finished adding the pictures, they will be available for use.

If PowerPoint did not recognize the new ClipArt package or you created your own pictures to add to the gallery, you will be prompted to input the drive and folder where the ClipArt is located. Follow these steps:

1. In the Add Pictures to ClipArt Gallery dialog box, select the drive and folder where the ClipArt is located and select the name(s) of the files you would like to add from the list. You can select more than one file by holding the **Ctrl** key and clicking on the files you want. After you have selected the files you want, click **Open**.

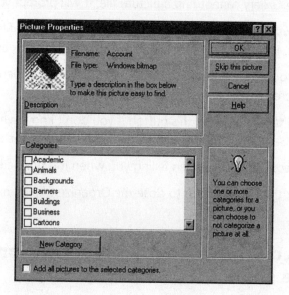

2. If you want, type in a description of the picture in the **Description** box.

3. Click the category that you want your picture to be in (it's easier to find your pictures later if you categorize). You can check more than one category or none at all. If you would like to add a new category, click the **New Category** button.

4. Click **OK**.

If you selected more than one picture in step one, repeat steps 2 through 4 until PowerPoint categorizes all of the pictures. Your pictures will now be available to insert in your presentation.

58: When I clicked on a picture in the ClipArt gallery and tried to insert it, PowerPoint told me that it couldn't find the picture.

The pictures in the ClipArt gallery do not match the actual ClipArt that is on your drive. You may have deleted some ClipArt or it could have been removed when you uninstalled a program. Click the **Cancel** button to close the Cannot Insert Picture message box. If you want to update the ClipArt gallery so it contains only pictures that are actually on your hard drive, follow these steps:

1. From the ClipArt Gallery dialog box, click the **Organize** button.

2. In the Organize ClipArt dialog box, click the **Update Pictures** button.

3. In the Update dialog box, click **Check network drives** if you want the Gallery to check your network for pictures, or click **Check removable drives** to check floppy drives, Bernoulli drives, CD-ROM drives, and so on. Click the **Update** button.

4. If the Gallery cannot find a picture file, it will prompt you to:

    Browse   Click this button if you moved the picture file to a different folder or hard drive. Enter the correct folder in the Open dialog box and click the **Open** button.

    Remove File   Click this button if the picture has been removed and you no longer want the preview in the Gallery.

    Skip this File   Click this button if you don't know what happened to the picture. The Gallery will leave the preview in and continue the search for other pictures.

5. A message box will open telling you when it is finished updating the Gallery. Click **OK**.

6. Click the **Close** button to close the Organize ClipArt dialog box.

59: I added ClipArt to my presentation, but it fills up the whole slide.

When you insert ClipArt on your slide, it is always the same size. It's pretty easy to change the size after you insert it. Just follow these steps:

1. Click the picture to bring up the sizing handles (sizing handles are the little squares that surround the picture).

2. Using the mouse, point to one of the sizing handles until the mouse pointer turns into a double-headed arrow. Click the left mouse button and drag the picture to the desired size. Use the corner sizing handles if you want the picture to change proportionally.

3. When you get the picture to the correct size, you may need to move it to a different location on the slide. Just click in the middle of the picture and drag the entire picture to the desired location.

60: I can't select some of the objects on my slide.

The objects you can't select are probably on the slide master. To select these objects, point to **Master** on the **View** menu and click **Slide Master**, or hold the **Shift** key and click the **Slide View** button to the left of the horizontal scroll bar. You will now be able to change the objects in the slide master. To get back to your slides, choose **Slides** from the **View** menu or click the **Slide View** button. Remember, any changes you make to the slide master will affect all of the slides in your presentation.

Schedule+ Problems

61: When I started Schedule+, it asked me if I wanted to work in group-enabled mode. What does that mean?

Schedule+ is a powerful scheduling program that allows you to manage your time more efficiently. It works well as a personal scheduling program. However, if you're using Microsoft Mail, you can schedule meetings and send requests to your coworkers and then track the status of their replies. Other Schedule+ users can view your schedule and schedule meetings with you if you give them permission. If you are connected to a Mail server, click the **Yes, work in group-enabled mode** option. If you're not connected to a Mail server, or you don't want to use this option, click the **No, work alone** option. If you will always use the same option, and you don't want this dialog box to open again, check the **Don't ask me this question again** check box. When you select the appropriate option, click **OK**.

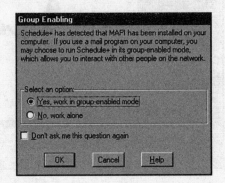

62: I want to view the yearly calendar, but the Yearly tab is not displayed.

Schedule+ allows you to customize the tabs that appear along the left edge of the window. You can add tabs for the views you will use most often. Follow these steps to change the tabs:

1. From the **View** menu, choose **Tab Gallery**.

2. In the Available tabs box, click on **Yearly Calendar** and click the **Add** button.

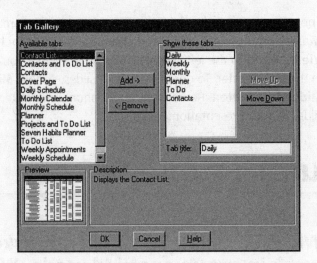

3. Click on **Yearly** in the **Show these tabs** box and use the **Move Up** or **Move Down** button to move the **Yearly** tab to the desired place. The tabs will appear in the same order as the list in the **Show these tabs** box.

4. Click **OK**. The **Yearly** tab will now be available.

63: My coworker can't view my schedule.

In order for other users on your network to access your schedule you must give them permission to do so. You can set one set of permissions for everyone, or you can give specific permissions to individual users. Follow these steps to change the permissions:

1. Choose **Set Access Permissions** from the **Tools** menu.

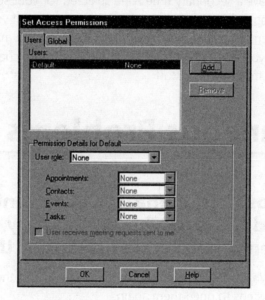

2. Choose the desired user from the list in the **Users** box. Choose **Default** to set the permissions for all of the users. If you need to add a user to the list, use the **Add** button.

3. Choose a desired role from the drop-down list in the **User role** box. The following is an explanation of the roles:

   • **None**   Gives no permissions to the user.

   • **Read**   The user can read your schedule except for private items.

   • **Create**   The user can read and add items to your schedule except for private items.

   • **Modify**   The user can read and change items on your schedule except for private items.

   • **Delegate**   The user can read and change all items in the chosen area.

- **Owner**   The user can do everything to your schedule that you can do except send and receive meeting messages for you.

- **Delegate Owner**   The user can do everything you can do.

- **Custom**   Allows you to set custom permissions using the **Appointments, Contact, Events,** and **Tasks** box.

4. Click **OK** to close the Set Access Permissions dialog box.

64: There are two different time columns listed on my schedule.

You have a secondary time zone selected for your schedule. The secondary time zone will appear on your Daily and Weekly calendars. If you frequently work with others in a different time zone, the secondary time zone can make it easy to tell what time they are on. If you find the extra time column confusing, choose **Second Time Zone** from the **View** menu to turn it off.

Miscellaneous Problems

65: I closed the What's New opening screen before I read it. Now when I open my Office program, the opening screen is no longer there.

The What's new screens give a great overview of the new features in Office. Follow these steps to open them again:

1. Choose **Answer Wizard** from the **Help** menu.

2. In the Help Topics dialog box, type in **What's new** in the first dialog box and click **Search**.

3. From the list of topics, select **What's new in** (whatever office program you are in).

4. Click the **Display** button to open the What's New screen.

66: The toolbar is in a box in the middle of the screen. How can I get it back under the menu bar?

If you double-click the toolbar it will turn into a toolbox. You can move the toolbox anywhere on the screen. Double-click in the title bar of the toolbox to change it back into a toolbar. If you can't find the toolbar at all, select **Toolbars** from the **View** menu, check the **Standard** check box, and click **OK**.

67: My toolbar no longer has the buttons I need. How can I get it back to the original configuration?

If you or someone else has changed the configuration of your toolbar, it's easy to reset the default configuration. Follow these steps:

1. Select **Toolbars** from the **View** menu.

2. In the Toolbars dialog box click the toolbar you want to change in the **Toolbars** section.

3. Click the **Reset** button.

4. A dialog box will open asking you what documents you want to change the toolbar for. Click **OK** to change the toolbar for all your documents.

5. Click **OK** to close the dialog box. Your toolbar will be as good as new.

68: Someone customized my menu. How can I get it back to the way it used to be?

To reset your menus, follow these steps:

1. Choose **Customize** from the **Tools** menu and click the **Menus** tab.

2. In the Customize dialog box, click the **Reset All** button. Word will ask you if you're sure you want to reset your menus. Click **Yes** and your menus will be back to their factory configuration.

Integration Problems

69: When I try to open a Word outline in PowerPoint it tells me that it cannot modify the file because it is in use.

You probably forgot to close the file in Word. PowerPoint cannot open a file that is open in another program. Click over to Word using your taskbar and close the file. Now you should have no problem using the outline in PowerPoint.

70: When I copy an Excel worksheet into Word, it doesn't update automatically when I edit it in Excel.

You need to create a *link* between Excel and Word. When you link an object, Excel will automatically update your worksheet. To link your Excel worksheet to Word, follow these steps:

1. Open the document in Word and move the insertion point where you want the Excel worksheet to be inserted.

2. If you want to insert an entire worksheet that you already have made up, choose **Object** from the **Insert** menu and click the **Create from File** tab.

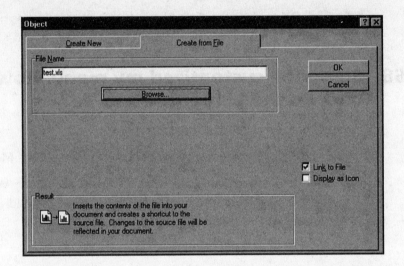

3. Enter the name and folder of your Excel file in the **File Name** box (if you don't remember where it is, click the **Browse** button). Be sure to check the **Link to File** check box.

4. Click **OK**. This will establish the link between the two files. Any changes that you make to your worksheet in Excel will be reflected in the Word document.

If you would rather link only part of the worksheet, follow these steps:

1. Select the desired range in Excel and click the **Copy** button on the toolbar.

2. Open Word and bring up the document that you want to link the Excel worksheet to. Move the insertion bar to the desired location in your document and choose **Paste Special** from the **Edit** menu.

3. When the Paste Special dialog box appears, choose **Microsoft Excel Worksheet Object** from the **As** box and click **Paste Link**.

4. Click **OK**, and the selected range in your worksheet will be linked to your Word document.

71: Now that I have my worksheet linked to Word, it still won't update when I edit it in Excel.

Somehow ,the link between the files has been broken. This may have happened if you renamed the Excel file or moved it to a different folder. You can try to relink the files by doing the following:

1. Choose **Links** from the **Edit** menu.

2. In the Links dialog box, click the link you are having trouble with in the **Source File** box.

3. Click the **Change Source** button and choose the name and folder where your worksheet is located.

4. Click the **Open** button.

5. Click the **Update Now** button to update the link. If the link is still not updated, you'll have to delete the Excel worksheet from your document and insert it again using the techniques in Quick Fix #68.

72: When I tried to copy an Excel worksheet into PowerPoint, the data was not lined up.

When you pasted the Excel data into PowerPoint, you probably used the **Paste** command from the **Edit** menu. This will not work correctly because the Paste command tells PowerPoint that you are pasting plain old text. You need to let PowerPoint know that you are pasting Excel data. To do this, follow these steps:

1. Highlight the range of data in Excel and click the **Copy** button in the toolbar.

2. Switch to PowerPoint, click where you want to insert your Excel data, and choose **Paste Special** from the **Edit** menu to bring up the Paste Special dialog box.

3. Click **Microsoft Excel Worksheet Object** in the **As** box (it should already be highlighted) and click **OK**. Your worksheet will be inserted as an object. If you need to edit the data, double-click in the middle of the Excel object.

73: I want to copy an Excel worksheet into PowerPoint, but it won't fit on the slide.

Edit your worksheet to remove any unnecessary data before you copy it to Power-Point. If you need all the data, you can reduce the size after you have inserted it into PowerPoint. First, be sure to copy your worksheet as an Excel Object (see Quick Fix #70). To change the size, single-click in the middle of the Excel worksheet in PowerPoint. You will notice little squares surrounding the picture. These are called sizing handles (see Quick Fix #61 for a picture of sizing handles). To change the size, click one of the sizing handles and drag the edge/corner until the data is the desired size. Be careful shrinking your data too much, though; it may make it so small that it is unreadable to your audience.

74: I used Find to search for a document, but it didn't find it.

You may not be searching enough places. Try choosing a drive in the Look in box and check the Include subfolders check box. It may take longer to search all the subfolders, but if the file is on the drive, it should find it. Also, click the **Date Modified** tab and select **All files**. Click the **Advanced** tab. Check that the **Of type** box is **All Files and Folders** and the **Containing text** and **Size is** boxes are blank. This will give you the widest possible search.

75: I want to edit a linked object, but nothing happens when I double-click it.

Whenever you double-click a linked object, the source application should open to edit the object (the source application is the one that created the object). If the source application doesn't open when you double-click the object, choose **Links** from the **Edit** menu. Click the **Open Source** button to bring up the source application.

76: When I double-click an Excel worksheet I have embedded in Word, it looks more like a worksheet, but Excel never opened.

This is one of those cases where Word and Excel work so well together that you can't even tell they are two different programs. When you double-click your embedded worksheet, look up at the toolbar. You'll notice that it is the Excel toolbar even though it looks like you are still in Word. Also, your embedded worksheet will change to show your column and row headings. You can edit the worksheet as though you were in Excel. When you are done, click somewhere else in your document and the Word toolbar will once again appear.

77: I can't change the name of the buttons on the Shortcut bar.

To rename a button on the Shortcut bar, you need to change the name of the shortcut used to open the file. If the button is an Office program, the shortcut can be found in the MSOffice\Office\Shortcut Bar\Office folder. To change the name, follow these steps:

1. From My Computer or Explorer, open the **MSOffice\Office\Shortcut Bar\Office** folder.

2. Find the shortcut that you want to rename and click on it.

3. Choose **Rename** from the **File** menu. Type in the new name and press **Enter**. The corresponding button on the Shortcut bar will now have the name that you specified.

Printing Problems

78: I can't print because the print option is grayed out.

You probably do not have a printer installed. To install your printer do the following:

1. From the Windows **Start** menu, select **Settings** and **Printers**.

2. Double-click the **Add Printer** icon.

3. The Add Printer Wizard will open to help you add your printer. Choose your printer from the list of **Manufacturers** and **Printers**. If you have a disk from your printer manufacturer, click the **Have Disk** button. After you have chosen your printer, click **Next**.

4. Choose the port that you want to use with this printer. Most printers are connected to the parallel port (LPT1). Click **Next**.

5. Type a name for the printer, and click **Yes** if you want to use this printer as the default printer. If this is your only printer, it is the logical choice. Click **Next**.

6. Click **Yes** to print a test page and click **Finish**. It is a good idea to print the test page to see if your printer will work correctly.

7. A dialog box will appear asking if your test page printed correctly. If it did, click **Yes** and your printer is set up. If it didn't print correctly, click **No**. Windows will bring up the Help menu to aid in troubleshooting the problem. Check to make sure that you attached the cable to the computer and the printer. Also, make sure that the printer is turned on, online, and loaded with paper.

79: My printer prints a blank page after my document is printed.

You probably have some blank lines at the bottom of your document. To check, click the **Show/Hide** button in the toolbar. If you see one or more paragraph marks on blank lines at the end of your document, highlight and delete them. You can see if this fixed your problem by choosing **Print Preview** from the **File** menu and scrolling to the last page to see if it is blank.

80: My pages print in reverse order when I print my Word document.

Your printer controls the order that your pages print. It can be annoying to have to re-order all your pages every time you print a document, so Word has given us a way to fix the problem. Follow these steps to change the print order:

1. From the **Tools** menu choose **Options**, and click the **Print** tab.

2. Click the **Reverse Print Order** check box to change it (uncheck it if it's checked; check it if it's not).

3. Click **OK** to close the Options dialog box.

81: When I create a table in Word, the gridlines show up on the screen, but they don't print.

Gridlines do not normally print. They are there to show the position of your table on the screen. To print the gridlines, follow these steps:

1. Select the table (click somewhere in the table, and then press **Alt+5** on the numeric keypad with Num Lock off).

2. Choose the **Borders and Shading** option in the **Format** menu.

3. In the Table Borders and Shading dialog box, click the **Borders** tab and choose **Grid** in the **Presets** box. If you want, you can change the thickness and style of the lines in the **Style** box.

4. Click **OK** and you'll have lines around your table suitable for printing.

82: When I print my document, it doesn't look as good as it does on the screen.

Your printer probably doesn't support the font you have chosen. Check the printer documentation to see what fonts your printer supports and use one of those. Another alternative is to use a *TrueType* font (the ones with **TT** beside them in the font list). These fonts will print well on virtually all printers. If you want to check which TrueType fonts are available for use, do the following:

1. From the Windows **Start** menu, select **Settings** and **Control Panel**.

2. Double-click the **Fonts** icon. A folder will open showing all of the installed fonts. The TrueType fonts will have **TT** in the icon. Standard fonts will have an **A** in the icon.

3. If you double-click one of the font icons, you see some information about the font and a sample of what the font looks like.

4. Click the **Print** button to print a sample.

5. When you finish, click the **Done** button.

83: When I print graphics, the lines are all jagged.

You may have the resolution set too low. The resolution is how many dots per inch the printer will use to print your graphics. The higher the resolution, the better it looks, but it will also take longer to print. To change the resolution, do the following:

1. From the Windows **Start** menu, select **Settings** and **Printers**.

2. Right-click the printer icon you are using to print your graphics and choose **Properties** from the menu.

3. Click the **Graphics** tab and click the drop-down list in the Resolution box. The list will show all of the resolutions supported by your printer. Click the highest one.

4. Click **OK** to close the dialog box.

84: When I try to print a PowerPoint slide on my laser printer, it only prints half the slide.

Your laser printer doesn't have enough memory to print the entire slide. Unlike dot-matrix or inkjet printers, laser printers have to load the entire page into their memory before they can print. The best way to fix the problem is to add more memory to your printer. Consult your printer documentation for information on what type of memory to buy. If you can't afford an upgrade right now, try printing with a lower resolution. Follow these steps to change the printer resolution:

1. From the Windows **Start** menu, select **Settings** and **Printers**.

2. Right-click the printer icon you are using to print your graphics and choose **Properties** from the menu.

3. Click the **Graphics** tab and click the drop-down list in the **Resolution** box. Choose a lower resolution from the list.

4. Click **OK** to close the dialog box.

More of your slide should print. If the full slide still doesn't print, you may have to choose a lower resolution than you did in step 3, or shrink the size of the slide so it doesn't take up the whole page.

85: I loaded 8 1/2-by-14-inch paper in my printer, but it only prints on the top 11 inches.

You have to tell Office when to change paper sizes. Follow these steps to let your Office application know there is different paper in your printer:

1. From the Office application, choose **Print** from the **File** menu.

2. Choose the desired printer from the drop-down list in the **Name** box and click the **Properties** button.

3. Click the **Paper** tab and click the appropriate paper size in the **Paper size** box. In this case, select **Legal**.

4. Click **OK** to close the dialog box. Remember to change the paper size back to 8 1/2-by-11-inches when you finish. You may also have to set up your printer to accept the larger paper. Consult your printer manual for information on how to do that.

86: The edges of my document do not print.

You are probably trying to print on too much of the paper. Most printers require you to have at least a 1/2-inch margin on all edges of the paper. Consult your printer manual for specifics. To fix this problem, the first thing you need to do is find out if your print driver has the correct settings for the unprintable area. Follow these steps to check:

1. From the Windows **Start** menu, select **Settings** and **Printers**.

2. Right-click the printer icon you are using to print your document and choose **Properties** from the menu.

3. Click the **Paper** tab and click the **Unprintable Area** button.

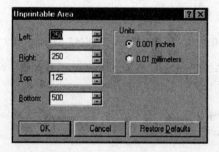

4. In the Unprintable Area dialog box, check your printer documentation and ensure that the values in **Left**, **Right**, **Top**, and **Bottom** are correct. The units are in .001 inches, so a value of 250 will be .25 inch (1/4-inch). You can also select the units in .01 millimeters by selecting it in the **Units** box.

5. Click **OK**; then click **OK** again to close the dialog boxes.

Once you are satisfied that you have the unprintable area configured correctly, you must change the margins in your document to match these settings.

87: I only want to print my embedded Excel chart, but it prints the whole worksheet.

To print a chart embedded in your worksheet, double-click the chart and choose **Print** from the **File** menu. Check that **Selected Chart** is highlighted in the **Print What** section of the Print dialog box. Click **OK** and only your chart will print.

88: When I print my Excel report, all the pages are numbered page 1.

Even though it seems obvious, you have to let Excel know that you want to number the pages continuously. To do this, follow these steps:

1. Choose **Report Manager** from the **View** menu.

2. In the Report Manager dialog box, choose the desired report from the **Reports** box and click the **Edit** button.

3. At the bottom of the Edit Report dialog box, check the **Use Continuous Page Numbers** check box and click **OK**.

4. Click the **Print** button in the Print Report dialog box to print out your report using continuous page numbers.

89: I have a date field in my document, but the correct date does not print.

The field has not been properly updated. The date that is printing is the date that was current when you inserted the field in your document. To update the field to today's date, highlight the field and press **F9**. If you would like your fields to be updated automatically when you print, choose **Options** from the **Tools** menu and click the **Print** tab. Under **Printing Options** check the **Update Fields** check box and click **OK**.

File Creating and Saving Problems

90: I want to save my document, but my application tells me I haven't chosen a valid file name.

With Windows 95, you can use long, descriptive file names to name your files. You can even use spaces in the names. There are still a few characters that you cannot use, however. You can pretty much use any character except a control character (for example, CTRL+A, CTRL+B, and so on) or the following: ?\<>l/*":;

91: I want to open a file, but it doesn't show up on the list of files in the dialog box even though I'm in the right folder.

You have probably saved your file with an extension other than the default for the program you are using (for example, XLS for Excel files). In the File Open dialog box, the program only shows files with the default extension for that program. To see all the files, select the drop-down list in the **Files of Type** box to display a list of choices. Choose **All Files** from the list and all the files in the folder will appear. In the future, you should let the application assign the extension for you when you save your files. This makes it less confusing when you are trying to open the file again.

92: I can't find the file I'm trying to open. What should I do?

You probably saved the file in a different folder than the one the program uses as the default. The easiest way to find it is to point to **Documents** on the **Start** menu in Windows. Windows will display the 15 most recently used files. If the file you are looking for is in the list, click on the name of the file to open it. If the file is not on the list, use the **Find** option. Follow these steps to find your file:

1. From the Windows **Start** menu, select **Find** and **Files or Folders**.

2. If you remember the name (or part of the name) of the file, click the **Name & Location** tab and type the name in the **Named** box. You can use wild cards if you like.

3. If you can't remember the name, but you remember when you worked on it last, click the **Date Modified** tab.

Click the radio button next to **Find all files created or modified**, and click one of the following options:

between   If you know that you last modified your file between two dates, select this option and type in the dates.

during the previous month(s)   Select this option if you want to find files that you modified within a certain number of months. Type in the number of months you want to look back.

during the previous day(s)   Select this option if you want to find files that you modified within a certain number of days. Type in the number of days you want to look back.

4. If you don't remember when you last worked on the file, click the **Advanced** tab. Choose one or a combination of the following options:

- If you know what type of file it was (such as a Word document), choose it from the drop-down list in the **Of type** box.

- If you know that the file contains certain text, type the text in the **Containing text** box; this search will take awhile because Windows has to search the contents of each file on the drive.

If you know that the file is greater than (or less than) a certain size, choose the appropriate entries in the **Size is** box. First, choose **At least** or **At most** from the drop-down list. Next, type in the size in KB (kilobytes).

You can also choose combinations of steps 2–5, for example, if you know the date the file was modified, and you know that it contains a certain text phrase.

5. Click the **Find Now** button to begin your search. A window will appear below the Find dialog box with a list of files that it finds. The window will show which folder the file is in. If you want to edit the file now, double-click it. The application that created it will open to edit the file.

93: I saved my file using a password. Now I've forgotten the password. Is there any way to open this file?

Unfortunately, you're out of luck. There is no way to open this file short of typing in every combination of characters and numbers until you come up with the correct password (this could take years). Next time, write down your password and put it in a place where you won't lose it.

94: My files always end up in different folders. How can I get the folder I want as the default?

By default, the Office applications save the files you are working on in the same folder that they store their program files. This can make it very hard to find your files later because these directories contain so many files. Therefore, it is a good idea to store your files in a different location. You can set the default location for your files, but each application does it a little differently.

For Word, follow these steps:

1. Choose **Options** from the **Tools** menu.

2. Click the **File Locations** tab. Click the folder you want to change under **File Types** and click **Modify**.

3. Choose the desired folder from the Modify Location dialog box (you can also create a new folder with the **Create New Folder** button in the toolbar). A good example would be a folder called **Documents** for Word files.

4. Click **OK** to close the dialog box; then click **Close**.

In Excel, follow these steps:

1. Choose **Options** from the **Tools** menu, and click the **General** tab.

2. Type in the desired drive and folder in the **Default File Location** box.

3. Click **OK** to close the Options dialog box.

In PowerPoint, follow these steps:

1. Choose **Options** from the **Tools** menu, and click the **Advanced** tab.

2. Type in the desired drive and folder in the **Default File Location** box.

3. Click **OK** to close the Options dialog box.

95: I can't get Word to open my Word for Macintosh document. It tells me that the disk drive is not valid.

The disk that contains your file is probably formatted for Macintosh. Windows-based computers cannot read Macintosh disks. Take a Windows formatted disk over to your Macintosh and tell it to save the file in MS-DOS format. If you have already done this, but you still get the error, you probably have a defective diskette. Get another one and try again.

96: I tried to copy a file to a floppy disk, but got an error message telling me that the disk is write-protected.

All floppy disks can be write-protected. When a disk is write-protected, it keeps you or someone else from accidentally deleting or changing files on that disk. It is a good idea to write-protect floppies when you have important data on them. If the data on the disk is not that important, or you just want to add a file to the disk, you can unprotect it. You do this differently depending on the type of floppy disk.

- For a 3 1/2-inch floppy disk, turn the disk to the back side. There is a square piece of plastic in the upper left corner of the disk that you can move to cover or un-cover a square hole. If the square hole is visible, the disk is write-protected. If the hole is covered by the plastic piece, the disk is not write-protected. Use your fingernail or the end of a pen to move the piece of plastic to the desired location.

- For a 5 1/4-inch floppy disk, there is a notch on the right edge of the disk about an inch from the top. To write-protect these disks, get a piece of tape and cover the notch (packages of disks come with pieces of tape for this purpose). To unprotect the disk, simply remove the tape.

System Problems

97: The screen redraws very slowly in Word. How can I speed it up?

When you have a lot of fancy fonts and graphics on the screen in Word, the screen can update rather slowly. To speed up the redraw, click the **Normal View** button in the lower left corner next to the horizontal scroll bar. Your fonts and graphics will not display correctly, but if you are just adding text, it won't matter. When you want to see how things actually look, or change the layout, switch back to **Page Layout View** by clicking on the **Page Layout View** button.

98: I can barely see the toolbar icons on the black-and-white screen of my laptop.

The colored icons in Office look great on a color monitor, but they are very difficult to see on a monochrome screen. To make them easier to see, choose **Toolbars** from the **View** menu; uncheck the **Color Buttons** check box and click **OK**.

99: When I double-click a document in My Computer or the Explorer, a dialog box pops up asking me what I want to open the file with. I know I created the document in Word. What's the problem?

You have probably saved your document with an extension other than DOC. The extension is the three characters to the right of the period in your file name. If your file has a DOC extension, Word knows that it needs to open when you double-click that file. If you choose another extension for your file, Word won't know to open. When a certain extension is associated with the program that created it, such as DOC for Word documents, it is known as *file association*. So, when you save your files in Office, don't put any extension on the file name. Then, the Office program will automatically put the correct extension on them and know to open when you double-click the file in My Computer or the Explorer. If you want to associate another file extension with one of the Office programs, follow these steps when you get the Open With dialog box:

1. From the list of programs, click the one you want to use to open this file. If the program is not on the list, click the **Other** button and navigate through the folders until you find your program.

2. If you check **Always use this program to open this file** check box, Windows will remember to use this program the next time you double-click the file.

3. Click **OK** to open the file using the program you chose in step 1.

100: When I try to select something using the left mouse button, a menu pops up next to the mouse pointer. Whatever I'm trying to select doesn't get selected.

When we refer to the left mouse button, we really mean the primary button. If you normally use the mouse with your left hand, and have your mouse set up that way, the right button will be the primary button. Therefore, whenever we tell you to click the left button, click the right button. If you don't want your mouse set up left-handed, do the following:

1. From the Windows **Start** menu, select **Settings** and **Control Panel**.

2. Double-click the **Mouse** icon.

3. Click the **Buttons** tab and click the radio button next to **Right-handed**.

4. Click **OK** and your mouse will be set up Right-handed.

101: When I got an error message, I clicked on Help in the menu bar, but nothing happened. Why can't I get help when I need it the most?

The **Help** command on the menu bar will not work when there is an error message on the screen. To get help, click the **Help** button in the error message box. If there is no Help button available, try pressing the **F1** key.

PART 4

Handy Reference

Use this handy reference section to help you with common shortcut keys, toolbars, and Excel functions. This reference section helps you find the more common shortcut keys for the tasks you perform in Word, Excel, and PowerPoint.

Also included in this section is a listing of all buttons on the major toolbars for Microsoft Word, Excel, PowerPoint, and Schedule+. The buttons are in the order they appear on each toolbar with a short description for each button. Don't forget that you can always use the ToolTip feature; just move your mouse pointer over the toolbar button and pause. The button's name appears on-screen. You can also click the **Help** toolbar button and drag it to a button you're unfamiliar with. Clicking the button will open a help screen designed especially for that button.

For those of you who want to become more fluent in the language of Excel functions, there is a listing of common functions. Categorized by subject, this list is handy when designing complicated worksheets. The major arguments for each function have been included where appropriate.

What You Will Find in This Section

Microsoft Office Shortcut Keys

General Shortcut Keys for All Windows Programs

Shortcut Key	Desired Command
Ctrl+Esc	Displays Task Bar and Start menu
Alt+Tab	Switches to next window
Ctrl+X	Cuts selection
Ctrl+C	Copies selection
Ctrl+V	Pastes selection

Word

Formatting in Word

Shortcut Key	Desired Command
Ctrl+E	Aligns center
Ctrl+J	Aligns justify
Ctrl+L	Aligns left
Ctrl+R	Aligns right
Ctrl+Shift+A	All uppercase letters
Ctrl+B	Bold applied to text
Shift+F3	Changes case
Ctrl+Shift+F	Font
Ctrl+Shift+P	Font size
Ctrl+I	Applies italic
Ctrl+J	Justifies paragraph
Ctrl+U (or Ctrl+Shift+U)	Underlines
Ctrl+Shift+D	Double underlines

Deleting, Copying, and Inserting

Shortcut Key	Desired Command
Ctrl+Shift+C	Copies formatting of text
Ctrl+Backspace	Deletes previous word
Ctrl+Delete	Deletes current word
Ctrl+Shift+Enter	Inserts column break

(continues)

Deleting, Copying, and Inserting *Continued*

Shortcut Key	Desired Command
Alt+Shift+D	Inserts date field
Ctrl+Enter	Inserts page break
Alt+Shift+T	Inserts time

Selecting Text

Shortcut Key	Desired Command
F3 (or Ctrl+Alt+V)	AutoText
F8 key	Begins selection
Shift+(Go to Key)	Extends selection
Ctrl+P	Prints
Ctrl+F2	Print Preview
Ctrl+S (or Shift+F12)	Save
F12	Save As
F7	Spell Check
Ctrl+Z (or Alt+Backspace)	Undo
Ctrl+Alt+N	View normal
Ctrl+Alt+O	View outline
Ctrl+Alt+P	View page layout

Moving in Word

Shortcut Key	Desired Command
Alt+Shift+C	Closes current window
Ctrl+W (or Ctrl+F4)	Closes document
Alt+Page Down	Go to end of column
Ctrl+End	Go to end of document
End	Go to end of line
Ctrl+Alt+Page Down	Go to next page
Ctrl+Alt+Page Up	Go to previous page
Alt+Page Up	Go to start of column
Ctrl+Home	Go to start of document
Home	Go to start of line
Ctrl+N	New document

Excel

Shortcuts for Entering and Manipulating

Shortcut Key	Desired Command
F2	Activates the cell and Formula Bar
Esc	Cancels an action
F4	Repeats the last action
Ctrl+Minus	Deletes the selection
Delete	Clears the selection of formulas and data
Shift+F3	Displays the Function Wizard
Alt+=	Inserts the AutoSum formula
Ctrl+;	Enters the date
Ctrl+Shift+:	Enters the time

Shortcuts for Moving and Scrolling Inside Worksheets

Shortcut Key	Desired Command
Ctrl+Backspace	Scrolls to display the active cell
Alt+Page Down	Moves right one screen
Alt+Page Up	Moves left one screen
Ctrl+Page Up	Moves to the previous sheet in the workbook
Ctrl+Page Down	Moves to the next sheet in the workbook
Home	Moves to the beginning of the row
Ctrl+Home	Moves to the beginning of the worksheet
Ctrl+End	Moves to the last cell in your worksheet
Ctrl+Spacebar	Selects the entire column
Shift+Spacebar	Selects the entire row
Ctrl+A	Selects the entire worksheet

Shortcuts for Working in a Cell or Formula Bar

Shortcut Key	Desired Command
=	Starts a formula
Ctrl+Del	Deletes text to the end of the line
Esc	Cancels an entry in the cell or formula bar
Enter	Completes the cell entry
Alt+Enter	Inserts a carriage return
Tab	Completes cell entry and moves to the next cell

(continues)

Shortcuts for Working in a Cell or Formula Bar *Continued*

Shortcut Key	Desired Command
Shift+Tab	Completes cell entry and moves to the previous cell
Ctrl+Shift+"	Copies the value from cell directly above

Shortcuts for Formatting Data

Shortcut Key	Desired Command
Ctrl+Shift+~	Applies the general number format
Ctrl+Shift+$	Applies the currency format with two decimal places (negative numbers appear in parentheses)
Ctrl+Shift+%	Applies the percentage format with no decimal places
Ctrl+Shift+^	Applies the exponential number format with two decimal places
Ctrl+Shift+#	Applies the date format with day, month, and year
Ctrl+Shift+@	Applies the time format with the hour and minute, and indicates A.M. or P.M.
Ctrl+Shift+!	Applies the two-decimal-place format with commas
Ctrl+B	Applies or removes bold
Ctrl+I	Applies or removes italic
Ctrl+U	Applies or removes underline
Ctrl+9	Hides rows
Ctrl+Shift+(	Unhides rows
Ctrl+0 (zero)	Hides columns
Ctrl+Shift+)	Unhides columns

PowerPoint

Shortcuts for Text Formatting

Shortcut Key	Desired Command
Ctrl+Shift+F	Changes font
Ctrl+Shift+P	Changes point size
Ctrl+Shift+>	Increases font size
Ctrl+Shift+<	Decreases font size
Ctrl+B	Applies bold
Ctrl+U	Applies underline
Ctrl+I	Applies italic
Ctrl+E	Centers paragraph
Ctrl+J	Justifies paragraph

Shortcut Key	Desired Command
Ctrl+L	Left-aligns paragraph
Ctrl+R	Right-aligns paragraph
Shift+F3	Toggles case

Shortcuts for Deleting and Copying

Shortcut Key	Desired Command
Backspace	Deletes character left
Ctrl+Backspace	Deletes word left
Delete	Deletes character right
Ctrl+Delete	Deletes word right
Ctrl+Z	Undo

Shortcuts for Selecting

Shortcut Key	Desired Command
Shift+right arrow	Selects right character
Shift+left arrow	Selects left character
Ctrl+A	Selects all objects (Slide view)
Ctrl+A	Selects all slides (Slide Sorter view)
Ctrl+A	Selects all text (Outline view)
Double-click	Selects word
Triple-click	Selects paragraph

Shortcuts for Slide Shows

Shortcut Key	Desired Command
<Number>+Enter	Go to slide <number>
A or =	Show/hide pointer
S or +	Stop/restart automatic show
Esc Ctrl+Break or - (minus)	End show
M	Advances on mouse click
H	Advances to hidden slide
Hold both mouse buttons down for 2 seconds	Go to slide 1
Mouse click, Spacebar, N, right arrow, down arrow, or Page Down	Advances to next slide

(continues)

Shortcuts for Slide Shows *Continued*

Shortcut Key	Desired Command
Click right mouse button, Backspace, P, left arrow, up arrow, or Page Up	Returns to previous slide

Toolbar Buttons

Microsoft Office Default Shortcut Bar

Icon	Program
	Starts a new document of your choosing
	Opens an existing document
	Sends an e-mail message
	Opens Schedule+ to the Appointment dialog box
	Opens Schedule+ to the Task dialog box
	Opens Schedule+ to the Contacts dialog box
	Accesses documentation on the Office CD-ROM
	Opens up the Answer Wizard online help system

Word Toolbar Buttons

Word's Standard Toolbar

Button	Description
	Creates a new document using the Normal template
	Opens an existing document or template
	Saves the active document or template
	Prints the active document using the current defaults
	Displays the active document as it will print
	Checks the spelling in the current document
	Removes the selection and places it in the Clipboard

Button	Description
	Copies the selection and places it in the Clipboard
	Inserts the contents of the Clipboard
	Copies and applies the formatting of the selection
	Reverses the action performed
	Reverses an Undo
	Automatically formats a document
	Inserts an address from your electronic address book
	Inserts a table at the cursor location
	Inserts a worksheet object
	Changes the column format of a selection
	Shows or hides the drawing toolbar
	Shows or hides all nonprinting symbols
100%	Allows you to see more or less detail by changing the scale of the sheet
	Opens the TipWizard bar
	Converts mouse pointer to a help selector (point-and-click on any item to display specific help)

Word's Formatting Toolbar

Button	Description
List Bullet	Lists the available text formatting styles
Times New Roman	Lists the available fonts
10	Lists available sizes for the font selected
B	Formats the selection bold
I	Formats the selection italic
U	Formats the selection with a continuous underline
	Highlights the selection like a highlighter pen
	Aligns the paragraph at the left indent
	Centers the paragraph between the two indents

(continues)

Word's Formatting Toolbar   *Continued*

Button	Description
	Aligns the paragraph at the right indent
	Aligns the paragraph at both the left and right indents
	Creates a numbered list
	Creates a bulleted list
	Decreases indent or promotes the selection
	Increases indent or demotes the selection
	Displays or hides the border toolbar

Excel Toolbar Buttons

Excel's Standard Toolbar

Button	Description
	Creates a new workbook
	Displays the Open dialog box so you can open an existing workbook
	Saves changes made to the active workbook
	Prints the active workbook
	Displays each page as it will look when printed
	Checks the spelling of text in worksheets and charts
	Removes the selection and places it onto the Clipboard
	Copies the selection and places it onto the Clipboard
	Pastes the contents of the Clipboard into the selection
	Copies only the formats from the selected cells or objects
	Reverses the last command you chose (if possible)
	Repeats the last command you chose (if possible)
	Invokes the SUM function and suggests the range of cells to be added
	Opens the Function Wizard and inserts the selected function into the Formula Bar or active cell
	Sorts the current list from lowest value to highest value

Button	Description
	Sorts the current list from highest value to lowest value
	Guides you through the steps required to create a new chart
	Opens the Data Map feature for inserting geographical maps into your worksheet
	Displays the Drawing toolbar
100%	Allows you to see more or less detail by changing the scale of the sheet
	Displays tips based on the actions you perform
	Converts mouse pointer to a help selector (point-and-click on any item to display specific help)

Excel's Formatting Toolbar

Button	Description
Arial	Lists the available fonts
10	Lists available sizes for the font selected
B	Applies bold formatting to selection
I	Applies italic formatting to selection
U	Applies a single underline to selection
	Aligns selection to the left
	Centers the contents of selection
	Aligns selection to the right
	Centers text horizontally across the selected cells
$	Applies current Currency style to selected cells
%	Applies current Percent style to selected cells
,	Applies current Comma style to selected cells
	Each click adds one decimal place to the number format
	Each click removes one decimal place from the number format
	Displays a palette of border styles
	Changes the color of a selected cell
	Displays a palette of colors for changing the font color of selection

Excel's Chart Toolbar

Button	Description
	Selection of 14 chart types to choose from
	Changes an active chart to the default format
	Creates or modifies an embedded chart on a worksheet
	Toggles major gridlines on and off
	Adds a legend to the right of the plot area

PowerPoint Toolbar Buttons

PowerPoint's Standard Toolbar

Button	Description
	Creates a new presentation
	Opens an existing presentation
	Saves the current presentation
	Prints a copy of slides automatically
	Runs the Spell Checker
	Cuts the selected item and copies it to the Clipboard
	Copies selected item to the Clipboard
	Pastes from the Clipboard
	Copies and then applies formatting of selected item
	Performs a single undo if possible
	Undoes an undo
	Inserts a new slide after the current slide
	Inserts a Word table
	Inserts an Excel worksheet
	Creates a Graph object
	Opens the ClipArt Gallery
	Applies a new template design

Button	Description
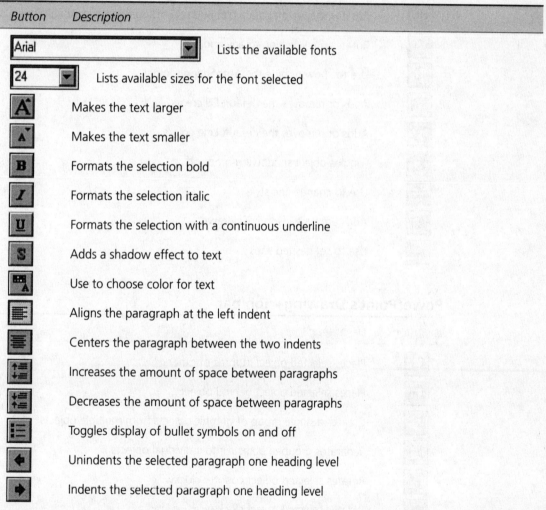	Opens the Animation Effects toolbar
	Saves slides as a Word outline without graphics
	Displays slides in black-and-white view
	Adjusts the size of your on-screen slide
	First click this and then click on item you need help with

PowerPoint's Formatting Toolbar

Button	Description
Arial	Lists the available fonts
24	Lists available sizes for the font selected
A	Makes the text larger
A	Makes the text smaller
B	Formats the selection bold
I	Formats the selection italic
U	Formats the selection with a continuous underline
S	Adds a shadow effect to text
A	Use to choose color for text
	Aligns the paragraph at the left indent
	Centers the paragraph between the two indents
	Increases the amount of space between paragraphs
	Decreases the amount of space between paragraphs
	Toggles display of bullet symbols on and off
	Unindents the selected paragraph one heading level
	Indents the selected paragraph one heading level

PowerPoint's Drawing Toolbar

Button	Description
	Use for editing and selecting objects
	Creates text objects
	Creates a straight line
	Creates unfilled rectangles or squares
	Creates unfilled ellipses or circles
	Creates unfilled arcs or circle segments
	Creates shapes that are a combination of freehand and straight lines
	Rotates the selection to any angle
	Use to show or hide the AutoShape toolbar
	Adds or removes the default Fill colors
	Adds or removes the default Line colors
	Toggles object shadowing on or off
	Use to change line style
	Adds arrowheads to lines drawn
	Use to set dashed lines

PowerPoint's Drawing+ Toolbar

Button	Description
	Places selected object in front of others
	Places selected object behind object
	Creates a single group of graphic objects from multiple objects
	Separates grouped objects into individual objects
	Rotates selected object counter-clockwise
	Rotates selected object clockwise
	Creates a right-left mirror image of selected object by flipping it
	Creates an up-down mirror image of selected object by flipping it

PowerPoint's Slide Sorter Toolbar

Button	Description
	Chooses transition effects for slide changes
No Transition ▼	Chooses special effects for slide changes
No Build Effect ▼	Chooses special effects for text building
	Skips the selected slide during the slide show
	Runs and rehearses a slide show
	Displays all character formatting

PowerPoint's Animation Effects Toolbar

Button	Description
	Causes the slide's title to drop down into the slide
	Inserts slide text one sentence at a time
	Inserts object into slide like a speeding car, complete with sound effect
	Object flies into slide
	Inserts object into slide with the sound of a camera click
	Flashes object onto slide, then off again
	Writes text onto slide with a laser-like effect and sound
	Inserts slide text one character at a time, like a typewriter, complete with typewriter sounds
	Builds your text block from bottom up
	Drops in each word one at a time
	Lets you order the effects assigned
	Opens the Animation Settings dialog box

Schedule+ Toolbar Buttons

Schedule+ Toolbar

Button	Description
Today	Opens the daily schedule to the current date
	Opens a calendar for selecting other dates to view in the daily schedule
	Opens a new schedule
	Prints the designated portion of the schedule
	Cuts selected data to the Clipboard
	Copies selected data to the Clipboard
	Pastes data from the Clipboard into the schedule
	Undoes the last action performed
	Opens the Appointment, Task, or Contact dialog box
	Deletes selected data
	Lets you edit the selected data
	Sets a recurring item on your schedule
	Sets a reminder for the item
	Sets the data as private information in your schedule
	Schedules the item as tentative on your schedule
	Opens the Meeting Wizard function for scheduling meetings on a network
	Opens the Timex Watch Wizard for using Schedule+ with the Timex Data Link Watch
	Lets you view network e-mail

Excel Functions

Financial Functions

Function	Arguments	Purpose
ACCRINT	(issue, first_interest, settlement, rate, frequency)	Calculates the accrued interest for any security that pays periodic interest
ACCRINTM	(issue, rate)	Calculates the accrued interest for any security that pays interest at maturity
CUMIPMT	(rate,nper,pv,start_period, end_period, type)	Calculates the cumulative interest paid between two periods
CUMPRINC	(rate,nper,pv,start_period, end_period, type)	Calculates the cumulative principal paid on a loan between two periods
DB	(cost, salvage, life, period)	Calculates the depreciation of an asset for a specified period using the fixed-declining balance method
DDB	(cost, salvage, life)	Calculates the depreciation of an asset for a specified period using the double-declining balance method or some other method you specify
EFFECT	(nominal_rate, npery)	Calculates the effective annual interest rate
FV	(rate, nper, pmt)	Calculates the future value of an investment
FVSCHEDULE	(principal, schedule)	Calculates the future value of an initial principal after applying a series of compound interest rates
IPMT	(rate, per, nper, pv)	Calculates the interest payment for an investment for a given period
IRR	(values)	Calculates the internal rate of return for a series of cash flows
NOMINAL	(effect_rate, npery)	Calculates the annual nominal interest rate
NPER	(rate, pmt, pv)	Calculates the number of periods for an investment
PMT	(rate, nper, pv)	Calculates the periodic payment for an annuity
PPMT	(prate, per, nper, pv)	Calculates the payment on the principal for an investment for a given period
PV	(rate, nper, pmt)	Calculates the present value of an investment
RATE	(nper, pmt, pv)	Calculates the interest rate per period of an annuity
RECEIVED	(settlement, maturity, investment, discount)	Calculates the amount received at maturity for a fully invested security
YIELD	(settlement, maturity, rate, pr, redemption, frequency)	Calculates the yield on a security that pays periodic interest
YIELDMAT	(settlement, maturity, issue, rate, pr)	Calculates the annual yield of a security that pays interest at maturity

Date and Time Functions

Function	Arguments	Purpose
DATE	(year, month, day)	Calculates the serial number of a particular date
DATEVALUE	(date_text)	Converts a date in the form of text to a serial number
DAY	(serial_number)	Converts a serial number to a day of the month
DAYS360	(start_date, end_date)	Calculates the number of days between two dates based on a 360-day year
HOUR	(serial_number)	Converts a serial number to an hour
MONTH	(serial_number)	Converts a serial number to a month
NETWORKDAYS	(start_date, end_date)	Calculates the number of whole workdays between two dates
TODAY	( )	Calculates the serial number of today's date
WEEKDAY	(serial_number, return_type)	Converts a serial number to a day of the week
WORKDAY	(start_date, days, holidays)	Calculates the serial number of the date before or after a specified number of workdays
YEAR	(serial_number)	Converts a serial number to a year

Math and Trigonometry Functions

Function	Arguments	Purpose
ABS	(number)	Calculates the absolute value of a number
ROUND	(number, num_digits)	Rounds a number to a specified number of digits
ROUNDDOWN	(number, num_digits)	Rounds a number down, toward zero
ROUNDUP	(number, num_digits)	Rounds a number up, away from zero
SUM	(number1, number2, ...)	Adds its arguments

Statistical Functions

Function	Arguments	Purpose
AVERAGE	(number1, number2, ...)	Calculates the average of its arguments
COUNT	(value1, value2, ...)	Counts how many numbers are in the list of arguments
COUNTA	(value1, value2, ...)	Counts how many values are in the list of arguments
MAX	(number1, number2, ...)	Calculates the maximum value in a list of arguments
MEDIAN	(number1, number2, ...)	Calculates the median of the given numbers
MIN	(number1, number2, ...)	Calculates the minimum value in a list of arguments

Text

Function	Purpose
CONCATENATE	Joins several text items into one text item
DOLLAR	Converts a number to text, using currency format
FIXED	Formats a number as text with a fixed number of decimals
LOWER	Converts text to lowercase
TEXT	Formats a number and converts it to text
UPPER	Converts text to uppercase
VALUE	Converts a text argument to a number

Logical

Function	Purpose
AND	Returns TRUE if all its arguments are TRUE
FALSE	Returns the logical value FALSE
IF	Specifies a logical test to perform
NOT	Reverses the logic of its argument
OR	Returns TRUE if any argument is TRUE
TRUE	Returns the logical value TRUE

Index

X-Y-Z

PLUG YOURSELF INTO...

The Macmillan USA Information SuperLibrary (tm)

See the new SuperLibrary Newsletter

THE MACMILLAN INFORMATION SUPERLIBRARY™

Free information and vast computer resources from the world's leading computer book publisher—online!

FIND THE BOOKS THAT ARE RIGHT FOR YOU!

A complete online catalog, plus sample chapters and tables of contents give you an in-depth look at *all* of our books, including hard-to-find titles. It's the best way to find the books you need!

- STAY INFORMED with the latest computer industry news through our online newsletter, press releases, and customized Information SuperLibrary Reports.

- GET FAST ANSWERS to your questions about Macmillan Computer Publishing books and software.

- VISIT our online bookstore for the latest information and editions!

- COMMUNICATE with our expert authors through e-mail and conferences.

- DOWNLOAD SOFTWARE from the immense Macmillan Computer Publishing library:
    - Source code and files from Macmillan Computer Publishing books
    - The best shareware, freeware, and demos

- DISCOVER HOT SPOTS on other parts of the Internet.

- WIN BOOKS in ongoing contests and giveaways!

TO PLUG INTO MCP: → **WORLD WIDE WEB: http://www.mcp.com**

FTP: ftp.mcp.com

Complete and Return this Card
for a *FREE* Computer Book Catalog

Thank you for purchasing this book! You have purchased a superior computer book written expressly for your needs. To continue to provide the kind of up-to-date, pertinent coverage you've come to expect from us, we need to hear from you. Please take a minute to complete and return this self-addressed, postage-paid form. In return, we'll send you a free catalog of all our computer books on topics ranging from word processing to programming and the internet.

Mr. ☐   Mrs. ☐   Ms. ☐   Dr. ☐

Name (first) ☐☐☐☐☐☐☐☐☐☐☐☐☐☐   (M.I.) ☐   (last) ☐☐☐☐☐☐☐☐☐☐☐☐☐☐☐☐

Address ☐☐☐☐☐☐☐☐☐☐☐☐☐☐☐☐☐☐☐☐☐☐☐☐☐☐☐☐☐☐☐☐☐☐☐☐

City ☐☐☐☐☐☐☐☐☐☐☐☐☐☐☐☐   State ☐☐   Zip ☐☐☐☐☐ ☐☐☐☐

Phone ☐☐☐ ☐☐☐ ☐☐☐☐   Fax ☐☐☐ ☐☐☐ ☐☐☐☐

Company Name ☐☐☐☐☐☐☐☐☐☐☐☐☐☐☐☐☐☐☐☐☐☐☐☐☐☐

E-mail address ☐☐☐☐☐☐☐☐☐☐☐☐☐☐☐☐☐☐☐☐☐☐☐☐☐☐

1. Please check at least (3) influencing factors for purchasing this book.

Front or back cover information on book .... ☐
Special approach to the content .... ☐
Completeness of content .... ☐
Author's reputation .... ☐
Publisher's reputation .... ☐
Book cover design or layout .... ☐
Index or table of contents of book .... ☐
Price of book .... ☐
Special effects, graphics, illustrations .... ☐
Other (Please specify): _____ ☐

2. How did you first learn about this book?

Saw in Macmillan Computer Publishing catalog .... ☐
Recommended by store personnel .... ☐
Saw the book on bookshelf at store .... ☐
Recommended by a friend .... ☐
Received advertisement in the mail .... ☐
Saw an advertisement in: _____ ☐
Read book review in: _____ ☐
Other (Please specify): _____ ☐

3. How many computer books have you purchased in the last six months?

This book only .... ☐   3 to 5 books .... ☐
2 books .... ☐   More than 5 .... ☐

4. Where did you purchase this book?

Bookstore .... ☐
Computer Store .... ☐
Consumer Electronics Store .... ☐
Department Store .... ☐
Office Club .... ☐
Warehouse Club .... ☐
Mail Order .... ☐
Direct from Publisher .... ☐
Internet site .... ☐
Other (Please specify): _____ ☐

5. How long have you been using a computer?

☐ Less than 6 months   ☐ 6 months to a year
☐ 1 to 3 years   ☐ More than 3 years

6. What is your level of experience with personal computers and with the subject of this book?

	With PCs	With subject of book
New	☐	☐
Casual	☐	☐
Accomplished	☐	☐
Expert	☐	☐

Source Code ISBN: 1-56761-6232

7. Which of the following best describes your job title?

Administrative Assistant .... ☐
Coordinator .... ☐
Manager/Supervisor .... ☐
Director .... ☐
Vice President .... ☐
President/CEO/COO .... ☐
Lawyer/Doctor/Medical Professional .... ☐
Teacher/Educator/Trainer .... ☐
Engineer/Technician .... ☐
Consultant .... ☐
Not employed/Student/Retired .... ☐
Other (Please specify): _____ ☐

8. Which of the following best describes the area of the company your job title falls under?

Accounting .... ☐
Engineering .... ☐
Manufacturing .... ☐
Operations .... ☐
Marketing .... ☐
Sales .... ☐
Other (Please specify): _____ ☐

Comments: _____
_____
_____

9. What is your age?

Under 20 .... ☐
21-29 .... ☐
30-39 .... ☐
40-49 .... ☐
50-59 .... ☐
60-over .... ☐

10. Are you:

Male .... ☐
Female .... ☐

11. Which computer publications do you read regularly? (Please list)

_____
_____
_____
_____
_____
_____
_____
_____

Fold here and scotch-tape to mail.